D1001313

MARGERY KEMPE AND THE LONELY READER

MARGERY KEMPE AND THE LONELY READER

REBECCA KRUG

CORNELL UNIVERSITY PRESS
Ithaca and London

Copyright © 2017 by Cornell University

All rights reserved. Except for brief quotations in a review, this book, or parts thereof, must not be reproduced in any form without permission in writing from the publisher. For information, address Cornell University Press, Sage House, 512 East State Street, Ithaca, New York 14850.

First published 2017 by Cornell University Press

Printed in the United States of America

Library of Congress Cataloging-in-Publication Data

Names: Krug, Rebecca, author.
Title: Margery Kempe and the lonely reader / Rebecca Krug.
Description: Ithaca ; London : Cornell University Press,
    2017. | Includes bibliographical references and index.
Identifiers: LCCN 2016039392 (print) | LCCN 2016040225
    (ebook) | LCCN 2016040226 (ebook) | ISBN
    9781501705335 (cloth : alk. paper) | ISBN 9781501708152
    (epub/mobi) | ISBN 9781501708169 (pdf)
Subjects: LCSH: Women authors, English—Middle
    English, 1100–1500—Biography. | Christian pilgrims
    and pilgrimages—Early works to 1800. | Christian
    women—Religious life—England. | Kempe, Margery,
    approximately 1373– Book of Margery Kempe | Kempe,
    Margery, approximately 1373–
Classification: LCC PR2007.K4 Z76 2017 (print) | LCC
    PR2007.K4 (ebook) | DDC 248.2/2092—dc23
LC record available at https://lccn.loc.gov/2016039392

Cornell University Press strives to use environmentally responsible suppliers and materials to the fullest extent possible in the publishing of its books. Such materials include vegetable-based, low-VOC inks and acid-free papers that are recycled, totally chlorine-free, or partly composed of nonwood fibers. For further information, visit our website at www.cornellpress.cornell.edu.

❦ Contents

 PREFACE

When I started work on *Margery Kempe and the Lonely Reader*, I wanted to answer one question: Why did Margery Kempe write her *Book*? An ever-growing body of scholarship considers various aspects of Kempe's life and her writing, but little of it gives consideration to the issue of the *Book*'s origins—at least not in the emotional and experiential terms that interest me. The *Book* just *is*—and it is so surprising, strange, and difficult that questions more answerable than mine have occupied critics since its rediscovery in 1934. Nonetheless, given both my previous work on women's literate practice and my own sometimes conflicted feelings about writing, it is, for me, an urgent question.

Why did Kempe, after twenty years, during which she received frequent encouragement to write her "felyngs" down but resisted doing so, finally decide, sometime in the late 1420s or early 1430s, to write her *Book*? Why not instead continue to read devotional books with her clerical friends, trade tales with spiritually like-minded acquaintances, discuss her revelations with her confessors, and share the "wonder"—as the *Book* calls it—of her spiritual life, as she had done for many years, with people at home and abroad? The *Book*'s preface says that Kempe was "bodyn in hyr spyrit for to wrytyn"—meaning God told her to write the *Book*. But how, then (even if this is an answer to my question), did she come to fulfill this command, finally, when she was sixty years old, and why, further, did this involve such a convoluted process—including her reliance on at least three scribes (one of whom wrote "neithyr good Englysch ne Dewch"; another who drafted one page and gave up; a third who resisted Kempe's requests for assistance for four years) and extending to the addition of a second book several years after the *Book* had, seemingly, been completed?

Kempe lived outside the social milieu of elite women who, at the encouragement of their confessors, may have done some writing and translating for spiritual edification. She was a late medieval laywoman with many spiritual friends but few acquaintances who were authors. Of those who were writers, such as the Carmelite friar Alan of Lynn, the disparity between their educational and institutional backgrounds makes it unlikely that Kempe decided to begin writing her *Book* merely because it seemed like "the thing to do." None of her *scholarly* friends were laypeople. And none of them were women (unless we include Julian of Norwich, whom Kempe visits seeking spiritual guidance; the *Book* makes no mention of Julian's status as an author). Whether she was completely illiterate in a strict sense or, as seems likely to me, perhaps able to make some sense of written language has little bearing on the question except to suggest even more pressingly how important it is.

Which brings me back to my original question: How did it become possible, desirable, necessary for her to write the *Book*? In *Margery Kempe and the Lonely Reader*, I try to provide an answer by thinking about Kempe's authorship in terms of the dynamic and changing nature of her literate practice, which includes the entire range of activities and social understandings related to written culture as it changed over the course of her life. My argument is, briefly, that Kempe wrote the *Book*, finally, as a revisionary act: she came, after many years of engagement with written culture as a reader and listener, to feel compelled to produce her own book of consolation, a type of devotional writing found in late medieval religious culture that taught readers how to seek spiritual comfort and, most important, how to *feel* about one's spiritual life. She did so out of a desire to experience spiritual comfort herself, and out of the impulse to find, sustain, and interact with fellow believers who, like Kempe, were also looking to live lives of intense, devout engagement.

Kempe's decision to write was tied to her belief in the validity and truthfulness of emotional experience. She discovered—and the *Book* insists—that expansive emotional expression is fundamental to a life of devotion. When a famous preaching friar attempted to force Kempe to say she was physically ill—to deny that God was the source of her revelations—she responded by refusing to disavow her feelings: she "hirself knew wel be revelacyon and be experiens of werkyng it was no sekenes, and therfor *sche wolde not for al this world sey otherwyse than sche felt*" (chapter 61, emphasis added). In writing the *Book*, Kempe composed her own book of consolation, one that would, in fact, "say" as she "felt"—if at all possible. In doing so, she wrote a book about, by, and for herself.

Kempe's reader, like Kempe herself, is both "outside" the life that is represented and simultaneously drawn into the represented experience of self. The *Book* draws attention to the provisional nature of every attempt to capture the truth of experience: Kempe reads, rereads, and revises the truth of this "creature," who she is and was (and believes she will in some way continue to be). The value the writer finds in this process of constant reinterpretation is thus extended to the reader. To put it another way, her subject is her own life and her experiences, but her representation of that self, as found in the *Book*, is constructed to reach out to and include the reader: "I write about my own life," Kempe might have said, "but it could just as easily be *your* life." This is why the prologue to the *Book* asserts that it is for the "solas and comfort" of the "synful wrecchys" who read it: the "grace that [God] werkyth in any creatur is ower profyth." Kempe thought of herself as such a wretch and believed that her readers were too.

Scholars of feminist autobiography use the term "autography" to refer to life writing in which the "I" of the narrative (the "creature's" in the case of the *Book*) is shared by author and reader. In place of a static, linear narrative history of Kempe's life, the *Book* presents a process of self-in-the-making in which the dynamic construction of identity is located both in lived experience and in the act of capturing and reenvisioning that life in writing. It makes it clear that Kempe's identity is not just reported (a stable, graspable object) but performed (a variable, not quite tangible thing). Its eager, contradictory, and sometimes frustrated attempts to uncover and construct the "creature's" identity are offered to the reader; the reader is, in turn, invited to take part in the same performative process as Kempe herself. The possibility of such self-creation and uncovering of emotional truth, the *Book* suggests, was missing from the books of spiritual consolation available to Kempe and her readers. This absence, or, in positive terms, the need for a lived life as a model for working through the problems of finding spiritual, emotionally felt comfort, became the grounds for writing her own book that would "say as she felt." Her *Book*, then, is the book of consolation that Kempe came to write after twenty or more years of thinking about reading and writing.

❧ ACKNOWLEDGMENTS

I have been teaching, lecturing, and writing about *The Book of Margery Kempe* for more than twenty years now—about the same amount of time that it took Kempe to get around to writing it. My debts are many and begin with the students who have read some or all of the *Book* with me. I wish I could name them all, because their thoughts—as well as the opportunity to respond to those thoughts—shape my argument in so many ways. I am particularly grateful to Elissa Hansen, Gabriel Hill, Kathleen Howard, Karolyn Kinane, Kathryn Mogk, Alex Mueller, Katie Robison, Amanda Taylor, and Ben Utter for being excellent "companions in the way."

Over the years, friends and colleagues invited me to speak and write about various aspects of this project. I thank audiences at Taipei Technical University's Forgotten Books and Cultural Memory Conference, the Plymouth Medieval Forum, the Great Plains British Studies Conference, Northwestern University's Medieval Colloquium, and the Medievalists' Writing Workshop for their engaged responses. I am grateful to the organizers of these events for their generous and insightful feedback: Sharin' Schroeder; Karolyn Kinane; Glenn Davis; Katy Breen, Barbara Newman, and Susie Phillips; and Seeta Chaganti and Claire Waters. For helping me think through tricky parts of my argument, I thank Elizabeth Allen, Katy Breen, Lyn Blanchfield, Jessica Brantley, Richard Kieckhefer, Kathy Lavezzo, Alex Mueller, Cathy Sanok, and Meg Worley. I am extremely grateful to the following editors and colleagues who worked with me on essays related to this project: Andy Galloway; Shannon Gayk and Kathleen Tonry; Larry Scanlon; and Jane Tolmie and Jane Toswell.

The cheerful and professional staff at Cornell University Press made it a pleasure to finish this book. I am especially grateful to my former editor Peter Potter, current editor Mahinder Kingra, Bethany Wasik, and Karen Hwa. My appreciation for and of Amanda Heller's masterly copyediting is boundless. I also thank the Press's anonymous readers for their thoughtful and learned reports. The first reader challenged me to make my argument clearer. The second reader's careful, sympathetic response and willingness to read the manuscript twice improved this book enormously.

I have the good fortune to have friends who are medievalists; my debts to them are both personal and professional. Glenn Davis, Elissa Hansen, and Ji-Soo Kang met with me for weekly lunches in the summer of 2012 and helped me tackle the framework for this book. Glenn's thoughtfulness and insight allowed me to see that I was writing a second book about literate practice; Elissa's and Ji-Soo's expert knowledge of Kempe meant I could discuss details of the project without having to explain myself. Their support was essential to this book's composition.

David Benson, Susie Phillips, and Theresa Kemp have talked with me about this project for as long as I have been working on it. David helped me remember that Margery Kempe had spunk and encouraged me at times when I desperately needed it. Susie was instrumental in sorting out my ideas about negative thinking and provided me with a set of loaded dice that would have been the envy of John Holmes's angel. Theresa sent me back to Adrienne Rich and reminded me why I write about women readers and writers. I also thank Kit French, Pam Benson, Rebecca Schoff Curtin, Katharine Horsley, Dan Donoghue, Derek Pearsall, and Nicholas Watson for kindnesses past and present. John Watkins and Shirley Garner have been allies and friends throughout my career at Minnesota. I am grateful to them and to Ellen Messer-Davidow, my department chair, who supported my efforts to finish this book. Publication costs have been subsidized by an award from the University of Minnesota's Donald V. Hawkins Fund. I thank the Hawkins estate and the University of Minnesota Department of English.

Like Kempe, I lost friends during the writing of my book, including my teacher Alfred David, who invited me, as his teaching assistant, to deliver my very first lecture—on Margery Kempe and Julian of Norwich; Larry Benson, who was always happy to tell me something entertaining and eager to hear about my latest projects; and my father-in-law, Michael Goldberg, who believed in the work that teachers do. They are sorely missed.

My friends and family kindly allowed me to talk about Kempe unceasingly and rarely asked me when I would finally be finished with this book. I am very grateful to them all, including my neighbors Deb Swenson and Basil, who now know more about Margery Kempe than most medievalists do; Christine Evert Thompson, who commiserated; the Eau Claire Kemps, Leisl, Theresa, Taylor, and Mike; and Susie Phillips, Dietmar Baum, and Johannes Baum. All offered much-needed fellowship and occasional comic relief. I am very grateful to my parents, Mary and Bill; my sister, Heather; my sister-in-law, Jessica; and my mothers-in-law, Rachel Goldberg and Janet Stamm, and Janet's husband, Bob, for their thoughtfulness and good humor. Brian Goldberg and Duncan have sustained me through the years.

MARGERY KEMPE AND
THE LONELY READER

Introduction

Adrienne Rich's celebrated essay "When We Dead Awaken: Writing as Re-Vision" draws attention to the moment *just before* readers recognize that they are having a collective, rather than peculiarly individual, experience.[1] The essay, first delivered at the Modern Language Association meeting in December 1971, reflects on the way women who are readers become writers. When Rich's hypothetical reader, who is also Rich herself, turns to books, she tries, Rich reports, to recognize herself in the books' pages—to find her own "way of being in the world"—but never does: when she reads, she fails to find the "drudging, puzzled, sometimes inspired creature" who "sits at [her] desk." Gradually and then suddenly, Rich's reader comes to realize that others are also turning to books and that they too are looking for, and failing to find, themselves. When the reader finally comes to this recognition, Rich explains, when she "awakes," it is "no longer such a lonely thing" for her "to open [her] eyes." After this moment of recognition, these now no-longer-lonely readers turn to writing, and in doing so, Rich argues, they have the ability to reshape both personal and collective identity.

Rich's is, of course, a feminist awakening, and particular to the latter half of the twentieth century, but despite this historical specificity, her essay offers

---

1. Adrienne Rich, "When We Dead Awaken: Writing as Re-Vision," *College English* 34 (1972): 18–30.

a powerful, broadly applicable description of the experience of realizing that what seemed like an individual, isolating experience is in fact shared with other people. Rich's "sleepwalkers," as she calls these readers, respond to both their sense of cultural limitation and their belief in their own value. The revisionary principles espoused in "When We Dead Awaken" are both optimistic (resting on the belief that books in which women's experiences are represented should and might be written) and critical (there is something wrong with a world in which the only books available exclude "real" women, and the situation requires redress).[2]

In *Margery Kempe and the Lonely Reader*, I argue that Kempe's *Book* is the product of a no-longer-lonely reader, that is, one who, as both an individual and a member of a larger community, is both hopeful about the future and critical of the present state of affairs.[3] *The Book of Margery Kempe* represents its author, like Rich's sleepwalkers, as discovering over the course of her life—gradually and then suddenly, in bursts and starts—that her dissatisfaction with mainstream religious culture and her desire to live a life of intense, deeply felt devotion were shared by other people. As the *Book* records Kempe's experiences, it shows us what seem, at first, to be isolated, individual cases of passionate spiritual desire but goes on to demonstrate that these instances are in fact examples of a new kind of ecstatic devotion shared by believers inside and outside of religious institutions.

The *Book* catalogues fellow participants in "Kempeian" spirituality, which revolves around intense emotionality and expressiveness, including Kempe's unnamed friend, a Dominican anchor; the "worshipful doctor of divinity," Alan of Lynn, compiler of indexes to Bridget's revelations and to the *Incendium Amoris*; Bishop Philip Repingdon, sometime defender of Wycliffite doc-

---

2. Ibsen's *When We Dead Awaken*, from which Rich takes her title, stands in stark contrast: Irena, the artist's model who says she is "dead" throughout the play, announces, "When we dead awaken . . . we see that we have never lived" (act 2). She and the sculptor Arnold Rubek are killed by an avalanche in the play's final scene.

3. *The Book of Margery Kempe*, ed. Lynn Staley, TEAMS Middle English Texts Series (Kalamazoo: Medieval Institute Publications, 1996). References to Kempe's *Book* are cited parenthetically in the text by chapter (common to all Middle English editions) and page number in Staley's edition. Staley's edition is searchable through the TEAMS website, http://d.lib.rochester.edu/teams/publication/staley-the-book-of-margery-kempe.

Kempe's *Book* consists of two parts, usually referred to as books one and two. I include the book designation only when the passage is from the second book. I also refer parenthetically by page to the other standard Middle English editions: *The Book of Margery Kempe*, ed. Barry Windeatt, Longman Annotated Texts (Harlow: Pearson Education, 2000); and *The Book of Margery Kempe*, ed. Sanford Brown Meech and Hope Emily Allen, EETS 212 (1940; London: Oxford University Press, 1993). Modern English translations are my own. The manuscript, British Library Additional Manuscript 61823, is now available digitally (edited by Joel Fredell) at http://english.selu.edu/humanitiesonline/kempe.

trine, who encourages Kempe to write her own book; the renowned Archbishop Thomas Arundel, fierce opponent of Lollardy, who entertains her in
his garden "until the stars come out"; anchoress Julian of Norwich, now well
known for composing her own book offering comfort; Richard Caister, vicar
of St. Stephen's in Norwich, the author of a well-known devotional hymn;
Kempe's "specyal frende," an unnamed "holy woman," for whom she prays;
the convert Thomas Marchale; her guide Patrick; and others with whom
Kempe shares stories, meals, and tears.[4] Though drawn from widely divergent
social spheres, all of these individuals are represented in the *Book* as sharing
the same enthusiasm, engagement, and eagerness to experience religious faith
directly, positively, and completely. As the *Book* unfolds, it invites its readers
to see themselves, too, as participants in this spiritual community, to imagine
themselves as companions on a spiritual quest, and to read themselves into
the pages of the *Book* itself as active agents participating in the same process
of reflection, revision, and self-creation in which Kempe, as both author and
reader, engages.

Kempe's spirituality can be placed in a broader, European context, supplementing the East Anglian one that has so fruitfully advanced our understanding of her *Book*.[5] John Van Engen, for example, describes the *Devotio Moderna* of the Netherlands and Germany in terms very similar to those found
in Kempe's *Book*. The "Devout," Van Engen explains, sought intense spiritual
experience as part of a way of life separated out from "but not finally separate from the world."[6] Similarly, Barbara Walters and her coauthors describe
the ways the institution of the Corpus Christi feast in Liège "galvanized and
channeled widespread and popular religious emotions," "gave rise to religious seekers," and fueled the search for "structure, meaning, and identities

---

4. Because emotional expression in Kempe's *Book* is much closer to modern "feelings" than to
earlier philosophical definitions in which passion is distinguished from affection, I use "emotion"
interchangeably with "affect"; see Erich Auerbach, "Passio als Leidenschaft," in *Gesammelte Aufsätze
zur romanischen Philologie* (Bern: Francke, 1967), 161–75. On the history of emotion, see William M.
Reddy, *The Navigation of Feeling: A Framework for the History of Emotions* (Cambridge: Cambridge University Press, 2001); and Barbara H. Rosenwein, *Emotional Communities in the Early Middle Ages* (Ithaca:
Cornell University Press, 2007). On "affect theory," largely derived from Deleuze, see Melissa Gregg
and Gregory J. Seigworth, eds., *The Affect Theory Reader* (Durham: Duke University Press, 2010). Anne
McTaggart, *Shame and Guilt in Chaucer* (New York: Palgrave Macmillan, 2012), applies this theory to
medieval literature.

5. See Clarissa Atkinson, *Mystic and Pilgrim: The Book and the World of Margery Kempe* (Ithaca: Cor-
nell University Press, 1983), esp. 67–101; Gail McMurray Gibson, *The Theater of Devotion: East Anglian
Drama and Society in the Late Middle Ages* (Chicago: University of Chicago Press, 1989), 47–65; Margaret
Gallyon, *Margery Kempe of Lynn and Medieval England* (Norwich: Canterbury Press, 1995); and Anthony
Goodman, *Margery Kempe and Her World* (London: Pearson, 2002).

6. John Van Engen, *Sisters and Brothers of the Common Life: The* Devotio Moderna *and the World of
the Later Middle Ages* (Philadelphia: University of Pennsylvania Press, 2008), 320.

that transcended . . . ordinary, disheveled, and prosaic pursuits."[7] In the same vein, Susan Karant-Nunn draws attention to the highly emotional qualities of late medieval German Catholicism, characterizing it as depending on "affective, dramatic demonstration of feeling." She observes that in such a religious climate, "emphatic sensations of sinews, nerves, and hearts" were called for; it was understood that the pious would "lose control, moan, and weep."[8]

This broader context for late medieval English devotion, crucial to unraveling the religious expression behind Margery Kempe's *Book*, is explored by Wolfgang Riehle in *The Secret Within: Hermits, Recluses, and Spiritual Outsiders in Medieval England*.[9] Revising his earlier view that Kempe was "neurotic and sick," Riehle places the author and her book within what he understands as the affective devotional traditions of late medieval European spirituality. He now includes her in the canon of late medieval devotional writers, Riehle explains, because he no longer reads Kempe's life "in isolation but [rather] from a European perspective" of devotional experience (280).

As part of his synthesis of late medieval affective devotion, Riehle describes similarities between Kempe and European holy women such as Marie of Oignies, Bridget of Sweden, Mechthild of Magdeburg, and Elizabeth of Hungary. Kempe, he argues, borrows "movable pieces" from the "collective fund" of Continental women's mystical experiences and folds this material into the *Book*'s account of her life (265). Riehle writes that he no longer finds her "sensational" and, except for the "intensity and frequency of her tears," not "exceptional" either. Kempe, he asserts, "should be judged as a woman who sought to lead as intense and authentic a life as possible, grounded in the faith and mentality of her day" (280).

The value of Riehle's approach is that it provides a context for considering Kempe's spirituality and allows us to see how certain aspects of her devotional practice, especially those that might seem surprising to modern audiences, were part of broader historical trends. *The Secret Within* draws attention to the outlines of late medieval spirituality and offers informed comparative analysis. Riehle notes, for example, that in contrast with those from other regions, English devotional writers placed a distinct emphasis on "joyful

---

7. Barbara R. Walters, Vincent Corrigan, and Peter T. Ricketts, *The Feast of Corpus Christi* (University Park: Pennsylvania State University Press, 2006), xv–xvi.

8. Susan Karant-Nunn, *The Reformation of Feeling: Shaping the Religious Emotions in Early Modern Germany* (Oxford: Oxford University Press, 2010), 60–61; on the association of the Virgin Mary with this kind of expressivity, see 159–65, 185–87. See also Kathryn Kerby-Fulton, *Books under Suspicion: Censorship and Tolerance of Revelatory Writing in Late Medieval England* (Notre Dame: University of Notre Dame Press, 2006), esp. 247–60 concerning Kempe, Alan of Lynn, and Thomas Netter.

9. Wolfgang Riehle, *The Secret Within: Hermits, Recluses, and Spiritual Outsiders in Medieval England* (Ithaca: Cornell University Press, 2014), cited parenthetically by page in the text.

sweetness" (302). He also describes the emotional outpouring of "tears of joy" in English writing and places this emphasis in the context of European devotion in which the desire for "spiritual freedom" and expression was essential (298–302). Riehle's method makes it possible to see what is shared and what is unusual in distinct religious cultures of late medieval Christianity, and offers a descriptive system in which individual cases like Kempe's can be understood and evaluated. In his reassessment, Kempe's *Book* is important because it tells us so much about late medieval religious experience.

Although I am indebted to scholars such as Riehle, Van Engen, Walters, and Karant-Nunn, the present book takes a different approach to Kempe's writing about her spiritual life. In it I reverse the emphasis on devotion—found, in particular, in *The Secret Within*—and maintain that late medieval religious culture is important because it tells us so much about Kempe and her *Book*. Kempe, no doubt, was "bound to show the influence of the times," as Riehle puts it, in writing about her spiritual practices and concerns (281). But, as I argue, despite her similarities with fellow believers, she was unusual precisely because she came to write *her own book* about her visions, feelings, and intense devotional experiences. It is remarkable, surprising, and in no way simply an aspect of the "times" that Margery Kempe—possibly illiterate and definitely in need of scribes to write for her—came to compose the story of her spiritual life. Kempe's is one of the first long prose books in English—sometimes referred to as the first autobiography in English—and it is one of only two extensive English-language works (Julian of Norwich's *Revelations* is the other) composed by women. There were, of course, other people who wrote about their extraordinary spiritual experiences, even in England. But Kempe's authorship of the *Book* is particular, hers alone—even as part of a collaborative process—and important for our understanding of whatever it means to *know* about the later Middle Ages.

We can, certainly, and should, try to see how historical circumstances contributed to the specific conditions under which the *Book* came into being, but this extends beyond an intellectual history of devotion. Social considerations, especially the conditions under which literacy was acquired, for example, shaped the nature of Kempe's engagement with the written word, and she shared these circumstances with other fifteenth-century women. For example, her growing involvement with books over the course of her life, despite her lack of formal training, follows patterns of involvement with the written word shared with other laywomen. Her engagement with written culture followed the familial construction of identity that was typical of the period: she refers to her lister, the young priest who read books aloud to her for seven or eight years, as her "son"; she imagines writing as extending her familial relationships with the divine—as a "daughter" of God, for instance. Her literate practice, like that of many late medieval women, was personally transformative. This was true, moreover, of her writing as well as her reading.[10] She was, as Riehle observes, a product of her times.

Nonetheless, I think it is of paramount importance to note how Kempe was, despite sharing attitudes about writing and devotion with other people, exceptional. Unlike the vast majority of late medieval women, she became a writer, and this alone distinguishes her from her contemporaries. Therefore, in contrast with Riehle, rather than grappling with the normalcy of her religious practices and sentiments, I ask a different question: Why was her quest for spiritual fulfillment predicated, finally, after decades of pursuing a life of passionate devotional engagement, on becoming the author of a book about her experiences?

This question is significant in two respects. First, it demands that we think about the ways in which books came to be composed in the later Middle Ages. The *Book* did not need to be written (I mean this in the sense that it was created and could, therefore, have not been created), and yet it was. Why? How did it happen that a laywoman who claimed that she could neither read nor write (even if she could) came to write a book? Second, it places emphasis on the fact that the *Book* was a *book*. We can, of course, learn all kinds of things about Kempe and her age by reading it, but unless we think about it as a written document (instead of a transparent vehicle for understanding late medieval devotion), we are overlooking an important historical fact. I see the *Book* as written by, for, and about Kempe—and not, as Lynn Staley has argued, a fiction created by Kempe about a character called Margery—but in my view it is nevertheless important to treat it as a *book* and not just a source of historical information or a straightforward transcript of life experience.

We continue to read Kempe's *Book* because it is *interesting*. The story of Kempe's life is moving and sometimes surprising. Her personal struggles and social interactions are absorbing, and even when we dislike her, as most readers do at times, we are also riveted by her responses. Despite the fact that she was born more than six hundred years ago, when we read the *Book*, it is as if we hear her speaking to us directly. Critics frequently comment on the sense of familiarity that readers feel toward her; habitual reference to her as "Margery" points at the sense of companionship and mutuality that many people experience as they read the *Book*.

---

10. See Rebecca Krug, *Reading Families: Women's Literate Practice in Late Medieval England* (Ithaca: Cornell University Press, 2002), 210–12. On a similar, personally transformative understanding of textual interactions, see Van Engen, *Sisters and Brothers*, 4.

But even as we think of her as a "real" person, our interest is not simply historical but, rather, produced by the language, images, and ideas found in the experience of reading. The *Book*'s prose is compelling, the dialogue is extraordinarily close to the rhythms of life—at least it seems so to me—and the analysis of Kempe and the people around her is revealing, thoughtful, and often funny. The *Book* is certainly digressive, episodic, and occasionally rambling, but it is also spirited, exciting, and action-packed. It is a remarkable piece of writing, and it holds our attention not just because Kempe is a remarkable historical figure but because the *Book* is a creative *literary* work.[11] And because it is, we should be as interested in understanding what kind of *book* it is as in what kind of person Kempe was. The present book, therefore, reflects both on the nature of the *Book* as a written text and on Kempe's engagement with written culture over the course of her life.

In *Margery Kempe and the Lonely Reader* I argue that Kempe's writing supplemented her reading and became the means by which she re-understood and reenvisioned both her self and the books she had read. Over the course of her life, she pursued her spiritual interests by turning to books: she was first a listener and conversationalist (hearing ideas found in books and discussing them with her spiritual friends), then a reader (encountering books more directly), and at last, years later, the author of her own book. I demonstrate that in writing the *Book*, she refused, finally, to be satisfied with other books' articulation of the nature of spiritual joy and comfort. She instead insisted that she must "say as she felt" by writing, and in doing so, she invites her *Book*'s readers, including herself and her scribes, to participate in the same process of revisionary reflection and self-construction.

A dynamic performance of self, the *Book* suggests, was missing from the books Kempe read and was, she came to believe, what she needed in her life. In the books she read, she looked to find a lived life, one represented as "in process," as a model for working through the problems of the need for consolation as part of the quest for spiritual joy. Without such a book, she came to write her own. Kempe and her scribes "read" her life, as she described it, and as it was shaped by and filtered through multiple experiences, including the explicitly textual models found in books. Her habitual retelling of her life—to herself, to spiritual advisers, and, finally, to the scribes writing the *Book* with

---

11. On the significance of the language of the *Book*, see Nancy Partner, "Reading *The Book of Margery Kempe*," *Exemplaria* 3 (1991): 29–66, and " 'And Most of All for Inordinate Love': Desire and Denial in the *Book of Margery Kempe*," *Thought* 64 (1989): 250–67. In the second essay, Partner argues that "repeated narrative motifs" are "clues to the structures of [Kempe's] inner life" (261). On style and late medieval devotional writing, see Elizabeth Robertson, *Early English Devotional Prose and the Female Audience* (Knoxville: University of Tennessee Press, 1990), esp. 195–98.

her—forms the fabric of the *Book*'s textualization of experience as a collaborative, social act in which Kempe, her scribes, and, ultimately, readers of the *Book* take part. Like Rich's lonely readers, she comes to write her own book, a book of consolation, the book she wished she had had all along.

By the time I finished a full draft of this project, I discovered that I had come to see Kempe's textual engagements—encounters with literate culture including activities beyond self-directed reading or writing such as aural reading, singing and recitation, attendance at worship services and cultural events, and conversation about books and ideas found in books—as *structuring* the *Book* in formal terms. Spanning across its textual surface, my chapters move from the preface's generic self-designation (as a book of consolation) to identification of the role that central devotional concepts (comfort, despair, shame, fear, and loneliness) played in both its emotional and textual articulations through the entire written work. I provide chapter summaries at the very end of this introduction that describe, briefly, what I see as the relationship between affective and textual reenvisioning developed in the *Book*. But first I place my approach to Kempe and the *Book* in the context of literary scholarship in the field, concentrating on three concepts: revision, collaboration, and autography.

Revision

The overarching argument of *Margery Kempe and the Lonely Reader*—that Kempe, in writing her *Book*, came to understand the work she was composing as her own book of consolation—is related to three issues that have occupied many of the *Book*'s critics: the concept of revision, the nature of collaboration, and the relationship between writer and readers.

An understanding of the *Book* as revisionary has fueled criticism, much of it concerned with women's authorship, for at least the past twenty-five years. Scholars have been especially interested in the ways in which cultural constraints and ideals are reimagined. In *Margery Kempe and Translations of the Flesh*, for example, Karma Lochrie argues that Kempe, rather than being silenced by women's traditional association with bodiliness in late medieval culture, "occup[ies] and exploit[s] her position as flesh" and in doing so discovers "a position from which to speak and write."[12] Lochrie's trenchant reflec-

---

12. Karma Lochrie, *Margery Kempe and Translations of the Flesh* (Philadelphia: University of Pennsylvania Press, 1991), 4. Lochrie's influence can be traced in scholarship about embodiment and the *Book*, for example, Vickie Larsen and Mary-Katherine Curnow, "Hagiographic Ambition, Fabliau Humor, and Creature Comforts in *The Book of Margery Kempe*," *Exemplaria* 25 (2013): 284–302; Liz Herbert McAvoy, *Authority and the Female Body in the Writings of Julian of Norwich and Margery Kempe*

tions on Kempe's writing as resistance and her articulation of the ways the *Book* speaks through "fissures" in patriarchal discourse continue to shape discussions about Kempe, including my own. Similarly, critics whose essays appear in Sandra J. McEntire's *Margery Kempe: A Book of Essays* are invested in discovering how Kempe reconceives of her experiences as a woman who writes.[13] The collection is particularly valuable for its exploration of issues related to vocation and personal psychology and, like Lochrie's book, continues to influence critics' understanding of Kempe as a writer who revises and resists medieval gender codes and conventions.

Lynn Staley in *Margery Kempe's Dissenting Fictions* also draws attention to the writer's ability to rewrite and reimagine reality. Staley employs the distinction between the author "Kempe" and her written subject "Margery" in her identification of the *Book* as a critique of late medieval social institutions, especially the late medieval Church. Staley argues that Kempe constructs a fictional account of Margery's experiences in order to imagine a new version of community, thereby revising existing ideas of collective life. Like Lochrie's *Translations of the Flesh*, Staley's book remains highly influential. My treatment of Kempe as an author searching for new kinds of spiritual community is indebted to her analysis.[14]

Recent interest in "vernacular theology" has encouraged scholars to return to the *Book*'s reception and reconfiguration of ideas about spirituality. This includes a wide variety of concerns. For example, Julie Orlemanksi relates Kempe's devotional "noise"—her sobbing—to shifts in the ways female sanctity was authorized.[15] David Lavinsky looks at the influence of devotional writing on the *Book*, examining Kempe's responses to Rollean ideas about affectivity.[16] Turning to Christian worship, in *Margery Kempe's Meditations*, Naoë Kukita Yoshikawa draws attention to Kempe's participation in communal religious traditions and argues that the *Book*'s structure depends on

---

(Cambridge: D. S. Brewer, 2004); and Kathy Lavezzo, "Sobs and Sighs between Women: The Homoerotics of Compassion in the *Book of Margery Kempe*," in *Premodern Sexualities*, ed. Louise Fradenburg and Carla Freccero (New York: Routledge, 1996), 175–98.

13. Sandra J. McEntire, ed., *Margery Kempe: A Book of Essays* (New York: Garland, 1992).

14. Lynn Staley, *Margery Kempe's Dissenting Fictions* (University Park: Pennsylvania State University Press, 1994). Staley's influence shapes literary/historical criticism about the *Book*; see, for example, Catherine Sanok, *Her Life Historical: Exemplarity and Female Saints' Lives in Late Medieval England* (Philadelphia: University of Pennsylvania Press, 2007), 116–44; Christine Cooper-Rompato, *The Gift of Tongues: Women's Xenoglossia in the Later Middle Ages* (University Park: Pennsylvania State University Press, 2010), 103–42; and Tara Williams, *Inventing Womanhood: Gender and Language in Later Middle English Writing* (Columbus: Ohio State University Press, 2011), 114–48.

15. Julie Orlemanski, "Margery's 'Noyse' and Distributed Expressivity," in *Voice and Voicelessness in Medieval Europe*, ed. Irit Ruth Kleiman (New York: Palgrave Macmillan, 2015), 123–38.

16. David Lavinsky, "'Speke to me be thowt': Affectivity, *Incendium Amoris*, and the *Book of Margery Kempe*," *Journal of English and Germanic Philology* 112 (2013): 340–64.

Kempe's redeployment of liturgical patterns.[17] Barbara Newman, reflecting on Kempe's involvement in personal rather than corporate religious practices, describes how Kempe experiments with various—sometimes conflicting—models of spiritual engagement, such as prophecy, mystical marriage, and spiritual sensation, pursuing one and then another, and recording this process in her book.[18] Sarah Salih, focusing on the relationship between texts and devotion, considers the ways in which the *Book* rewrites conceptions of virginity and argues for Kempe's gendered revision of religious discourse.[19]

Like the critics just mentioned, I understand Kempe's writing as revisionary in broad terms—as reinterpreting, reflecting on, and reshaping received ideas—but I also think of this "rewriting" in a narrower and primarily textual sense. My focus is on Kempe's composition of the *Book* as a process through which she reconceives of and reenvisions ideas found in books—and, by extension, in the text-based practices associated with literate culture through which such ideas are confronted. In my account, as it is for Rich, revision is overtly textual: it comes from interaction with books, and it results, at least in some cases, in writing that has the potential to reshape personal and collective understandings.

As I suggest in the chapters that follow, Kempe's reading, aural or otherwise, was extensive and included many works beyond those referred to in the short syllabus found in chapters seventeen and fifty-eight.[20] Ideas articulated in books of devotion that Kempe read or heard about in some other, second-hand way—like the scribe's recounting of his reading of Marie of Oignies's life, for example—are reexamined, reworked, and newly expressed in the

---

17. Naoë Kukita Yoshikawa, *Margery Kempe's Meditations: The Context of Medieval Devotional Literature, Liturgy and Iconography* (Cardiff: University of Wales Press, 2007). Kempe's reimagining of religious influences was the focus of the earliest positive assessments of Kempe's *Book*; see Hope Emily Allen's references to Continental holy women throughout the EETS edition of the *Book*.

18. Barbara Newman, "What Did It Mean to Say 'I Saw'? The Clash between Theory and Practice in Medieval Visionary Culture," *Speculum* 80 (2005): 1–43.

19. Sarah Salih, *Versions of Virginity in Late Medieval England* (Cambridge: D. S. Brewer, 2001). The relationship between spirituality and embodiment is a central theme in *A Companion to* The Book of Margery Kempe, ed. John H. Arnold and Katherine J. Lewis (Cambridge: D. S. Brewer, 2004), which includes a chapter by Salih, "Margery's Bodies: Piety, Work and Penance," 161–76.

20. I discuss all the works on Kempe's syllabus, but I also refer to works for which there is no explicit "proof" that they were read by Kempe, an idea I discuss later in this chapter. On reading, see Windeatt, *Book*, 7–18; A. C. Spearing, "Margery Kempe," in *A Companion to Middle English Prose*, ed. A. S. G. Edwards (Cambridge: D. S. Brewer, 2004), 89; Alexandra Barratt, "*Stabant matres dolorosae*: Women as Readers and Writers of Passion Prayers, Meditations and Visions," in *The Broken Body: Passion Devotion in Late-Medieval Culture*, ed. A. A. MacDonald, H. N. B. Ridderbos, and R. M. Schlusemann, 64, 67; Jacqueline Jenkins, "Reading and the *Book of Margery Kempe*," in Arnold and Lewis, 113–28, esp. 120–25. On illiteracy/Latinity, see Jenkins, "Reading and the *Book of Margery Kempe*," 126; Lochrie, *Translations of the Flesh*, 126; Cooper-Rompato, *The Gift of Tongues*, 122–23.

Book's chapters.[21] Although the *Book* certainly encapsulates ideas found, often with close linguistic similarity to lines and phrases, in other books, I argue that it comes to newly created understandings as Kempe reflects on her reading and her life *as she writes*. The books she encountered became part of her understanding of herself—an identity, in turn, subsequently created, discovered, and reshaped by the revisionary act of writing.

Collaboration: Reading

In the context of the present discussion, the term "collaboration" is important, first, for understanding the nature of late medieval reading. With a few exceptions, Kempe's reading practice—not just a list of books read or influencing the *Book* but the active, lived experience of textual consumption and absorption—has received little sustained attention. One useful exception is Anne Clark Bartlett's *Male Authors, Female Readers*. Bartlett proposes that late medieval women, including Kempe, read according to a "discourse of familiarity" in which female readers experienced books as part of spiritual friendships with male clerical readers.[22] Her analysis places reading in the social context of friendship. Another is Jacqueline Jenkins, "Reading and the *Book of Margery Kempe*." Jenkins, too, argues for collaborative reading as a distinct feature of Kempe's relationship with her lister, the young priest with whom she read books for seven or eight years. Her essay draws attention to the structures of power that shape the experience of reading. She observes, in relation to Kempe's tutorials, that " 'being read to' by a spiritual adviser does not necessarily mean 'being led by' " and "reading-through-hearing . . . is by no means an intellectually passive act."[23] Like Bartlett and Jenkins, I maintain that Kempe's reading was thoroughly collaborative; I develop this idea, briefly, in relation to late medieval literate practice.[24]

In a culture in which aural reading was common, the definition of reading extends well beyond the modern sense of silent, isolated engagement with a written text. Although underexamined in literary criticism, the subject has

---

21. In some cases, the *Book* records conversations and represents the topics discussed as if they were commentaries on written works. See, for example, chapter eighteen.

22. Anne Clark Bartlett, *Male Authors, Female Readers: Representation and Subjectivity in Middle English Devotional Literature* (Ithaca: Cornell University Press, 1995), 110–14.

23. Jenkins, "Reading and the *Book of Margery Kempe*," 117.

24. In contrast with "literacy," I use "literate practice" to refer to "the complex, sometimes contradictory, and socially shaped nature of medieval textual engagement" (Krug, *Reading Families*, 5). My use of the term is based on anthropological theory, such as that of Brian V. Street, which follows an "ideological model"; see *Literacy in Theory and Practice* (Cambridge: Cambridge University Press, 1984), 2–3.

been treated extensively by scholars concerned with the history of literacy; in relation to aural reading in the later Middle Ages, Joyce Coleman's analysis is among the most important.[25] Looking at both France and England, Coleman demonstrates that fourteenth- and fifteenth-century audiences showed a marked preference for "public reading"—aural reading experienced in group settings—over private textual consumption. The intimate and exclusive relationship between reader and book that defines modern reading is shown, in her analysis, to be historically constructed and particular to modernity. Medieval readers, in contrast, looked for opportunities to read books communally.

All aural readers, not just those listening in large groups, depend on sight readers for access to the content of books, allowing us to extend Coleman's identification of this preference to Kempe's aural reading with the young priest. If Kempe was indeed able to read on her own, as many scholars suggest, she must have *preferred* to listen to the young priest reading aloud. Coleman's thesis draws our attention to the social nature of this experience, and it becomes easier to see how the situatedness of reading matters as much as the content of the books read. In Kempe's case, it is a reminder that books encountered aurally are read in various ways; their meaning is dependent on the nature of the reading exchange, the participants in the reading experience, and the relationships that develop around interactions with books.

So, for example, Kempe's relationship with the young priest who reads to her for seven or eight years comes into focus as a shared interaction. The *Book* represents Kempe as selecting the books to be read; she "cawsyd" the young priest to read "meche good scriptur" and "many a good doctowr whech he wolde not a lokyd at that tyme had sche ne be" (chap. 58, 141). Furthermore, it notes that their tutorials were not just for Kempe—a favor the priest undertook—but, rather, mutually satisfying. The priest is said to have found "gret gostly confort" in their relationship; their reading brought him "gret encres" in "cunnyng" and "meryte" and served him well later in life (chap. 58, 141). The *Book* carefully observes that the relationship grows over time: Kempe and the young priest come to support and depend on each other. He becomes her advocate and defends her against detractors. She in turn prays for him, recounts her great anxiety when he falls ill, and dwells on her sadness when he leaves for another position.

One of the most interesting aspects of collaborative reading is that it is dynamic: as texts are experienced communally and listener/readers reflect and respond, meaning can be endlessly transformed. This can be true even

---

25. Joyce Coleman, *Public Reading and the Reading Public in Late Medieval England and France* (Cambridge: Cambridge University Press, 1996).

when participants come to the situation with fixed ideas about the material under consideration. In collaborative exchanges, even the "dominant participant"—this can be different participants at different times, depending on what is being read and with whom—who actively engages with the ideas of others may come to new understandings and see things from different perspectives. This is not to say that all public reading works this way, only to observe that symbiotic, collaborative reading is possible and that it is identified as the way in which Kempe learned to read books.

Collaboration: Writing

In contrast with scholars' general understanding of Kempe's reading as collaborative, there is no consensus about the usefulness of the term in relation to the *Book*'s composition. Rather, critics have been vocal in their disagreements about this process and continue to ask, "Who wrote it down?" and "Whose words are recorded?" So much, in fact, has been written on the subject of the *Book*'s composition that it is useful to think about it in terms of what I will call a "scale of collaboration."[26]

On the extreme ends of the scale, there is little collaboration of even a tangible, practical sort: scribes / male clerics—not Kempe—wrote (or rewrote so thoroughly that it might be said to be their work) the *Book* (John C. Hirsh; Sarah Rees Jones), or, at the other end, Kempe wrote it herself, and the scribes in the text are fictional tropes inserted to deflect criticism that would be directed at a female author (Staley). As we move to the middle of the scale, Kempe and her scribes both take part in the process of composition. In this middle range, either Kempe dictated the book to the scribes and we are able to distinguish the bits by Kempe from those by the scribes (Nicholas Watson); or, alternatively, there was some kind of collaborative process but not a "simple dictation model—she speaks, he writes" (Felicity Riddy), and, moreover, although the book "arose out of and was embedded in social interactions" (Riddy), there is no need to think of Kempe as a "real woman" writing "in a realistic mode" (on what grounds could such a claim be made if there is no

---

26. I list the references in order of their appearance in the text: John C. Hirsh, "Author and Scribe in *The Book of Margery Kempe*," *Medium Aevum* 44 (1975): 145–50; Sarah Rees Jones, "Margery Kempe and the Bishops," in *Medieval Women: Texts and Contexts in Late Medieval Britain*, ed. Jocelyn Wogan-Brown (Turnhout: Brepols, 2000), 371–91; Lynn Staley Johnson, "The Trope of the Scribe and the Question of Literary Authority in the Works of Julian of Norwich and Margery Kempe," *Speculum* 66 (1991): 820–38; Staley, *Dissenting Fictions*; Nicholas Watson, "The Making of *The Book of Margery Kempe*," and Felicity Riddy, "Text and Self in the *Book of Margery Kempe*," in *Voices in Dialogue: Reading Women in the Middle Ages*, ed. Linda Olson and Kathryn Kerby-Fulton (Notre Dame: University of Notre Dame Press, 2005), 395–434, 454–57, 435–53, 454-57.

documentary record of Kempe's existence outside the *Book*?) about herself (Riddy again).[27]

Rather than giving a full response to each position, I will simply list my objections in a general way and then explain how I think the process of composition is collaborative.[28] First, I see no reason to think there was not an actual, historical person named Margery Kempe or, a softer version of this, to assume that when she wrote a book describing her life, these were not her experiences. The *Book* states explicitly that these experiences were hers and insists that they are important precisely *because they happened*: they are evidence of God's grace, according to the preface, and significant as proof of God's mercy. Since purposefully fictional accounts of revelation, such as the dream visions *Pearl* and *Piers Plowman*, circulated during the later fourteenth century, it is hard to think of reasons to pass off this aspect of the *Book* as true if it was not.

All writing can be said to be "fiction" in the sense that textual construction *is* construction; that is no reason to dismiss the author's attempts to tell her story. It is for this reason that I refer to both the subject of the *Book* and its author as "Kempe." This is not to say that there are no differences between what "really" happened and what is represented in the *Book* but, rather, to emphasize the significance of the author's investment in the reality of her experiences and to draw attention to her sense of herself as continuous: changing over time but, nonetheless, in some way essentially the same person throughout her life.[29]

Second, I see no reason to recast the existence of the scribes as tropes. Many people, including men who were quite able to read and write on their own, employed amanuenses in the Middle Ages; technologically, writing was vastly more difficult on rough parchment or paper with stylus than it is now.

---

27. Riddy, "Text and Self," 457, 435–36.

28. Sue Ellen Holbrook's important essay "'About Her': Margery Kempe's Book of Feeling and Working," in *The Idea of Medieval Literature*, ed. James M. Dean and Christian K. Zacher (Newark: University of Delaware Press, 1992), 265–84, has shaped my thinking here and throughout this book.

29. Just as there was value in Talbot Donaldson's distinction between Chaucer-the-poet and Chaucer-the-pilgrim, Staley's insistence on the difference between Kempe and Margery usefully reminded scholars to think about the textual, constructed nature of the *Book*. I think it has outlived its usefulness, but if critics do continue to employ the distinction, it should be with the awareness that doing so has the effect of privileging the world "outside" Kempe's *Book* (documentation and "history" are associated with "Kempe"; records made by others are valued more highly than the "fictive" *Book*) over the particular creative act of writing to convey personal experience and understandings as expressed in a book (first-name-intimate "Margery") and over the textual nature of the *Book* itself. Given standard practice, the distinction is also problematic in terms of gender and the authorship of books related to self. For example, compare the Margery/Kempe distinction with our usual habit of referring to Petrarch, Rousseau, and Wordsworth by their last names.

At about the same time Kempe was writing, the undeniably literate (in every sense of the word, including facility with Latin) lawyer John Paston sometimes employed scribes. Even literate writers who hoped their compositions would remain private were known to use scribes. One woman demands her letter's recipient show the letter to "non erthely creature safe only your-selfe," and yet we know that at least one other person surely saw it: it was penned by her father's scribe.[30]

Third, although the act of writing was difficult and required training, there is no reason to believe that clerics wrote Kempe's *Book* without her input or that Kempe was uninvolved in the process. The record of her difficulties in acquiring scribes to assist her, traced in the prefaces, would be at least odd and certainly perverse if this had been the case. Furthermore, the *Book* is replete with personal detail and personal anecdotes of a disturbing nature that seem unlikely to have been known by anyone except the author herself.

Fourth, although I have no doubt that Kempe composed the *Book* in collaboration with clerical amanuenses, I am also certain that it is impossible, except in very specific cases in which the text marks voice explicitly, to separate Kempe's words from the scribes'. At certain points it is very clear (in the preface, for example) when the scribe represents his role in the process.[31] In most cases, however, divvying up of lines according to collaborator cannot be done with any degree of certainty. Anyone who has written an essay for an "interventionist" editor, taken dictation for a supervisor who encourages silent editing, or, at another's request, composed a letter in that person's name knows just how tangled the process of identifying "ownership" of words can be.[32] Furthermore, "dictation" is not synonymous with "transcription"; it can encompass a vast range of levels of interaction between speaker and scribe and varies from situation to situation.[33]

---

30. This example concerns John Paston II's future sister-in-law, Margery Brews; see Krug, *Reading Families*, 40.

31. Although critics generally ignore the second scribe (who writes only a page or so), I found it helpful to remind myself there were at least three scribes, and I therefore use "third scribe" to refer to the amanuensis who recopies (and probably expands) the rough draft of the first book written by the "first scribe," who may have been Kempe's son. The "second scribe" is an acquaintance of the third and had some familiarity with the first amanuensis's scribal hand. For further discussion, see chapter 5, "Loneliness." Critics have been eager to pursue the identities of the scribes. For a recent example, see Sebastian Sobecki, "'The writyng of this tretys': Margery Kempe's Son and the Authorship of Her *Book*," *Studies in the Age of Chaucer* 37 (2015): 257–83. Sobecki's essay appeared as I was completing revisions on the present book.

32. Watson's temptation to identify Latinate vocabulary with the scribe instead of Kempe is a case in point.

33. Even transcription isn't necessarily word-for-word recording; a good transcriptionist will modify, smooth over, and correct what is missing, irregular, or muddled. Kempe and her scribes work

In the present book, I understand the process of the *Book*'s composition as collaborative—just as the experience of reading was—in material and social terms. In writing, just as in reading, there is a pragmatic, physical dimension: Kempe was unable or unwilling to write with her own hand and depended on scribes to help her compose her book. This material dimension also has social consequences. In some cases the relationship between author and scribe might be heavily weighted toward the authority of the person dictating the work, and in others it might, just as possibly, be concentrated in the scribe. In the *Book*, however, the interaction between Kempe and her scribes is represented as shifting and changing. Collaboration does not simply mean "working together" but implies much more than this: the sharing of experience that is liable to change over time. When the third scribe—the one who writes the prefaces and who used his "inability" to read the hand in which the draft was written as an excuse not to get involved—finally finishes the project, he has been *changed* by his interactions with Kempe and their shared reading of her life. He goes from resisting her spirituality to weeping along with her as they write. This, too, is collaborative.

Some critics insist that Kempe's voice dominates—I often refer to it as "her" *Book*, and I do think this is the case—but it is important to acknowledge that the process of composition is nonetheless collaborative: the *Book* focuses on her life, and was motivated by Kempe's desire to fulfill God's command to write, but its composition involves shared experiences of writing down and reinterpreting that life.[34] The scribes become part of the text simply by taking part in the process of writing. They, and their reading and life experiences and professional concerns, are woven into the *Book* as part of an ongoing collaborative experience of spirituality and understanding that makes it difficult if not impossible to trace out clear distinctions between overlapping processes of reading, remembering, reconstructing, explaining, and composing.[35]

---

over the manuscript multiple times. (There is, to be clear, no reason to assume, on the basis of my reading of his essay, that Watson, as Riddy suggests, thinks of "dictation" as a process free of collaborative interventions.) Even if we think the first version was "pure" transcript, the final version is not.

34. On voice, see David Lawton, "English Literary Voices, 1350–1500," in *The Cambridge Companion to Medieval English Culture*, ed. Andrew Galloway (Cambridge: Cambridge University Press, 2011), 237–58, esp. 251–57 about Kempe and Julian of Norwich. See also Diana R. Uhlman, "The Comfort of Voice, the Solace of Script: Orality and Literacy in *The Book of Margery Kempe*," *Studies in Philology* 91 (1994): 50–69.

35. Riddy explains that the "boundaries" between "writing, narrating and reading" are "blurred" in the *Book*. This, as she points out, differs from the way other "authoritative" devotional books, such as the *Cloud of Unknowing*, are constituted ("Text and Self," 440–41).

Autography

Readers of the *Book*, as well as Kempe and her scribes, are invited to take part in the same self-construction the author claims for herself as reader and writer of her life. This is the kind of life writing that scholars of feminist autobiography call "autography": "These writers make 'I' and 'we' signify both continuity with an ongoing life in a body and a community, and dissociation within that life—gaps, amputations, silences. . . . The texts produced by this process simultaneously reshape female subjectivity and agency while reinscribing the possibility, experience, and value of being a 'self.' "[36] Like contemporary autography, in place of offering a static, linear narrative history of her life, Kempe's *Book* represents a process of self-in-the-making in which the dynamic construction of identity is located both in lived experience and in the act of capturing and reenvisioning that life in writing.[37]

Although the term "autography" is fairly new, scholarship about Kempe's *Book* has long taken note of this aspect of her writing, that is, of the indistinctness of the line between readers and writers. Clarissa Atkinson, for instance, first drew attention to the strangeness of this "autobiography" in which the author refrains from calling herself "I" and leads us to wonder who the *Book* was about and for whom it was intended.[38] Kate Greenspan has considered the "autohagiographical tradition" in relation to this aspect of Kempe's *Book* as well, providing a useful analysis of the role of the third person in women's devotional writings.[39] Riddy, too, reflects on continuities between writer and reader: "There is the formal oddity that the narration is in the third person and not the first, keeping 'who speaks?' and 'who perceives?' distinct."[40] Gail

---

36. Jeanne Perreault, *Writing Selves: Contemporary Feminist Autography* (Minneapolis: University of Minnesota Press, 1995), 4. In *Living Autobiographically: How We Create Identity in Narrative* (Ithaca: Cornell University Press, 2008), Paul John Eakin discusses the relationship between textualization and identity formation in terms of a "mutually enhancing interplay between what we are and what we say we are" (2). His term "identity narratives," in which "the content of self experience" is not limited to the "I," is a useful extension of "autography"; see esp. 76–79. See also Sidonie Smith, *A Poetics of Women's Autobiography* (Bloomington: Indiana University Press, 1987); and Leigh Gilmore, *Autobiographics: A Feminist Theory of Women's Self-Representation* (Ithaca: Cornell University Press, 1994). A. C. Spearing's use of the term "autography" differs from that of feminist scholars: he refers to first-person narration that resists predictable conclusions in favor of inconsistency and "lived" experience; see A. C. Spearing, *Medieval Autographies: The "I" of the Text* (Notre Dame: University of Notre Dame Press, 2012).

37. Riddy, in "Text and Self," observes, "It is in writing that the self is made" (443).

38. Atkinson, *Mystic and Pilgrim*, 21.

39. Kate Greenspan, "The Autohagiographical Tradition in Medieval Women's Devotional Writing," *a/b: Auto/Biography Studies* 6 (1991): 157–68.

40. Riddy, "Text and Self," 442–43. A number of critics have noticed, mostly in passing, the links created between writer and reader. See Watson, "The Making," 423; Lochrie, *Translations of the Flesh*, 145; Staley, *Dissenting Fictions*, 119; and Jessica Rosenfeld, "Envy and Exemplarity in *The Book of Margery Kempe*," *Exemplaria* 26 (2014): 117.

McMurray Gibson emphasizes the "usefulness" of the *Book* to readers for whom, she argues, it is "an indispensable guide."[41]

Kempe's *Book* invites readers to see themselves as similar to the book's subject in terms of their emotional uncertainties, sense of self, and understanding of that self in relation to the divine. This is why the prologue to the *Book* asserts that it is for the "solas and comfort" of all "synful wrecchys" who read it: the "grace that [God] werkyth in *any creatur* is ower profyth" (17, emphasis added). Kempe, a writer who is a reader, who writes about her younger self from the perspective of her older self, and who spends her life actively searching for spiritual comfort, reaches across her book's pages to the reader, who, she seems sure, must feel the same way Kempe herself has felt.

My sense of the continuity between Kempe and her readers is related to, but distinct from, that of the critics in the middle of my "scale of collaboration," Watson and Riddy. Watson, approaching the issue in theological terms, notes that the "hermeneutic instructions provided readers by the *Book* are . . . no different from those that God offers Kempe."[42] Focusing on the spiritual lessons encoded in the *Book*, he argues that the similarity between Kempe and the reader is based on the truths they share as believers. "Despite her singularity," he asserts, Kempe stands as "a type of devout lay living"; she represents the "ordinary Christian."[43] His concern is with narratives of shared Christian experience; keenly interested in the broader context of "ambitious" late medieval spirituality, he places Kempe and her readers in that social milieu. Watson's reader, like Kempe herself, is above all searching for spiritual understanding, and he therefore works to explicate the *Book*'s theological message in his account of its creation.

Riddy, by contrast, is fascinated by Barthesian theories of authorship that refuse to fix meaning in an author and, despite some impassioned remarks about the significance of gender for understanding the *Book*, resists treating Kempe as a historically "real" person. Her *readers* are, like Kempe's *Book*, producers of meaning, but she is uneasy with the idea of Kempe *herself* as a creator of meaning. What we encounter, she insists, is a book and not a person:

41. Gibson, *The Theater of Devotion*, 48–49. I have also described the *Book*, somewhat experimentally, as a "treatise"—not an autobiography—that aims to teach readers; see Rebecca Krug, "Margery Kempe," in *Cambridge Companion to Medieval English Literature, 1100–1500*, ed. Larry Scanlon (Cambridge: Cambridge University Press, 2009), 217–28.

42. Watson, "The Making," 423. See also Lochrie, *Translations of the Flesh*: Kempe directs "the same solace at her readers that she seeks for herself" (145); and on "interdiction" of Kempe's voice "between text and reader . . . into the writing and reading processes to authorize itself at the same time that it instructs the reader's desire" (100–101); and Rosenfeld, "Envy and Exemplarity," 105–21.

43. Watson, "The Making," 423–25.

"We have a 'Mar. Kempe of Lynne' in the text, but no evidence at all for an author of this name outside it."[44]

I am sympathetic to both viewpoints, but because I am most concerned with how Kempe, as an author, found ways to "speak" what she "felt" by writing, I diverge from both. Instead of tracing out theological principles in this book, I notice how ideas of self—both communal and individual—and self-expression are created in the *Book*. Kempe is concerned with religious experience but, as far as I can tell, not especially interested in systematized theological principles. Rather, her goal is to find spiritual comfort and community, and the approach in the *Book* is to reflect on religious understanding through experience.[45] If Kempe is Watson's ordinary Christian, I argue she is such in the sense that all believers undergo the same emotional difficulties and struggles. The *Book* is more therapeutic than theological and, in my account, shows the reader what it is to live with feelings of worthlessness, anxiety, and imperfection as part of efforts to find spiritual joy.

Like Riddy, I understand—with a few exceptions, including recent discoveries of documents related to the life of Kempe's son—that we can know Kempe only through her book and that there is no reason to think this is a "transcript" of her life. Any written work, as theorists have argued for my entire life as a scholar, involves creative construction: texts are never purely, directly mimetic; their language necessarily "mediates and selectively represents" that to which they refer.[46] I am nonetheless concerned with what we *can* know about Kempe from her *Book*. I do not *need* Kempe, as author, to anchor meaning in the *Book*. I *want* her to be its author because, unless we find some other way to learn to travel back in time, attending to the words a particular woman wrote about herself and her life is surely among the best ways—if it is to be possible at all—to gain historical knowledge.[47]

---

44. Riddy, "Text and Self," 436. Sobecki, "The writyng of this tretys," describes historical documents that suggest Kempe's first scribe was, as Allen suggested in the EETS notes, Kempe's son.

45. But perhaps the search for comfort is a kind of theology. See Berndt Hamm, "Was ist Frömmigkeitstheologie? Überlegungen zum 14. bis 16. Jahrhundert," in *Praxis Pietatis: Beiträge zu Theologie und Frömmigkeit in der Neuzeit; Wolfgang Sommer zum 60. Geburtstag*, ed. Hans-Jörg Nieden and Marcel Nieden (Stuttgart: Kolhammer, 1999), 9–45. Ronald Rittgers draws attention to Hamm's importance in this context; see *The Reformation of Suffering: Pastoral Theology and Lay Piety in Late Medieval and Early Modern Germany* (Oxford: Oxford University Press, 2012), 6.

46. Ralph Hanna, "Brewing Trouble: On Literature and History—and Alewives," in *Bodies and Disciplines: Intersections of Literature and History in Fifteenth-Century England*, ed. Barbara A. Hanawalt and David Wallace (Minneapolis: University of Minnesota Press, 1996), 1–17, esp. 3. Hanna offers a succinct and useful account of the ways that the methods of literary study, with their emphasis on texts as linguistic constructions, are important for understanding the past.

47. See Marea Mitchell, *The Book of Margery Kempe: Scholarship, Community, and Criticism* (New York: Peter Lang, 2005); and Holbrook, "About Her," esp. 279–80.

Kempe, I argue, wrote a book in which she came to see herself, along with her readers, as finding her "own way of being in the world." Through the revisionary, collaborative experiences of reading and writing, despite the unlikeliness that she would do so, she came, after years of reflection, conversation, and spiritual revelation, to write her own book of "solas and comfort." The *Book*, finally, invites readers, whom it identifies as part of the same community as Kempe and her scribes—no-longer-lonely readers—to experience the same sense of particularity, significance, and creative self-exploration that motivated its author to turn from reading to writing.

In *Margery Kempe and the Lonely Reader* I argue that Kempe came, over the course of her life, to feel compelled to produce her own book of consolation. She did so out of a desire to feel comfort and, as part of this desire, to find, sustain, and interact with fellow believers who were also looking to live lives of intense spiritual engagement. Over time, Kempe grew dissatisfied with books that were unable to match her own experiences—books that did not speak "so hyly of lofe of God" as she experienced it—and came, finally, to write her own book in an attempt, "yf sche cowd," to show how "sche felt" (chap. 17, 51).

The *Book* revises five categories of emotional engagement found in devotional writings that offer spiritual consolation: comfort, despair, shame, fear, and loneliness. In her reconsideration and rewriting, these concepts become both emotionally and textually significant, changing Kempe's understanding of herself and structuring the written instantiation of experience in her *Book*.

My first chapter, "Comfort," is about the offer of consolation in late medieval devotional writing. Here I distinguish between classical traditions, in which consolation was meant to eradicate grief and return the bereaved to civic life, and medieval ones, in which comfort was to be found in the recognition of both God's infinite goodness and the intense depravity of sinful humans. Medieval books of comfort sought to teach readers how they should feel about their "wretchedness"; the preface to Kempe's *Book* identifies it as offering "solace" to the "sinful wretches" who read it, to Kempe herself, and to her scribe. This chapter tracks the *Book*'s exploration of communal experiences of high devotional desire, comfort, joy, and emotional expression as a replacement for isolated individual experiences of "wretchedness." The search for a solution to the problem of wretchedness, in Kempe's case, was to turn to writing. I argue that Kempe and her scribes came to understand the *Book* itself as a work of consolation, a distinct category of devotional writing offering comfort, which, through the collaborative process of emotional, devotional intensity, was collectively experienced.

The second chapter, "Despair," locates the *Book*'s origins in the emotional/ spiritual experience of intense isolation and speechlessness, conditions associated with despair and, if despair was left unchecked, with suicidal inclinations. I suggest that this "temptation" toward suicide was Kempe's "secret sin" and that her decision to write the *Book* is an attempt to replace the silencing of confessional discourse, which had led her to a moment of near-suicidal crisis, with self-expression. Looking for ways to escape from definitions of self imposed from the outside upon a twenty-year-old woman (married to a "worschepful" citizen and soon thereafter pregnant as "kynde wolde" [chap. 1, 21]), the *Book* identifies despair, in retrospect, as an event that allowed its author to begin again. In struggling to "say what she felt," Kempe responds to the advice found in books of consolation: these warned against the damaging effects of despair but did little to explain how to escape its destructive power. She represents her discovery of the difference between "telling"—the process of saying how the condition felt—and enumerative confession that silenced and defined without allowing such expression as a solution to the problem. For Kempe, despair is the moment, as reconstructed in her *Book*, that explains how she was compelled to start writing and the point, in narrative terms, at which her story of becoming an author begins. Nevertheless, despite the positive results that accompany this "token" of God's love, the *Book* also insists on the ongoing experience of pain, even in the context of promises of new beginnings.

Chapter 3, "Shame," untangles the relationship between conflicting explanations of the value of this emotion, as found in devotional writing, and Kempe's methods for resisting its destructive power. Despair let Kempe initiate the process of rewriting her life, allowing her to see her self as dynamic and ever-changing (a self-in-the-making); shame was the condition that defined her and the emotional experience that united her with potential readers. The *Book* models two approaches to shame. The first is to represent this experience as a cause for celebration. Suffering scorn, debasement, and humiliation became a sign of divine favor and replaced feelings of shame. But because this reinterpretation required Kempe to suppress the lived experience of shame, that is, to replace actual experience with allegory, this approach is supplemented by another. The second method treats shame as an opportunity to re-understand self-identity—Kempe's own and her reader's—in relation to ideas of future spiritual perfection. The approach involves the repetition of phrases (lyrics, verse, proverbs, sayings) that allow Kempe and her reader, as part of the search for spiritual joy, to move beyond constraining, "worthless," shame-based identities. In textual terms, this strategy extends her efforts in the *Book* to "say as she felt" by turning to shared linguistic experiences to explore the process of self-making. The latter half of the chapter offers a catalogue of these verbal "remedies" against the destructive force of shame and returns, finally, to the second book's concluding re-exploration of the subject in terms of social interaction and personal history.

In the third chapter I argue that Kempe relies on ideas about the future to reexamine traditional understandings of the value of negative emotional experiences; my fourth chapter, "Fear," traces her efforts to focus on the present moment. The *Book* represents fear as alive and lived in an ever-returning present. Kempe is "evyr feryd," and Jesus speaks to her "evyr among," that is, always-in-the-middle-of, those fears. According to devotional writers, fear was, on the one hand, spiritually hygienic and, on the other, an obstacle to genuine love of God. Fear's importance, for these writers, was in its meaning (not in the experience of fear itself). Kempe wrestles with both the positive and negative definitions but focuses primarily on the experience, rather than the meaning, of fear. The *Book* is filled with "believer-in-crisis" episodes, and the excitement and pleasure of dramatized fear encourage readers to identify with the *Book*'s author/reader, reinforcing the exemplary function that the author and her scribes claim for its composition. In the first part of the *Book*, Kempe learns to cope with fear. In the second part, she explores less dramatic fears (of traveling and weather) in the context of the everyday and "unheroic." Rather than highlighting the excitement of terror, these episodes, by virtue of their very mundaneness, become opportunities, which come constantly and which Kempe and her readers might experience at every moment, to practice faith.

Chapter 5, "Loneliness," looks at Kempe's search for spiritual joy and companionship in conjunction with contradictory advice, offered in books of consolation, about interpersonal relations. One model insisted that the highest form of spiritual love could be found only in solitude—in a relationship with "Jesus Alone"; another recommended that believers seek out the fellowship of "right-minded men." Kempe's *Book* traces her struggle to live in accordance with both models. This involves, first, separation from family and home, followed by a series of pilgrimages, and, second, upon her return to Lynn, reintegration into English devotional and familial communities.

Following a period of loneliness and isolation, Kempe's decision to write her own account of her life is bound up in her desire to continue to experience the joy and companionship of fellow seekers after passionate, emotionally felt devotion. Her scribes become part of this process.

Ultimately, the *Book* itself is represented as Kempe's solution to the problem of loneliness. By creating a community of like-minded readers, the written text attempts to resolve the problem of loneliness by offering a permanent solution to the fracturing of friendship and fellowship. Kempe and her chosen readers become companions with perfect—and identical—understandings of one another. But the finality and permanence of this solution to loneliness is also thrown into question by what serves as a coda to the first eighty-nine chapters—book two—in which the distinction between textualized conclusiveness conflicts with representation of the always unfinished nature of lived life. This coda leaves us with a question: Is it possible for one to fend off loneliness by treating a physical book, as a writer or as a reader, as a vehicle for companionship?

Finally, a note about quotations, translations, and editions. At the beginning of several chapters, I provide my own translation of a passage that establishes elements of the argument that follows. In these translations I attempt to convey the meaning of the passages, and, although I try to be literal, I also try to make the meaning as clear as possible. Within the chapters themselves, I quote the *Book* in its original Middle English—standard practice in the field—and include bracketed glosses of especially difficult words.

My quotations of the *Book* by chapter and page number are from Lynn Staley's (TEAMS) edition of the Middle English text. I also refer to Barry Windeatt's (Longman) and Hope Emily Allen's (EETS) editions, and because chapter designations are consistent throughout all Middle English editions, readers who wish to look for citations may use these as well. Staley's edition is searchable through the TEAMS website (and I used this feature extensively). Windeatt's notes are more comprehensive than Staley's, and his edition includes a great deal of useful information, such as a chronology of Kempe's life and chapter summaries. The EETS edition includes detailed notes and references.

Editions of other devotional works to which I refer (such as *The Prickynge of Love*) employ a bewildering variety of editorial practices. I cite the edition listed in my bibliography and, when necessary for comprehension and ease of understanding, I silently emend quotations as needed.

CHAPTER ONE

Comfort

Some books ask us to forget that they were written over time. The *Book of Margery Kempe*, in contrast, demands that readers notice the link between its production—a lived performance occurring at specific moments and in particular contexts—and the finished work. The three passages excerpted here illustrate this point. Considered in chronological order of composition, the passages form a narrative of textual production in which reading and writing are part of a search for joy, wholeness, and comfort that spans thirty years, from the early decades of the fifteenth century, when Kempe—an aural reader—began to hear books read aloud, to completion of her *Book* in the late 1430s. The sequence demonstrates that Kempe's attraction to books was predicated on a belief in the ability of writing to offer "solace and comfort," and it outlines a transitional process in which Kempe-the-reader became a writer.

1. "She never heard any book—neither Hilton's book, nor Bridget's book, nor the *Pricking of Love*, nor the *Fire of Love*, nor any other book that she heard read aloud—that spoke more highly of the love of God than—if she knew how to or otherwise might have shown her feelings—she felt it working in her soul" (chap. 17, 51).
2. "And she was many times sick while this treatise was being written, and as soon as she would begin to go about the writing of this treatise, she was suddenly hale and whole" (chap. 89, 205).

3. "Here begins a short treatise and a comforting one for sinful wretches wherein they may find great solace and comfort for themselves" (preface, 17).

The first passage, from chapter seventeen of book one, refers to Kempe's reading of well-known devotional works.[1] Early in the fifteenth century, the *Book*'s author began visiting with an unnamed Dominican anchor who "many tymes refreschyd" her with God's "holy worde"—an expansive term that includes other "holy books."[2] Several years later, the anchor, who had brought her such "solas and comforte" (chap. 58, 140), died. After his death, Kempe and another friend, a young priest, began, around 1413, to read devotional books together, including those named in chapter seventeen (and fifty-eight, where a similar list appears)—and did so over the course of seven or eight years. In the context of this syllabus, her eagerness for reading books is emphasized and the great value of the tutorials for both Kempe and her "lister"—her reader, the young priest—described.

Yet, despite her enthusiasm for reading, the *Book* indicates that Kempe found, over time and on reflection, that her encounters with devotional works were never completely satisfying. In retrospect, the books seemed an imperfect match with her emotional experiences: they left her, despite her deep desire to hear them read aloud, "hungry" and longing for something more (chap. 58, 140). Kempe, according to chapter seventeen, experienced a distance—a difference at least—between her own understandings of spiritual joy and those represented in the books she and her friends read together. She felt "as hyly" as the descriptions of spiritual joy articulated by the books' authors, equal to the representations, that is, in degree but at the same time, different from them in kind. As a result of this lack of identity between the reader and her books, the chapter suggests, Kempe felt compelled to put her own feelings into words.

Presented in retrospect, chapters seventeen and fifty-eight explain that Kempe came to write her own book because she could no longer countenance the disjunction between her personal experiences of joy and comfort and the descriptions in written accounts. Her inability, emphasized in chapter

---

1. See also chap. 58, 140, where a similar syllabus appears. Windeatt describes the nature of these reading lists: "Here Kempe apparently refers to the *Revelations* of St Bridget of Sweden, some work by the fourteenth-century English mystic Walter Hilton, the pseudo-Bonaventure's *Stimulis Amoris*, and the *Incendium Amoris* of Richard Rolle" (*Book*, 10); chapter fifty-eight adds "many a good boke of hy contemplacyon and other bokys, as the Bybyl wyth doctowrys thereupon . . . and swech other" to the list in chapter seventeen.

2. The anchor was attached to the Dominican friary in Lynn. Kempe made the anchor's acquaintance sometime around 1409; see Goodman, *Margery Kempe and Her World*, 102.

seventeen, to describe the precise nature of her dissatisfaction and the round-about phrasing in which speaking and writing both seem to be implied—" yf sche cowd or ellys mygth a schewyd as sche felt" (chap. 17, 51)—draw attention to her struggle to find ways to make sense of the differences between the authority of the books she read and her experiences. These chapters show Kempe, over the course of more than twenty years, coming to see reading as a catalyst for textual production. By the time the *Book* records her thoughts on the subject, instead of allowing books to speak for her, she had begun to write her own.

The second passage, from the very last chapter of the *Book*'s first part, describes the consolatory effects of composition. As Kempe, depicting her much older self (she was in her early sixties by this time), neared completion of this part of the treatise, she experienced the act of writing as deeply therapeutic. Now that she has learned to "schew as sche felt" in the process of composing her own book, the chapter explains, composition has become a remedy for ongoing "sickness." Writing makes her "heil and hoole"—vocabulary that draws attention to its ability to heal and restore. In this passage, Kempe's earlier uneasiness about the imperfect ability of reading to reflect her own experience is supplanted by the efficacy of composition: solace comes from recounting her feelings in writing. Because individual experience is particular, singular, and idiosyncratic, it is in need of written articulation if someone desires to "say as she felt." Composition, the chapter suggests, allows for private expression and personal emotional fidelity.

And yet the *Book* locates the consolation of writing in communal sharing as well as personal expression. As Kempe and her scribe work together to compose and revise her "tretys in felyng and werkyng"—as they read over "every word" (preface, 20) of the draft, according to the preface—they both experience "holy teerys and wepingys" (chap. 89, 205–6). The shared circumstances of composition, the mutual investment in describing how Kempe felt in written words, draws author and scribe together in an emotional outpouring that merges their separate identities. Although we might understand the *Book* as Kempe's alone—that is, as her own hygienic encounter with her earlier life—in refusing the distinction between author and scribe/writer/reader, chapter eighty-nine underscores the collaborative, therapeutic aspects of writing. Kempe's feelings and reflections are the catalyst for writing, but as amanuensis and author work through her recollections, they both become active participants in the consolatory process.

This consolatory sharing occurs over time. Before becoming engaged in the work of writing the book, the scribe had been critical of Kempe. Swayed by popular opinion and official condemnation of her by a famous preaching friar, the scribe was "in purpose nevyr to a levyd hir felyngys" and he "fled and enchewyd [avoided]" her whenever possible (chap. 62, 149–50). But as they worked together, he changed his opinion about her, first, by reading books about spiritual ecstasy, like *The Prickingye of Love* (chap. 62, 150), which helped him understand her experiences, and then, as the excerpt quoted earlier suggests, by participating actively in the *Book*'s composition. In the second passage, books and personal experience become one, and the consolation of reading makes the consolation of writing possible.

Finally, the last of the three excerpts shows that the *Book*'s consolatory fusion of writing and reading is extended to the *Book*'s implied readers. In the *Book*, it is usually *people* who bring Kempe "solas and comfort." The phrase is used, for example, in chapter fifty-eight to refer to Kempe's friend and first reader, the Dominican anchor. Similarly, in chapter eighty-five, consolation comes from a person, in this case a childlike angelic figure who "gaf" her "comfort" by showing her, in a dream vision, that her name was written in the "boke of lyfe" (chap. 85, 195). Furthermore, the *Book* records Kempe's frequent requests that Jesus should ease her fears and bring her assurance, and she herself comforts many individuals including her guides, fellow pilgrims, and fellow parishioners.

In contrast, in the passage from the preface, readers are invited to find "solas and comfort" in the pages of the *Book*: instead of a person, the book itself brings consolation. The scribe's identification of the *Book*'s genre—a book of comfort—comes after the fact of composition, of course: the scribe wrote the revised preface after having read through the draft with Kempe, after having written a shorter, original proem, and after having rewritten the first "qwayr" of the *Book*.[3] By the time the revised preface was composed, Kempe and the scribe had come to associate *their own book* with the kind of solace that Kempe had, before, gotten from other people. The preface's generic identification focuses attention on the link between the *Book*'s author, who writes to find comfort, and her readers, who are invited to read to find solace.

In this story of textual production, Kempe's dissatisfaction with other people's books results in the composition of a book that provides her with solace of the same kind that she had found in her personal relationship with the anchor. Her *Book* will, in turn, allow its readers (beginning with Kempe herself and her scribes) to be comforted. It identifies itself as written *by readers for readers* and outlines the active and ongoing search for consolation as *shared* by

---

3. Windeatt suggests that the first quire ended somewhere between chapters sixteen and eighteen (*Book*, 50, n. 149).

authors, scribes, and readers. Although the *Book* is, finally, completely drafted, and therefore "finished," in this narrative of textuality, writing and reading are conceived of as dynamic, unending, and ever-changing. The act of writing becomes part of the ongoing search for spiritual comfort and understanding. She thus records successes and failures, joy and misery, wholesome emotions and destructive tendencies. As she does so, Kempe invites those who read her *Book* to claim for themselves its assertion of the right to speak the truth of one's feelings, to share in spiritual communities of desire, and to continue to explore the possibilities of finding comfort.

Writing her own book of consolation became the means by which Kempe sought, discovered, and created communal relationships in which she could share her desire for sustaining, emotionally realized spiritual joy. But how did she come, over the course of her life, to experience writing as comfort? What made her feel that she, and everyone she could imagine reading her book, *needed consolation*—a need so pressing that the *Book* repeats the word "comfort" nearly 150 times—if they were reading as part of a quest to experience spiritual joy? How did writing her own book make it possible for her to provide comfort for herself, her scribes, and the community of readers she imagined as her audience?

To answer these questions, the first half of this chapter traces the emphasis in the later Middle Ages on what I refer to as "the positive power of negative thinking," a concept of central importance to late medieval writing offering spiritual comfort. I then turn in the second half of the chapter to the historical circumstances, as encoded in the *Book*, which led Kempe—an unlikely candidate for authorship—to write her own book of consolation. I argue, finally, that after years of spiritual searching, she came to write her book out of a vocational sense of collective spiritual obligation as part of her quest to find comfort.

Consolation

In the later Middle Ages, two broad strains of consolatory writing shaped readers' ideas about the nature of loss and suffering. The first, and by far the most familiar to modern scholars, derived from classical traditions linking rationalist philosophy and civic life. The purpose of ancient consolations, as Han Baltussen observes, was to "rationalize the cause of grief and give meaning to it by exhorting the addressee to redefine or reconceptualize" loss.[4] Clas-

---

4. Han Baltussen, introduction to *Greek and Roman Consolation: Eight Studies of a Tradition and Its Afterlife*, ed. Han Baltussen (Swansea: Classical Press of Wales, 2013), xiii–xv.

sical consolations sought to eradicate feelings of loss. Ancient writers, including Cicero, whose own *Consolation* is often referred to in such discussions, understood grief as an "inconvenient and disruptive emotion" that needed to be controlled and eliminated.[5] Although these writings offering solace were formally diverse and served multiple purposes—making definition of consolation as a genre difficult—it is possible, as J. H. D. Scourfield observes, to generalize about underlying concerns.[6] Classical consolations exhibit a general lack of descriptive particularity—the individualized conditions resulting in grief are minimized in these works—and they emphasize social utility over personal experience.[7] The classical tradition of consolation remained important in the later Middle Ages and was especially influential in fictional literary writing.[8]

In contrast, late medieval books offering spiritual comfort, such as those mentioned in the syllabus found in chapters seventeen and fifty-eight of Kempe's *Book*, directly addressed the personal, affective dimensions of suffering and were far less concerned with philosophical reflection and civic integration.[9] Rather, the aim of such consolations was to alleviate anxiety felt with regard to one's spiritual life and, especially, to offer assurance of forgiveness for sin.[10] The solace that they offer concerns the feeling of "wretchedness" that medieval Christians believed was necessary but that, they felt, at the same time threatened to overwhelm the individual at any moment.[11] The books offered emotional security and certainty about divine forgiveness—not just the truth of such promises but, rather, the *feeling* of surety.

---

5. Ibid., xiii. Cicero's *Consolation*—now lost—written on the death of his daughter and long thought to be uniquely personal in its consolatory aims, is now considered, like his other treatises, to perform a public function; see Yelena Baraz, *A Written Republic: Cicero's Philosophical Politics* (Princeton: Princeton University Press, 2012), 86–95.

6. J. H. D. Scourfield argues for "social practice" as the defining feature of classical consolations: "At the centre of the consolatory map lies a range of texts (prose letters and similar material, poems, speeches, inscriptions) which may differ greatly from one another in certain respects but which share a common task" (20); see "Towards a Genre of Consolation," in Baltussen, *Greek and Roman Consolation*, 1–36.

7. On lack of particularity, see A. R. Wilcox, "Sympathetic Rivals: Consolation in Cicero's Letters," *American Journal of Philology* 126 (2005): 237–55, esp. 242.

8. Chaucer is particularly notable for the influence of this tradition on writing from the earlier parts of his career, such as *Book of the Duchess*, as well as much later, such as *Troilus*.

9. For the sake of clarity I have overemphasized the distinction between the two traditions. There is no question that they were intertwined in the later Middle Ages. Chaucer's *Book of the Duchess* and the anonymous *Pearl* are good examples of this fact.

10. See Thomas N. Tentler, *Sin and Confession on the Eve of the Reformation* (Princeton: Princeton University Press, 1977), esp. xvi, 13–15, 76, 114–15.

11. Julian of Norwich's assurance that "all shall be well" is the best-known expression of this need for comfort.

Later medieval consolations diverged from the classical tradition in three fundamental ways.[12] First, the need for consolation was based on human sinfulness, an ongoing condition rather than an event or occurrence, and not, as in the classical tradition, on eradicating grief or eliminating suffering. As a consequence, the comfort promised in these works is deeply desired, emotionally experienced, but temporary. Second, the aim of the devotional consolatory tradition was to intensify personal affective engagement: the goal was to *heighten* emotional response, not to eliminate it, because the consolatory dynamic focused on the individual's awareness of her feelings. Third, the purpose of late medieval consolations was to bring the "wretched" individual to a renewed state of faith: the goal was emotionally realized spiritual transformation. Such renewal, according to medieval books offering comfort, required constant, unwavering attention to *both* one's own fallen sinfulness *and* God's infinite goodness. The pursuit of spiritual joy therefore required the experience of both wretchedness and comfort.[13]

When Kempe began to read books offering spiritual comfort, she joined growing numbers of people in the Christian West searching for new ways to understand their personal relationship to belief. Given this dissatisfaction with prevailing categorizations of devotional experience—including distinctions between religious and lay, male and female, literate and non-literate—which had come to seem emotionally and spiritually constraining rather than natural and sustaining, the rise of new forms of passionate engagement with religion was increasingly widespread.

For spiritual seekers, devotional reading was a particularly important practice because it offered individuals outside of religious and cultural institutions guidance. Like modern self-help literature, medieval books offering comfort were eagerly consumed by readers looking to find personal fulfillment. Growing numbers of people, as Vincent Gillespie observes, turned to vernacular

---

12. Ralph Hanna observes that the need for sharp distinctions between classical and Christian ideas about patience (a virtue associated with consolation) declined in the later Middle Ages. Christian tradition frequently borrowed from classical sources; see "Some Commonplaces of Late Medieval Patience Discussions: An Introduction," in *The Triumph of Patience: Medieval and Renaissance Studies*, ed. Gerald J. Schiffhorst (Orlando: University Presses of Florida, 1978), 65–87.

13. See Julian of Norwich's explanation of the redemptive possibilities of human depravity: if we focus on God's love, God "loveth us now as welle while that we be here as he shalle do when we be there before his blessed face. But for failing of love in oure party, therfore is alle oure traveyle. Also God shewed that *sinne shalle be no shame, but wurshipe to man.*" *The Writings of Julian of Norwich: A Vision Showed to a Devout Woman and A Revelation of Love*, ed. Jacqueline Jenkins and Nicholas Watson (University Park: Pennsylvania State University Press, 2006), 237, emphasis added. In relation to this passage, see Annie Sutherland, "'Oure feyth is groundyd in goddes worde': Julian of Norwich and the Bible," in *The Medieval Mystical Tradition in England*, Exeter Symposium VII, *Papers Read at Charney Manor*, ed. Edward Alexander Jones (Cambridge: D. S. Brewer, 2004), 13.

religious works in order to pursue lives of "ambitious devotionalism."[14] The phenomenon is well documented.[15] "Devotional reading was everyone's reading," as Mary Erler observes, and because of this, books offering spiritual guidance "are found very widely and somewhat indiscriminately in male and female, lay and clerical hands."[16]

Readers of these works came from a wide variety of backgrounds: "By the fifteenth century the readership of works in the English vernacular was made up of an increasingly broad spectrum of social groups."[17] This "growing community of readers," as Watson argues, exhibited "deep interest in theological and ecclesiastical matters" and extended to include believers outside "the circle of privilege comprising aristocracy, gentry, and urban merchant classes."[18] According to Gillespie, such readers formed a newly emerging "audience aware of its own spiritual potential, eager to realise it, newly hungry for signs of divine grace and for communion with the deity"; for these readers, books "telling them how to avoid temptation or to deal with tribulation were part of the answer to their needs."[19]

Books of comfort assume readers turn to written works because they are looking for solutions to problems. Individuals may, of course, read books for other reasons—entertainment, nostalgia, habit, and so on. But the perspective from which books offering comfort are written is one in which readers are "sick" or lacking in some way—uncertain, uncomfortable, distressed—and read in order to improve their present condition.[20] Explicitly oriented toward results rather than the experience of reading, the books constitute a heterogeneous group, defined on the basis of their offer to help readers find spiritual comfort, and include remedies, books of comfort/tribulation/consolation,

14. Vincent Gillespie, "Religious Writing," in *The Oxford History of Literary Translation in English*, vol. 1, ed. Roger Ellis (Oxford: Oxford University Press, 2008), 269.

15. George R. Keiser, for example, links the growing centrality of printed works to emerging classes of late medieval manuscript readers; see "The Mystics and the Early English Printers: The Economics of Devotionalism," in *The Medieval Mystical Tradition in England*, Exeter Symposium IV, ed. Marion Glasscoe (Cambridge: D. S. Brewer, 1987), 7–26. Mary C. Erler has documented the dramatic rise in women readers, both religious and lay, of spiritual writing in the fourteenth through sixteenth centuries; see *Women, Reading, and Piety in Late Medieval England* (Cambridge: Cambridge University Press, 2002), esp. 4–5, 116–17.

16. Mary C. Erler, "Devotional Literature," in *The Cambridge History of the Book in Britain*, vol. 3, 1400–1557, ed. Lotte Hellinga and J. B. Trapp (Cambridge: Cambridge University Press, 1999), 495.

17. Jocelyn Wogan-Browne et al., *The Idea of the Vernacular: An Anthology of Middle English Literary Theory, 1280–1520* (University Park: Pennsylvania State University Press, 1999), 112.

18. Nicholas Watson, "The Politics of Middle English Writing," ibid., 339, 345.

19. Vincent Gillespie, "Anonymous Devotional Writings," in Edwards, *A Companion to Middle English Prose*, 131.

20. See Michael Solomon, *Fictions of Well-Being: Sickly Readers and Vernacular Medical Writing in Late Medieval and Early Modern Spain* (Philadelphia: University of Pennsylvania Press, 2010).

and even mystical treatises.[21] Although generically diverse, all the books on
Kempe's syllabus invite readers to find comfort in their pages. It is inelegant
to lump together books we have traditionally sorted into separate categories,
but the point remains: Kempe and readers like her were looking for spiritual
comfort, and they read books, of whatever variety, that promised to teach
them how to find it.[22]

Despite being generically dissimilar, medieval books offering comfort nevertheless articulate characteristic ideas about the need for comfort. Their primary basis of affiliation is their shared sense that people are always in need
of consolation and that books are vehicles by which it can be found.[23] Written explicitly for believers who, like those described in Misyn's translation
of Rolle's *Incendium Amoris* (Fire of Love), were "more besy to con lufe god
[more busy to know the love of God] then many thinges to knawe," vernacular books of comfort synthesize complex ideas about consolation for inde-
pendent study.[24] Although some offers of comfort, like those in Julian of Nor-

---

21. Scholars increasingly avoid the term "genre" to describe consolatory works; see Scourfield,
"Towards a Genre of Consolation." On late medieval devotional writing and the usefulness of other
types of categorization, see Vincent Gillespie, "Vernacular Books of Religion," in *Book Production
and Publishing in Britain, 1375–1475*, ed. Jeremy Griffiths and Derek Pearsall (Cambridge: Cambridge
University Press, 1989), 317–44; and Ralph Hanna, "Miscellaneity and Vernacularity: Conditions of
Literary Production in Late Medieval England," in *The Whole Book: Cultural Perspectives on the Medieval
Miscellany*, ed. Stephen G. Nichols and Siegfried Wenzel (Ann Arbor: University of Michigan Press,
1996), 37–52. A thematic emphasis on comfort allows us to notice that many of the categories, such as
"temptation" and "tribulation," overlap in P. S. Jollife's important and useful catalogue of devotional
writing *A Check-List of Middle English Prose Writings of Spiritual Guidance* (Toronto: Pontifical Institute,
1974).

22. Manuscript evidence suggests that the books on Kempe's syllabus were often found with
other books of comfort. Cambridge University Library MS Hh, for example, includes Flete's *Remedy*,
The Mirror of the Blessed Life of Jesus Christ, a translation of Suso's *Horologium*, selections from *The Prickynge of Love*, and *Qui Habitat*; see Edmund Colledge and Noel Chadwick, "Remedies against Temptations: The Third English Version of William Flete," *Archivo Italiano per la Storia della Pieta* 14 (1967):
206–7. MS Bodley 423 includes *The Contemplations of the Dread and Love of God*; an excerpted Middle
English version of Bridget's *Revelations*; several pieces in the consolation tradition such as *The mirrour
and the mede of sorow and of tribulacion*, the *Boke of Tribulacyon*, Flete's *Remedy ayenst the troubles of
temptacyons*; and selections from Rolle's *Form of Living*. Dated circa 1450, the manuscript is too late for
Kempe to have seen it, but its contents are certainly suggestive; see *Aelred of Rievaulx's De Institutione
Inclusarum*, ed. John Ayto and Alexandra Barratt, EETS 287 (Oxford: Oxford University Press, 1984),
xix–xxvi. On the inclusion of the *Contemplations* with other books of consolation (including those on
Kempe's syllabus), see Margaret Connolly, "Mapping Manuscripts and Readers of the *Contemplations
of the Dread and Love of God*," in *Design and Distribution of Late Medieval Manuscripts in England*, ed.
Margaret Connolly and Linne R. Mooney (York: York Medieval Press, 2008), 261–78.

23. K. S. Whetter provides a useful definition of genre as "a communicative resource leading to
understanding" that involves a "community of users" including "authors and their initial audiences";
see *Understanding Genre in Medieval Romance* (Aldershot: Ashgate, 2008), 16, 21.

24. *The Fire of Love and The Mending of Life or The Rule of Living of Richard Rolle, Translated by
Richard Misyn*, ed. Ralph Harvey, EETS o.s. 106 (London: Kegan Paul, Trench, Trübner and Company,

wich's *Revelations*, are complex and nuanced, many of the books accomplish their goals by proffering clear, intimate-seeming, and succinct directions for the individual trying to work things out on her own.[25]

Books of consolation offered readers acknowledgment of the emotional struggles involved in pursuing a life of devotion. In particular, they recognize that readers often feel a disjunction between their desire for deeper spiritual connections and their perceived ability to pursue such goals effectively. *Contemplations of the Dread and Love of God*, for instance, explains that contemporary readers see themselves as "more fieble" and "more unstable" than "holi fadres" from the past but encourages them nonetheless to imagine themselves as capable of loving God "with al desir" and of experiencing the sweetness and joy of "parfit love."[26] The books validate the readers' feelings of inferiority and worthlessness but also encourage them to see themselves as justified in their desire for the same close affiliations with the divine that, they believe, characterized the relationship between the "holy fathers" and God. Books offering comfort taught readers that their desire for deeper spiritual connections was laudable and that improving one's devotional life was possible for anyone who cared to try to do so. They urged their audiences to struggle against their sense of themselves as unstable and to begin the search for perfect love.

Hilton's *Scale*, for example, guarantees that comfort will come even when the reader feels "forsaken" and "lost." Hilton promises his reader that "whanne thou art brought so lowe bi traveil in temptacion that thee thenketh noon help ne comfort," if she remains hopeful and prays, "sotheli thou schalt sodaynli springe up as the dai sterre in gladnesse of herte."[27] The attractive image of joy as the morning star—a bright light suddenly appearing in the darkness—conveys the optimism and comfort that Hilton's *Scale* offers its readers. *The Prickynge of Love*—also, like the *Scale*, on Kempe's syllabus—is even more explicit in its repeated excursions into the sweetness and pleasure of moments of comfort and solace. The reader is urged to "entre into the loue of crist" to find "ioie endeles" and to visit the

1896), 3. The difficulty of Rolle's Latin in the original coupled with the theme of continual study of spiritual matters (*Fire*, 8, for example) tempers this idea.

25. Gillespie, "Anonymous Devotional Writings," notes that works such as Flete's *Remedies against Temptations* appealed to readers responsible for providing spiritual guidance as well as those "devout and literate laymen self-diagnosing the symptoms of their own spiritual wellbeing" (131).

26. *Contemplations of the Dread and Love of God*, ed. Margaret Connolly, EETS 303 (Oxford: Oxford University Press, 1993), 5–6, 18, 22–25.

27. *Walter Hilton's* The Scale of Perfection, ed. Thomas H. Bestul, TEAMS Middle English Texts Series (Kalamazoo: Medieval Institute Publications, 2000), 72.

"spicer's shop" of Jesus' passion, where she will find sweet-tasting medicines that heal, restore, and console.[28]

Like many readers, Kempe was attracted to this joyful variety of comfort, so much so, in fact, that the *Prickynge*'s language of sweet intoxication is embroidered into the *Book*'s articulation of the nature of devotion. Chapter sixty-two's description of spiritual desire (as filtered through the lens of the scribe's reading) is a good example: "Lofe governyth me and not reson . . . thei that se me irkyn and rewyn, not knowyng me drunkyn wyth thi lofe."[29] Kempe enthuses over heaven's honeyed "sownd of melodye so swet and delectable" (chap. 3, 26); and chapter twenty-two offers a delighted recounting of Jesus' promise that she is his "synguler lofe" and will be "fulfyllyd of al maner lofe" that she "cove[ts]" (chap. 22, 60–61). From beginning to end, the *Book* celebrates spiritual consolation as rapturous joy. Its final prayer marvels over the magnitude of God's mercy and the inadequacy of Kempe's boundless desire to think in her "hert" and "spekyn" with her "mowth" in his praise, honor, and reverence (bk. 2, chap. 10, 233). She claims the promises made in these books as her own, accepting their truthfulness and celebrating their guarantees that comfort and joy can be experienced.

Books of consolation invited readers like Kempe, who looked for ever greater solace and delight, to see themselves as God's beloved friend. They represent passionate spirituality as an intimate personal relationship between reader and the divine, and God's loving companionship as the highest form of comfort.[30] During times of trouble, such books promise, God will be the sufferer's "felawe in tribulacion."[31] In books offering comfort, trials and temptations are deemed desirable—not merely endurable—because they bring the divine ever nearer to the reader and in doing so bring her closer to the appealing warmth and security of God's personal devotion.

The positive, consoling force found in these books makes comfort synonymous with God's infinite goodness, mercy, and love. Solace, they argue, is love, and to find it, the reader must experience the divine emotionally as well as intellectually. For this reason, the books cultivate images of God that speak to their readers' affective apprehension of divine presence as the deepest form

28. *The Prickynge of Love*, ed. Harold Kane (Salzburg: Institut für Anglistik und Amerikanistik, 1983), 10–11.

29. *Book*, chap. 62, 150; see also *Prickynge*, 20.

30. See Rittgers, *The Reformation of Suffering*, on the late medieval view that suffering was "salvific" (12–83).

31. *The Book of Tribulation*, ed. Alexandra Barratt (Heidelberg: Carl Winter, 1983), 41. The idea is commonplace and frequently traced back in books offering comfort, as it is in *The Book of Tribulation*, to Psalm 90 [91]:15, which is known by its opening words in Latin, "Qui Habitat." The psalm and an anonymous exposition of it (sometimes identified as Hilton's) are discussed later in this chapter.

of devotion.[32] Intellectual knowledge, they argue, is useful and important, but the spiritual growth they believe their readers are searching for is understood as dependent on embodied emotional experience.[33] God is a friend, beloved companion, parent, and teacher; the reader is encouraged to feel gratitude and love toward him and to congratulate herself on her good fortune at having the opportunity to understand and feel that this is the case.[34] She is instructed to pursue this intimate relationship by learning to understand her feelings—both positive feelings like joy and negative feelings like unworthiness and instability. In this way, books offering consolation invite readers to see emotional self-expression as necessary to spiritual life.

Little wonder if believers like Kempe, eager to discover new ways of feeling "as highly" as they might, turned to books of comfort to look for deeper understanding of their ability to experience such joy and love.

Little wonder, that is, except that the method prescribed for feeling "as highly" as one might was, paradoxically, to feel "as lowly" as one could.

Wretchedness

Consolations invariably frame the pursuit of spiritual comfort in relation to human corruption and divine perfection.[35] In fact, in attempting to teach readers that their sinful natures allow for spiritual renewal, the books emphasize the loathsomeness of human depravity over spiritual joy.[36] The *Prickynge*, for example, declares that it is difficult to explain "thourghe wrytynge of a penne" the "gladsomnesse" and "swetnesse" readers can expect to feel if they practice these exercises, but has no trouble articulating the vileness of fallen humanity.[37] Similarly, in *The Scale of Perfection*, even as Hilton is careful to assure

---

32. Riehle, *The Secret Within*, observes that for Hilton, love is a precondition for knowing (190).

33. The *Prickynge*, for example, describes comfort as bodily and spiritual (11).

34. Readers are assured this is so even when, and sometimes especially when, God allows them to suffer. Kempe, for example, is told by her friend the anchor that her confessor's "sharpness" is due to the fact that God, for her "merit," has made him her "scourge." He compares the confessor with a smith who uses a file to make iron bright—a comparison common in consolations like the *Book of Tribulations* that list the "profits" of suffering. The anchor describes himself, in contrast, as her "nurse" and "comfort" (chap. 18).

35. See Richard Kieckhefer, *Unquiet Souls: Fourteenth-Century Saints and Their Religious Milieu* (Chicago: University of Chicago Press, 1984), for an important and influential discussion of this subject.

36. Nicolette Zeeman provides an extensive and illuminating analysis of the link between the experience of one's sinfulness and spiritual benefit; see *Piers Plowman and the Medieval Discourse of Desire* (Cambridge: Cambridge University Press, 2006), esp. 1–108. Linda Georgianna, *The Solitary Self: Individuality in the* Ancrene Wisse (Cambridge: Harvard University Press, 1981), esp. chap. 4, "Self-Awareness and Sin," 120–42, is also important and useful.

37. *Prickynge*, 15.

the reader that she should feel optimistic about God's mercy—"hopen stide-fastli"—and encourages her to actively pursue the joys of heaven, he returns frequently to the theme of human depravity. The reader is instructed to think of herself as "so greet a wrecche" that she is "worthi to synke to helle."[38] Human "wretchedness" is foundational: in the *Scale*, original sin is referred to as falling into "foulness" and "bestiality"; the soul itself is an unclean house full of "mulle [garbage]" and "filthe and smale motes."[39] Casual references to extreme self-abjection abound in these works. *The Faits and the Passion of Oure Lord Jesu Christ*, like the *Scale*, encourages its recipient to count herself as of "lesse pris"; the believer "schulde alwey sette lest of hemself" and she should consider herself, of all creatures, "most sinful."[40] Hilton goes even further, urging the reader who wants to find closeness to God that she must think of herself as a "wrecche, outcaste and refuse of alle men and women"; she is to "holden" herself as "not oonli . . . the moste wrecche that is but also as nought."[41] She is filthy, worthless, depraved, and, finally, nothing at all.

A sense of utter worthlessness, not just sinfulness, is at the heart of late medieval writers' emphasis on negativity.[42] *The Fire of Love*, for example, advises its reader to recognize her "frailtes" and consider herself "wars then all other"; true saintly meekness, according to Rolle, requires one to call one-self "lawest of all and unworthiest."[43] This applied to the high as well as the low. Despite her being recognized as the "Queen of Heaven," late medieval devotional writers frequently associated the Virgin, for example, with this extreme version of worthlessness. In Love's *Mirror*, Mary describes herself as the lowest of the low, a person who, "in hire awne sight," is "more foule and

---

38. *Scale*, 54. Modern self-help theory, in contrast with medieval negative thinking, is largely "positive." As the psychologist Julie K. Norem observes, belief in the benefits of optimism has been central to both popular and academic psychology for at least the last thirty years. Her theory of "negative thinking" or "defensive pessimism," in contrast, focuses on potential negative outcomes; see *The Positive Power of Negative Thinking* (Cambridge, Mass.: Basic Books, 2001). Popular responses to the pervasive demands of optimism include Barbara Ehrenreich, *Bright-Sided: How the Relentless Promotion of Positive Thinking Has Undermined America* (New York: Metropolitan Books, 2009); and David Rakoff, *Half-Empty* (New York: Doubleday, 2010).

39. *Scale*, 78, 86.

40. Alexandra Barratt, "The Faits and the Passion of Our Lord Jesu Christ," excerpted in *Women's Writing in Middle English: An Annotated Anthology*, ed. Alexandra Barratt (London: Longman, 1992), 205–18.

41. *Scale*, 47, 177.

42. See Andrew S. Galloway, "Petrarch's Pleasures, Chaucer's Revulsions, and the Aesthetics of Renunciation in Late-Medieval Culture," in *Answerable Style: The Idea of the Literary in Medieval England*, ed. Andrew S. Galloway and Frank Grady (Columbus: Ohio State University Press, 2013), 140–66, on "the varying categories of 'purity' and renunciation" as part of the "general shape of emotions" in the period (143).

43. *Fire*, 63.

more wrecched" than all others.[44] The Middle English version of Bridget's *Revelations* externalizes this lack of worth in the image of the Virgin Mary's "despisable" outer coat. The coat, Mary explains, is her "mekenes," and though it is "full despisable" to "louers of the worlde," it is worn to "plese noone" except her "sone."[45]

For late medieval writers, feeling one's own worthlessness was seen as the first step toward spiritual transformation. If human selves are, by definition, corrupt, a true understanding of self must be based on a clear view of one's utter culpability. To achieve this goal, devotional writers strive to represent the loathsomeness of sin as a personal, rather than abstract, problem, and they return to this idea habitually. The *Prickynge*, for example, makes a case for ongoing consciousness of oneself as "vileste and most wrecche of all other"; the reader must think of herself as ever "ful of synne and overleyd with uggli merkenesse [murkiness]."[46] The experience of self-loathing was so important and so widely discussed that the Middle English verb *uggen*—to fear, to dread—became identified with this kind of self-revulsion: the *Prickynge* advises the reader that it is a "grete gifte of god" to despise "thiself wilfulli so mykel that thou *uggest* of thiself and unnethes mai suffre [can barely stand] thiself."[47]

For spiritual healing to take place, emotional and physical suffering were deemed necessary. Painful, negative self-reflection, as the key to renewed spiritual vigor, was the concept that directed writers' energies. Furthermore, self-loathing was not merely a topic in books, not just an intellectual concept, and not simply an allegory about the soul's relationship to God. Rather, it was a way of interpreting oneself, the world, and one's reading, and it colored late medieval perception of reality at every level. Investment in personal loathsomeness constituted a prevailing emotional and spiritual discourse in the

---

44. *Nicholas Love's Mirror of the Blessed Life of Jesus Christ*, ed. Michael G. Sargent (New York: Garland Publishing, 1992), 19–20. When she is asked about her "manere of lyuyng" and if her life has been "ful of grace and of alle vertues," Mary responds, "Wit thou wele for certayne, that I held myself als gilty, most abiecte, and unworthi the grace of god." Mary Magdalene, one of Kempe's favorites saints, is also described in these terms. See Theresa Coletti, *Mary Magdalene and the Drama of Saints: Theater, Gender, and Religion in Late Medieval England* (Philadelphia: University of Pennsylvania Press, 2004), 151–89. There is a substantial literature on medieval women's relationship to literary models. See for example Amy N. Vines, *Women's Power in Late Medieval Romance* (Cambridge: D. S. Brewer, 2011).

45. *The Revelations of Saint Birgitta*, ed. William Patterson Cumming, EETS, o.s., 178 (London: Oxford University Press, 1929), 101.

46. *Prickynge*, 89, 91. Emphasis on degradation continues into the sixteenth century. See, for example, Thomas Betson, *Treatyse to Dyspose Men to be Vertuously Occupyd* [STC 1978]: "By reason of thy body ye were foule slyme of the erthe and now thy body is the house of fylte and derte and herafter it shall be wormes mete" (b1).

47. *Prickynge*, 94–95, emphasis added.

later Middle Ages, and it was understood as vital to a life of intense, emotionally realized devotion.

A Middle English exposition of Psalm 90 [91], *Qui Habitat*, provides a useful illustration of the influence and pervasiveness of insistent emphasis on sinful wretchedness in the period.[48] The psalm itself asserts the active power of God's protection. Its first verse promises, "He that dwelleth in the aid of the most High, shall abide under the protection of the God of Jacob." The subsequent fifteen verses describe the ways God shields the believer from danger. The psalm's tone is confident throughout—"A thousand shall fall at thy side, and ten thousand at thy right hand: but it [the forces of danger] shall not come nigh thee"—and its message of protection so strong that early Christians had it written on amulets (Psalm 90 [91]:7).[49]

The Middle English exposition, in startling contrast, presents a reading of the psalm focused on human suffering and sinfulness rather than divine aid. *Qui Habitat*'s first lines declare that all Christians will suffer persecution. Life is dangerous: inner and outer enemies lie in wait; the believer needs to be constantly vigilant. We might assume, given the psalm's guarantee of God's protective care, that the exposition would go on to develop this theme in relation to trials and tribulation. But instead of explaining how God comes to the aid of his chosen ones, *Qui Habitat* emphasizes the believer's imperfection and sinfulness. The reader is told that he must be meek, "forsake" himself, and experience his own "unstrengthe" (2). Rather than offering assurance, *Qui Habitat* teaches readers to understand divine protection as the revelation of human culpability. The "rihtwyse man" thanks God for showing him the "horiblete" of his "synnes." God is our "uptaker," protecting us from ourselves by revealing the "meschef" to which we are blind (4). In the exposition, only he who "dispiseth himself as he hath ben and as he is of himself" can count on God to defend him

---

48. *An Exposition of "Qui Habitat" and "Bonum Est" in English*, ed. Bjorn Wallner, Lund Studies in English 23 (Lund: C. W. K. Gleerup, 1954), cited parenthetically by page number in the text. The Vulgate, referred to in the *Exposition*, follows the Greek numbering of the psalms; Protestant translations of scripture follow the Hebrew numbering. I include the bracketed reference to Protestant translations. John P. H. Clark argues that Hilton is the author of the commentary in "Walter Hilton and the Psalm Commentary *Qui Habitat*," *Downside Review* 100 (1982): 235–62. Zeeman, *Piers Plowman and the Medieval Discourse of Desire*, discusses the exposition in the context of the sin-renewal dynamic (47–48).

49. The psalm was "an apotropaic song used to protect the faithful from malevolent spirits." Kevin J. Cathcart, "The Phoenician Inscriptions from Arslan Tash and Some Old Testament Texts," in *On Stone and Scroll: Essays in Honour of Graham Ivor Davies*, ed. James K. Aitken, Katharine Julia Dell, and Brian A. Mastin (Berlin: Walter de Gruyter, 2011), 87–99. Cathcart notes that the psalm was also inscribed on a Jewish incantation bowl and on Aramaic magical bowls.

(43). Oppositions are collapsed, and positive and negative become one and the same: "mournynge" is "murthe," "wo" is "wele," "serwe [sorrow]" is "glad" (44, 47–49). All "feeling" in this life is tribulation, and tribulation, *Qui Habitat* insists, *is* comfort.

The exposition leaves readers looking for comfort with little to go on. Who needs apotropaic songs if suffering is joy? How can the reader feel good if she should feel bad? Some books of comfort ask the same question. Many authors were aware of the power and intensity of emotions and of the difficulties caused when one felt "otherwise" than one supposedly should.[50] The narrator of *The Book of Tribulation*, for instance, acknowledges the accuracy of his "reader's" sense that humans experience the negative more intensely than the positive. The "reader" exclaims, "Sir, the presence of tribulacion I fele wel," but God's companionship "feel I not." If, the reader asks, God means for us to feel the "swetnes of his presence" in our hearts when we suffer, why is it that we do "not moor fele him?"[51] When readers are miserable, it is because of sin, but if sin motivates spiritual renewal, it is of fundamental importance to remember that this is the case: wretchedness was to be desired.

The books' authors grappled with the emotional burdens of the sin-renewal dynamic. Some works insist that when the promise of God's love and mercy is recalled, negative feelings will melt away. Chaucer's Parson, for example, recognizes that when a person feels "hevy thoghtful, and wraw [anxious]," those emotions may lead one to feel defeated but insists the cure is simple: "Allas, kan a man nat bithynke hym on the gospel. . . . Allas, what nedeth man thanne to been despeired, sith that his mercy so redy is and large? Axe and have."[52] Others acknowledge the initial utility of feelings of worthlessness, misery, and self-loathing but argue that such emotions must be purged when they are no longer useful. In *The Revelations of Saint Birgitta*, for example, negative feelings must, once the sinner is motivated to reform, be dug up, like weeds, by the root or hacked to pieces with axes.[53] Still others articulate theories in which negative feelings are constitutive of the soul's identity but at the same time separable from self-understanding. In *The Prickynge of Love*, for instance, the reader is told to hold herself in the lowest estimation possible yet, simultaneously, to distinguish sin from self: "Thou shalte hate thi

---

50. On the intractability of emotions in the *Book*, see chap. 61, 147; chap. 76, 159; chap. 68, 161.

51. *Book of Tribulation*, 42–43.

52. Geoffrey *Chaucer, The Parson's Tale*, in *The Riverside Chaucer*, ed. Larry D. Benson (Boston: Houghton Mifflin, 1987), ll. 677, 310; ll. 700–705, 311–12.

53. *Revelations of Saint Birgitta*, 21.

synne [but] thou shalt not hate thi-selfh."⁵⁴ Although the books differ in their approaches to the problem, they all tend to offer cognitive "workarounds" to emotional obstacles which limit devotional experience. Their advice falls into three categories: ignore your feelings, destroy your feelings, or pretend they are not really your feelings at all.

How could late medieval readers have eagerly turned to books offering this sort of cold comfort? What made it possible to benefit from such books? Why might Margery Kempe, in looking for comfort and joy, find herself "hungry" for this kind of advice?

Well and Woe

The yoking together of opposites was common in literature of the later Middle Ages. We might think, for example, of the Towneley (Wakefield) *Second Shepherd Pageant*'s masterly lashing together of the everyday world of the thief Mak and the miraculous birth of the savior. The coupling of seeming opposites (felix *and* culpa; Eva *and* Ave; tree of knowledge *and* cross) was so familiar that the oppositions required no explication. In the short call-and-response lyric *Adam Lay Bound*, for example, the logic behind associating the *celebration* of Mary as Queen of Heaven with Adam's crime and punishment is asserted but not explained: it was all for an apple.

In the context of communal performances, the logic behind the pairing of opposites is unexpressed, but the purpose is clear: these are celebrations of God's remarkable mercy. The depth of human depravity is asserted, but the collective, joyous expression of mercy punctuates these performances. What might seem startling—like the carol *Nova, nova, Ave fit ex Eva* (News, news! Ave has been made from Eve!)—provocatively announces the spectacular nature of God's transformation of evil into good. That which is lowest has been made highest, and this is cause for unbounded happiness. The divine performance of the impossible has, as it always will, saved the day.⁵⁵ In these celebratory events, the individual's reception of the seeming opposition between depravity and spiritual joy is filtered through the communal event

54. *Prickynge*, 96. The *Remedy* makes a similar distinction: "ye" do not consent to sin, but "it is the sensualite that dooth it in you" (229). Throughout this book I refer to Flete's English translation as "Remedy" and cite Colledge and Chadwick's edition. Santha Bhattacharji offers a brief but provocative discussion of this division: "Is there a part of the self that defines itself over and against its thoughts and emotions?"; see *Approaching Medieval English Anchoritic and Mystical Texts*, ed. Dee Dyas, Valerie Edden, and Roger Ellis (Cambridge: D. S. Brewer, 2005), 54.

55. Translated in Edith Rickert, ed., *Ancient English Christmas Carols, 1400–1700* (New York: Duffield and Co., 1915), 30–31.

(call-and-response recitation, attendance at plays, carol singing). As consola-tion for sin, the joyous collective reception of this message exceeds isolated individual responses to the binary opposition: "well" always triumphs over "woe," and participants in these events *feel* this as well as know it.[56]

Work by historians on religious expressiveness and emotion sheds impor-tant light on the social and pastoral importance of this kind of collective comfort in the late medieval and early modern periods. Building on Bar-bara Rosenwein's description of emotional communities, Karant-Nunn, for instance, discusses the role of communal experience in "cement[ing] groups" together; she draws attention to the way such experiences nurture and sus-tain individual emotion.[57] In the context of late medieval Catholicism, she argues that "willing, socially reinforced activities" and "the societal binding power of confraternities and processions . . . lent additional structure to com-munal existence" and, furthermore: "Inner and outer forms of culture can-not exist apart from one another. Feeling and expression are inseparable."[58] Gervase Rosser's book about English guilds, *The Art of Solidarity*, is similarly engaged with collective experience and communal ideals in the later Middle Ages. Rosser points out that social groups like the guilds depended on ideas of Christian friendship "as a means to break down the selfishness of individual isolation." He argues that friendship and empathy left "traces in the mind and body, fostering a physical and mental process of intersubjective exchange and transformation." The guilds, in cultivating communal friendship as a mode of living, served purposes that were, he argues, "at once personal and social."[59]

Rosser's and Karant-Nunn's attention to collective experience helps us understand how the *social* experience of books offering comfort made writ-ten consolations attractive to Kempe and readers like her. The consolatory dynamic as *lived*, experienced in a group and not in isolation, allows for a

56. Mervyn James argues that Corpus Christi plays involve "a mythology and a ritual in terms of which the opposites of social wholeness and social differentiation could be both affirmed and also brought into creative tension"; see "Ritual Drama and Social Body in the Late Medieval English Town," in *Society, Politics and Culture: Studies in Early Modern England* (Cambridge: Cambridge University Press, 1986), 16–47. On the formal patterning of "well and woe" in the *Book*, see Timea Szell, "From Woe to Weal and Weal to Woe," in McEntire, *Margery Kempe: A Book of Essays*, 73–91; and Partner, "Reading *The Book of Margery Kempe*." Consolation, as Julian of Norwich describes it in perhaps the now best-known book of comfort, is a process of trusting in the "mervelous medelur both of wele and of wo"; see *Writings*, 289). Julian's wry comment on tribulation is pertinent: God "saide nought 'Thowe salle not be tempested, thowe shalle not be travailed, thowe shalle not be desesed,' bot he saide, 'Thowe shalle nought be overcomen'" (113).

57. Karant-Nunn, *The Reformation of Feeling*, 4.

58. Ibid., 9.

59. Gervase Rosser, *The Art of Solidarity in the Middle Ages: Guilds in England, 1250–1550* (Oxford: Oxford University Press, 2015), 90, 94, 97.

sharing of wretchedness (I am a sinful wretch but so is everyone around me) that disperses the individual burden of this recognition and, in fact, makes the shared burden intensely pleasurable.[60] In group experience, the positive expands and makes the negative a cause for even greater unity.

In contrast, when read in isolation, books of consolation—as static written documents—maintain the hierarchical distinction between authoritative author and reader-in-need-of-solace and, necessarily, lack the affirmative nature of lived communal experience. Although the books often address the reader as "friend" and employ the second person in their efforts to create community, the reality of the solitary experience of reading is palpable. Furthermore, even when these books were read communally (and they often were), the author himself is absent—his presence only a fiction.[61] What most of the books offer in place of collective experiential sharing and acknowledgment are the advantages of textuality: the fixedness, authority, and iterability of the written. In their articulation of the nature of the comfort they bring, the books identify regular, repetitive concentration on individual sinfulness as the mechanism by which readers find solace. The books' objective is the same as that offered in communal experiences of "well and woe," but if they are read in isolation, the weight of their depictions of sinful abjection might easily smother readers as they try to find their way to spiritual comfort and joy.

Critics have frequently noted, for example, that Nicholas Love's *Mirror of the Blessed Life of Jesus Christ* seems to restrict its readers' intellectual activity; many of the books of comfort and remedies are even less concerned than the *Mirror* with analysis and explication. *The Twelve Profits of Tribulation*, for one, is little more than an outline of points (the first benefit of tribulation being that it is the "trew socoure of help sent from god to delyuer the soule") alongside authoritative citations relating to "profit."[62] Similarly, although remarkably sensitive to the reader's emotional needs in many ways, the vernacular versions of Flete's *Remedy against Temptations* is, nonetheless, also restrictive. The reader is urged to refrain from curiosity; searching for causes and reasons,

---

60. For a literary example of the dynamic, see Benjamin D. Utter, "Gawain and Goliath: Davidic Parallels and the Problem of Penance in *Sir Gawain and the Green Knight, Comitatus* 44 (2013): 121–55.

61. Erler, *Women, Reading, and Piety*, observes, for example, that the Duchess of York's regimen specified daily collective reading from Hilton's *Scale of Perfection* and other devotional books (5).

62. *The Twelve Profits of Tribulation*, in *Yorkshire Writers: Richard Rolle of Hampole and His Followers*, ed. Carl Horstmann, 2 vols. (London: Swan Sonnenschein, 1896), 2:46. Horstmann also published a second version of this work (2:389–406). On the differences between the two, see Barratt, *The Book of Tribulation* (which is another version of the material), 29; on the history of these related works and their popularity, see Barratt, 7–31.

the *Remedy* explains, will lead her to fall into "errouris" and "angwyschis."[63] Books offering consolation are adamant about the reasons why comfort is needed. They fix blame, often with energetic relish, on the individual believer, and because of this, their content can seem harsh and excessively negative.

It would be easy, at this point, to insist that Kempe's desire for comfort led her to reject the negativity of the books outright. Kempe, according to this way of thinking, decided to write her own "book of consolation" in order to bring negativity to the forefront and manage it. She understood the theory of negativity from her reading of books of consolation, and it is encoded in her writing—the *Book* is filled with stylized narratives of her childhood, for example, in which she identifies herself as the most wicked, dissolute, and sinful of girls—because she was incapable of ignoring, removing, or wishing away her feelings of self-loathing and finding the "comfort" for which she longed.[64] The decision to write the *Book*, then, came out of her desire to reject the "theory of negativity."

Neat as this sounds, however, it is an oversimplification of the *Book*'s rewriting of this material and a distortion of the social experiences in which Kempe came to read and reflect on books offering consolation. This is important, given the well-and-woe dynamic described earlier, because, as I have argued, content alone does not determine how ideas are experienced or how books are read. It is particularly significant for works, such as the consolations, that are meant to be *used* by their readers. The context in which textual consumption takes place, the frequency of interaction with writing, and the "constellation" in which a book is placed by its readers—among other books of varying types or alongside works belonging to similar genres or incorporating common themes—are as important as content in creating meaning.

I will mention just a few situations that reshape the meaning of books. Works read in isolation shape the reader's experience differently from books read communally. Works read in consultation with authorities influence understanding differently from those read with equals or subordinates.[65]

---

63. *Remedy*, 221. The *Remedy* is aware of the restrictive aspect of the written consolations and reminds its audience, "Though sometyme ye heren speke or reede in bokes sharpe wordes and harde sentencys, comforteth youre self, and thenke weel, many wordis that semen ful harde ben ment ful tendirly in good vndirstondyng" (225).

64. Kempe's revision of the ideas about negative thinking is progressive and changes over time, but she does not necessarily "reject" the earlier ideas out of hand. The *Book* provides ample evidence that she holds seemingly contradictory ideas at once without any suggestion that this is a problem. Riddy, "Text and Self," notes that in the *Book*, selfhood is not "integrated and consistent" but rather "in process—experimental, tentative, and contradictory" (443).

65. For some readers, these books were integrated into regular patterns of communal and daily living. When Cecily Neville, the Duchess of York, listened to Hilton and "Bonaventure"—referring

Works read in isolation from other books—some devotional writers claim their book is the *only one* a reader will need—present reading as contained in a single textual universe. These books insist on a monovalent view of meaning. In contrast, those that are read in the context of other books (this might, but need not, include those found in the same manuscript) are variously shaped by the books with which they are bound—or read—together. Books encountered only once or merely through secondhand description influence readers differently from books read repeatedly.

Kempe's *Book* offers its own evidence against a simple equation between discontent with books of comfort, as containing static, monolithic meanings, and her decision to write. The ecstatic language of joy, that is, the promise offered in books of consolation, is so common in Kempe's *Book* that it is clear she had found ways to experience comfort during the years *before* she began to write. The *Book*, as I argue in subsequent chapters, certainly revises concepts of negative emotion found in books of comfort, but it also reports that she felt "more highly" than the books she read; she was not mired in negative feelings but frustrated by the books' failure to live up to her own experiences of high desire.

Timeline

The message of negativity encoded in the books of consolation did not overwhelm Kempe because she received that message in the context of collective searches for and experiences of joy. She lived in various communities and interacted with many people, who, at least for a time, allowed her to manage the well and the woe of the consolatory dynamic. Collaborative reading, consultations and conversations with authorities and friends, and attendance at events like sermons and plays were all part of a dynamic communal exploration of what it meant to live with wretchedness as well as joy. For this reason, to understand the changes that led her to write her own book of comfort, we need to see how the communal experience of consolation worked in her life. What aspect of those experiences made it possible for her to keep a balance between wretchedness and comfort, and how, then, did this change over

---

probably to either *Love's Mirror* or *The Prickynge of Love*—at dinner, she did so as part of a life of regular interactions with other people. These included her chaplain and other members of her household, to whom she "recyteth" the material she had heard read earlier at suppertime and with whom she later enjoyed some "honest mirth" before drinking a glass of wine an hour before bed, praying alone, and retiring at eight o'clock; see "Ordinances and Rules of the Princess Cecill," in *A Collection of Ordinances and Regulations for the Government of the Royal Household Made in Divers Reigns from King Edward III to King William and Queen Mary*, ed. John Nichols (London: Society of Antiquaries, 1790), 37–39.

time? How does the *Book* make her rewriting of ideas of consolation both a personal quest and a commitment to a community of readers?

High Desire: 1413–1421

The years between 1413 and 1421, as recorded in the *Book*, represent the pinnacle of Kempe's engagement with diverse individuals, communities, and institutions. During this time, she grew ever more involved with others seeking spiritual understanding and solace and became increasingly vocal about her devotional outlook. (For this reason, these are also the years in which she faced the greatest dangers from the legal/clerical establishment.) In the spring of 1414, she sailed from Venice to the Holy Land and then from the Holy Land to Rome. In Rome, Kempe found the devotional intensity and communal joy that she had sought at home, looked for during her visits with spiritual advisers like Julian of Norwich, and pursued (but failed to discover) while she was in Jerusalem.

There is a fairy-tale-like quality to the chapters about Rome: Kempe is led into the city by a broken-backed guide, Richard, and travels with a mysterious lady, Margaret Florentyne, who is accompanied by a host made up of gentlewomen and Knights of Rhodes (chap. 31, 85). Once in Rome, casual strangers strike up conversations with Kempe, even those who speak little or no English. She is repeatedly invited to dinner by people who, having merely witnessed her devotion, want to spend more time with her. Strangers give her money. People cry along with her as she talks and tells stories. She has merely to walk the streets of Rome to discover friends, sweet dalliance, great devotion, and "hey comfort and consolacyon" (chap. 38, 97). Even her experiences of poverty feel like blessed opportunities. This was a time so enjoyable to her, and to those around her, that the city itself, as represented in the *Book*, feels like a refuge against the depredations of a worldview based on personal wretchedness. Maybe suffering really was joy and wretchedness a problem caused not by sin but by other people.

The *Book* presents Kempe's emotional symmetry with the Romans as its ideal version of communal interaction. These are *her* people because they are responsive, expressive, and driven by an outlook that expects the best, even when they are confronted with things they do not understand, such as her crying and dressing in white. It is unsurprising, then, that when she returns to England, she keeps finding herself in situations in which people "convert" to her spirituality of high desire. Given her experiences in Rome, these are the kind of people for whom she would have looked. The best example of this is found in the portrait of Thomas Marchale in chapter forty-five. After talking with Kempe "oftetymes," Marchale, moved by her words of "swetnes and of devocyon," becomes a "new man" (chap. 45, 110).

They meet in Bristol, just as Kempe prepares to go on pilgrimage to San-tiago, during the Corpus Christi celebration in 1417. Marchale is attracted by her extraordinary devotional expression: during the procession, she weeps and swoons, so overcome with emotion that she "myth not beryn it" and has to be carried inside. There she cries out, "I dey, I dey," causing people to have "gret merveyl what hir eyled" (chap. 45, 110). Although many bystand-ers react to her with irritation and surprise, Marchale is among those who are caused by God to "lofe hir and cherschyn hir ryth meche" on account of this episode. Like the Romans, the sympathizers at the celebration, includ-ing Marchale, invite her into their homes and feed her, eager to listen to her "dalyin in owre Lord." Drawn by her "good wordys that God put in hir to sey," Marchale, in particular, is "al mevyd *as he had ben a newe man* wyth terys of contricyon and compunccyon, bothe days and nyghtys, as owr Lord wolde visiten hys hert wyth grace" (chap. 45, 110, emphasis added).

Marchale's conversion is described in the language of affective extremes frequently found in late medieval writings offering spiritual comfort.[66] As he alternates between tears of contrition and ecstasies of sweetness and grace, Marchale, like Kempe at the Corpus Christi procession, is overcome by his emotions, so much so that, according to chapter forty-five, he sometimes went out "in the feldys" and "wept so sor for hys synnes and hys trespas that he fel down and myth not beryn it" (chap. 45, 110–11). The passage—very similar to one in chapter three in which Kempe reflects on her lifetime of "wykkednes" and can do nothing "but sorwyn and wepyn and evyr preyn for mercy and forgevenes" (chap. 3, 27)—draws attention to his membership in the company of sinful wretches: he had been, he tells Kempe, "a ful rekles man and mysgovernyd, and that sore rewyd hym" (chap. 45, 111).

And yet, as part of the sequence beginning with Corpus Christi Day, a fes-tival honoring the joyous aspects of the Eucharist and celebrating Christian unity, Marchale's transformation is laden with celebratory significance, and his wretchedness itself becomes part of the energizing rush of "grace" with which "owr Lord wolde visiten hys hert" (chap. 45, 110).[67] The *Book* draws attention to his conversion, first, in the context of the larger Christian com-munity's corporate celebration and, second, within Kempe's intimate world of spiritual seekers. Marchale becomes part of the *Book*'s network of partici-

---

66. In chapter 5 I argue that Marchale is one of Kempe's "spiritual sons."

67. On Corpus Christi, as a feast instituted "in a socio-historical context that gave rise to religious seekers," see Barbara R. Walters, Vincent Corrigan, and Peter T. Ricketts, *The Feast of Corpus Christi* (University Park: Pennsylvania State University Press, 2006), xv; the feast emerges as "a ritual of iconic unity" out of responses by a "rising stratum of urban bourgeoisie" to "an already established patrici-ate," which the authors connect with growing lay literacy (xvi).

pants in "Kempeian" high desire, joining her on the pilgrimage itself and supporting her in her legal difficulties when she returns to England.

As subsequent chapters unfold, we learn, upon their return from Santiago, that Marchale, Kempe, an unnamed man from Cambridgeshire, and Kempe's guide, Patrick, suffer together at the hands of the officials in Leicester. Following the release of the unnamed man and Marchale from jail, and on hearing the happy news that Kempe would not be burned as a heretic, they celebrate their "victory" over their "enmyis." Marchale, Patrick, and Kempe spend the entire night "hyly thankyng God" and "enjoy[ing] in owr Lord" (chap. 49, 119). In these chapters, as Kempe and her friends suffer persecution together, they experience and embody tribulation as redemption. Neither penitents nor ascetics, they simultaneously displace blame onto their persecutors and, through their full-throttle embrace of the justice behind their suffering, affirm their understanding of the paradoxical nature of their own sinfulness as profit.[68]

The *Book*'s description of the companionship between Marchale, Patrick, and Kempe allows us to round out our sense of Kempe's response to traditions of comfort. The episode provides a basis for identifying the affective appeal of the spirituality of high desire, that is, of a dynamic of intense visceral awareness of sin coupled with the sweetness of companionship and the pleasure of personal triumph over enemies.[69] Like Kempe, Marchale discovers the centrality of communal interaction for pursuing a life of devotion that sets him apart from the world. Chapters forty-five through forty-nine concentrate on this aspect, signaling that the weight of sin and the rhetoric of depravity are sustainable and productive for Kempe, Marchale, and Patrick through collective affirmation. The chapters demonstrate an awareness of community in which the pleasure and excitement of suffering are amplified by group celebration and solidarity. These are the same chapters in which Kempe is called a "loller" by the mayor of Leicester, a term synonymous, at least on the Continent, with spiritual intensity and zeal. Like the Devout on the Continent, of whom the term was used, her friends sought to turn

---

68. Amy Appleford distinguishes between, on the one hand, "a spiritually ambitious mode of personal asceticism" in which "disengagement with the world" was encouraged and, on the other, penitential discourse that is "rooted in the practice of confession"; see *Learning to Die in London, 1380–1540* (Philadelphia: University of Pennsylvania Press, 2014), 103; also 98–136. But the distinction does not apply to Kempe and her friends: they neither withdraw from the world nor focus on "moral self-analysis" (103). On confessional practice and self-definition, see Katherine C. Little, *Confession and Resistance: Defining the Self in Late Medieval England* (Notre Dame: University of Notre Dame Press, 2006), 17–48.

69. See Riehle, *The Secret Within*, on "sweetness" (302).

"inward" by forming intense spiritual communities while still living in the world—not in isolated religious enclosures.[70]

The *Book* makes it clear that Kempe found solace through affirmative interactions with fellow spiritual seekers. By the time she returned from her pilgrimage to Santiago in August of 1417, she had discovered ways to embrace the positive aspects of the consolatory dynamic and found strategies for living with the negative ones. This makes it unlikely that the composition of the *Book*, in and of itself, was conceived of as a direct solution to the problem of isolation and the experience of self-loathing. What does seem to be true, however, as I discuss shortly, is that *the isolation itself* that characterized Kempe's life in subsequent years resulted in her decision to begin writing.

Once Kempe's friend the young priest, her lister, left for another position sometime in the early 1420s, Kempe grew increasingly lonely. After his departure, and without the sustaining support of regular interaction with friends like Marchale and Patrick, her life looks more and more like that of the imaginary isolated reader of books of consolation that I described earlier in this chapter. Thrown back on her own resources, Kempe discovers that the negative aspects of consolation propel her forward, just as they had in the years recorded at the beginning of the *Book*, sending her on another quest to find new avenues of communal support, social engagement, and personal affirmation.[71]

Isolation: 1420s–1430s

The *Book* identifies the years from 1420 or so to the early 1430s as intensely lonely. In about 1421, the young priest who had read with Kempe left for a benefice elsewhere; at the same time, Kempe was attacked by a famous preaching friar, and her friends, including the priest who later became her third scribe, failed to support her. The *Book* itself seems to lose interest in things at this point in the narrative. It records few details about Kempe's life between 1421 and the early 1430s, with the exception of her visit to Richard Caister's grave, her abuse at the hands of the Franciscan friar, and the miraculous quenching of the fire at the church in Lynn in 1421.

---

70. Van Engen, *Sisters and Brothers*, 1–2.

71. On isolation, see Holbrook, "About Her," esp. 276. Holbrook argues that this period of isolation led Kempe to study spiritual matters on her own. Book one, Holbrook argues, was written in secrecy; book two, in contrast, is a sign of public validation that demonstrates the truth and value of Kempe's revelations (277). The care and fearfulness to which the scribe alludes support Holbrook's claim about secrecy, but this does not explain why Kempe started to write in the first place.

In place of the close accounting characteristic of most of the *Book*, the chapters covering the "missing" years lack detail and instead allude to absence and isolation using broad brushstrokes. In chapter sixty-three, for instance, Kempe's confessor, Robert Spryngolde, is recorded as asking her what she will do because only "the mone and seven sterrys" are left to become her enemies; everyone else has already turned against her (chap. 63, 151). The motif dominates the sparse narration of this "absent" period. Spiritual friends leave town; intimate friends and advisers are forbidden, on account of malicious gossip, to speak with her. Kempe, miserable and alone, describes herself as having "no comfort neithyr of man ne of childe" (chap. 69, 163).

Kempe's exile from friends is coupled with the cares of advancing age. After her own recovery, sometime around 1426, from an illness lasting many years, she begins to tend to her sick and elderly husband, John, and lives with him until his death in the early 1430s. The *Book* spares no words in describing how onerous this duty was: she had "ful mech labowr wyth hym," and his care took up all her time. This went on for many "yerys aftyr, as long as he levyd" (chap. 76, 173). At the end, John "turnyd childisch agen and lakkyd reson," lost control of his bodily functions, and "as a childe voydyd his natural digestyon in hys lynyn clothys ther he sat be the fyre er at the tabil" (chap. 76, 173). Unable to travel with abandon, as she had in her forties, sometimes ill herself—so sick that at times she believed she would die—and caring for an aging and incontinent husband, Kempe remained at home alone.

Yet even as the *Book* underscores the loneliness and desolation of this period, it identifies these years with spiritual growth. Kempe prays and meditates, as she had done "mor than twenty-five yer whan this tretys was wretyn," week in, week out, in "qwyet of sowle" unless she "wer ocupiid wyth seke folke, er ellys wer lettyd wyth other nedful occupasyon as was necessary unto hir er to hir evyn crystyn." In fact, her "contemplacyonis," the chapter notes, were now "mech mor sotyl," than before (chap. 87, 202). Chapters seventy-six through eighty-seven, which correspond with this time period, describe a series of meditations focused on events leading up to the Crucifixion. The busyness of her life at home, and her inability to leave the house much of the time, pushed her inward but also enriched her spiritual life.

The *Book*, in fact, goes even further than this, labeling the period of isolation as not merely beneficial but transformative. Echoing the breakdown and renewal recorded in chapter one, chapter eighty-seven describes another situation in which Kempe believes she will die. She succumbs to illness "dyvers tymys" and, as in chapter one, is so hopeless about her condition that "sche wend to a ben ded." But in contrast with the suicidal despair and subsequent breakdown she experienced early in her adult life, in this chapter hopelessness does not overwhelm her. Despite her repeated fears of dying, on each of these "dyvers tymys" she pulls through. Each time, she discovers anew "that sche schulde not deyin," and in fact, learns that "sche schulde levyn and far wel, and," the *Book* confirms, "so sche dede." Finally, not only does she find reassurance, but also, as part of this experience of illness and isolation, she revels in inner experiences of comfort and joy and delights in intimate communication "in hir sowle" with God (chap. 87, 202).[72]

Chapter eighty-seven identifies the period of isolation as the necessary prelude to what comes *after* the repeated instances in which Kempe believed she would die. The "comfort" that she felt "in hir sekenes," brought directly by the Virgin, Peter, Paul, Mary Magdalene, Katherine, Margaret, and every "seynt in hevyn that sche cowde thynke on" as they speak to her soul, as glorious as this experience is, leads her to choose a new path. The "missing years" and the promise that she will not just live but thrive remind her of the joy found in communal interaction.

The very next chapter, chapter eighty-eight, in fact, identifies the experience of writing, which she takes up after this illness, as allowing her to grow spiritually. What the missing years provided was time to reflect on her life. Without the solace and comfort of friends like Marchale, the lister, her friends in Rome, Caister, and the Dominican anchor, the memory of the negative aspects of the woe-well dynamic came back into focus. Beaten down by illness and worn out with caring for her husband, Kempe nearly succumbed to the unrelenting sense of hopelessness that isolated experience (and reading) foregrounded. If the saints "rescued" her from herself, they also reminded her of the satisfaction she found in interaction with other people pursuing lives of high desire. She did not retreat to her "inner Jerusalem." Instead, at this point, writing became the way to begin the search for fellow spiritual seekers all over again.

House Guests: The Early 1430s

Hope Emily Allen suggested that Kempe's son may have been her first scribe; the preface's description of the scribe as "a man dwellyng in Dewchlond whech was an Englyschman in hys byrth and sythen weddyd in Dewchland and had ther bothe a wyf and a chyld" and as having "good knowlach of this creatur" (preface, 19) certainly fits her son.[73] But even if, as is entirely possible,

---

72. The link back to the initial breakdown seems intentional: the chapter continues by observing that "sche had levar a servyd God, yyf sche myght a levyd so long, an hundryd yer in this maner of lyfe *than oo day as sche began fyrst*" (chap. 87, 202, emphasis added). The point of drawing the comparison is about the passage of time: it is forty years later and things are different.

73. Watson, "The Making," notes the discrepancy in chronology that has to be accounted for if the son was indeed the first scribe and argues that the scribe who rewrote the first book and was

he was not her son, the first scribe, and the scribe's wife, according to the preface, came to England and "dwellyd wyth the forseyd creatur tyl he had wretyn as mech as sche wold tellyn hym for the tym that thei wer togyder. And sythen he deyd." The scribe was "mevyd" by Kempe's "desyr" to have the book written; until he arrived, she could find "no wryter that wold fulfyllyn hyr desyr ne geve credens to hir felingys" (preface, 19).

The scene of writing, as described in the preface, is domestic. If the scribe was her son, then the second book's description of his visit to see his mother, accompanied by his German wife, reveals even more about the social nature of the process of writing the *Book*. There is no detailed record of the visit, but the *Book*'s brief account of the day on which Kempe's son fell ill indicates, despite chapter eighty-seven's portrait of quiet withdrawal from the world, that her house had been a whirlwind of activity: "On the next day that was the Sonday, whil thei wer at mete at noon with other frendys, [Kempe's son] fel in gret sekenes that he ros fro the tabyl and leyd hym on a bed, whech sekenes and infirmité ocupiid hym abowte a monyth" (bk. 2, chap. 2, 210).

It is difficult to see this as a period of total isolation: in addition to Kempe, her incapacitated husband, and her son and his wife, the house was filled with dinner guests.[74] And in fact, at the same time that the *Book* presents a stylized portrait of its author as quiet, contemplative, withdrawn from the world, it never lets its readers forget how much this final stage of involvement with written culture is about the conditions under which writing takes place. For Kempe, writing was necessarily collaborative and communal, but there is more to this than necessity: she actively chose to write because it allowed for social engagement.

The *Book* suggests that the intensely social nature of the process of composing the first draft was incidental. Kempe and her scribe/son worked at her house because it was convenient. But the *Book* also draws our attention to her habitual desire to share her life with other people, to the period of isolation, and to the pleasure she took in the company of fellow spiritual seekers. In this way it indicates that Kempe's decision to write was motivated by her desire to return to greater involvement with fellow spiritual seekers, and was therefore wrapped up in her desire to escape from loneliness. In composing the *Book*, Kempe and her scribes work together on the "text" of her life in a manner that replicates the social experience of her tutorials with the young priest.

---

entirely responsible for the second simply made a mistake (399). See Sobecki, "The writyng of this tretys," for documents that seem to confirm the son's role in the *Book*'s composition.

74. Riddy, "Text and Self," draws attention to the busyness of Kempe's life during the time of writing the *Book* and observes that "producing a book in these circumstances must have been a physically and emotionally fraught business" (437).

It would be glib to claim that Kempe came to write the *Book* merely because she was lonely or to suggest that she rounded up the scribes simply so she would have someone with whom to talk. What does seem true, however, is that she came to write the *Book*, at least in part, because during the "lonely years," she had time to think about the difference between past intense, joyful experiences of community and the isolation of the present. The memory of times when "well" outweighed "woe" made her reflect on those experiences—and on the books—that were part of that past. She must have thought about the ways she herself had changed over time, and as she did, her understanding of the books that told her how she should feel changed as well.

Vocation: Late 1430s

By the time Kempe and her scribe finished the second part of her *Book*, sometime after April 1438, her understanding of comfort as fleeting, the model found in books of comfort like the *Scale*, was replaced by a sense of the possibility of perpetually renewing ecstatic spiritual experience. This indicates that the process of writing, rewriting, and reflecting on her life allowed her, over the years in which the *Book* was composed, to revise her understanding of the meaning of consolation that she had originally encountered in books. By the late 1430s, as the second book argues, comfort is an ongoing, dynamic process—a constant part of life rather than a series of singular events. The second book demonstrates this by drawing attention to the last leg of Kempe's final pilgrimage before she returned home to Lynn. Her visit to Syon Abbey at Lammastide "for to purchasyn hir pardon" and her homecoming are described in the *Book*'s final chapters as part of the necessary, ongoing experience of finding joy and consolation in communal spiritual engagement.[75]

For a spiritual seeker looking to find comfort, Syon's Lammastide pardon was extremely attractive: it offered plenary remission, meaning that it removed all the temporal punishment due for sin whose guilt had been forgiven.[76] Syon itself was, furthermore, a magnet for believers eager to pursue lives of high spiritual desire. Founded by Henry V, Syon, a Bridgettine double monastery, relocated in 1431 from Twickenham to Isleworth on a very visible site just across the river from the Carthusian Charterhouse of Sheen. It was thought of, as Jeremy Catto notes, as "a gigantic power-house of

---

75. Salih, "Margery's Bodies," observes that Kempe "never abandons the world or the body as points of reference, but continues to rely on social interaction for both affirmation and rejection" (175).

76. Susan Powell, "Preaching at Syon Abbey," *Leeds Studies in English*, n.s., 31 (2000): 231.

prayer."[77] Having stopped in London on her way back from the Continent, Kempe made her way to Syon three days before the feast day. It was assuredly a side trip that she had planned to make.

In chapter ten's recounting, Kempe, a powerhouse of devotion herself, shares the spectacular imaginative representation with the abbey. Upon entering the church, she wept "plentiuows teerys of compunccyon and of compassyon" and experienced "gret devocyon and ful hy contemplacyon"— which by this point readers of the *Book* recognize as a formula used repeatedly to describe the spectacular "wonder" of Kempe's devotion (chap. 10, 228). The public nature of that devotion is as important as the moment of personal grace: in the *Book*'s final chapter, the "occupasyon" of Kempe's "sowle," as the chapter calls it, becomes linked with both the transformation of strangers and the pleasure of shared spiritual friendship.

At Syon, a young man, unknown to Kempe, witnesses this "wondyr" and is "mevyd thorw the Holy Gost" to ask her, with "fervent desir," why she weeps: "Modir, yf it lyke yow, I pray yow to schewyn me the occasyon of yowr wepyng, for I have not seyn a persone so plenteuows in teerys. . . . And, modir, thow I be yong, my desir is to plesyn my Lord." Kempe's response is tied firmly to the idea that one's wickedness—hewing to the counsel found in the books of comfort—must be ever present in one's mind. The cause of her weeping, she tells the young man, is "hir gret unkendnes agens hir maker," her repeated offenses against God's "goodnes," and "the gret abhominacyon that sche had of hir synnys" (bk. 2, chap. 10, 229).

But in addition to its enunciation of the theory of negative thinking, the passage is also an exposition of the communal comfort of the feast day and, even more pointedly, of Kempe's personal interaction with the zealous young man. The chapter draws attention to his eagerness to know her—the same kind of eagerness expressed in earlier chapters when she had visited with devout figures like Julian of Norwich and Richard Caister. It draws attention to his eagerness by reporting the young man's exact words: "I prey yow beth not strawnge unto me. Schewith modirly and goodly yowr conceit unto me as I trust unto yow." Kempe is moved to tell him "many good wordys of gostly comfort," and they dine together, the anecdote concluding with the observation that the young man, who planned to become a priest, was "ful glad to ben in hir cumpany" (bk. 2, chap. 10, 229). She seems to have seen in him a younger, male version of herself.

77. Jeremy Catto, "Religious Change under Henry V," in *Henry V: The Practice of Kingship*, ed. G. L. Harriss (Oxford: Oxford University Press, 1985), 111.

The young man's pleasure in her consoling discourse is associated, in the same chapter, with Kempe's own delight at seeing her friend Reynald the hermit on Lammas Day. As she catches a glimpse of him, she approaches him "wyth gret joy of spirit" and welcomes him "wyth alle the myghtys of hir sowle" (bk. 2, chap. 10, 229). Despite her warmth, Reynald, put out because he got into trouble for helping Kempe leave Lynn without her confessor's permission, at first gives her the cold shoulder. When she asks him to accompany her on her way home from London, he retorts, "I was blamyd for yowr defawte whan I led yow last; I wil no mor," and then warns her that she will find "lityl frenschep" when she gets home. Nevertheless, Kempe offers to pay his way and he begrudgingly agrees to accompany her. On her return home, she finds, after some "ful scharp wordys" from her confessor, that "sche had as good love" from him, despite Reynald's warning, and "of other frendys aftyr as sche had beforn" (bk. 2, chap. 10, 230).

The sequence caps off the second book's definitive statements about the nature of comfort—statements, interestingly enough, that seem to reinstate the civic, social impetus motivating ancient writing about consolation. In the *Book*, comfort, finally, is identified as communally as well as individually experienced, and the effort to find it is not just a personal whim or egocentric desire but a shared obligation. In chapter three of book two, in a glance back at the revised preface's wind-tossed reed, God tells Kempe to "suffer paciently a while," "trost in my mercy," and "wavyr nowt" in faith (bk. 2, chap. 3, 214). This is the language of books of consolation like the *Twelve Profits*, but the *Book* reanimates these quasi-stoical truisms by reflecting on the positive, immediate, and transformative promise of this kind of comfort. In chapter three of the concluding book, God tells her that when she remains steadfast, not only will she find "gret comfort" in herself but also she will have the ability to "comfortyn al" her companions. Having become an expert in finding comfort and "hy devocyon" of the sort that brought her "ful meche grace in this lyfe" and allowed her to feel assured that she would have "joy and blysse wythowtyn ende" (bk. 2, chap. 9, 228) in the afterlife, she is bidden to recognize her ability and her obligation to help others find solace (bk. 2, chap. 3, 214).

The fact that Kempe records this idea in the final pages of the *Book* indicates that the process of finding comfort, which initiated her movement away from her domestic life in Lynn and out into the world to seek advice, validation, and assurance, has been reevaluated over time. As a written text, the *Book* shapes this search into a narrative that—despite the assertion that the *Book* is written not in order but rather according to seemingly spontaneous acts of memory—has a level of systematic coherence. Kempe's experiences, as written, textualized narrative, begin with uncertainty and struggle as she wrestles, in isolation, with her feelings of despair and desperation as a young woman. Although the spiritual closeness to God, through prayer, contemplation, and revelation, that Kempe finds is celebrated in the *Book*, its ephemeral and isolating nature demands supplementation in communal interactions. Compelled to find comfort, she ventures out into the world, turning first to spiritual authorities, then to books, and on to companions and friends with whom to share her desire for a life of high devotion.

The sequence in book two underscores the significance of Kempe's status as a laywoman in her decision to choose to write; it is an act of consolation for herself *and* her readers. The young man who makes her acquaintance can turn to life as a priest—he tells her he plans to "takyn the abite of this holy religyon"—to fulfill his desire for a life of passionate spiritual engagement (bk. 2, chap. 10, 229). Similarly, Kempe's friend Reynald, the unenclosed hermit, is, like the young man, able to pursue a life of spiritual intensity through his vocation.

The "occupation" of Kempe's "soul," in contrast, finds expression in the wider community of believers. We can see her as limited by gender and life experiences that excluded her from religious vocations aligned with the institutional Church, but we can also see her as enabled by the same factors. The *Book* gets written precisely because it becomes a possible way, an avenue of opportunity—even in spite of the difficulties she confronts in finding scribes to write for her—for Kempe to find and share her experiences of devotional intensity with the *Book*'s readers. In his discussion of solidarity and the English guilds, Rosser argues that in the later Middle Ages an understanding of communal obligation and collective spiritual engagement "saw lay men and women taking ownership of collective purposes and projects which had previously tended to be the preserve of ecclesiastical institutions."[78] In writing her *Book*, Kempe embarked on such a project.

This active communal impulse dominates Kempe's life, as recorded in the *Book*, from the time she began to read books with spiritual advisers in her early thirties. The question that compelled her to read books and consult authorities was how to *feel* God's presence in order to experience comfort. Without that feeling, she found it impossible to know how to respond to spiritual truths that she *knew*. The *Book* traces the path toward living—not merely finding, but creating, solving, and continually experiencing—an answer to this question. As part of the quest to feel God's presence and to understand

---

78. Rosser, *The Art of Solidarity*, 209.

herself and her experiences, the *Book* tells the story of her search for friend-ship and community. That, in turn, reshaped her understanding of who she was and what it meant to find solace and comfort in the face of the emotional isolation and anxiety that the first chapters of the *Book* identify as disabling.

In telling her story, Kempe filters the events recorded through the culmi-nation of her experiences (lived and read) over the course of twenty or more years. Although the *Book* sometimes feels as if it offers a record of events as they happened, its chapters create and construct Kempe's life.[79] Her dis-tance from the events allowed her—forced her—to think of herself as both the reader of her life story and its writer. In this way, the *Book* reaches out to and includes its readers as part of the life it creates.

Jesus tells Kempe, addressing her in the second person, that she has "gret" and even "grettyr cawse" to love him because "thu schalt heryn that thu nevyr herdist" and "se that thu nevyr sey" and "felyn that thu nevyr feltist" (chap. 35, 93). The problem of sin, as it is discussed in devotional writing from the books on her syllabus, is part of Jesus' message in this passage—he lays blame on Kempe just as the books of consolation did—but it is the stirring guarantees of entirely new experiences and sensations that make the *Book* so appealing. Although Jesus' promise of remarkable feelings, emotions so unprecedented that the chapter insists on their sensual novelty repeatedly, is made to Kempe personally, it functions as a guarantee that extends to the *Book*'s readers. The promise works retrospectively for Kempe herself, validating her earlier experi-ences and reframing her understanding of her feelings in terms of the excite-ment of such promises. And it also works for the book's reader, who can apply the promise to his or her own life and who benefits from its "writtenness"—just as the scribes, Kempe's first readers, do. When the *Book* makes promises to Kempe, it extends those promises to readers as well.

There is a stirring, heroic quality to Kempe's life, as described in the *Book*, that is not just personal megalomania—although there is that, too—but an emotional pact with the reader: "we," the *Book* might have stated, "who want to experience God's love are special, and whatever hardships we face, we are chosen for exceptional experiences." When Kempe stands up to enemies who mock and abuse her, the reader is invited to see herself in this heroic position. When Kempe is frightened by roadside bandits or stormy seas, the comfort

---

79. Naoë Kukita Yoshikawa observes, in her discussion of Kempe's "meditations," that the pas-sages are shaped by her liturgical knowledge and that, as narration, they are written "in retrospect after having practised or having considered the meaning [of the meditations] for twenty-five years or longer," and that Kempe's "meditational experience seems to affect the way she selects and handles the events of her life in her creative act of recollecting them" (*Margery Kempe's Meditations*, 4–5).

that God brings her is to be understood as the reader's, too. When God talks directly to Kempe, the reader is reminded that God talks to her, too, directly. This is not limited to instruction; rather, it is the remarkable, all-consuming, and heroic nature of Kempe's life that the *Book* invites her readers to share as their own.[80] This is not to say that there are no difficulties, struggles, or problems (indeed, it is in the common sense of trying to sort out one's feelings in relation to the complexities of the world, the incomprehensible nature of God, and the messiness of being human that Kempe and her reader often come together) but rather that what the *Book* offers to its author and her readers is hope. What Kempe and her *Book*'s readers want, finally, is to feel joy and to find a way to accept their fallenness without letting this negative sense of self destroy them. What the *Book* does is try to find how Kempe did this, at least partially, and how her life could be read by others in order to find this for themselves.

---

80. Lochrie and Staley, though offering very different discussions of Kempe and her *Book*, are both intensely aware of this aspect and trace its effects on the text. See Lochrie, *Translations of the Flesh*, esp. 97–166; and Staley, *Dissenting Fictions*, esp. 1–82. See also Barry Windeatt, "'I Use but Comownycacyon and Good Wordys': Teaching and *The Book of Margery Kempe*," in Dyas, Edden, and Ellis, *Approaching Medieval English Anchoritic and Mystical Texts*, 115–28. Windeatt concludes: "Despite all her frequent frustrations and anguish, this [optimism] derives not least from Margery Kempe's glorious readiness to see God's work in all and any humdrum incident, however banal. For insofar as *The Book of Margery Kempe* records, in its own way, a triumphant life, it is also a joyous book" (128).

✶ CHAPTER TWO

Despair

> When this creature was twenty years of age or some-
> what older, she was married to a worshipful burgess and was with child within a short
> time, as nature would have it. And after she had conceived, she was labored with great
> attacks of illness until the child was born. And then, what with the difficulty she had in
> giving birth and on account of the sicknesses beforehand, she despaired of her life, believ-
> ing she might not live. And then she sent for her spiritual father, for she had a thing on her
> conscience which she had never revealed before then, not in her whole lifetime (chap. 1, 21).

Where do we begin the stories of our lives? The place where we start, the
point at which a writer chooses to fix her origin, determines the shape of
the story that gets told. It does this simply by declaring itself *the beginning.*
Genesis, for example, takes as its starting point the moment when heavenly
and terrestrial worlds come into existence: "In the beginning God created
heaven and earth." Individual lives, of course, have beginnings as well. Sometimes the origin is located at the moment of birth, but in many cases it is a
point that marks a new psychic—rather than biological—beginning. Dante,
for example, begins the *Inferno* with a moment of awakening: "Midway along
the journey of our life / I woke to find myself in a dark wood, / for I had
wandered off from the straight path."[1] Closer to Kempe in time and geog-

---

1. Dante Alighieri, *The Divine Comedy*, vol. 1, *Inferno*, ed. Mark Musa, rev. ed. (New York: Penguin,
2003), canto 1, 1–3.

raphy, Rolle begins the *Incendium* with his first experience of mystical "fire": "Mor haue I merualyed then I schewe, fforsothe, when I felt fyrst my hert wax warme, and treuly, not ymagynyngly."[2]

Kempe, in contrast, marks her beginning with a passage that announces its author's failings. In her very first chapter, we learn that, following a difficult childbirth, she is exhausted and so unwell that she "dyspered of hyr lyfe." Rather than feeling joy at the child's birth, she represents herself as overtaken by anxiety concerning a secret, long-unconfessed sin. Afraid she will die, she calls for a priest to make her last confession, but she finds no relief; instead her desperation grows yet more unbearable. When the priest arrives and she is about to reveal "that thing whech sche had so long conselyd," she stops because the confessor was "a lytyl to hastye." Instead of hearing her out, he "gan scharply to undyrnemyn [reprove] hir," and she, as a result, is incapable of saying the things she needed to say. Able only to begin her confession and not complete it, she locates her *Book*'s origins in her *inability to tell her story*.

Although the first chapter draws attention to the imperfect nature of the situation—the priest pressed her too hard, rushed her, was overly zealous in his reproof—it, more significantly, underscores the linguistic nature of Kempe's dilemma. She knows her "entent" but finds herself incapable of getting those feelings into words. Divided against herself—"sche *wold* no mor seyn for nowt" her confessor "mygth do" (chap. 1, 22, emphasis added)—she is unable to continue speaking. Both of her options, to speak or to accept the consequences of failing to speak, are impossible, and "for dreed sche had of dampnacyon on the to syde and hys [the priest's] scharp reprevyng on that other syde, this creatur went owt of hir mende" (chap. 1, 22). Instead of finding relief, she is trapped, as she had been the whole time she kept the sin a secret, by silence.

Once both alternatives are refused, Kempe's speechlessness is transformed into linguistic excess. Her inability to tell the truth about her sins initiates a sharp downward spiral into slander and lies. At the urging of devils and evil spirits, she forsook her family and denied God and her faith; "slawndred hir husbond, hir frendys and her owyn self"; and "spak many a reprevows worde and many a schrewyd worde" (chap. 1, 22). Eight months pass, and the *Book*'s description of that time is static, collapsed into an eternal present. Kempe's entire existence, as recorded in the first chapter, is taken up by verbal destructiveness—malicious language directed at herself and those she loves—in which words and deeds appear interchangeable. Her efforts to destroy herself verbally are matched by attempts to destroy herself physically.

---

2. *Fire*, 2.

The demons that possess her are figured as speech that comes from her mouth, but that speech is not actually *hers*. Overtaken by someone else's words—those of her "enemy"—Kempe spends three quarters of a year trying to kill herself.

The only escape from this situation, according to the *Book*, is to reclaim the power to listen and to speak. During a seemingly random and unexpected break from self-destruction, the frenzied cascades of verbal abuse are replaced, in turn, by a kind of silence different from the speechlessness that had prevented her from completing her confession. Alone in her room, with no one by her side, her "kepars" all away from her, Kempe silently watches as Jesus appears to her and says "thes wordys" to her, the only example of direct discourse in the chapter: "Dowtyr, why hast thow forsakyn me, and I forsoke nevyr the?" (chap. 1, 23). Precipitated by her inability to speak, her despair is resolved by Jesus' miraculous speech, as the chapter goes on to note, repeating the adverb "anon" to emphasize the connection between his words and her recovery: "Anoon, as he had seyd thes wordys"; "anoon the creature was stabelyd in hir wyttys and in hir reson as wel as evyr sche was beforn" (chap. 1, 23). Firmly linking spoken language with Kempe's restoration, the first chapter of the *Book* concludes with Kempe's return to health via her visionary and auditory experience, but it *begins* with despair that leaves her speechless.[3] It is a beginning, then, that draws attention to the necessity of speaking, the consequences of failing to speak, and the power of listening to another's speech.

Figured through the emotional experience of despair, the *Book*'s first chapter establishes the dynamic relationship between Kempe—as author and reader of her own book—with her readers. As part of this self-construction, despair is central to the *Book*'s opening scenes because it is the emotional experience, retrospectively considered, that most profoundly challenged the principles that had shaped Kempe's understanding of herself as a believer and, less obviously, as a reader. For this reason, despair is integral to the *Book*'s reshaping of ideas about emotional life *and*, more surprisingly, literate practice. Following her initial encounter with despair, she learns she has been mistaken in her feelings about her experience but refuses to dismiss the feelings as invalid, inauthentic, or unimportant. Despair is identified as the point of origin because in it the reader/Kempe locates the disparity between her experiences *as she felt them* and the information she read in books. The

---

3. In the Middle English life of Marie of Oignies, the story of a young virgin who is attacked by devils and falls into despair is told. The virgin, like Kempe, is unable to confess, but it is Marie's intervention, rather than God's, that cures her. See Marie of Oignies, "Life," in "Prosalegenden: Die Legenden des MS. Douce 114," ed. C. Horstmann, *Anglia* 8 (1885): 144. This is relevant to Kempe's life as a token against despair, discussed later in the present chapter.

Book "watches" Kempe as she wrestles with despair, as a lived experience that requires exploration and understanding rather than silencing, and invites the reader, in turn, to claim the right to speak.

Kempe writes in response to late medieval works that draw attention to the hazards of "wanhope," the Middle English word found in both literary and devotional works alongside the more familiar term "despair." Books offering consolation warned against despair, murmured about its dangers, and hurriedly urged readers to step away from this "temptation" by holding fast to faith. For these writers, despair must be *ended*, and the voices luring the reader to listen to her feelings must be shut out. This, they argued, required an act of will and a rational decision. For Kempe, in contrast, despair is the moment, as reconstructed in her writing, that explains why she was compelled to start writing and the point, in narrative terms, at which her story of becoming a writer begins. This is because for Kempe, despair is associated with the need to talk (to herself, other people, God) about herself. In the *Book*, despair is linked with kinds of "telling"—speechlessness, slander, self-narration, confession, finally writing—that are central to the act of textualized self-(re)construction.

Feelings of despair, carefully distinguished from suicidal impulses, are represented in the *Book* as unavoidable, frightening, and at the same time profitable in their ability to insist on the individual's reevaluation of what constitutes "normal" life. Despair, like writing itself, provides Kempe with a method for re-beginning and re-understanding her experiences so that she can come to terms with the sense of culpability that books of consolation assigned to individuals. Furthermore, it becomes the starting point for the self-making that Kempe *shares* with her readers.[4] But as I discuss in the second half of this chapter, despair as articulated by traditional writings on the subject (as an either/or proposition, an absolute state) can only be heuristic; it has no explanatory power for the individual in despair. The *Book*, in contrast, works to create a space of performed experience in which readers find themselves at odds with the sort of narration that involves linear, cumulative accounting. It turns, instead, to a kind of recounting that, despite its seeming irrationality, allows for "telling"-as-one-feels as an ongoing process of beginning again and

---

4. Barbara Rosenwein provides an outline of scenes of despair in the *Book*; see "Transmitting Despair by Manuscript and Print," in *Crying in the Middle Ages: Tears of History*, ed. Elina Gertsman (New York: Routledge, 2012), 249–57. I was fortunate to hear Emily Huber's talk on this subject, "Margery Kempe's Institutional Sorrow," at the Medieval Academy of America in 2009. See also Rebecca Krug, "The Idea of Sanctity and the Uncanonized Life of Margery Kempe," in Galloway, *Cambridge Companion to Medieval English Culture*, 131–33.

again, at different points and with different results, that invites reinterpretation, reconstruction, and continual discovery.

The Secret Sin

Medieval writers associated despair with the keeping of secrets. In *Suicide in the Middle Ages*, Alexander Murray unravels this relationship between secrecy and despair through reference to a story about a "holy nun," the fourteenth-century Dominican Adelheid Langmann.[5] According to the story of Langmann's life, a man from Nuremberg, Marquart der Tokler, sought her advice about a "great temptation" that had troubled him for nine years.[6] As Murray tells it, the man "said he had never confessed" this secret sin "to his priest, nor revealed it to anybody else, and did not even wish to identify it to Sister Adelaide herself. She nevertheless divined it. It was the temptation to suicide, she said."[7]

Although Kempe's undisclosed sin is never named, and despite the fact that modern readers tend to assume this sin was sexual, the similarities between the *Book*'s representation of Kempe and the story of Marquart der Tokler's suicidal despair are striking. Like the German man, Kempe, first, describes her long struggle with her conscience; second, never revealed her "crime" to anyone, including her confessor; and third, despite drawing attention to the centrality of this experience, leaves its meaning to be teased out by the reader instead of identifying the sinful desire as the temptation toward

---

5. On Adelheid Langmann, see Leonard P. Hindsley, *The Mystics of Engelthal: Writings from a Medieval Monastery* (New York: St. Martin's, 1998), 49–64. Langmann's "Gnadenvita" and Kempe's *Book* share a number of similarities. Rebecca L. R. Garber mentions Kempe in passing in her discussion of Langmann; see *Feminae Figurae: Representations of Gender in Religious Texts by Medieval German Women Writers, 1100–1475* (New York: Routledge, 2003), 127–56.

6. "Temptation" is the term used in books of consolation to refer to sinful enticement; it can be alluring, but it is also, and more frequently, used to describe suffering, trials, and tribulation with little emphasis on enjoyment. Zeeman observes that there is no strict distinction between temptation and sin: "The line between sinning and merely being tempted" is "often blurred . . . sin and temptation can both be understood simply as a form of tribulation" (*Piers Plowman*, 39).

7. Alexander Murray, *Suicide in the Middle Ages*, vol. 1, *The Violent against Themselves* (Oxford: Oxford University Press, 1998), 34. The German original reads: "Ain man was zu Nüerenberg der hiez Marquart der Tokler. der kom hintz dem closter zu der swester . . . und er sagt ir, er wer in grozzer anfehtung. si het in vor nie gesehen und von im nie gehört . . . si fragt in. waz anfehtung er het. er sprach: 'ich hon si neun jor gehabt und hon si nie gepeiht noch menschen nie gesagt. ich nem kein gut dor um daz ich eu ez sagt.' zu hant tet ir unser herre uf sein gnade und sein permhertzigkeit, daz si bekant alz sein leiden und si sprach: 'we eu! armer mensch, wolt ir euch dem teufil also haben lozzen überwunden leib und sele?' und sprach: 'ir habt di korung, daz weiz ich worz wol daz ir euch selber toten wolt'" (*Quellen und Forschungen zur Sprach und Kulturgeschichte der germanische Völker* 26 [1878]: 45).

suicide.[8] Kempe's silence, it should be added, is in direct contrast with the *Book*'s extensive cataloguing of other temptations that she faced during her lifetime, including those that seem particularly shameful (to a modern audience at least), such as the urge to commit adultery and sexual fantasizing.[9]

Rather than announcing Kempe's temptation to kill herself as her secret sin, the *Book* provides a visual representation of her breakdown that emphasizes her desire for self-annihilation and complements the *Book*'s attention to patterns of "telling." Stating very literally that she has tried to "fordon hirself" (do away with herself) following her inability to confess, the first chapter goes on to represent her physical state in terms of well-known visual images associated with suicide. Kempe's biting of her own hands and tearing at her own flesh, for example, are stylized gestures common in depictions of the damned in Last Judgments; in these representations, the damned were understood as destroying themselves through despair.[10] The extremity of Kempe's suicide attempts, like those of the damned, is emphasized in terms of the lasting effects of her violence against herself: "Sche bot hir owen hand so vyolently that it was seen al hir lyfe aftyr" (chap. 1, 22). The extent of her desire is so great that she makes use of the only "tool" available to her, her fingernails, with which she tears the skin over her heart; even "wers sche wold a don saf [she would have done even worse except for the fact that] sche was bowndyn and kept wyth strength bothe day and nygth" (chap. 1, 22–23). These visual representations reinforce our sense that Kempe's suicidal attempts were ongoing.

The severity of Kempe's illness itself, even before the episode of self-destructive madness, also marks her, at least potentially, as suicidal. Murray notes that suicide was linked in medieval narratives with seemingly incurable illness. The *Book* correlates Kempe's despair of her life with her illness before and after childbirth. Despair of health left one seemingly without choices: suicide,

---

8. The identification of suicide/temptation toward suicide as *sin* is, of course, a medieval and not a mainstream modern notion.

9. On silence, see Theresa D. Kemp, "The Knight of the Tower and the Queen in Sanctuary: Elizabeth Woodville's Use of Meaningful Silence and Absence," *New Medieval Literatures* 4 (2001): 171–88; and Jamie Taylor, *Fictions of Evidence: Witnessing, Literature, and Community in the Late Middle Ages* (Columbus: Ohio State University Press, 2013), 55–85. Suicidal despair was associated with a sinful past; sexual indiscretions may, of course, have been part of Kempe's past. There is circumstantial evidence for this, including her affinity with "fallen" women such as Mary Magdalene and the woman taken in adultery; her agitation over her ongoing sexual involvement with her husband; and the *Book*'s association of several subsequent episodes of despair with sexual desire (her near seduction by a friend in chapter four and her inability to control sexually charged thoughts in chapter fifty-nine, discussed later in this chapter).

10. Moshe Barasch, *Gestures of Despair in Medieval and Early Renaissance Art* (New York: New York University Press, 1976), 1–5; Murray, *Suicide in the Middle Ages*, 1:46.

writers suggested, might strike the terminally ill as the only available option.[11] Drawing on a range of suicidal "touches," the *Book*'s first chapter places Kempe, if we think of despair as encompassing emotional responses from sadness to self-annihilation, at the most extreme end of the scale. Kempe's history of suicidal inclinations frames her self-portrait in the first chapter as a woman devoid of alternatives.[12] Extreme isolation and secrecy; violent attempts at self-mutilation; illness that leads to despair; the sense that individual choice is impossible: all were associated with suicide in the period and occur in the *Book*'s first chapter.

But why, since Kempe, as the *Book* describes in great detail, escapes from her dilemma, recovers from her illness, refrains from injuring herself (and in fact over the course of her life comes to avoid physical pain as much as she can), enmeshes herself in multiple local and devotional communities, speaks with almost reckless abandon, and goes to the extent of writing down even the least flattering aspects of her life, does the *Book* open by linking narration, despair, and suicide?

The answer lies in the *Book*'s insistence on the uncoupling of despair from suicide as part of the "upsodown" structure—as the preface refers to the narrative pattern of comfort and upheaval that Kempe and her scribes argue characterizes her life—that is, the model of "well and woe" that drives the act of "telling" and telling again.[13] Rejecting the constraints of devotional rhetoric that, if one is to find forgiveness, demand insistent counting and cataloguing of sins, and rejecting, along with those constraints, the pressure to tell something once and be done with it, the *Book* returns to despair as a reminder of the limits of speechlessness. To stay alive, to find spiritual comfort and joy, and to keep trying to do these things, according to Kempe, demands that the believer reject both silence about emotional experience and conceptions of self that are unchanging.

The *Book*'s distinction between suicidal impulses and despair rests on Kempe's rejection of the nearly irresistible force of suicidal inclinations. This is a complex dynamic, however, as I argue later in this chapter, because at the

---

11. Alexander Murray, *Suicide in the Middle Ages*, vol. 2, *The Curse on Self-Murder* (Oxford: Oxford University Press, 2000), 374–75. Murray observes that "in miracle stories *desperatio* is employed frequently in respect of a sickness thought incurable before the miracle." Caesarius von Heisterbach's *Dialogue on Miracles* includes many stories of near suicide; the exemplum about John Holmes, discussed later in this chapter, is similar to narratives in the *Dialogue*.

12. Late medieval writers often draw attention to women's relation to suicide. Malory, for example, inscribes this pattern in the *Morte*, most famously, of course, in relation to Elaine of Astolat, but the pattern extends to Isolde (on the brink of self-destruction) and Lanceor's lady (who kills herself after Lanceor's death). In Malory, these female characters are represented as believing they have no other choice but to kill themselves.

13. On this pattern, see Szell, "From Woe to Weal and Weal to Woe."

same time that suicide is rejected, the initial suicidal event is enshrined in the *Book* as a memorial "token" that guarantees God's love and Kempe's faith. The propulsive force of secrets, speechlessness, and self-destruction found in the *Book*'s first chapter is revalued to mark a point of origin, but because the initial episode fulfills a memorial function, it can be read only *after* the fact of the experience. Kempe's failure to accomplish the act of self-destruction becomes meaningful as a sign of God's grace only in retrospect.

After she realizes she is still alive—after she has not found herself condemned to hell on account of the unconfessed sin—Kempe understands that episodes of despair function as proof of faith; in a Pauline sense, the episodes are "the substance of things hoped for [we might read 'desired'], the evidence [here, 'proof'] of things not seen" (Hebrews 11:1). Recounting near-suicidal events—she falls repeatedly "half in despair"—and in turn, analyzing, exploring, reimagining them, becomes an extension of this faith in the validity and significance of her feelings. That assurance is shared explicitly (as a guarantee and promise) with the *Book*'s readers. To understand how this works, we need to have a sense of late medieval writers' account of the spiritual significance of despair.

Dangerous Despair and Perfect Sorrow

Late medieval representations of the association between despair and suicide were remarkably consistent. In the morality play *Mankind*, for instance, the title character's despair, like Kempe's, starts with the failure to confess and seek mercy. He finds himself frustrated, weary, and unsure what steps he should take after Mercy has left his side and he must make his way on his own. Mankind's dramatic plunge into "wanhope" neatly underscores the emotional trick that the failure to believe in mercy plays on believers. As if mesmerized, Mankind, following the lead of the vice figure New Guise, places a rope around his own neck and is saved from self-destruction only by Mercy's fortuitous appearance.[14] The play provides a useful shorthand

---

14. *Mankind*, in *Medieval Drama*, ed. David Bevington (Boston: Houghton Mifflin, 1975), 901–38). Chaucer's *Book of the Duchess* and Malory's *Morte* are further examples of literature that articulates the same basic pattern. In *Book of the Duchess*, the Man in Black's grief over White is understood by the narrator, without Black's having once mentioned actual self-destruction, as suicidal despair. It is enough for Black to declare that, because there is nothing that can cheer him, his wish is to "deye soone" (*Riverside Chaucer*, ll. 690–709); the narrator recognizes this as suicidal and anxiously insists that he should not "for sorwe" murder himself (and if he did, the narrator observes, he "sholde be dampned" [ll.724–25]). Malory is similarly confident that little is needed to convey the link between despair and suicide. He requires only a few lines and offers no explanation, for instance, for the representation of Lancelot's grief and his decision to jump out the window upon discovering he has slept

account of the potential deadliness of late medieval despair. Its propulsive force, the ability of despair to drive one quickly into feelings of excessive sorrow and dread—as Chaucer's Parson, for instance, also describes it—takes on a life of its own.[15] The rapidity with which despair pushed its victims into danger was matched by its ability to first distort and then mask emotional awareness. Its hazards lay in the speed with which it overtook individuals and in its ability to escape detection—especially by the person it victimized.[16] It is surprising how widespread the image of suicide is in late medieval writing and the visual arts. Self-annihilation (or its threat) features so prominently in literature of the period that it is clear its imaginative power over late medieval audiences was substantial. Both devotional and literary writers represent despair as life-threatening, as in the cases just described, but also, if one survived the experience, as transformative and spiritually renewing.

At the same time that devotional and literary writers warned of the dangers of undetected despair, they advised readers to embrace the therapeutic value of "parfite sorow," as the author of *The Cloud of Unknowing* calls it, an emotional condition that might be easily confused with the desire to destroy oneself. In perfect sorrow, the believer comes to a clear understanding of her "owne beyng" as sinful and becomes "al forsobbid and forsonken" on account of this knowledge.[17] The experience is painful: in it the believer "findeth evermore" that his consciousness of and feelings about himself seem as if they "were ocupied and fillyd with a foule stinkyng lumpe of himself," and this in turn makes him feel worthy to "alweis be hatid and be dispisd and forsaken" (ll. 1567–69). The importance of complete immersion in this self-loathing is made explicit by the adverbial constructions: this should happen *without* ceasing; it must *always* be practiced.

Visceral, insistent awareness of sinfulness, which puts the believer on the brink of despair again and again, leads, according to books like the *Cloud*, to spiritual renewal. The *Cloud* draws attention to the irresistible force of near-suicidal feelings in its depiction of the beneficial aspects of perfect sorrow. In the *Cloud*, the believer's feeling of beneficial self-hatred causes him to go "ni wood [nearly insane] for sorow"; he will cry, complain, and curse,

with Elaine of Corbin (*Le Morte D'Arthur*, ed. Stephen H. A. Shepherd [New York: W. W. Norton, 2004], 472).

    15. Chaucer, *Parson's Tale*, l. 693, hereafter cited parenthetically in the text.
    16. *Mankind*'s head demon, Titivillus, goes about in a cloak of invisibility, a clear indication of despair's ability to escape detection.
    17. *The Cloud of Unknowing*, ed. Patrick J. Gallacher, TEAMS Middle English Texts Series (Kalamazoo: Medieval Institute Publications, 1997). l. 1540. Subsequent citations are given parenthetically in the text. On perfect sorrow, see Tentler, *Sin and Confession*, 233–300.

thinking he bears a terrible burden, but he "rechith never what worth of hym" (he does not care at all what happens to him) as long as God is "plesid." Although the *Cloud* carefully distinguishes between perfect sorrow and suicidal despair, insisting that one should never desire "to unbe," because this is the "develles woodness [madness] and despite unto God," the line between the two is very fine (ll. 1570–1574). The *Cloud* author warns his addressee, the "young disciple," against deception that would destroy body and soul on account of "pride" and "fleschlynes and coriousté of witte" (l. 1587), indicating conscious awareness of the dangerousness of flirtation with inclinations toward self-destruction. The intensity of the emotional experience was the point: extreme self-loathing, leading to reckless abandon of attachment to oneself, was effective precisely because it was so intensely felt.

Devotional writers were aware that their advice on this subject was powerfully suggestive. Vulnerable readers, in fact, needed to be shielded from some details associated with despair because their influence might be too strong. When *The Chastising of God's Children* describes the sufferings that befall "goostli lyuers" in particular, it does so in general terms to protect those who have not had these experiences. The *Chastising* author observes that he has intentionally refrained from offering specifics about "such dredeful thoughtis" because those who have had such experiences will already "wite in her soule" what he means, and those who have not should not be "traueiled" with such imaginings; they would never have been disturbed by these ideas except "bi other mennys tellynge."[18] Furthermore, certain people were thought to be more susceptible than others to spiritual maladies like despair and vainglory, and writers were especially careful to suggest that observers be sure to take into account the delicate nature of these people. The Middle English life of Marie of Oignies, for instance, draws attention to the susceptibility of the spiritual to despair and observes that sometimes "good minds" think they are guilty when they are not.[19]

Even as devotional writers display awareness of the risks of despair-like emotions and the particular vulnerability of certain persons to this condition, they nonetheless insist on personal culpability for sin, and place blame on the despondent individual. *The Chastising of God's Children*, for example,

---

18. *The Chastising of God's Children*, ed. Joyce Bazire and Eric Colledge (Oxford: Blackwell, 1957), 119. The spiritual woes mentioned in the *Chastising* are all similar to things described in Kempe's *Book*; see, for example: "to sum goostli lyuers ther fallen many dredis, both wakynge and slepynge: to sum bi orribil sightis, to sum bi wondirful heerynge, and to sum bi dredeful bodili felynge. Also to sum in her bigynnynge comen imagynacions of dredeful thinges whiche thei mow nat put awei" (117–18). This is similar to Kempe's own "horrybyl" temptations and visions.

19. Marie of Oignies, "Life," 139.

acknowledges the intensity of spiritual distress yet reproaches the reader for her condition. Noting that some people suffer terrible "temptacions" that "passen al disease," so much so that "for drede and doute al comfort is lost," the *Chastising* nonetheless instructs the reader that the first step must always be for "euery man to rette [count] it to his owne defaute that grace is withdrawe, bi sum maner necligence, of for a special defaute."[20] Its author goes on to suggest various failures that may have caused the reader's despair and advises her to confess her sins openly and frequently. Although the *Chastising* follows this up with gentler advice—work hard no matter how you feel; eat sufficient food and get sufficient rest; seek out spiritual advisers who will help you with these problems—this moderation is followed by renewed emphasis on personal worthlessness. "Another remedie" for a person in distress, for example, is for the despondent individual to "sette himself at nought" and to remind himself that "nought he hath, ne nought he hadde, ne nought he may haue."[21]

In addressing the issue of despair, writers came up against disparities between the goals of individualized pastoral care and the public, institutional expression of sound doctrine. Books of consolation needed to find ways to describe the possible emotional consequences of their suggestions concerning "perfect sorrow" without admitting—or at least recognizing—that religious orthodoxy and clerical authority might be unable to cure despair.

Failure to confess, for instance, was routinely offered as the cause for despair in devotional and popular literature. *Mankind*, again, offers a useful example. The play draws its audience's attention to the connection between despair and confession and does so in terms of the social relations that the title character should reject—the vice figures Nought, New Guise, and Nowadays—and the appropriate, semi-familial, and hierarchical relations he should cultivate, through confession and other institutional practices, with the clergyman Mercy. Other works such as the *Gesta Romanorum* and Mirk's *Festial* also underscore the relationship between despair and confession in terms of institutional authority: despair in these works dissipates once the individual hiding secret sins comes clean and confesses.[22]

In terms of pastoral care, confession is represented as therapeutically valuable for the person in despair not only because it addresses the problem of sin but also because it functions as an enabling strategy, that is, a method for escaping from the burdens of extreme negative self-identity. Chaucer's Parson, for example, recognizes that when a person feels "hevy thoghtful, and

20. *Chastising*, 110–11.
21. Ibid., 112.
22. See Krug, "Margery Kempe," 222, and "The Idea of Sanctity," 132.

wraw [anxious]," those emotions may lead one to feel defeated without cause: "He that despeireth hym is lyk the coward champioun recreant [the fearful combatant who believes himself defeated before the match is over], that seith 'creant' [I give up] withoute nede" (ll. 677, 698).[23] Confession makes it possible to confront these feelings because it provides a space for stepping outside the persona of fearful "champioun recreant"—it stops the "match" and invites the believer to see herself as she truly is—and it does so in an institutionally sanctioned arena.

For the Parson, faith is clear and easy: just believe and choose not to have this miserable, desperate feeling. Confession (asking and having) is so attractive, he explains, because it is so straightforward. The Parson's version of pastoral care speaks to complex and serious issues by helping believers choose to act rather than remain caught in the emotional/spiritual tangle of false feelings. Although, on an emotional and theological level, the Parson seems aware of the labyrinthine depths of despair—it is "horrible," the "moost displesant to Crist" and "most adversarie" (ll. 704, 697)—despite this awareness, he argues that the cure is easy: remember the crucifixion, including Jesus' mercy toward his enemies, ask for mercy, and confess. The Parson's upbeat advice assists the individual believer by encouraging her to see what is good and inspiring. There is no condescension here, just firm belief in the truth and a very optimistic understanding of the troubled believer's ability to turn toward that truth.

But in reality, the solution to despair—or the means for preventing perfect sorrow from becoming despair—seems not to have been as easy as the Parson suggests. Kempe's clerical advisers, for example, like the author of the *Cloud*, acknowledged the risks of celebrating the positive power of near-suicidal despair. Perfect sorrow, with its emphasis on self-recrimination, coupled with the understanding that it might result in a compulsive fascination

---

23. The Parson's comments are made in relation to *acedia*, spiritual "sloth," which was directly tied to despair. See Siegfried Wenzel, *The Sin of Sloth: Acedia in Medieval Thought and Literature* (Chapel Hill: University of North Carolina Press, 1967). Susan Snyder observes that the theological and emotional connotations of the word "despair" became entangled, and this "duality . . . became a commonplace" beginning in the earlier Middle Ages; see "The Left Hand of God: Despair in Medieval and Renaissance Tradition," *Studies in the Renaissance* 12 (1965): 20. Snyder makes her observation in relation to the sin of *tristitia*, which Gregory the Great had merged with *acedia;* see Morton Bloomfield, *The Seven Deadly Sins: An Introduction to the History of a Religious Concept* (1952; repr., East Lansing: Michigan State University Press 1967), 72. Watson argues for a "laicized understanding" of late medieval despair as a "difficult passage in life's journey," distinct from a more sophisticated and serious version important to "religious specialists"; see Nicholas Watson, "Despair," in *Cultural Reformations: Medieval and Renaissance in Literary History*, ed. Brian Cummings and James Simpson (Oxford: Oxford University Press, 2010), 342–57. My sense is that in the later Middle Ages the traditions were less distinct than Watson suggests.

with self-destruction—and its evil twin, despair—placed a heavy burden on spiritual advisers' shoulders. Kempe's confessor, for instance, watches her anxiously when she has "gret trubbyl wyth swech felyngys" and "fer[s] that sche schuld a fallyn in dyspeyr" (chap. 23, 64). Much as modern people think of illnesses like cancer and heart disease as silent killers, the danger of falling into despair was thought to be widespread and the stricken individual's ability to recognize her symptoms deemed low. Despair could happen to anyone (Kempe, Lancelot, Mankind) at any time—some people were deemed more likely to succumb to the temptation than others—and early detection was infinitely better than obliviousness to one's condition.[24] Emphasis, therefore, was placed on uncovering its presence, and confession, following the medical analogy, was the place where this problem could be diagnosed and treated.

This was, then, the mainstream view, but it is not, in fact, how Kempe's *Book* represents her solution to the problem at its point of origin. Rather, although her initial episode of despair results from her belief that her sins are unforgivable—an extreme and mistaken version of setting oneself at naught—it is resolved by miraculous divine intervention. Not only does confession fail to offer a solution to her problems, but also, in her first chapter, it precipitates the episode in which she falls into despair. This escalation of perfect sorrow/despair was, of course, necessary, at least in terms of doctrine—self-administered penance was not doing the trick (nor could it, according to the Church)—but this is in no way a version of the Parson's simple, institutionally mandated solution. In fact, after her initial attempt to confess, Kempe does not mention institutionalized confession again, in relation to her secret sin, until the *Book*'s third chapter.[25] Rather, *the initial episode of despair itself*—not the act of confessing—is represented, with its miraculous

---

24. In *The Chastising of God's Children*, the author describes six general temptations in physiological *and* emotional terms. The sixth of these is despair: it is termed "greuous" and is found on the left side of the body. The author notes that some people are more susceptible to certain of these temptations because of "disposicion of kynde"—physiological makeup—and God's "ordinaunce." Colledge notes that this physiology of sin is probably not original to the *Chastising* (*Chastising*, 116–17). Interestingly, *The Pricke of Conscience* links illnesses such as dropsy, gout, and leprosy with mortal sins (ed. Richard Morris [Berlin: A. Asher, 1863], 81–83).

25. The third chapter mentions that Kempe was "schrevyn sumtyme twyes or thryes on the day, and in specyal of that synne wheche sche so long had conselyd and curyd" (chap. 3, 27). Frequent confession is included among other pious practices such as bodily penance, fasting, and waking. The third and fourth chapters draw attention to the futility of mere human effort. For the first two years after her breakdown, she was able to stick to her ascetic practices. But, finally, rigorous asceticism fails to keep her from being "smet wyth the dedly wownd of veynglory," which she "felt . . . not." Vainglory becomes coupled with "the snar of letchery." From here she falls, again, "half in dyspeyr" and imagines "sche wold a ben in helle for the sorw that sche had" and begins to believe, again, that she is not worthy of mercy (chap. 4, 28–30).

resolution, as the moment that initiates change, and that moment marks a permanent break with the dynamic of speechlessness/slander that precipitated Kempe's suicidal confinement.

Supplementing confession, despair becomes a vehicle for explaining Kempe's feelings because it allows her to recognize that she feels "discomforted" instead of simply pushing negative emotions aside.[26] In making this emendation, the *Book* partially lessens the intense weight of blame associated with feelings of despair and, like many of the works she read with her lister, identifies Kempe's feelings of distress with possibility.[27] Revelation can come only *after* despair. Recognizing the extreme nature of the first chapter's opening allows us to understand just how far Kempe has come by the fifth chapter: she falls into despair (at least "half" despair) again and again, but by this point she does not feel that her life is over (or wish that it was over). Instead, although she can hardly bear the experience of these "wondyrful"—meaning "dreadful" or "horrible"—temptations, she copes with her feelings of desolation, albeit with "mourning and sorrow."[28] She has come, then, by the fifth chapter, to see the possibilities in "negative thinking" while at the same time refusing to dismiss her own emotional responses.

The new beginning encoded in the first chapter is re-encoded in the fifth: by this point, despair was still possible but suicide was no longer an option. In interpreting her own life experiences, Kempe draws attention, in retrospect, to the conscious refusal of suicide after the issue of the secret sin is addressed in the first chapter. With self-inflicted death "off the table," the emotional experience of despair is presented as powerful, transformative, but not laden with personal recrimination that forces her into silence. Knowing that she has not killed herself and addressing readers who also know this (obviously true, or she could not have written the *Book*), she demonstrates that, whether she thinks she can or not, she has learned to "beryn" her feelings of desolation, the sense of having been abandoned by God, and to cope with the feeling of alienation from the people around her.

---

26. On confession and consent, see Tentler, *Sin and Confession*, esp. 148–61. On confession and self-identity, see Little, *Confession and Resistance*.

27. Some devotional writers approached the subject by drawing attention to the uncertain nature of human emotions. In *The Prickynge of Love*, the despairing person is told not to "deme" [judge] himself or herself because the "felynge of thyn owne thoughtes" may be "neuer so sooth [true]"; we do not know what God thinks, and therefore must keep "al in nonn-certeyn until goddis doom" (170). This long-term solution is problematic, of course, if one is actually in despair.

28. "Wonderful" is one of the adjectives in *Chastising*'s list of six general temptations. They are reprovable, wonderful, dreadful, unseemly, moveable, and grievous (this is the adjective used to describe despair). See *Chastising*, 116–17.

Kynde

The first step in finding ways to "say as she felt" involved a gradual process of redefining the person who Kempe understood herself to be. This, too, is part of the *Book*'s opening chapter. Beyond facticity, the *Book*'s representation of feelings of isolation, despair, and forsakenness, as an ongoing part of her life, allows Kempe to explore the emotional experience as a condition that can be treated but not cured. In this revision, the *Book* moves to soften the sense of what we might think of as *affective culpability* associated with sinfulness. She comes to understand herself as different from her feelings and not simply worthless because of them.[29]

What Kempe required was a new way of thinking about her life, and the opening chapters are particularly concerned with drawing attention to the various "ruptures" in the normal routines of the life of this seemingly bourgeois laywoman. There is no "return to normal" for her, and that is the point. Following her first revelatory experience, she returns to the minutiae of daily life immediately after her senses are restored: she "preyd hir husbond as so soon as he cam to hir" for the keys to the pantry "as sche had don beforn." Her husband, overruling the servants, lets her have them. After eating and drinking, she then tells her "frendys," her "meny" (servants), and "all other that cam to hir" of Jesus' grace to her during her time of "tribulacyon" (chap. 1, 23). It looks as if the problem has been solved.

This return to normal life, however, including witnessing to others about God's mercy, only appears to be a resolution. The passage states that following the restoration of her senses, Kempe "dede alle other ocupacyons as fel for hir to do wysly and sadly inow" (chap. 1, 23). This matches the chapter's opening, in which she is represented as a "normal" woman of her class and age: "wysly" and "sadly inow" underscore the appropriateness of her efforts to take up her household responsibilities. It looks as if the "jolt" provided by the episode of despair has produced the exact sort of spiritual renewal that is supposed to accompany perfect sorrow. Kempe's return to ordinary bourgeois life, however—both mundane and spiritual—is presented as only a temporary resolution. The chapter concludes by indicating that her escape from despair and return to normalcy seem to be positive efforts, but as the narrative of her life continues, we discover that they are, in fact, insufficient. As the first chapter observes, although she conducts herself properly accord-

---

29. The *Prickynge*, as mentioned in the previous chapter, insists on a similar separation of one's sense of self from one's sense of sinfulness; the *Book* explores the way this idea might work as a lived experience of resisting despair.

ing to prescribed practices for women of her social milieu, she "knew not veryli the drawt of owyr Lord" (chap. 1, 23). In this passage, despite returning to everyday experience—represented explicitly by her return to eating and drinking—Kempe had not yet truly "drunk" in God. The point is pressed home to the *Book*'s readers: hers is a model of searching that, at this point in the narrative, is incomplete because it involves the return to acceptable, respectable behavior but has not been transformative.[30]

In constructing the narrative of Kempe's breakdown, the *Book* rejects the social and spiritual rules of "kynde," but it is not, strictly speaking, a conversion narrative. "Conversion" suggests a permanent, completed change; but this is not the result of her revelatory experience. Instead, the first few chapters of the *Book* underscore the significance of further transformation and emphasize the *incompleteness* of the effects of the first vision. In place of a straightforward conversion—an instantaneous movement from darkness to light—these chapters demonstrate the ongoing and unfinished nature of Kempe's attempts to find a "new way." The (now well-known) accounts of her endeavors and spectacular failures in the business world, her unsuccessful efforts to brew beer (it always went flat) and grind corn (the horse refused to pull the mill), as well as her ongoing enthusiasm for fashionable dress, are described in the *Book*'s first chapters. The tentativeness, incompleteness, and mistakenness of her understanding of the revelatory experience is emphasized.

The second chapter's description of Kempe's failed business ventures places her, yet again, outside mainstream society's conventions. The chapter notes that her fellow townspeople look on her with a mixture of fear and animosity. After the horse responsible for grinding the corn refuses to walk forward, Kempe's servant—standing in for bystanders in general—leaves "hys servyse and wold no lengar abyden wyth the fornseyd creatur [Kempe]." She has become the subject of widespread gossip, and the *Book*'s careful description of the scene indicates that it is another turning point. Her own rejection of kynde requires the world's rejection of *her*. Some people, the chapter notes, "seyden sche was acursyd; sum seyden God toke opyn venjawns upon hir." Only a few "wyse" people, the chapter notes, remarked that it was Jesus' "hey [high] mercy" that called Kempe "fro the pride and vanyté of the wretthyd world." It is only after these subsequent failures, the *Book*'s second beginning, that Kempe came "to entyr the wey of evyrlestyng lyfe" (chap. 2, 25).

---

30. The chapter employs imagery associated with drinking to point metaphorically at the need for further change. The keys she had gotten from her husband were for the "botere" (buttery, from "butt," meaning "barrel"), which is the room in which barrels of alcoholic beverages were kept.

Finding a new path, she discovers, at least in retrospect, requires rejection of the world's values and a thick skin.

Despair takes hold of Kempe in the *Book*'s initial point of origin because the naturalness of bodily, temporal existence distorts perception; she worries about what other people see and not what God sees. Although later in the *Book* physicality will be directly tied to sexuality, in the first chapter bodily existence is part of *social* life. The casualness of the opening chapter's sense of what is normal, including its estimate of her age at marriage—"twenty yer of age or sumdele mor," a typical age for marrying and so commonplace that there is no reason to be exact—coupled with her pregnancy "wythin schort tyme," similarly normalizing, mark this chapter as concerned with distinguishing between the mundane and the extraordinary. Up to the point of her breakdown, she has lived "as kynde wolde," that is, according to the normal course of life for a young woman from Bishop's Lynn, and whatever self-awareness she has is based on the established norms of behavior that dictated what a person, the daughter of a former mayor, should expect from her life as a wife and mother.[31]

What seems normal from this perspective (to marry and bear children) is explicitly tied, in the *Book*'s first chapters, to public perception and its ability to fix identity. Kempe's strenuous efforts to hide her "secret sin" from the people around her are figured in this passage as normal: it is normal to do what everyone in one's social group does, and it is normal to want the people around you to respect you according to the social group's terms. This is taken for granted to such an extent in the *Book*—and in our own lives, for that matter—that we sometimes miss the stark contrast between the "normal" people and Kempe. In the textualization of her life, however, this distinction is made repeatedly, and once we look for it, it is difficult to miss. Later in the *Book*, she is taunted about her decision to live her life differently and is told, "Forsake this lyfe that thu hast, and go spynne and carde as other women don" (chap. 53, 129).[32] The reader, siding with Kempe, of course, is asked to identify with the outsider, the person who chooses to go her own way, who chooses even to annoy the

---

31. William Provost, "Margery Kempe and Her Calling," in McEntire, *Margery Kempe*, 3–15, draws attention to the lack of "vocational clarity" in Kempe's life and observes that this is as important as gender in shaping her experiences (11). Her vocation as "wife" is, of course, already a gendered category. Tara Williams, in *Inventing Womanhood: Gender and Language in Later Middle English Writing* (Columbus: Ohio State University Press, 2011), argues that Kempe, like the Virgin Mary, locates her authority in her roles as mother and wife (114–48). See also McAvoy, *Authority and the Female Body*, 28–63, which suggests that this motherhood extends to the *Book* itself as the last of Kempe's "children" (63).

32. Martin L Warren, *Asceticism in the Christian Transformation of Self in Margery Kempe, William Thorpe, and John Rogers* (Lewiston, N.Y.: Edwin Mellen Press, 2003), describes the way that "cenobitic asceticism" is empowering (59).

people around her, and sometimes to change her mind. It is, of course, possible to resist this invitation, but if we do so, we choose, from the perspective of the *Book*, the conventional, safe, and predictable. The choice of socially comfortably kynde is the option that Kempe herself refuses even when she longs for it.

The *Book*'s emphasis on domestic life, extending even to visionary experiences—Kempe provides the Virgin Mary with a hot drink to help ease her grief, for example—traces the depth of her desire for a life lived according to kynde. The spiritual can be, and often is, figured domestically in its chapters but, at least in terms of social life in this world, it represents this desire as a problem. The longing for normalcy and acceptance was, for instance, responsible for Kempe's failure to confess the secret sin in the first place: it is the social pressure of hiding her "secret sin" from the prying eyes of her confessor that is finally too much for her and precipitates her breakdown. *Kynde* would have her keep up appearances for other people. *Despair* lets her stop pretending and offers her the chance to start over.

Kempe's despair, as distinguished from temptations toward suicide, redefines her "perfect sorrow" as ongoing and presents despair and recovery from despair as *always* possible. Episodes of despair appear throughout the *Book* and are included with the specific aim of refusing the silence of books of consolation concerning the lingering effects of feelings of despair. The early chapters of the *Book* show her escaping from *desperatio* of the sort that leads to suicide attempts, but these chapters also insist on the possibility of desolation, the feeling of being alone and forsaken, as a regular part of life: one of the conditions of human kynde, according to the *Book*, is to feel desolate, abandoned, forsaken, excluded. Kempe's extreme despair can only be treated as an ongoing condition, not cured. The *Book* goes to great lengths to emphasize this point.

Early on in its textualization of this condition, it makes some effort to trace out causal patterns for the periods of despair that Kempe experiences. The fifth chapter, for instance, describes the onset of further "temptations" following two years during which she had "gret qwiete of spyryt" and had endured physical torments. An explanation is offered: the temptations came, according to the *Book*, because during the two years, she was overly confident in her own spiritual strength to the point of "presumpcyon"; she believed at that time that "sche lovyd God mor than he hir" (chap. 4, 28).[33] Similarly, in chapter twenty-three the *Book* identifies despair's origins. Here it is

---

33. Spiritual presumption, vainglory, and impatience are discussed at length in my fourth chapter, "Fear."

Kempe's failure to trust in the verity of her visions, on account of her fear of "illusyons and deceytys of hir gostly enmys" (chap. 23, 63), that causes her to become despondent. Another failure, her inability to drive sexual images out of her head, a "punishment" for refusing to believe that some people will be damned, as God has told her, is offered as the reason she is "ner at dispeyr" in chapter fifty-nine (chap. 59, 143).

Yet, although the *Book* looks for explanations for Kempe's feelings, especially in the earlier chapters, the proposed explanations are represented as attempts to account for experiences that are fundamentally inexplicable—as if the events were experienced by someone other than Kempe herself. This is directly tied to the ways in which motivation and choice function. So, for example, the temptations described early in the *Book* include sexual desire and its existence apart from autonomy over conscious decision making. The fourth chapter describes her desire for a man who was not her husband. Although she does not engage in sexual activity with him—she does not actively commit the sin—she had, nonetheless, "consentyd in hir wyl for to don synne" (chap. 4, 30). This experience leads her to fall "half in dyspeyr" and has long-lasting results: she is "labowrd wyth horrybyl temptacyons of lettherye and of dyspeyr," and she loses her ability to respond to God's love for her on an emotional level. Instead, she is as far from "felyng grace" as those persons who had "nevyr felt noon" (chap. 4, 30).

The "willing" represented earlier is active but seemingly accomplished by someone other than the *Book*'s author herself. Emotions take hold of Kempe as if occurring in a space that is entirely beyond her control: "willed" in some sense, but "unwilled" as well. The *Book* renders this as part of the "upsodown" pattern of her life that causes her to experience despair repeatedly. Except for the times when "sche felt grace," she explains, her experience of trying to resist temptations and sinful feelings, which she experienced as beyond her control, was so "wondyrful"—astonishingly frightening—that she could not "beryn" it and "therfor alwey sche dyspeyrd" and felt "as thow God had forsakyn hir" (chap. 4, 30).[34] Desperate emotions and sinful desires are part of human life and sometimes beyond individual control. This, in fact, as far as the *Book* is concerned, becomes the true definition of what is really shared by humans in terms of kynde.

The *Book* insists that Kempe discovers the value of preparing for and developing strategies for separating negative emotional experiences from spiritual truth through her own life's example. The redefinition of kynde found in the

---

34. There is a marginal comment in the manuscript next to this passage (fol. 8v): "dyspare."

Book is concerned not only with redrawing the nature of domestic experience but also, therefore, with articulating what constitutes the nature of discovering and revealing emotional truth. If books of consolation, such as *The Chastising of God's Children*, tried to help readers know how they *should* feel, Kempe's *Book*, instead, looks for ways to say how she, and readers like her, actually experienced these feelings. Ultimately, the consolation that the *Book* offers is a sense of empathy concerning negative emotional experiences: no one escapes from these feelings. Despair is not an exceptional case but something that the believer should expect to experience over the course of her life. Even for individuals like Kempe who are shown special grace, negative emotional experiences are seriously troubling and require active and ongoing management.

"Discover" Your Heart

The institutional remedy for sin was, of course, confession. Books of consolation tend, however, to address themselves to what we might think of as the preconditions for sin.[35] Their method is to prepare readers to manage potentialities and situations that lead to sin. One of their primary avenues for managing such conditions is conversation.

Although there are obvious similarities between therapeutic talking and confession, devotional as well as literary writers distinguished between the two. In some versions of the *Remedy against Temptations*, for instance, a story of a man in suicidal despair is appended to the ninth chapter as an example of "comfort" sent to those in despair. In the story of the distraught "John Holmes," an angel advises that when a man is in "discomfort and heuynesse," he should always "discouere his herte to somme creature that myght ese hym"; according to the angel, "thorough good counsel" a man might find "good remedy" and feel anew "comfort" and "heele."[36] *The Chastising of God's Children* offers a similar discussion of the importance of revealing one's problems to a fellow "gostli lyuer": no man or woman falls "in myschief" and is overcome except those who "gooen forth and wil nat shewe her herte to no man." It is, according to the *Chastising*, "good to ask counseil in eche neede."[37] In both examples, unburdening one's heart, telling the story of one's "woe," is not

---

35. See Georgiana, *The Solitary Self*, 123–42, for a discussion of the distinction as it appears in the *Ancrene Wisse*.

36. *Remedy*, 236.

37. *Chastising*, 155.

straightforwardly confessional. Instead, it is through the process of talking, in the act of conversing itself, that the person in despair finds relief.

Late medieval literature, including literary writing, is replete with scenes in which talking is shown to assuage feelings of grief, anger, and general distress.[38] In Chaucer's *Book of the Duchess*, the narrator invites Black to "discure"—reveal—his "woo" in order for the narrator to help him "amend" his heart. The narrator offers the Black Knight his services as confidant: "to make yow hool / I wol do al my power hool / And telleth me of your sorwes smerte; / Paraunter hyt may ese youre herte / That semeth ful sek under your syde" (ll. 548–58).[39] The dream vision *Pearl*, too, another literary book of consolation, represents conversation as solace: the Dreamer had been accustomed to having his "wrange" relieved by the now lost pearl, and his vision is presented as a chance to resume the therapeutic talk.[40]

The *Book* depicts Kempe's concerted efforts, after her initial speechlessness and suicidal behavior, to "discover" her heart. Before the writing of her *Book*, Kempe's method, as recorded in the *Book* itself, is to take a confessional approach to this unveiling, even when the circumstances are not strictly confessional. Following her suicidal despair, she links culpability and self-expression, imitating confessional practice. That is, she tries to articulate her worthlessness and her "perfect sorrow" for sin, described earlier in relation to *The Cloud of Unknowing*, as cumulative and allowing for precise tabulation. In this model, sins are like "charges" on an account. This model is familiar to students of medieval literature. In the morality play *Everyman*, for example, sins are counted up, and a "receipt" of Everyman's life is drawn up; in the Towneley *Last Judgement*, the devil Titivillus collects briefs totaling up deadly sins committed. The bureaucratic nature of such accounting is frequently part of the point, and scenes in which such accounting takes place are represented as confessional even when, strictly speaking, they are not.

In Kempe's *Book*, accounting is both self-imposed and reinforced by institutionalized "bookkeeping" strategies. Kempe's habitual narration of her sins from a young age is a case in point. Although in the third chapter she finally

---

38. See Susan E. Phillips, *Transforming Talk: The Problem with Gossip in Late Medieval England* (University Park: Pennsylvania State University Press, 2007), esp. 147–202, for an important discussion of this idea. On conversation as a means of "inducing cheerfulness," see Glending Olson, *Literature as Recreation in the Later Middle Ages* (Ithaca: Cornell University Press, 1982), esp. 55–64.

39. The "smerte/herte" rhyme appears three times in Kempe's *Book*. Chaucer frames his "remedy" in relation to Ovid's *Remedia Amoris* (*Book of the Duchess*, l. 568).

40. *Pearl*, in *Poems of the Pearl Manuscript*, ed. Malcolm Andrew and Ronald Waldron, York Medieval Texts, 2nd ser. (Berkeley: University of California Press, 1982), ll. 14–18; as the vision begins, she "profered" him "speche" (l. 235), and in the following stanza the Dreamer describes the time before this "return" when he was alone and "playned" his loss by himself (ll. 241–45).

confesses her secret sin, she still attempts, at least in part, to manage her sinful condition on her own. For example, by tallying up her offenses, she reminds herself of her sinful wretchedness. Since original sin means this began at birth, "sche bethowt hir fro hir chyldhod for hir unkyndnes as ower Lord wold put it in hir mende ful many a tyme" (chap. 3, 27). In "beheldyng [beholding] hir owyn wykkednes," she could do nothing but "sorwyn and wepyn and evyr preyn for mercy and forgevenes." In a state of perfect sorrow, she experienced "gret compunccyon" and wept "plentyuows teerys" with many "boystows sobbyngys" because of her "synnes" and her "unkyndnesse ageyns hir maker" (chap. 3, 27). In Kempe's self-narration, the listing of sins from childhood is identified as a method for staving off despair. The litany of sins acts as a catalyst for remorse and a method for rediscovering forgiveness. Fresh repetition of her crimes is a mechanism that jolts her immediately, as she recalls it, back into perfect sorrow; this initiates a cycle of remorse, prayer, and the feeling of being forgiven that keeps her from falling into suicidal desperation. Her habitual reflection on her "unkyndnesse ageyns hir maker" is accompanied by a description of her efforts to engage in penitential practices that reinforce her accountability to the Church. Not only did she perform "gret bodyly penawnce," but also "sche was schrevyn sumtyme twyes or thryes on the day" (chap. 3, 27).

The wickedness-from-childhood narration is clearly patterned on institutional confession, but what is most striking about the practice—and about the early chapters of the *Book* in general—is the emphasis placed on quantification. Like confessional discourse, Kempe's efforts are enumerative: hers is a long-concealed sin, seemingly hidden for years according to the first chapter—and reiterated in the third ("that synne whech sche so long had conselyd and curyd [covered up]" [chap. 3, 27]). In battling that sin, she confesses twice and sometimes three times a day, even after Jesus has come to offer her miraculous reassurance; turning to self-narration as a strategy against the memory's ability to drag her back into despair, she recalls her sins from childhood, moving through them item by item, cataloguing them, managing data.

In chapters seventeen and eighteen, Kempe's efforts to adapt quantitative methods in her attempts to balance out perfect sorrow and despair are explored further. Referring to the same stylized narrative of unkindness-from-childhood employed earlier, the chapters experiment with enumeration as a strategy for coming to *complete* understanding of the relationship between sinfulness and assurance. In these chapters, she visits with spiritual authorities looking for confirmation that her revelatory experiences were indeed divinely ordained. During these interviews, she again recounts her sinful life story from childhood. In her discussion with the "holy man" Richard Caister, vicar of St. Stephens in Norwich in 1413, she shows him "al hyr maner of

levyng fro hyr chyldhod as ny as it wolde come to hir mende" (chap. 17, 50).
She does the same thing during her visit with the Carmelite priest William
Southfield, telling him as well, "as sche had don to the good vykary [Caister]
beforn" (chap. 18, 52).[41]

The spiritual framework for telling Caister and Southfield about her life
concerns the validity of Kempe's revelatory experiences, and the litany of sins
from childhood functions as a contextual guarantee for her audience. The episodes are clearly concerned with the issue of "discernment of spirits"—verifying the truthfulness and divinely sent nature of Kempe's visions—as Nancy
Caciola and Rosalynn Voaden have demonstrated, but the assumption behind
these episodes is more broadly concerned with representing the truth.[42] They
focus in particular on completeness and accuracy as achieved through quantification and repetition. The assumption in these chapters is that providing
Caister and Southfield with precise measurements of sinfulness will enable
them to draw the most truthful conclusion possible. As experts, they are given
the oral equivalent of Kempe's "receipts": records of her feelings, actions,
and intuitions that will allow them to make a proper determination about her
spirituality. The relationship between Kempe and spiritual experts like Caister
and Southfield is therefore nearly identical with that involved in confession.[43]

Kempe seems to use the same wickedness-from-childhood trope when she
meets the high-ranking German priest Wenslawe while she is in Rome in
1414. In her first confession to the German priest, she reveals "alle hir synnes
as ner as hir mende wold servyn hir fro hir childhode" (chap. 33, 88). Similarly,
the new priest at the Gesyn Chapel of St. Margert's Church hears "al hir lyfe
as ner as sche cowde fro hir yong age, bothe hir synnes, hyr labowrys, hir

---

41. Caister is referred to as a "holy man . . . whom God hath exaltyd and thorw mervelyows
werkys schewyd and prevyd for holy" (chap. 17, 51). Southfield is a "good man and an holy levar"
(chap. 18, 52). A cult arose around Caister's tomb, and Southfield was known to have "received supernatural visitations"; see Goodman, *Margery Kempe and Her World*, 139; and Windeatt, *Book*, 117, n.
1297. Both Caister and Southfield are discussed in chapter 3, "Shame."

42. Nancy Caciola, *Discerning Spirits: Divine and Demonic Possession in the Middle Ages* (Ithaca: Cornell University Press, 2003); Rosalynn Voaden, *God's Words, Women's Voices: The Discernment of Spirits
in the Writing of Late-Medieval Women Visionaries* (York: York Medieval Press, 1999).

43. Riddy, "Text and Self," describes Kempe as a "compulsive autobiographer" in relation to her
habitual retelling of her sinful life "fro hyr chyldhod"; she also notes the fact that the *Book* opens with
childbirth, in contrast with episodes in which Kempe tells the story of sinfulness from her own youth
(45). Salih, in *Versions of Virginity*, argues that the repeated instances in which Kempe retells her life
from beginning to end are part of attempts to tell "the story of herself in a search for a complete narrative" (179). Mary Beth L. Davis also discusses Kempe's "compelling need to talk"; see "Spekyn for
Goddys Cawse: Margery Kempe and the Seven Spiritual Works of Mercy," in *The Man of Many Devices,
Who Wandered Full Many Ways: Festschrift in Honour of János M. Bak*, ed. Balázs Nagy and Marcell Sebök
(Budapest: Central European University Press, 1999), 251. Sidonie Smith refers to the "self-effusive
rather than self-effacing" nature of Kempe's *Book* and concludes that it "speaks of the unbounded
possibilities of female storytelling" (*A Poetics of Women's Autobiography*, 82–83).

vexacyons" and the contemplations, revelations, and grace shown to her by God (chap. 69, 163).

Yet in recording these later instances in which Kempe confesses her "wickedness" from childhood to the present, the *Book* increasingly blurs the distinction between confession and "telling" as it appends Kempe's miraculous experiences of divine grace to her self-narration. She discloses "the prevyté of hert" to a young priest who, while she is on pilgrimage in Rome, travels from England and tracks her down because he has heard so much about her miraculous experiences, telling him "what grace God wrowt in hir sowle" and "sumwhat of hir maner of levyng" (chap. 40, 101). In book two, she "openyd hir hert" to her biological son, revealing "how owr Lord had drawyn hir thorw hys mercy and be what menys, also how meche grace he had schewyd for hir" (bk. 2, chap. 2, 209); finally, in the very last chapter of the *Book*, during her visit to Syon Abbey, she tells the earnest young man, who has a "fervent desir to have undirstondyng," a short version of her life in answer to his questions concerning the reasons why she cries (bk. 2, chap. 10, 229).

In place of strict enumeration, these episodes become instances of sharing and reinterpretation. Even when she assumes the role of a teacher, an older holy "levar" who instructs others, she supplements quantitative, confessional rhetoric with "telling" that opens up personal experience and makes it available to her audience for reflection. Although she continues to rely on the vocabulary of secrets as part of this revelation, these secrets are no longer her own personal burden of sin but rather information about herself that she shares. She discloses her "privity"; she "opens her heart"; she explains things about herself rather than simply counting up her failings. Even when she literally confesses, as she does to the German priest Wenslawe, the purpose seems to be communal, that is, to share her experiences with the person to whom she tells her story rather than to catalogue sin.

For Kempe, repeatedly telling the story of her wickedness functions as protection against speechlessness and despair, but this changes over the course of the *Book*. In the early years, the method is based on adherence to the dictates of confessional culture; later, she comes to associate this pattern with shared conversation and exploration. Over time, she undercuts the confessional, enumerative pattern by replacing her own "wickedness" with miraculous intervention. The seemingly exaggerated depictions of her sinfulness, in which she describes herself as, for example, God's enemy (chap. 77, 175) and as so wicked that "yf al this world knew" of it they would "merveylyn and wonderyn" that God had shown her such "gret goodnes" (bk. 2, chap. 10, 232), are used to highlight the wonder of divine mercy. Although the miracle of God's love is wrapped in the language of sin, the *Book* resists the sense of blame and self-recrimination that devotional writers often encouraged. Rather than concentrating on the cumulative weight of transgression, the *Book* places the wickedness-from-childhood trope in the liberatory frameworks of despair and divine intervention. Both freeing and enabling, despair and miraculous intervention are the secrets Kempe shares with her readers. This is what she shows them when she reveals the "privite" of her feelings.

A Game of Dice

Kempe's *Book* works toward eliminating her fear of speechlessness in the presence of others—the linguistic equivalent of despair—as part of its retrospective, autographic self-construction, which depends on drawing the audience/ reader into the unveiling of hidden or undiscovered narratives of selfhood that supplement, and sometimes supersede, the accounting-like methods of confession. In this way, it differs from seemingly similar accounts of the central role of conversation in managing spiritual despair in its insistence on what David Lawton has called "a religious faith in vocality."[44] For Kempe, the shared, collaborative, and ongoing experience of conversing about, writing, and re-understanding despair resists the restraint and completeness associated with confessional discourse. In traditional books of comfort, the sharing is, in contrast, hierarchically structured and finite.

The story of John Holmes, who was "in poynt to spille [kill] hym self," appended to some versions of the *Remedy against Temptations* and alluded to earlier, is a case in point. The exemplum identifies Holmes as a "synful man" who, upon "beholdynge of his synnes and be the feendes temptacions," had fallen into despair for forty days, during which time he could neither eat nor sleep. Taking pity on him, God sends an angel disguised as a man to offer him the opportunity to unburden himself. The angel asks Holmes why he is so distraught, but Holmes refuses to tell him. The angel then insists that a "man schulde . . . alwey in discomfort and heuynesse discouere his herte to somme creature that myght ese hym, for thorugh good counsel, he myght . . . recouere bothe to comfort and to heele, or in sum wyse haue good remedy." Holmes, fearing that upon hearing of his condition the man/angel might say "som word that schulde vtterly haue disesed hym," continues to refuse to tell him.[45]

---

44. Lawton, "English Literary Voices, 1350–1500," 257. Lawton's distinction between the conversations between Kempe and Julian and those between Kempe and Southfield and Caister draws attention to the potentially gendered nature of this kind of "telling."

45. *Remedy*, 236. All references to the *Remedy* in this section are from 236–37. The *Contemplations of the Dread and Love of God* makes a similar point (35). Chaucer's *Book of the Duchess*, a literary book of consolation, also draws a connection between the importance of talking to a confidant and the

In contrast with Kempe's *Book*, the exemplum draws attention to the limitations of both conversation and narration. What we might expect next in the narrative, given the angel's endorsement of conversation, is a tactic designed to compel Holmes to reveal his feelings. What we get instead, however, is the angel's announcement, like Sister Adelheid's to Marquart der Tokler, that he already knows what the problem is. He tells Holmes, "Thou art . . . in dispeir of thi sauacion." The angel goes on to assure him that God is merciful, but Holmes is not convinced because he knows that God is "rightful." Still despairing of God's grace, he listens to the angel tell "many exaumples" of God's mercy, but "this squier . . . was soo deeply fallen in heuynesse and in dreed that he kowde take no comfort of no thing that he seyde."

After Holmes remains, despite the angel's efforts, unable to trust in God's mercy, the angel, unwilling to give up, moves from narrative proof to a game of chance. He persuades the man to play a game of dice in which the high scorer will be assured of salvation. The angel rolls first, and the three dice come up sixes, the highest score possible. Holmes, exhibiting heightened suggestibility, panics and refuses to take his turn because he considers the odds of winning slim to impossible. "Dar I not," he says to the angel, because "I wot wel, though I caste the dise," that it is impossible to beat the angel's throw. Despite Holmes's objections, the angel urges him, nevertheless, to take his turn. He encourages him to imagine the impossible, and when Holmes finally rolls the dice, each breaks in two in such a way that "on eche dee was sixe, and so he hadde the double that the aungel hadde." Holmes's score with the magical dice is thirty-six, twice the angel's perfect score.[46]

This is the miraculous proof Holmes needs, and the exemplum concludes by relating that the "man" vanished and Holmes knew that this was an angel sent by God "to brynge hym oute of his wo." This gives him instant reassurance: "He caughte so gret comfort and ioye in the mercy of god, and in the goodnesse of his grace, that alle his sorwes and dredis wenten clene awey." He becomes a servant of God—a "blissed leuere"—and before his death he has his tombstone inscribed as follows: "Here lieth John Homelies, that of the mercy of god may seyn a largeis [give thanks for his largesse]." The narrator offers personal testimony concerning the tombstone's inscription,

---

staving off of suicidal despair. Interestingly, it also turns to games (the game of chess in Chaucer) to reflect on the situation.

46. These are of course supernatural dice, so anything is possible, but if they were dice of this world, the score would have been only twenty-one. Opposite sides of dice traditionally add up to seven; if broken in half, the opposite sides from the sixes would have been ones (three sixes plus three ones for a total of twenty-one).

declaring that he himself knew a "wurchipful persoone" who had seen it with his own eyes.

Like Kempe's miraculous rescue in her *Book*'s first chapter, Holmes's, too, is predicated on divine intervention that trumps the individual's refusal to speak. The story appended to the *Remedy*'s discussion of despair, however, in no way unravels Holmes's sinfulness or "confesses away" the grounds of his despair. Instead, the purpose is to offer a *better* narrative about God's mercy to readers, one that will encourage the next Holmes to "take comfort" without the reader's need to experience the actual miracle herself or to confront the necessity of verifying the validity of the inscription personally. Holmes's story is exemplary and, although promoting conversation to ward off despair, is in fact entirely unconvincing in regard to the usefulness of talking things over for the despondent individual. The conversational sharing found in Kempe's *Book*, as we will see, is, in contrast, insistently focused on drawing author and reader together as if they were one and the same. The experience of the miraculous as an antidote for despair, in her estimation, has to be shared and discussed.

Her Life as a Token

Kempe's life story is, like John Holmes's, exemplary: the *Book* calls it a "token," that is, narrative proof against despair. But in contrast with the story in the *Remedy*, where pedagogic value is associated with the exemplum's reader and with passersby who see Holmes's tombstone, the *Book* argues that this particular token works for her in the same way that it works for her readers. Despair draws writer and reader together as they strive to understand and benefit mutually from Kempe's experience.

In chapter seventy-seven, Jesus describes five signs by which Kempe will know that God "sett[s] but the mor prys" by her—values her highly—even if other people "settyn lityl" by her. Four of the five of these "tokens" are Kempe's own actions and feelings: (1) tears as a token of love, (2) "roaring" to induce compassion, (3) sorrow for passion/refraining from sin promises salvation, (4) pain in heart means no pain in afterlife or in dying. The four are both diagnostic and prognostic: they identify the nature and cause of her experiences or feelings and they predict outcomes. They are also exemplary in the sense that they are characteristics of Kempe's spiritual life that function as evidence or proof demonstrating God's power to all Christians. Kempe's tears, for example, are a token of God's love for humanity and are available for spiritual benefit to all. They are a sign for the Christian community: they are meant to be "read" but do not need to be directly experienced by anyone besides the *Book*'s author herself.

The remaining token is the promise that readers of the *Book* will avoid suicidal despair, just as Kempe has, by studying her life.[47] Chapter seventy-seven explains that any earthly person, even so "horrybyl a synner," will never fall into hopeless despair if he or she "wyl takyn exampil of" Kempe's "levyng" and try to live his or her life "sumwhat theraftyr" (chap. 77, 175). The promise comes up again, slightly altered, in chapter eighty-four, which places even greater emphasis on the reader's intentions: since God has been "so gracyows and mercyful" to Kempe, people are guaranteed to escape from despair and find "mercy and grace yyf thei wil [desire it for] hemself" (chap. 84, 195).

Although the idea of the story of Kempe's life as a token against despair seemingly places Kempe in a superior position to her audience, the *Book* undercuts this aspect of God's promise. Instead, the "token" is offered in the context of shared emotional relationships. In Kempe's experience, recorded at various points, Jesus speaks to her "veryly as o frend spekyth to another be bodyly spech" (chap. 17, 51). She in turn talks to her readers with the same intimacy and directness, inviting them to use her life as a charm against suicidal despair. The sense of equality and similarity makes her token distinct from Holmes's angel's dice: Kempe's life is her own to offer; she needs no angel to interpret it or prove that it is divinely ordained through a game of chance. Its meaning is hers to explore and discuss with her readers.

This is due in large part to the exploratory nature of the *Book*'s representation of despair. For Kempe, the meaning of her experiences remains open to reflection and re-inspection. In the *Remedy*, the angel's dice—the punch line—compete with the exemplum's articulation of an ethos of sharing and disclosure. The *Book*, in contrast, comes to a conclusion about despair—it is a token—but keeps looking for ways to live with the possibility of unpredictable and debilitating emotional experience. For this reason, it takes the advice offered in the *Remedy* very seriously: Kempe keeps trying to "discouere [her] herte to somme creature that myght ese [her]." She does this, ultimately, through her collaborative relationship with her *Book*'s readers.

The *Book* invites its readers to help Kempe understand events in her life that remain inexplicable to her. Among the most troubling to her are the "evyl thowtys," recorded in chapter fifty-nine, that unsettle her and bring her to the brink of despair. The episode is of the disturbing sort that books

---

47. It is fourth in the list of tokens as presented in chapter seventy-seven, after sorrow for passion and before pain in her heart.

of consolation such as the *Chastising* and *Remedy* maintain should be treated obliquely. Earlier in the *Book*, a sense of delicacy similar to that of the consolations' authors drives Kempe and her scribe to explain why they tell the story of her near seduction by a friend: this anecdote, "on of the hardest" that they relate, is "wrytyn for exampyl of hem that com aftyr" so they know not to fall into the same "snare" (chap. 4, 28). By chapter fifty-nine, the pressing need to understand her own experiences of desperation compels Kempe to ignore this sort of discretion.

The chapter begins by celebrating the "holy thowtys" that come to her increasingly over time and associates them with the "heryng of holy bokys" and "holy sermownys" (chap. 59, 141–42).[48] It quickly shifts focus, however, and turns to her struggle with "evyl thowtys" that trouble her for twelve days following her refusal to accept that anyone "schulde be dampnyd" and her desire for "alle men to be savyd" (chap. 59, 142). She refuses to believe God when he tells her she must think about the damned as well as the saved, and as a consequence, "owr Lord drow fro hir alle good thowtys . . . and suffryd hir to have as many evyl thowtys as sche had beforn of good thowtys" (chap. 59, 142). Rather than "holy spechys and dalyawns," she is haunted by visions of "letchery and alle unclennes," including the "beheldyng of mennys membrys and swech other abhominacyons" (chap. 59, 142). The "cursydnes" of these "horybyl syghtys and abhominabyl" drives her near "dispeyr," and she cries out, "Alas, Lord, thu hast seye befortyme that thu schuldyst nevyr forsake me" (chap. 59, 142–43). Here, "befortyme," of course, refers to the first chapter and Jesus' rhetorical question "Why hast thow forsakyn me, and I forsoke nevyr the?" (chap. 1, 23.)[49]

Critics have focused on the issue of "universal salvation" raised in this passage, and Kempe's unwillingness to hear about those who are damned certainly suggests that this was one of her concerns. But most of the chapter is taken up with the precise nature of the visions—of clerics' penises, in particular—and Kempe's inability to control her own thinking.[50] "Horrybyl syghtys and cursyd mendys [thoughts]" (chap. 59, 143) control her just as suicidal despair did in chapter one. She is unable to stop the visions, just as she was unable to control her speech in chapter one, and she finds herself powerless to understand or change what is happening to her. She cannot "sey nay"

48. Kempe's syllabus appears in the previous chapter.
49. Chapter eighty-seven, discussed in my first chapter, "Comfort," also refers to the beginning of the *Book* in this way.
50. Nicholas Watson, "Visions of Inclusion: Universal Salvation and Vernacular Theology in Pre-Reformation England," *Journal of Medieval and Early Modern Studies* 27 (1997): 145–187, esp., on Kempe, 152–53.

and feels bound to do the devil's "byddyng," even though she "wolde . . . not a don it for alle this worlde" (chap. 59, 142). And, as the chapter observes, it was even worse than being unable to stop this: she found the sights "delectabyl."

In chapter fifty-nine, despite Kempe's horror at this "cursydnes," she insists on telling her story as completely as she can. Refusing to protect us from something we probably never imagined, the *Book* insists that we confirm Kempe's sense of anguish, guilt-ridden pleasure, and relief by understanding precisely how such unwilled, obsessive thoughts feel. The contrast between Kempe's collaborative sharing with the reader, in this context, and the story in the *Remedy* is, again, useful for understanding how this matters. Holmes does not need us to experience his suicidal despair, but we (despairing souls that we are if we are reading this particular chapter of the *Remedy*) are primed to learn from him. In the *Book*, an angel comes to Kempe—much like John Holmes's angel—to explain what is happening to her, but it is Kempe herself (not a divine emissary) who constructs the meaning of this incident in the presence of her reader.

Kempe needs her reader as much as, or perhaps even more than, the reader needs her. For her "telling" to work, it has to make us accomplices in despair, and it does this by refusing to allow us to pass judgment on her. Critics some-times read the scene in chapter fifty-nine as "comic." Although this seems to me entirely wrongheaded—at least if the passage is read from Kempe's perspective—such readings evoke the essential lack of moral judgment that the chapter requires of readers. Instead of categorizing her thoughts as sin or sickness—the two options that Kempe's unsympathetic contemporaries offer to explain her experiences—the narrative demands that the reader take part in Kempe's inability to choose how she feels about the onslaught of obsessive imaginings of the penises belonging to "dyvers men of religyon," both Chris-tians and non-Christians. Refusing categorization entirely, judgment itself is associated, in chapter fifty-nine, with the devil: he forces Kempe to choose "in hir mende" which of the men's "bar membrys" she found most pleasing.

In contrast with her "enemy," Kempe refuses to make the relative attrac-tiveness of the men's private parts the issue. Instead, the emphasis is placed on her *inability to choose* how to feel about the experience: "Hir *thowt* that he seyd trewth." The passage represents her as helpless and incapable of resist-ing: "sche *cowde not sey nay*; "sche *must nedys* don hys byddyng" (chap. 59, 142, emphasis added). Even as she desires, emphatically, *not* to go along with the devil's prompting, she nevertheless "*thowt* that thes horrybyl syghtys and cursyd mendys wer delectabyl" (chap. 59, 143, emphasis added). Although this was all "ageyn hir wille" (chap. 59, 143), and although she tries to avoid such thoughts, they "abedyn wyth hir" and follow her. Nothing can stop them.

Even when she prays or tries to do other good deeds or simply, passively, sees the sacrament, "evyr swech cursydnes *was putte* in hir mende" (chap. 59, 143, emphasis added). Kempe goes to confession and "dede al that sche myth," but the thoughts continued to come to her and "sche fonde no relesyng tyl sche was ner at dispeyr" (chap. 59, 143). Helplessness is coupled with fascinated and horrified pleasure in the fantasies, and the reader is asked to reflect on this experience, identify with the feeling, and become complicit in this conflicted desire.

By this point in the chapter, it is clear that the experience of selfhood that Kempe constructs depends on the belief that other people share her feelings and, even more important, share with her the intractability of emotional experience.[51] But she also creates a shared self-representation, an experience of "we" rather than "I," that encourages the reader to think along with and through her past successes at escaping from suicidal despair. Desperate and suffering so much that the "peyn that sche felt and the sorwe . . . sche was inne" could not "be wretyn," she invites the reader to think back to the first episode of despair and, along with her, to call on God to fulfill his promise not to "forsake" her (chap. 59, 143).

Chapter fifty-nine illustrates how Kempe's textualized identity is variable and created through the process of writing. As the narrative reflects on the twelve days of uncontrollable pain, it proceeds as if the author herself is trying to sort out the meaning of the events in the company of her reader. The theological argument in the chapter, the event that precipitated her emotional turmoil, is nearly beside the point. Kempe is of course familiar with ideas about damnation and knows she is supposed to believe that it is possible. Instead, what appears to be unknown to her is how she should feel about the entire experience of being "punished" for something beyond her control (and, to go back to the theological point, how she feels about a God who imposes this kind of punishment). It is as though she "discusses" the subject with the reader—a reader who, like Kempe herself, understands that describing despair as sin is neither true to experience nor helpful to the person in despair.

As Kempe and her audience muse over the relationship between intention and emotion, pushing aside the theological issue in favor of the personal, reflecting back to the earlier moment of suicidal despair, our attention as

---

51. The same dynamic is readily observable in the episode, mentioned briefly earlier in the text, in which a male friend pretends to try to seduce Kempe; not knowing that he is merely "testing" her, she succumbs, and in reporting the scene constructs it, like the episode in chapter fifty-nine, as an open invitation for the reader to help her sort out why she feels the way she does (chap. 4).

readers becomes fixed on divine arbitrariness and human vulnerability. Many devotional works try to smooth over these issues by insisting that God, as Kempe's Jesus in fact explains in chapter eighty-six, receives "every good wyl as for dede" (chap. 86, 200).[52] But chapter fifty-nine makes it clear that, however consoling this might seem, there is actually a problem with this logic, for if you are unable to control your ideas and unable to know how you feel at all, how is it possible to know what it means to have "good wyl"? In working through the experience of despair, the *Book* invites the reader to help Kempe sort out this problem by affirming the meaningfulness and validity of her emotional representations. For Kempe, of course, this sorting through is partially retrospective (author Kempe writes for and about both earlier versions of her self and the self at the moment of writing), but the narrative's exploration of the subject looks to its (non-Kempeian) readers for this confirmation as well.

The *Book*'s answer to the question of the relationship between intentions and emotional truth involves conversation as a process of speaking and responding—telling a story, listening to responses, and telling the story again. Knowing if you have a "good wyl" is represented as the process of sifting through layer after layer of experience, noticing the details of emotional response—the contradictions as well as the clear bits—in an ongoing effort to uncover/discover the truth of the heart. Late medieval devotional works frequently describe the bond between believer and savior in terms of "inscription," the writing of the truth upon one's heart, but in the *Book*, truth is unearthed and reconstructed through repeated attempts at talking about the meanings of experience.[53] This is why Kempe keeps telling the story of wickedness-from-childhood-to-present. Each retelling is a way of discovering anew what the truth of her experience actually is and requires audience response. If retelling's truth is "inscribed," that inscription is not clear enough to be simply read once and understood. Each telling is a reconstructing, a new attempt to puzzle over the meanings of her life, and that puzzling is done along with her reader, in her own thought and inner conversation, and in the writing of the *Book*.

Kempe's model for communication is conversation—not writing—even when she decides to write, because conversation allows her to refuse hierarchical divisions between speaker and hearer. Although some books of consolation

---

52. Allen refers to this phrase as "highly characteristic of medieval English mysticism"; see *Book*, n. 212/11.

53. In chapter fourteen, Jesus refers to Isaiah 49:16: "I may not foryetyn the, how thow art wretyn in myn handys and my fete" (chap. 14, 43).

frame their advice through the fiction of friendship between reader and writer, they tend to be written from positions of authority. However intimate they may seem, the "friend" in these books is addressed by a narrator who knows more than his friend. Kempe's method, in contrast, to borrow Derrida's terms as read by Leonard Lawlor, is both "univocal" and "equivocal": "Inside myself when I speak to myself, I make no actual vocalisation. . . . In this experience, according to Derrida, I must hear myself speak at the very moment I speak. It is the same me speaking as hearing. Univocal. Yet, given that I am not the one speaking when I am the one hearing and vice versa, it is the same me speaking as hearing: equivocal. Because there is always a retention inseparable from the now, from the very moment in which I am hearing, there is always an other in me, in the same, speaking to me."[54] Kempe speaks/writes for, to, and with the reader: despite recording the "privy" knowledge given to her by God, the *Book* rejects distinctions between author and reader based on expert knowledge or identity. In this way, Kempe's memory of despair is a token that she and her readers share as the foundation for finding new beginnings, a starting point that allows for new reflections on the past, present, and future.

From Talking to Writing

Kempe's attempt to live through episodes of despair, and to find new beginnings, propels her to search repeatedly for "comfort" through conversation. According to the final chapters of the first book, the writing of the *Book* itself becomes the means, in both practical and imaginative terms, of extending this conversational search for solace. The *Book* traces connections between inner thoughts and speech, intimacy and listening, and recovery and writing as it constructs the relationship between author and readers as conversation.

Chapter eighty-seven returns to "inner" dialogue of the sort found throughout the *Book*—and discussed earlier in relation to Kempe's "evil thoughts." In this chapter, conversation with Jesus is identified as the experience that has sustained her and given her "comfort" for "mor than twenty-five yer whan this tretys was wretyn" (chap. 87, 202). It is precisely "speche and dalyawnce" that make her "mythy and strong" in devotion, and the chapter opens with

---

54. Leonard Lawlor, "The Beginnings of Thought: The Fundamental Experience in Derrida and Deleuze," in *Between Deleuze and Derrida*, ed. Paul Patton and John Protevi (London: Continuum, 2003), 79. The discussion in this paragraph is drawn from Rebecca Krug, "Jesus' Voice: Dialogue and Late-Medieval Readers," in *Form and Reform: Reading across the Fifteenth Century*, ed. Shannon Gayk and Kathleen Tonry (Columbus: Ohio State University Press, 2011), 110–29.

Kempe in church "heryng and undirstondyng" the "swet dalyawnce in hir sowle as clerly as on frende schulde spekyn to an other" (chap. 87, 201). Although this exchange appears to be almost entirely one-sided—Jesus making "gret behestys [promises]" to her and Kempe thanking him for them—it is, more particularly, a conversation in which listening is identified as active and as important as speaking. "Gret qwyet of sowle," the chapter explains, is necessary for this kind of conversation, and this quiet comes only through "long excersyse" (chap. 87, 202).

The effort and importance of speaking, highlighted in the *Book*'s first chapter, becomes associated with the strenuousness, necessity, and satisfaction of listening. In chapter eighty-seven the saints as well as Jesus "spokyn to the undirstondyng of hir sowle" (chap. 87, 202), and Kempe listens, learns, and responds to these inner voices. The saints "enformyd hir how sche schulde lovyn God" and "answeryd to what that sche wolde askyn of hem." The conversations are informative but also pleasurable: Kempe enjoys them so much that she loses all track of time, thinking that a mere hour has passed when it has actually been five or six; she never grows "irke" of talking with her holy friends, and "the tyme went awey" but "sche wist not how" (chap. 87, 202).

The act of writing the *Book*, in contrast with this timeless talking, is first introduced in chapter eighty-seven as temporally bound and burdensome. Kempe and the scribe begin the *work* of writing "weke be weke and day be day" (chap. 87, 202). Composition is at first an "interruption," like other "nedful occupasyons" such as caring for the sick. "Whan this booke was first in wrytyng," chapter eighty-eight relates, "the sayd creatur was mor at hom in hir chambre wyth hir writer and seyd fewer bedys for sped of wrytyng" (chap. 88, 203). The hurry to get this writing over with suggests that it is work that is unpleasant. Yet the sense of writing as burdensome, as something that gets in the way, is revised over the next few chapters. Jesus reassures Kempe that no devotional act will please him more that the effort of composing the *Book* and invites her to see writing itself as the same as speaking to him: it is "preyin" with her "hert" (chap. 88, 203). It is, like prayer, a way of understanding what is true.

In chapter eighty-nine, the last chapter of book one, composition takes on the same consoling function as speech. As Kempe and her scribe write, she has ecstatic, revelatory experiences—"holy teerys and wepingys," flames of fire in her heart—that are shared with "he that was hir writer." The scribe, too, "cowde not sumtyme kepyn hymself from wepyng" as they write together (chap. 89, 205), and the burden of writing dissolves completely into the pleasure of shared experience. As the *Book*'s first readers (with the exception of Kempe herself), the scribes take part in the same process of self-making upon which Kempe herself embarks. Together they write, as the prologue calls it, their "schort tretys" for the "solas and comfort" of "synful wrecchys," among whom they count themselves (preface, 17).

The "solace" that the *Book* offers Kempe and her scribes, as I have argued in the previous chapter, comes through the act of writing itself, and the consolation offered is not just imaginative but physical. Writing, in fact, cures illness. In chapter eighty-nine Kempe is again physically ill. In this chapter, writing, like Jesus' speaking in the very first chapter of the *Book*, is represented as instantly, physiologically restorative. Although the solace offered by the *Book* might be seen as didactic, in the sense that the reader learns from Kempe's life, the sense of healing found in the process of composition lets us see how the text incorporates the reader into its ongoing self-construction.

Instead of providing didactic answers, the *Book* invites its readers into a therapeutic process. The means for finding solace come explicitly via textualized experiences in the *Book*, and Roland Barthes's sense of the "writerly" text is at least partially useful for understanding this: Kempe's continuous rediscovery of herself as writer and reader, in the act of composition, is like Barthes's "production without product."[55] The reader of the *Book* encounters herself in the disorienting miraculousness of the healing process of writing that Kempe and her scribes enact. Reading the *Book* as if the reader were its author is like Kempe's refusal of speechlessness and despair. The embodied description of the act of writing resists the settled answers that the reader might expect from other books of consolation and replaces those answers with a process of ongoing self-discovery.

Hurt

In this chapter I have argued that Kempe identifies the "origin" of her life in despair and does so because she needed a way to understand what it was that she felt. The differentiation of despair from suicide in the *Book* initiates a process of telling and telling again that becomes associated not just with speech but with listening and with writing, and which makes the reader, in turn, complicit in self-making. The reader is Kempe's collaborator in discovering and uncovering the nature of emotional truth, a partner in the process

---

55. Roland Barthes, *S/Z: An Essay*, trans. Richard Miller (New York: Hill and Wang, 1975), 5.

of turning aside from the tendency to sanitize the emotional, found in books of consolation, and in exposing the related untruth: that turning aside from negative feelings is easy and obviously beneficial.[56]

Kempe's reimagining of despair involves resistance to personal blame, and therefore displacement of an important dimension of the theories of "negative thinking" which formed the basis for ideas about suffering that underwrote so much devotional literature from the period. It is worth noting, however, that her reconfiguration, as desirable as it seems to be, is incomplete, and so, therefore, is her refusal of self-harm. To the very end of the *Book*, she is compelled to tell the story of her wickedness, and this narrative form competes with the ongoing process of telling-as-she-felt. For example, in the last of these stories recounted in the *Book*, she tells the young man at Syon that "hir gret unkendnes agens hir maker," through which she had "many tymys offendyd" God's "goodnes," was the cause of her "wepyng and sobbyng"; that the "gret abhominacyon that sche had of hir synnys" as well as God's great mercy were the reasons. This, she explains, is "no merveyl" but is to be expected (bk. 2, chap. 10, 229).

In recounting this event, Kempe embraces the negative thinking that I argue the *Book* resists. She does the same thing in chapter eighty-nine, where the healing power of writing is coupled with representation of the "gret hevynes" and dread Kempe experienced when, for "many days togedyr," she "knew not how" she should understand her "felyngys" (chap. 89, 206). When this happened, the chapter relates, she wished that "hir hed had be smet fro the body" until God "declaryd" the meaning "to hir mende" (chap. 89, 206).[57] Although we might read past this comparison as a mere figure of speech, the violence of the imagined separation of body and head occurs in the same chapter in which the act of composition is physically restorative. Not knowing, then, becomes associated with the speechlessness of despair, found in chapter one. The residual traces of the pain felt in that first chapter cannot be so easily removed from the narrative of self-construction. This is because, however many times Kempe tells a new version of self, the initial episode of suicidal despair is still the point of origin, and as such, carries along both the memory of pain as well as the sense of possibility that I have described.

---

56. In Kempe's *Book*, the anguish of emotional suffering is pervasive and extends beyond deep despair over her own sinfulness to perception of pain in others. Even Jesus' "owyn modryr" must suffer. Kempe asks the Virgin how she can bear to see Jesus in such pain and tells Mary, "I may not dur it, and yyt am I not hys modyr" (chap. 79, 180).

57. See my fourth chapter, "Fear," for further discussion of Kempe's experiments with pain.

It is possible to read this theologically, that is, as Kempe intentionally inflicting pain, at least imaginatively, upon herself in imitation of Christ. There is certainly precedent for this in the *Book*, including Kempe's repetition of a rhyme about Jesus' wounds: "Lord, for thi wowndys smerte, drawe alle my lofe into thyn hert" (chap. 88, 204).[58] But the eagerness with which she describes herself seeking out comfort again and again suggests there is more to it than this. And so does Jesus' promise in the same chapter that he will comfort her himself if need be and that he cannot bear to allow her "to have peyne any while" without finding a "remedy" (chap. 88, 205).

Instead, it seems to me that the memory of such pain functions, in spite of herself, as Kempe's own promise to remember not merely Jesus' sacrifice for her but *hers* for him. In Kempe's choosing to move from despair to her redefinition of "kynde," the loss of the comfort of a normal life was part of the price paid. Along with the rewards of the choice, Kempe opened herself up to the uncontrollable and inexplicable demands of being given secret knowledge. When, in chapter eighty-eight, Jesus reframes the promise of chapter one in this way, "forgete me not, dowtyr, for I forgete not the" (chap. 88, 205), his emphasis on remembering is tied, at the end of the chapter, to *his* obligation to her: "Yyf *thu* wilt be buxom to my wil *I* schal be buxom to *thi* wil" (chap. 88, 205, emphasis added). Although it is easy for us to ignore the active nature of her choice, to see the pain of despair as motivation enough, to assume that the rewards of a life devoted to God are obvious, the *Book* never completely forgets any of this. Kempe's experience of pain, and her desire to have it stop, continue throughout the *Book*. But over the course of the *Book*'s composition, she and her scribe reenvision what it means to feel such pain.

In traditional books of consolation, the promise of relief is made but never shown. In contrast, in the *Book* the experience of comfort is represented vividly and in context. Looking back at her life and describing her feelings in no way decreased the intensity of those experiences, but it offered an example—a token—for the reader and the writer herself to keep in mind. The *Book*'s "guarantee" of relief was the lived experiences of Kempe, who experienced despair repeatedly but who could look back and see how each event constituted both a beginning and an end. In this way, Kempe comes much closer (closer than I imagined was possible when I began working on this chapter)

---

58. For further discussion of the rhyme, see chapter three, "Shame."

to the ecstatic embrace of "bitter sorrow" found in works such as *The Cloud of Unknowing* and the reveling in self-loathing central to *The Prickynge of Love*. As Kempe's own "tretys" of "comfort," the *Book* offers the solace of choosing to do something that is difficult and sometimes painful. For this reason, the *Book* is as much a token *of* despair as a token *against* it.

❧ CHAPTER THREE

Shame

Medieval writers recommended shame for its spiritual benefits. In the *Summa Virtutum de Remediis Anime*, the primary source for Chaucer's *Parson's Tale*, the author employs an analogy to explain that feelings of embarrassment teach humility. The peacock, he observes, "when it looks at its shining feathers, has reason for pride; but when it looks at its black feet and listens to its awful voice, it has reason to blush." The peacock's shame, brought on by recalling the ugliness of his own feet and voice, is identified in the comparison as spiritually useful because it reminds him not to feel overly pleased with himself on account of his beautiful feathers. Studying one's faults, according to the *Summa*, and feeling ashamed of those flaws will improve one's spiritual life by keeping feelings of self-worth in check: spiritual gain comes as the result of emotional discomfort over personal imperfection. This, the *Summa* explains, helps us understand Paul's advice to the Galatians: "'Considering yourself, lest you also be tempted,' . . . see what you have of your self, and not only of your self but from the gift of grace" (Galatians 6:1).[1]

---

1. *Summa Virtutum de Remediis Anime*, ed. S. Wenzel (Athens: University of Georgia Press, 1984), 86–87: "Per exempla potest humilitas edoceri, ut siquis eleuetur de gracia sibi collata, humilietur de culpa perpetrata. Pavo enim si lucentes pennas respiciat, habet unde superbiat; si nigros pedes et horribilem uocem attendat, habet unde erubescat. Ideo signanter dicit Apostolus, [Galatarum fine]: 'Considerans teipsum ne et tu tempteris,' quasi: vide quid sit ex te, et non solum quid [ex te set quid] ex dono gracie."

The *Summa*'s claim is consistent with the general sense found in books of consolation that consideration of one's failings is essential for spiritual growth. But the analogy also leaves us with a question: What, we might ask, about creatures who have "reason to blush" but who lack the peacock's beauty? How useful is shame, to follow the *Summa*'s example, if it is all a bird has to offer? More to the point, what is the good of self-mortification if it constitutes a totalizing vision of identity, that is, a state of being rather than a temporary response to a lapse? What is the point of reflecting on one's shameful failings if there are no opportunities for redress or improvement?

In this chapter I argue that Kempe rejects a static version of shame-based personhood. Instead, the *Book* represents episodes in which the author felt shame as an opportunity to reinterpret self-understanding in relation to ideals of spiritual perfection. Retrospectively, shame—as a response to sin and to feelings of social inadequacy and inferiority—is replaced in the *Book* by identification with a future, perfected self. This attempt to exchange a fixed sense of identity with one that is fluid (hopeful about the future and untrapped by the present) is consistent with Kempe's reenvisioning and revision of the message of books of consolation. Her search for comfort and joy taught her to find ways to express her feelings; battling suicidal despair allowed her to initiate the process of rewriting and re-understanding her life as dynamic and changeable; and struggling against shame, as I argue in this chapter, united her with potential readers of her *Book* as they, and the author herself, experimented with strategies to resist feelings of worthlessness.

The *Book* outlines two approaches to shame. The first involves a cognitive strategy in which scorn and humiliation are reinterpreted as signs of divine favor. In this method, allegorical "readings" displace the discomfort and misery of experience by translating shame into joy *as a textual effect*. In the first method, shame is translated into triumph through storytelling that distances lived experience from its meanings. The second approach, in contrast, resists the impulse to allegorize and eliminate the lived experience of humiliation and turns instead to strategies for coping with feelings of worthlessness. In the second method, Kempe employs patterned phrases—much as New Age proponents use daily affirmations—as defenses against shame. Linguistic multiplicity—the structuring and restructuring of verbal patterns and meanings—allows for movement beyond shame-based identity. Through the encoding of phrases, lyrics, and proverbs, the composition of the *Book* becomes part of a process that allows its author and her readers to revise and re-understand the experience of shame. Both strategies acknowledge that the individual involved is *not yet perfected* but must keep trying, despite this, to *see* herself as she will be in the future; but the second has the advantage of bringing the reader closer to a personalized experience of future perfection.

The Experience of Shame

Like modern theorists of performance, Kempe was intensely aware of the embodiedness of religious practice. Her struggle with female bodiliness is of particular importance in regard to her efforts to find spiritual comfort and joy. The shame that she experienced in relation to her sexuality defined her temporal existence and is represented, at least indirectly, as defining the identity of readers as well. In the first chapter, for instance, the physical conditions of pregnancy are presented as the shared experience of the *Book*'s readers. Similarly, her description of the desperation she feels when she has unwelcome fantasies about priests' "bare members" assumes an audience that identifies with her problems. Male readers can certainly understand her feelings of extreme discomfort, but these instances are written from a woman's point of view and take for granted a female audience. In these episodes, humiliation is gendered and it comes as part of the necessary experience of physical existence.

This is true as well when Kempe retells the story of her seduction and rejection by a male friend. The episode has all the emotional charge of actual illicit desire and, subsequently, the lived, visceral experience of shame. In chapter four's description of the event, she is compelled by her "friend's" insistence that he will "ly be hir and have hys lust of hys body, and sche schuld not wythstond hym," freshly ashamed to have acquiesced, and newly wounded by his rejection. The chapter's blow-by-blow account of the sequence, using location, date, and time—on Saint Margaret's Eve at evensong, after evensong, in bed with her husband that night, and so on—presents the incident as if she is replaying for herself what happened: Why, she seems to ask, did she agree to meet him? How did she feel about it? Why, she muses, did she consent to have intercourse with her friend, when, as she notes further in the passage, sexual relations with her husband seemed "abhomynabyl" even though they were "leful" (lawful) (chap. 4, 28–30)?

As Kempe tries to understand the event anew, the *Book* fills in explanations for her feelings and actions. First, her mind is described as clouded by "the mannys wordys": he has told her that he will have sex with her either now or later and that "sche schuld not chese." Her confusion, the *Book* recounts, became so great that she was unable to hear evensong or say her prayers or think a single good thought. She finds herself unable to recognize what is true, and she believes "God had forsake hir."[2] Following this logic of despair, chapter four explains that she gave in to temptation by "the devyl"—the term is clearly meant in context to refer to Satan, of course—but the passage conflates the human vehicle and the source. The power of the friend's suggestion was so great that it occupied her mind and "inasmech as he had spoke to hir" she was "labowrd" to "syn" with him. Unable to think because of the "noise" of her seducer's words, she is incapable of resisting temptation. The decision is made, seemingly, against her will (chap. 4, 29–30).

Kempe's representation of her inability to control the situation is in keeping with arguments made by devotional writers about will. Books of consolation frequently explain that sinful, inappropriate, or troubling thoughts may come to one unbidden. In the *Remedy*, for example, the reader is assured that as long as she does not consent to "wikked thoughtes," she is protected by her "good wil."[3] Kempe, however, has in fact consented to sin and is unable to pretend that she had not desired to have sex with her friend. The struggle is represented with frankness, and despite her efforts to interpret the event according to the advice found in her devotional books, it continued to trouble the *Book*'s author. She is unable to find a way to sort out how this might have been both out of her control and an act of consent, and so the turmoil of the episode is unrelieved by an appropriate conclusion. Even the natural impulse to blame the friend is taken from her. The chapter describes him as an instrument of God sent to test her, and for reasons that elude her, she has failed the test.

This failure before God is accompanied by extreme feelings of shame after the "friend" rejects her. When they meet and she offers to sleep with him, the *Book* repeats his refusal in colloquial phrases that capture the immediacy of the event. He tells her "he ne wold for al the good in this world" have slept with her, and "he had levar ben hewyn as smal as flesch to the pott" than to have done so (chap. 4, 29). The brutality of the rejection and the cruelty of this plan to prove her spiritual steadiness stand in stark contrast to her feeble attempts to reinterpret the scene according to the advice about temptation from the books of consolation. If suffering shame is to bring joy, as the books all maintain, this is another instance of that model's failure to describe real emotional experiences. While the narrative shakily sticks to the lesson and declares that "sche went away al schamyd and confusyd in hirself, seyng hys

---

2. Lochrie labels this episode (and the one in which Kempe has what are to her terrifying visions of priests' penises) "comic" as part of her argument about "laughter"; it produces unease and illustrates the *Book*'s "ongoing dismantling of the language and authority of the magisterium" (*Translations of the Flesh*, 153). See also Larsen and Curnow, "Hagiographic Ambition," 284–302.

3. *Remedy*, 229.

stabylnes and hir owyn unstabylnes" (chap. 4, 29), the moral is undermined by the shame and confusion the passage describes.

The intensity of Kempe's experience of shame—an intensity that devotional writers were clearly aware of when they suggested it was spiritually valuable—made it impossible for Kempe to embrace the jubilant reveling in shame described by books offering solace, such as *The Prickynge of Love*. That book's over-the-top delight in shame is of the sort that Alexandra Barratt suggests readers might, from the point of view of their clerical authors, "misread." Writers like the author of the *Prickynge*, Barratt explains, "exaggerated and troped Christ's sufferings in an attempt to evoke a response from readers desensitised, even jaded, by repeated exposure to meditative texts" from a "highly emotionsalised affective tradition."[4] The *Prickynge* insists that the best course is to meditate on the horribleness of sin in order to feel shame and self-loathing without ceasing. We should all, its author declares, feel "for-wondrid of owre-self" and "trede . . . doun oureself in oure thought and in oure-self as the vilest thynge that mai be."[5] He announces excitedly that he himself "shal ay lothe myself als vile stynckande filth" and encourages the reader to do the same. The *Prickynge* couples self-punishment with punishment by others. Its author proclaims it his mission to seek out opportunities to feel ashamed: "I shal gedere alle creatures on an hepe and preie hem alle that thei wole despise me & punysshe me & chastise me." It will be, he enthuses, "my tresour & my delices for to stire & gregge alle creatures agen me."[6]

Kempe, and readers like her, in contrast, remained outsiders to this "hyperbol[ic]" symbolic mode, as Barratt calls it. Indeed, from the perspective of any person who has experienced the misery of shame firsthand, Kempe's response makes much more sense than the *Prickynge* author's playful gathering of "all creatures in a heap" in order to enjoy the pleasure of being shamed by them. Neither the enjoyment that the author of the *Prickynge* takes in self-loathing nor the absence of shame's lingering effects, as described in some works, accurately reflects Kempe's emotional experiences. Shame, as represented in the *Book*, was destructive, confusing, and long-lasting; its effects lingered decades after the events described. For this reason, instead of reveling in humiliation, Kempe and her readers needed some kind of strategy to avoid its crippling effects, and the *Book* explores methods for doing so as part of an ongoing process of resisting and reinventing the value of "negative thinking."

---

4. Barratt, *"Stabant matres dolorosae,"* 67.

5. *Prickynge*, 3, 54.

6. Ibid., 58.

It is perhaps surprising, given the episodes just described, that the *Book*'s first method for reconceiving of shame has little to do, at least in a direct fashion, with sexuality. Female bodiliness is relatively unimportant to Kempe in this context because she *assumed* that (illicit) sexual activity was shameful. The *Book* is uncompromising in its identification of sexual desire with sin and, for this reason, spends little time on the subject in its discussion of interactions between people.[7] Kempe, like the devotional writers whose books she read, saw shame as useful in some cases because it could correct sinful behavior. The *Book* is in full agreement, for example, with Rolle, who observes that shame is appropriate when God's "true lover" succumbs to temptations because the feeling underscores the importance of resisting sin.[8]

Although it is similar to the *Summa*'s representation of shame, Rolle's principle is based on changeability instead of static identity. Kempe, too, follows this principle and distinguishes between episodes of appropriate and inappropriate shame. The *Book* shows us, for example, that her sense of confusion and mortification for having agreed to engage in extramarital relations is deserved. So is the shame she feels about her secret sin: she *should* feel ashamed, because she has kept it a secret instead of confessing and finding forgiveness. Her sense of shame before her confessor, by contrast, is not appropriate. No one should feel ashamed to confess and accept God's mercy; whatever her crime, she has no business worrying about the confessor's human response. Kempe of course knew this. That is why she sent for the confessor in the first place. The problem she confronts in the *Book* has to do with emotional experience, not knowledge. What the *Book* shows are her efforts to search out strategies for understanding why she feels shame as well as her attempts to find methods for feeling differently about "unproductive" shame.

Unworthy People

As unpleasant as deserved shame felt, the suffering was productive. Its value lay in creating opportunities for spiritual renewal, and its beneficial effects made up for its emotional cost. Kempe, however, felt shame even when there were no grounds for feelings of abjection. When other people—cruel people, ungodly people—were unkind to her, the *Book* represents her as feeling wounded and unworthy. This is easily observed in the chapters describing her pilgrimages outside of England. In chapter twenty-six, for example, she has

---

7. As I argue, however, Kempe's sexuality is of paramount importance in relation to her feelings of shame before God.

8. *Fire*, 19, 83.

barely left home when her fellow travelers begin to treat her with disdain. Angry that she follows a vegetarian diet, cries, and talks of God's love at meals and elsewhere, her companions "schamfully . . . reprevyd hir and alto chedyn hir" and declare that they will not "suffren hir as hir husbond dede whan sche was at hom." After she calmly observes that she has grounds to speak of God's love abroad and at home, they become even "wrothar than thei wer beforn." Kempe is terribly upset by this, and their "wreth und unkyndnesse" are "to this creatur . . . mater of gret hevynes." To make things worse, she is disappointed in them all the more because, despite all evidence to the contrary, they are "holdyn ryt good men, and sche desyred gretly her lofe" (chap. 26, 70).

At first, Kempe continues to worry about their opinion of her. She takes one of the men aside "specyaly" and says to him, "Ye do me meche schame and gret grevawns" (chap. 26, 70). Very much like her early inclinations to live according to "kynde," her sense of shame at the hands of her fellow pilgrims, at this stage, compels her to try to smooth things over, that is, to follow the normal course of social interaction. Distressed by her companions' hostile reactions to her spiritual practices, she asks them to consider *her* feelings. Perhaps, she seems to think, they will stop treating her this way if they *understand* how painful it is to her. This attempt at smoothing over social relations is shown to be unsustainable as part of a life in pursuit of extraordinary devotion.

Instead, pointed contrasts are drawn between her "enemies," who are nearly always thwarted, and Kempe herself, who, against all odds, triumphs. When, during the same pilgrimage, her companions try even harder to humiliate her by cutting "hir gown so schort that it come but lytil benethyn hir kne" and attempt to make her seem to be a "fool," Kempe, the *Book* notes, was nonetheless held "in mor worshep" than her fellow pilgrims "wherthatevyr thei comyn" (chap. 26, 70).[9]

By the time she returns from the Holy Land, Kempe represents herself as no longer experiencing the social shame she felt when she set out on her travels. For instance, in chapter fifty-two, a monk in York who had "herd meche slawndyr and meche evyl langage" about her spoke out against her during his sermon "so openly that the pepil conceyved wel it was for cawse of hir." Although his denunciation made her friends feel "ful sory and hevy therof," she dismisses him as "unworthy" and declares herself delighted to be treated

---

9. For a discussion of similar "social elevation" due to exclusion from community, see Katharine Horsley, "Poetic Visions of London Civic Ceremony, 1360–1440" (Ph.D. diss., Harvard University, 2004), 20–23, 96–113.

this way. Rather than feeling upset and ashamed, she says, she was "meche the mor mery" to bear his attacks because this abuse provided her with the opportunity "to prevyn hyr paciens and hir charité" (chap. 52, 124).[10] The idea—the more scorn she suffered, the greater would be her reward—is straight out of books of consolation that address the grounds for suffering. *The Book of Tribulation*, for example, asserts that "encressynge in grace and of vertu" is found "in susteynynge of the tribulacion"; in suffering temptation, the steadfast individual will win the "auauntage."[11] The experience of shame is transformed into spiritual victory over one's enemies. This becomes so central to the *Book*'s representation of Kempe's feelings that, as Windeatt observes, joy in tribulation becomes "a leitmotif" of her narrative.[12]

Other people are rendered powerless in their attempts to humiliate Kempe because she re-categorizes and reinterprets their contempt. Instead of producing feelings of humiliation, the scorn of others, according to the *Book*, brings her a sense of happiness and, finally, triumph. As she reflects on her past experiences in writing, she celebrates her tribulation at the hands of (obviously wicked or at least mistaken) people; rather than dreading "the schamys of the world" (chap. 15, 47), she explains that she has come to "lawghe" when she would before have felt humiliated, because she has learned "the mor schame I suffyr and despite, the meryar may I ben in owr Lord" (chap. 54, 134).[13] Although this may have a perverse ring to modern readers, such scenes are commonly inserted in saints' lives. The world of hagiography was divided between the righteous (who are few) and the wicked (who are many). Kempe embraces this idea wholeheartedly, and the *Book* represents her gleeful denunciation of people who are, to her mind, ungodly, superficial, and spiritually comatose.

Kempe learns to take the lived experience of shame and transform it into a generic trope. In chapter thirteen she describes her joy at being despised when she tells a "tale" about a man whose confessor had commanded him to pay people to "chyde hym and reprevyn hym for hys synnes." One day, she relates, this man fell in among a group of people, "many gret men as now ben her," she notes, who mocked and shamed the man "as," she observes to her

---

10. This kind of misreading by unenlightened observers is characteristic of the triumphant saint; see Rebecca Krug, "Natural Feeling and Unnatural Mothers: *Herod the Great*, The Life of Saint Bridget, and Chaucer's *Clerk's Tale*," in *Laments for the Lost in Medieval Literature*, ed. Jane Tolmie and M.J. Toswell (Turnhout: Brepols, 2010), 225–41.

11. *Book of Tribulation*, 43.

12. Windeatt, *Book*, 43, n. 50.

13. The bishop of Lincoln "dredyth mor the schamys of the world than the parfyt lofe of God" (chap. 15, 47). See also chapter 64, where Jesus observes, "He that dredith the schamys of the world may not parfytely lovyn God" (chap. 64, 154).

audience, "ye do me." The man, she says, had "gret cause to lawh," just as she does. Kempe then delivers the punch line: the man tells those who mistreat him how pleased he is to suffer shame at their hands, because instead of paying money to be reproved, "this day I may kepe my sylver in my purs; I thank yow alle" (chap. 13, 41).

The *Book* shows Kempe applying this generic transformation, in which abuse becomes a badge of honor instead of a cause for fear and alarm, to her own experiences. After telling this story, chapter thirteen takes what was surely a frightening experience and turns it into another anecdote about the value of suffering. Upon concluding Kempe's tale about free abuse, the chapter describes the crowd's response to it. As she leaves the monastery, the people in the crowd cry out, "Thow schalt be brent, fals lollare. Her is a cartful of thornys redy for the and a tonne [barrel] to bren the wyth" (chap. 13, 41–42). Though presented as a realistic record of events, chapter thirteen clearly offers interpretive analysis and the reframing of emotional experience as part of the history it reports. Kempe presents her own tale of abuse and triumph with a storyteller's perfect pitch, offering a precise and evocative rendition of the words of the crowd.

The retrospective nature of the narration is even more apparent when Kempe relates her experiences of being arrested after returning from Santiago. Chapter fifty-five describes her return to Lynn in 1417, following her arrest as "a loller" and her release, as a time when "sche suffryd meche despite, meche reprefe, many a scorne, many a slawndyr, many a bannyng, and many a cursying" (chap. 55, 135). The catalogue of terms associated with abuse is followed by a colorful vignette—its narrative status signaled by the phrase "And on a tyme"—in which a "rekles man, litil chargyng hys owyn schame," dumped a bowl of boiling water on her head "wyth wil and wyth purpose" as she walked in the street. Rather than show her becoming angry at the abuse or feeling ashamed by his mistreatment, the *Book* represents Kempe as "no thyng mevyd therwyth" and has her simply declare, "God make yow a good man." The chapter ends by commenting that she thanked God "heyly [highly] therof" and did so "many mo other tymes" (chap. 55, 135-36).

This same chapter opens with a passage in which Kempe repeats Jesus' advice to his disciples, "Stody not what ye schal sey" (chap. 55, 134), but the *Book*'s representation of shame at the hands of "reckless" people like the man with the boiling water is entirely "studied." Kempe's textualization of suffering is thoroughly in keeping with the attempts in books of consolations to rationalize tribulation.[14] Instead of an absurd universe or one that exclusively

---

14. By the mid-fifteenth century, the idea was so commonplace that it can be found in personal letters alluding to God's "visitation," that is, to the divine infliction of suffering and its benefits; see,

heaps blame on the person suffering misfortune, books of consolation insist that believers are culpable and suffer for sin but are also loved by God. Kempe studies this model and applies it to situations in which she feels suffering is undeserved. The feelings of shame may not disappear, but their meaning changes.

As part of this retrospective translation, the *Book* celebrates the joy of realizing that the *pain* of humiliation can be re-understood and reexperienced as comfort.[15] The twentieth-century psychologist Silvan Tomkins observes that the conversion of shame into joy is a typical response to the contempt of others. According to Tomkins, "For the contempt of the other to evoke shame . . . the other must be an actual or potential source of positive affect."[16] Kempe, seemingly "following" Tomkins's model, describes the way that she relinquished her desire for the approval of her fellow pilgrims. No longer seeing her companions as a potential source of comfort or identification, Kempe can enjoy the abuse of her fellow pilgrims precisely because, she insists, she has come to see that their approval is not of value. The *Book* identifies her traveling companions as "unworthy"—in sharp contrast with its labeling of the "worthy" religious figures whose good opinion Kempe seeks out.[17]

There is, however, a doubleness to this realization about shame. It is one thing to say, after the fact, that shame *brings* joy, but it is quite another to say that joy *replaces* shame. The *Book*'s value as a model comes through the incomplete nature of the life it represents. Part of its reflection on the past requires Kempe to relive and reexperience the difficulties of shame. For this reason, despite offering allegorical models for translating shame, the *Book* is careful to note that this is a struggle. So, for example, when Jesus instructs the nearly fifty-year-old Kempe, who had eaten a vegetarian diet for years and fasted once a week, to go back to eating meat, she tells him that she is afraid of public scorn. People, she says, "wil have gret merveyl and, as I suppose,

---

for example, Agnes Paston's letter to her son that includes the proverbial phrase "Qhom God vysyteth, him he loueth." *The Paston Letters and Papers of the Fifteenth Century*, ed. Norman Davis, 2 vols. (Oxford: Clarendon Press, 1971), vol. 1, no. 30.

15. Jesus suggests that his love is measured in pain: "Dowtyr, thes sorwys and many mo suffyrd I for thi lofe, and divers peynys, mo than any man can tellyn in erth. Therfor, dowtyr, thu hast gret cawse to lovyn me ryght wel, for I have bowt thi lofe ful der" (chap. 79, 182). Some books of consolation emphasize the special love shown by God when the believer suffers. *The Book of Tribulation* draws attention to the "many profits" of tribulation and the manner in which they are sent in order to help ("yholpen"), serve, and succor believers (39). Others, like *The Chastising of God's Children*, emphasize the corrective aspect of suffering (149–50).

16. Silvan Tomkins, *Shame and Its Sisters: A Silvan Tomkins Reader*, ed. Eve Kosofsky Sedgwick and Adam Frank (Durham: Duke University Press, 1995), 157–58.

17. Staley, *Dissenting Fictions*, notes that Kempe often relies on a "private vocabulary" in the same manner that Lollard groups did (10); "unworthy" is a good example of this.

despisyn me and scornyn me therfor" (chap. 66, 157). Jesus' answer offers tacit acknowledgment of her fear: "Thu schalt non heed takyn of her scornys but late every man sey what he wyl."[18] But with this comment he also insists that she confront her own feelings of shame: *she* needs to learn not to feel their scorn. As she expected, she suffers at the hands of the people around her for giving up her vegetarianism, but her reluctance to "etyn as other creaturys" disappears after her confessor commands her to do so.

It all works out, of course, but Kempe's fear of shame precedes the event. The push of official advice and pull of emotional experience are articulated in the *Book* as part of the retrospective point of view: both, as far as Kempe is concerned, are true, and she and her readers need to think about both. Even if those who mock Kempe for giving up her vegetarian diet are not "worthy" people, and even though Kempe, as Jesus reminds her, was able to "enduryn" her "perfeccyon of wepyng" (chap. 66, 157), the sting of others' negative perceptions requires her to perform a cognitive translation of her emotional experiences. Although Kempe's *Book* presents abuse by others in positive terms, it is unable to divorce humiliation from the deeply felt experience of actual, lived shame. *Past* shame caused by unworthy people can and should be reinterpreted positively, but in the *Book*, the lived experience of shame also retains its overwhelming power to terrify and confuse.

Future Perfect

It was possible for Kempe to recategorize those who caused her shame as unworthy and to re-describe the pain of humiliation as joy, but it was not possible for her to perform the same transformation in relation to the divine.[19] God was *not* unworthy, and she felt the overwhelming weight of shamefulness in his presence. The *Summa*'s peacock helps explain why this was the case. The bird who is taunted by other birds on account of his ugly feet and wretched voice can declare that this abuse is *not* abuse but a sign of his great worth; he cannot, however, claim that he has beautiful feet and a pleasing voice. The other birds know better, and so does the peacock. Kempe's shame is like that of the peacock: God knows the difference between the sinful and the

---

18. Jesus does, however, offer her an explanation: she needs to eat meat to maintain her bodily strength because her crying is so debilitating (chap. 66, 157). For similar remarks, see *Fire*, 25. Rolle, too, seems sensitive about his relationship to food, and denies the truth behind gossip about his supposed desire to be "delicately fed" (26).

19. "The future perfect tense is used to express action (or to help make a statement about something) which will be completed in the future before some other future action or event." *Warriner's English Grammar and Composition* (New York: Harcourt Brace, 1951), 149.

righteous, and all humans are sinful. Kempe's problem, as the *Book* explains, is actually a perceptual one. She finds it impossible to look at things from the point of view of a God who sees her in all her shamefulness and nonetheless loves her. The *Book*'s solution to this perceptual problem was to imagine things from God's perspective, and it does this by representing its author's attempts to view herself as perfected in the future rather than flawed in the present. In this way, she pushes aside the advice of books of consolation to dwell on sinfulness and turns, instead, to the future of imagined possibility and perfection.[20]

It is somewhat surprising, then, since this is the case, that Kempe's Jesus actually speaks in several instances exactly like the books of consolation that she resists because they demand concentration on one's utter unworthiness. Jesus tells her, for example, in chapter twenty-one that she should "have mende of [her] wykydnesse and thynk on [his] goodnes" (chap. 21, 59).[21] This admonition is found frequently in devotional writing and appears, for example, in the *Prickynge*, where the author instructs the reader to think of two things and to make them the "ground of al thi thoughtes." The first, he explains, is "thyne owne synne & thi wrecchidnesse." The second is "the charite of ihesu crist & his goodnesse." As the reader thinks of both of these, she is instructed to "thynke ai of thi-self als euel as thou can thenke & thynke ai of criste als mykel good as thou may."[22]

Devotional writers framed the juxtaposition between God's goodness and the believer's wickedness in terms of its restorative power. Medieval healing, based on the curative power of contraries, provided a model for this (meditating on Jesus' goodness will cure Kempe's wickedness), and the pain caused by the practice was, similarly, part of the process of healing. Hilton, for example, instructs the reader on the necessity of seeing "the ground of al synnes litil or mykil," that is, "the wrecchidnesse and the myschief of synne," which is,

---

20. See Krug, "Margery Kempe," 222–24, on future perfection. See also Watson, "The Making," esp. 418–24, for his discussion of the *Book*'s use of similes—"as" and "as if"—to shape its representation of human inadequacy and "infinitude" (with direct consequences for the nature of reading). On imperfection in late medieval writing, see Benjamin D. Utter, " 'Fawty and Falce': Sin, Sanctity, and the Heroic in Late-Medieval English Literature" (Ph.D. diss., University of Minnesota, 2016).

21. These words are repeated in chapter 85 when she asks Jesus in prayer how she might best please him.

22. *Prickynge*, 86. A similar statement occurs in *Contemplations of the Dread and Love of God*, for example, in the AB section (part of the treatise that appeared frequently in excerpted form): "Thenk also how sinful thou art, and . . . ther is no more sinful than thou art . . . yif thou haue eny vertu or grace . . . thenke it cometh of Godis sonde and nothing of thiself" (41). Kempe's Jesus makes a similar comment when he explains that he is a "hyd God": "I wythdrawe sumtyme thi teerys and thi devocyon that thu schuldist thynkyn in thyself that thu hast no goodnes of thiself but al goodnes comyth of me" (chap. 84, 194).

according to him, a necessary "peyne" that leads to recovery.[23] Paraphrasing John 12:25, he "quotes" Jesus as saying, "Whoso wole come aftir Me, forsake hymsilf and hate his owen soule . . . suffre the peyne of this *for awhile*, and thanne folwe."[24] Hilton insists that this personal misery will be temporary and lead to spiritual health, but writers held various views on the subject.

Chaucer's Parson tries to avoid the topic altogether by concentrating on God's goodness. For him, it is evident that such pain is nothing compared to God's great mercy; the believer need only pay attention to that greatness and focus on the divine to the exclusion of the personal. Still others, like the author of the *Prickynge*, employ heightened rhetoric to evoke an individualized emotional response. He confesses that his own heart is filled with poison, malice, and bitterness and has become a breeding ground for "wicked thoughtes" and "fleshli yernynges as a stynkande carion bredith ful of wormes and of mathis." These feelings, he declares, "freten" and "gnawen" him like "wormes in a stomak" and keep him from "the swete felynge of thyn holi grace."[25] Tucked within his baroque images of decay, his advice about God's goodness and our wickedness seems almost like an afterthought.

Kempe's *Book*, in contrast, exhibits strong awareness of temporal shame as a fundamental problem: if sinfulness is a basic condition of human existence, it is not actually possible to escape from a sense of shame in the present. If human beings are sinful and God hates sin, it is impossible to escape from shame. If ongoing meditation on one's wickedness is required, it does not seem possible to move beyond feelings of shame. Kempe puzzles over these problems and works in particular through her gendered experiences of sexuality, which function as constant reminders of shame, in relation to promises of future perfection.

Chapter twenty-one recalls the shame Kempe felt when she was pregnant. Her inferiority as a married woman, according to the traditional idea that virgins were superior to married women and widows, made her feel ashamed before Jesus and unworthy to engage in intimate conversation with him. The doubleness of advice about human wickedness and God's goodness is thematized in this chapter: even as Jesus assures her that he wants her to continue bearing children, he tells her that virgins *are* worthier than other women *and also* tells her that he loves her "as wel as any mayden in the world." Further confusing the issue, the paradoxical statement about virginity is framed by Jesus' challenge to human definitions of divine love: no man, he asserts, may

23. *Scale*, 76. On curing by contraries and spiritual renewal, see Zeeman, *Piers Plowman*, 41–42.
24. Ibid., 77, emphasis added.
25. *Prickynge*, 85–86.

stop him from loving "whom I wele and as mech as I wil" (chap. 21, 59). Jesus claims the right to love without regard to rules that define who is most lovable, even if those rules have divine authority behind them. The chapter keeps stumbling over the paradoxes: Are they rules if Jesus does not agree with them? How can virgins be superior to wives if Jesus loves pregnant Kempe as well as a virgin?

Jesus offers a solution: stop trying to make sense of the paradoxes. Instead of allowing her marital status to become an obstacle, he presents Kempe with the advice described earlier: she need only "have mende" of her "wykydnesse" and "thynk on" his "goodness." This, he insists, is the best way to love God. The fixity of the advice, however, has the same effect as the paradoxes. Unable to understand this as reassurance, and stricken by Jesus' attention to her wickedness, Kempe "seyd ageyn, 'I am the most unworthi creatur that evyr thow schewedyst grace unto in erth.'" She is not able to work through her bafflement until he reframes his admonition. After she repeats that she is the most unworthy, Jesus replies, "A, dowtyr . . . fere the nowt, I take non hede what a man hath ben, but I take hede what he wyl ben" (chap. 21, 59).

Kempe's concentration on her present physical condition is set aside in this way: if Jesus is able to look at Kempe as perfected, then she must also relinquish the present version of herself in favor of an understanding of her identity as the "future" Kempe, that is, as the Kempe she "will be."[26] The same phrase is repeated in chapter thirty-six, where Jesus insists that she put aside her shame before him and claims his right to "be homly" with her as "hir husbond." They must, he insists, "rest togedir in joy and pes," and she must understand that it does not matter if she sees herself as a "powr" woman and considers him "so gret a lorde" because, he explains, "I take non hed what thu hast be but what thu woldist be" (chap. 36, 94).

"Having mind" of her wickedness is necessary just as shame is in the opening story: it keeps her from misunderstanding her sinful condition. But, like her earlier sense of shame, Kempe's feelings of unworthiness are useful only if they are not obstacles to feeling the enormity of divine mercy. Insofar as shameful emotions limit her ability to love God, they lose their effectiveness. For this reason, the *Book* counters the orthodoxy concerning shame, even as it acknowledges its importance, by returning repeatedly to divine response as *different* from human understanding. Of particular importance is Jesus' insistence on his love for her as uninflected by her past and present: God attends to

---

26. The phrase (discussed later in this chapter) can be traced back to Isidore of Seville's *Sententiarum II* and is translated in *The Chastising of God's Children*, 152.

individuals in the conditions in which they find themselves.[27] The reader who feels, like Kempe, dismayed by her physical (and necessarily sinful) existence is encouraged to look beyond such emotions in order to imagine herself from God's perspective.

The task is, then, to discover what it means to see oneself as God does, and what the *Book* offers are methods for imagining oneself as perfected in the future. Rather than repeatedly dwelling on wickedness—even as it acknowledges the truth of Jesus' admonition—it draws attention to the possibilities of new kinds of self-understanding that free the believer from the agonizing experience of shame before God.[28] The *Book* does this by inviting readers to move outside the constraints of the immediate moment by shifting their focus from spiritual answers to, perhaps surprisingly, linguistic exploration.

Hooking Up Phrases and Clauses That Balance

It is, of course, impossible to see one's self exactly as God does. The impossibility of exact replication of another's understanding holds even for human individuals, who can never know if they "see" things just as others do, but the disparity between human and divine perspectives made the issue even more pressing for Kempe. If the only way to escape from shame is to imagine a future self, one that God sees but the believer does not, it becomes necessary to find ways to try to approximate divine perspective. The *Book* turns to proverbial phrases, lyrics, scriptural tags, and devotional imagery to accomplish this.

Although scholars frequently acknowledge late medieval authors' heavy reliance on authoritative writing, they rarely take up the subject in relation to Kempe's *Book*.[29] Nonetheless, the *Book* uses verbal phrases from other books to construct the life presented and to revise and reframe the nature of its author's personal understanding of spiritual truth. Jesus' explication of future perfection in chapters twenty-one and thirty-six is a useful example. Jesus' words, throughout the *Book*, are presented as direct speech, addressed to Kempe, but they are often, in fact, quotations or near quotations. This, as discussed earlier, is the case with "have mende" of your "wykydnesse" and "thynk on" my "goodnesse"; it is also true of chapter twenty-one's "I take non

---

27. In contrast, see the *Prickynge*: "How myghte hit be thenne but that thou shuldest hate thi-self yif thou be-thoughte the innerly what thou hast been and what thou arte?" (95). The emphasis is on the past and the present and their fixedness.

28. The EETS notes, which seem to me quite wrong in this case, insist that "'Haue mende of thi wykydnesse and thynk on my goodnes' . . . bears no special relation to what may be called Margery's characteristic piety" (281, n. 49/16).

29. Lochrie, *Translations of the Flesh*, is an important exception.

hede what a man hath ben, but I take hede what he wyl ben," originally from Isidore of Seville's *Sententiarum II*.

Kempe's reimagining of Isidore's claim is based on the reading of this material in *The Chastising of God's Children*. Arguing that no one should "mystrust of forgeuenesse," the *Chastising* uses Isidore to reframe the writings of Augustine and others who emphasize sinfulness as constitutive of human identity. "Al be it," the *Chastising* notes, Augustine and others "speken harde" about those who are in sin "al the daies of her lif," nonetheless ("yit"), the "hooli clerk" Isidore says "that a man shulde neuer mystrust, though he be nat turned to the last ende, so that bi the leeste tyme of repentaunce he shal be receyued into mercy."[30] Framed by "al be it" and "yit," this passage of the *Chastising* adds to and reshapes the point of view found in Augustine and the "other doctours," who argue for the need to think constantly on one's wickedness without dismissing their teachings. They are right, the *Chastising*'s author asserts, but so is Isidore. In this way, the *Chastising* shifts attention to the incompleteness of life, and thus the ongoing possibility of mercy until the very end. It develops this idea at length and offers a translation of Isidore to reinforce the point: "Therfor seith this same clerk [Isidore]: In eche mans lyueng we shulen *take heede of the ende*, for oure lorde lookith nat oonli hou we han lyued in oure lijf tofore, but rather he taketh heede what we bien in the ende of oure lijf."[31]

The *Chastising* models a method for breaking through the impasse of verbal phrases that become "stuck" in the reader's head. Emphasizing the linguistic packaging in which this advice appears, and drawing attention to the way language captures the reader's attention, the passage from the *Chastising* illustrates the ways in which late medieval writers could use authoritative language to reshape and reinterpret meaning. Like the *Chastising*, the *Book* shows Kempe learning to work with language in this way. Jesus' repeated quotation of the *Prickynge*'s advice—about "having mind" of one's wickedness and thinking of divine goodness—is a case in point.

Identified as a way out of the paradox concerning virgins and married women in chapter twenty-one, the phrase gets redeployed throughout the *Book*. As it is repeated, its meaning is transformed. In its original appearance in chapter twenty-one, discussed earlier, the phrase is the answer to the question of how best to please God. When the question is repeated in chapter seventy-seven, in contrast, Jesus tells Kempe only, "Kepe me alwey in thi mende as meche as thu mayst." He says she may "nevyr plesyn" him "bettyr" than to "havyn" him "evyr in [her] lofe," but refrains from insisting she think of her own wretchedness (chap. 77, 176). Back in chapter twenty-one he said

---

30. *Chastising*, 151–52.
31. Ibid., emphasis added.

the same thing ("thow mayst no bettyr plesyn God than contynuly to thinkyn on hys lofe"), but when she asked how she should do this, he said she needed to think of *both* her wickedness and his goodness (chap. 21, 59). In chapter seventy-seven, in contrast, *her wickedness* seems to have disappeared from the equation.

When the phrase appears yet again, her wickedness has not simply disappeared but been re-understood. In chapter eighty-five she prays and asks Jesus "how sche myght best plesyn hym," and he responds, again, "Have mynde of thi wykkydnes and thynk on my goodness" (chap. 85, 196). Her wickedness is reinstated, but instead of feeling rebuked as she did earlier in the *Book*, Kempe now records the way the phrase helped her find comfort by allowing her to reconfigure the meaning of the relationship between her wickedness and God's goodness: "Sche preyd many tymys and oftyn thes wordys, 'Lord, for thy gret goodnes have mercy on al my wykkydnes as wistly as I was nevyr so wykkyd as thu art good ne nevyr may be thow I wolde, for thu art so good that thu mayst no bettyr be" (chap. 85, 196). The logic is comparative and stretches out to infinity: I, Kempe tells Jesus, can *never, ever* be as wicked as you are good.

Verbal repetition and wordplay become tools for escaping from static notions of self. The passage is in fact a short poem. The rhythmic quality of the lines is somewhat obscured in prose, but breaking the lines up exposes the nature of the rhyme:

> I was nevyr so wykkyd as thu art good
> ne nevyr may be thow I wolde,
> for thu art so good
> that thu mayst no bettyr be.

Rhythm and repetition reinforce the phrase's efficacy, turning aside the damaging rebuke of self found in the twenty-first chapter by focusing on an imbalance between the human and the divine.[32]

Multiple variations on phrases appear throughout the *Book*. For example, when the young man at Syon approaches Kempe, described in chapter ten

---

32. On rhyme in the *Book*, see Robert Karl Stone, *Middle English Prose Style: Margery Kempe and Julian of Norwich* (The Hague: Mouton, 1970), 84–88. Seeta Chaganti's discussion of the relationship between agency and collectivity in late medieval lyric describes the performative nature of this process; see *Medieval Poetics of the Reliquary: Enshrinement, Inscription, Performance* (New York: Palgrave Macmillan, 2008), 155–69. See also Bruce Holsinger's discussion of "musicality" in *Music, Body, and Desire in Medieval Culture: Hildegard of Bingen to Chaucer* (Stanford: Stanford University Press, 2001), esp. 196–202.

of the second book, to learn why she weeps, she extemporizes yet again on the wickedness/goodness proverb. She cries on account of the "gret abhominacyon that sche had of hir synnys [her wickedness]" and "also the excellent charité of hir redemptowr [his goodness]" (bk. 2, chap. 10, 229). By this point in the *Book* the phrase has become "wordys of gostly comfort" instead of a reproach, and the sting of Jesus' seeming rebuke in chapter twenty-one is entirely assuaged by the familiarity of the sound of the lines.

"Thinking on Jesus' goodness" stands as shorthand for the promise of future perfection in the *Book*, and Kempe's imaginative practice of seeing herself outside of the present allows her to move beyond the constraints of negative emotion. Her clever dismantling of wickedness in the rhyme serves to transform the advice found in books of consolation by recontextualizing that advice. It is an example of the way phrases trigger emotional responses and draws attention to how verbal cues redirect such responses.

Underlying this reinterpretive practice is the *Book*'s understanding of language itself as capable of creating emotional responses through linguistic form. Words themselves have a palpable presence in the *Book*, and that presence extends beyond paraphrasable meaning. Kempe, for example, prays, asking God to make the people receive the words of human preachers as if they were God's: "Lorde, make thi holy word to *sattelyn* in her sowlys as I wolde that it schulde don in myn" (chap. 61, 146, emphasis added). "Sattelyn" means to be seated or fixed; the sense is that once the words are heard, they must find their place in the listeners' souls to be effective. The same phrase is used in chapter eighty-six. In this instance, Jesus reminds Kempe that he receives "every good wyl as for dede" (chap. 86, 200) and encourages her to pray that other people might have the same experience of his words "settling" in their hearts that she does.[33]

These words take up space; they fill up the heart and the mind. The *Book*'s frequent, repeated quotation of itself and other sources is, likewise, an attempt to "fill up" Kempe and her readers. Just as images may trigger visionary experiences, words evoke powerful emotions in the *Book*. Phrasing such as "Tho wordys wrowt so in hir mende" as applied, for example, to themes from sermons (chap. 78, 177) indicates how important this response was to Kempe.

---

33. The passage equates the success of her crying in drawing people to God with the hoped-for success of the preacher. For a similar discussion of words' effect on her, see book two, chapter two: "thorw the whech wordys sche was the mor steryd to obeyn the wil of God and parformyn hir entent" (212). The power of words to reshape one's emotional state was emphasized in books of consolation. See, for example, the *Remedy*, chap. 10: "Haueth tho wordes in youre mynde that often ben seyd in this writynge" (239).

The *Book*, however, also suggests that it is impossible to maintain a sense of oneself as perfected in the present if this identification hinges on only a few verbal concepts (wickedness/goodness and not-what-you-are-but-what-you-will-be). This would result in nearly the same problem that a single saying or idea creates. Instead, the *Book* illustrates the power of *multiplicities* of linguistic phrases to approximate a sense of perfection in the present. One of Kempe's primary methods for understanding herself from the divine perspective (as worthy and unashamed before God) is to maintain heightened emotional receptivity by employing multiple phrases as reminders or triggers that help her do the "thinking in her mind" that she had been directed to do and that are, in turn, modeled for the *Book*'s readers.

We might think of the web of phrases as a kind of soundtrack for the *Book*. What follows is a discussion of several of these "tracks" that intersect with Kempe's efforts to feel unashamed before God. Many phrases are repeated throughout the *Book*, and there are several that are closely associated with attempts to feel and understand future perfection as it is framed by the idea of "keeping Jesus in one's mind." I discuss six of these, and although they are representative, it is worth noting that the process of linguistic reshaping in the *Book* is less structured than my discussion of these categories. As the *Book* points out, despite the fact that it represents a rough chronology of her life, Kempe's approach is to write "not in ordyr as it fellyn but as the creatur cowd han mend of hem whan it wer wretyn" (preface, 21). "Having mind" of things did not require the kind of logical patterning for which modern readers look. Instead, as the *Book* shows, the process of remembering is layered, initiated by association as much as logic, and thickly clustered rather than linear. Instead of thinking through one phrase at a time, the *Book* deploys cascades of verbal constructions that repeat, intersect, and overlap with one another. The strands of associative phrases, described in what follows, weave in and out of one another as they become part of Kempe's strategy against static categorization of shame/self.

Near and Far

God's "hiddenness" was a common concern among devotional writers in the later Middle Ages. The *Book* refers at several points to this "hid" God, and the desire for immediacy is articulated even when that presence is in Kempe's "mind," as the *Book* describes interior thought, rather than in a visionary experience. Rhymed phrases, elaborately constructed strings of alliterating words, opposing terms, questions, and simple repetition remind readers that the problem of God's hiddenness is in fact a problem of human perception.

Jesus' first appearance in the *Book*, for example, has him asking this (rhetorical) question: "Why hast thow forsakyn me / And I forsoke nevyr the?" (chap. 1, 23). Kempe's belief that she is unworthy of God's mercy is shown to be, instead, her own choice to hide from God. This is underscored by the scribe's remark characterizing the problem of perception through spatial opposition: "Whan men wenyn [believe]" that God is far from them, he is nonetheless "ful nere" (chap. 1, 23).

Similarly, Kempe's couplet "I have ronnyn awey fro the / And thow hast ronnyn aftyr me" (chap. 22, 60) identifies God's seeming absence as, in reality, the human believer's decision to absent herself. In his response, Jesus reminds her that her sins are forgiven and that the two of them are "onyd [one-ed: united] together"; both their love and his grace are "singular": "Thu art to me a synguler lofe, dowtyr . . . thu schalt have a synguler grace in hevyn, dowtyr" (chap. 22, 60).[34] By embedding language that unifies the human and the divine in spatial and linguistic terms, the *Book* modifies the passages in which Kempe separates her wickedness from God's goodness, as in the poem in chapter eighty-five, and shifts the emphasis from difference to similarity.

Insistence on the identity between God and heaven becomes a touchstone for Kempe's efforts to survive the pain of imperfection and temporal separation from divine presence. Told she is a "mayden" in her "sowle" (chap. 22, 62) and Jesus' "derworthy derlyng" who, as the string of alliteration continues, is "her to dwellyn" with him "and nevyr to departyn," she is encouraged to imagine heaven on earth. The *Book* insists on identity between God and heaven: in chapter fifteen Jesus tells Kempe that despite the fact that he is "not yet" ready to take her "sowle owt of" her "body" and bring her there, she should understand that "nevyrtheles whersoevyr God is hevyn is, and God is in thi sowle" (chap. 14, 44). Similarly, in chapter thirty-five God and heaven are again equated: "For wherso God is hevyn is, and wher that God is ther be many awngelys, and God is in the and thu art in hym" (chap. 35, 93). The language of definition (God is. . God is) works to produce a rhythm that stands in for the imagined future to come. Jesus' "yet" in chapter fourteen— "that wyl I not *yet*"—is similar to the "yet" between Augustine and Isidore in the *Chastising*: a bridge to a possibility that seems logically impossible (or at least implausible) but which "nevertheless" gets at the truth.[35]

---

34. "Synguler" love, reward, and worship reappear in chapter twenty-two (62).

35. The *Book* takes up this idea by stating that intentions are more important than actions. For example, in chapter eighty-four Jesus tells Kempe that her reward will be based on her "good desyrys" to perform acts of devotion "as yyf thu haddist don hem in deed" (chap. 84, 193). Rolle makes a similar remark in *The Fire of Love* (bk. 1, chap. 22, 48). The idea appears in many other works including the *Remedy*, *Contemplations*, and *Chastising*.

The imagined mutuality between human and divine is intensified further by linguistic flourishes in which space itself is eliminated and Kempe and God are described as present in each other. When Jesus assures her, with another rhyme, that an enemy's antagonism toward her should cause her no concern because "I am in the and thu art in me" (chap. 34, 90), the *Book* is far from representing Kempe as a mere vessel for the divine presence.[36] Rather, it insistently draws attention to the relational nature of this "indwelling" and identifies the experience as reciprocal.[37] When Jesus tells her he will be "buxom" (chap. 14, 44) to her, like a child to his father, in chapter fourteen, it carries the same sense of responsiveness and obedience that it does when Jesus uses the word again in chapter sixty-four and tells Kempe, "Yyf thu wilt be buxom to my wyl, I schal be buxom to thy wil" (chap. 64, 153).[38]

Jesus est amor meus

Jesus' promised "buxomness" and the seeming mutuality it suggests is nevertheless tangled up in the problem of inequality and shame. Chapter sixty-four opens with Kempe offering yet another version of her question about the best way to please God.[39] She says, "I wolde I knew wherin I myth best love the and plesyn the and that my love wer as swet to the as me thynkyth that thy love is unto me" (chap. 64, 153). The fact that the question of how best to please God is repeated numerous times throughout the *Book* might suggest that it has become, in Kempe's usage, simply a way of choosing to move toward practices that allow for a sense of self as perfected through compliance with a model of behavior.

---

36. The phrase is from Canticles. The *Prickynge* goes even further, bringing together reflection on wickedness and indwelling as a sense of becoming divine ("thus nought" oneself and "magnyfie god so that he be as he were turned in-to god that he [the believer] se noon othir thynge ne fele but god" [chap. 22, 120]).

37. Earlier in the *Book* this is not nearly as clear. The phrase appears in chapter ten, too, for example, but in the context of verifying Kempe's words as God's to assure her she is not suffering from vainglory (see chap. 9, 36). Elizabeth Psakis Armstrong, "Understanding by Feeling," in McEntire, *Margery Kempe: A Book of Essays*, observes that this is characteristic of the *Book*: "These are the kind of touches of godliness Margery Kempe prefers, and they all go the other way—not she in heaven's realm, but God in hers" (23).

38. The EETS edition glosses buxom as "gentle" in the first instance, but as I go on to discuss, "obedient to" makes better sense. Emma Lipton, *Affections of the Mind: The Politics of Sacramental Marriage* (Notre Dame: University of Notre Dame Press, 2007), 129–60, describes Kempe's *Book* in relation to "compatibility" and "a new bourgeois model of marriage" (130–31).

39. The *Prickynge* takes a systematic approach to the question of how to please God best and lists ten points beginning with holding oneself most vile, having sorrow for sin and joy in tribulation, desiring poverty, and being indifferent to outward things (these four are of greatest importance to Kempe). The next three involve sympathy for fellow believers. The last three are about mindfulness of God and gratitude for his love.

Feeling future perfection might, then, be seen as an affective experience produced through practice and repetition. This certainly seems to be at least partially true. But what is also true—and embedded in the statement following the question from the passage in chapter sixty-four—is the incompleteness of this model in terms of emotional response. Knowing you are doing the right thing is one matter; but, the *Book* keeps asking its author and its readers, how do you feel it? In this passage, a sense of inadequacy emerges as an addendum to the question: Kempe wants to know how to please Jesus, but she also wants to know that *he loves her* in exactly the same way *she loves him*. Jesus' answer is a partial rejection of her equation: "Beleve wel, dowtyr, that my lofe is not so swet to the as thy lofe is to me" (chap. 64, 153). The point is that they are in fact *not* the same: she cannot experience the same "sweetness."

The question of pleasing God becomes a staging ground for sorting out the problem of submerging Kempe's wickedness in the vastness of God's goodness; far greater goodness means far greater love than that which she experiences. This is standard doctrine and constantly represented in discussions of mercy and forgiveness in the later Middle Ages. It is the truth, for Kempe, and the books she had read and the religious figures from whom she learned agreed on this: God's love is greater than humans can imagine. When, in chapter four, Kempe is "smet wyth the dedly wownd of veynglory," believing "sche lovyd God mor than he hir," the moral of the story is that, however she feels, she must understand the distance between God's love for her and hers for him (chap. 4, 28).

But the *Book* goes beyond restating the theological grounds for this belief in God's boundless love and turns instead to attempts to *feel* how divine love differs from human love. When Jesus reinstates the divide between the human and the divine, he conveys this message by telling her she would *explode* if she felt the same love that he feels: "It may not be knowyn in this werld how meche" his love "is, ne be felt as it is, for thu schuldist faylyn and brestyn [burst] and nevyr enduryn it for the joye that thu schuldist fele." That experience, he assures her, will come to her "in an other worlde," but for now he carefully "mesur[s]" it out to her to give her "most ese and comfort" (chap. 64, 153).[40]

The *Book* is pushed and pulled by the weight of advice about God's love, the human need for love, God's need for love from us, and the pressing issue of trying to understand the imbalance. Phrase upon phrase, drawn especially

---

40. See also chap. 86, 200: if people knew the grace "put in" Kempe at "that tyme, thei schulde rathyr wondyr that thin hert brost no asundyr." "Burst" is the verb used in the *Book* to describe emotional experiences that are beyond Kempe's control.

from devotional lyrics, is introduced to explain what it might mean to try to love God perfectly, given human imperfection. Two in particular are repeated multiple times in the *Book*: "Jesus est amor meus" (along with its translation into English, "Jesus is my love," and variations on the phrase), and the rhyming lines "Lord, for alle thi wowndys smert, drawe al the love of myn hert into thyn hert," which occur three times.[41] Out of context, both seem concerned with the believer's "mind" of Jesus, that is, with humans' love for God, and not, at least directly, with God's love for humans. Furthermore, the phrases are presented as ways of fulfilling Jesus' request, repeated at intervals in the *Book*, for Kempe to give him her heart completely: "I aske no mor of the but thin hert for to lovyn that lovyth the, for my lofe is evyr redy to the" (chap. 36, 95). This is traditional advice that excuses fallen humans from doing any more than loving God and reminds believers that God's love is unconditional.[42]

The *Book* supplements this idea with representation of intense emotional neediness. The first phrase, "Jesus est amor meus," is used to draw attention to Jesus' "wooing" of Kempe. This is somewhat surprising, since the saying was usually associated with the *believer's* love for God. It was linked to Saint Ignatius, whose name, as the *Golden Legend* explains, "comes from *ignem patiens*, which means being afire with love of God," and who, in contrast with those writers who insisted on the term *dilectio* (*agape*) in place of *amor* (*eros*), wrote, "My Love (*amor meus*) has been crucified."[43] Allen notes that the phrase was inscribed on prayer beads left to Arundel by William Wykeham, bishop

---

41. Douglas Gray observes that the Carthusian MS Additional 37049 includes pictures that "illustrate the words 'Jesus est amor meus'" (210); see "Medieval English Mystical Lyrics," in *Mysticism and Spirituality in Medieval England*, ed. William F. Pollard and Robert Boenig (Woodbridge, Suffolk: D. S. Brewer, 1997), 203–18, esp. 210–16. Jessica Brantley provides an extensive analysis of the manuscript; see *Reading in the Wilderness: Private Devotion and Public Performance in Late Medieval England* (Chicago: University of Chicago Press, 2007).

42. See EETS edition, 302, n. 90/25, on Jesus asking no more of believers than their hearts. The phrase, like much of the *Book*'s discussion of love and hearts, comes from the *Prickynge* and also appeared in devotional lyrics. See, for example, the lyric *Brother Abide*, which includes these words spoken by Jesus: "Off tendure love, all this I dyd endure; / Love dyde me lede, love dyde me thus constrayne; / And, for my ded and grevouse adventure, / More aske I nott but love for love a-gayne"; in *Religious Lyrics of the Fifteenth Century*, ed. Carleton Brown (1939; repr., Oxford: Clarendon, 1952), no. 110 (175). Hilton, in book one of *Scale*, discusses the impossibility of doing this and explains why he thinks God "bad us for to love soo" despite this (chap. 33, 65). Yoshikawa observes that "both [Saint] Bridget and Margery receive a revelation which emphasizes an exchange of hearts and wills" (*Margery Kempe's Meditations*, 56).

43. Jacobus de Voragine, *The Golden Legend: Readings on the Saints*, trans. William Granger Ryan, vol. 1 (Princeton: Princeton University Press, 1993), 140–41.

of Winchester, at his death in 1404, and this too points toward the believer's love for God and not the reverse.[44]

The *Book*, however, does not employ the phrase in the standard context of *human* attachment to Jesus. Rather, it is used to draw attention to Jesus' pressing need for Kempe. The saying first appears in chapter five of the *Book*. Here he orders her to use the phrase, saying, "I bydde the and comawnd the, boldly clepe me Jhesus, thi love, for I am thi love and schal be thi love wythowtyn ende." The passage uses the language of the wedding ceremony to emphasize Jesus' decision to "wed" this "wife": "I swer to the be my magesté that I schal nevyr forsakyn the in wel ne in wo" (chap. 5, 31).

The association of the phrase with Jesus' desire is reinforced by its next appearance, in chapter thirty-one, in the context of his demand that Kempe wear a ring on which the phrase is engraved. This looks something like what seems to be a general devotional attitude represented by Wykeham's inscribed prayer beads: a symbolic object is possessed to exert emotional force on its owner. But, again, the *Book* associates "Jesus est amor meus," despite its literal meaning, with Jesus' desire for Kempe. It is, as I have noted, associated explicitly with marriage. The Latin phrase is engraved on her "bone maryd ring," which he presents to Kempe: "Owyr Lord had comawndyd hir to do makyn [the ring] whil she was at hom in Inglond and dede hir gravyn ther upon, 'Jhesus est amor meus.'" She wears it at "hys byddyng" and does so even though she herself had "purposyd befortyme er than . . . nevyr to a weryd ryng" (chap. 31, 84).

The motto appears for a third time, in chapter sixty-five, and here, once again, it occurs in the context of representation of Jesus' devotion to Kempe. The "mayst boldly"–call-me phrasing from chapter five is repeated, and this time the emphasis on mutual obligation is made explicit. Jesus reminds her that she has "gret cawse" to love him, including her chaste life and her husband, John's, continuing health, but he also places the phrase in the context of his gratitude toward Kempe. She is "bowndyn" to thank him, but "nevyrthelesse yet I thank the for the gret lofe thu hast to me" (chap. 65, 155).

44. EETS, n. 78/12, 297. Kempe, of course, had been welcomed into Archbishop Arundel's garden in 1413 and stayed "tyl sterrys apperyd in the fyrmament" (49). Besides his anti-Lollard stance, Arundel was associated with devotional interests similar to those found in Kempe's *Book*. A northerner, he was, for example, an early reader of Rolle; the recipient of Love's *Mirror of the Blessed Life of Jesu Christ*, presented to him in 1411; and, it seems, committed to the brand of "negative thinking" associated with books of consolation. According to the entry by Jonathan Hughes in the *DNB* (online ed., May 2007), Arundel's will shows "a preoccupation with penance and personal unworthiness." This is in keeping with the lessons of the books Kempe and her lister read together.

This is the first in a series of things for which he thanks her, and as he goes on, he asks her especially not to be "yrke" (irritated) with him as she sits "alone" and thinks of his love because he himself is not "yrke" with her (chap. 65, 156).

Jesus compares his position to that of a married man whose beautiful wife arouses the "envye" of other men: "I far liche a man that lovyth wel hys wyfe, the mor envye that men han to hir the bettyr he wyl arayn hir in despite of hir enmys" (chap. 32, 87). The wife in the comparison is a prize to be displayed—in her glorious array—to other men. Kempe and Jesus may be different from each other, but at the level of desire, they both look for certainty and mutuality and both worry about the other's love. In chapter eighty-eight he reminds her she is "sekyr of my lofe . . . no thyng is so sekyr to the in erthe," and assures her that if she will "gevyn me al thyn hool hert," he wants "nothyng ellys" and will give her his whole heart in return (chap. 88, 205). This chapter circles back to Jesus' promise of "buxomness" in chapter sixty-four, promising that "yyf thu wilt be buxom to my wil I schal be buxom to thi wil, dowtyr" (chap. 88, 205).

Heart/Smart

The passages in which "Jhesus est amor meus" appears maintain the distinction between sinful human (with limited capacity to love) and perfect divine (with unlimited capacity). Rather than stopping at this distinction, however, the *Book* goes on to describe longing as both human and divine. Similarly, its incorporation of verses rhyming "smart" and "heart" navigates between identity and difference as a path to practicing belief in future perfection in the imperfect present. The phrase first appears in chapter sixty-five, the same chapter in which Jesus reminds Kempe to "boldly" call him her "love" and thanks her for her love. In this chapter, Jesus reminds Kempe of the way she has been able to "cryen" to him in times of suffering, saying, "Lord, for alle thi wowndys smert, drawe al the lofe of myn hert into thyn hert" (chap. 65, 156). Rhymes between "smart" and "heart" were extremely popular in the later Middle Ages and appear in texts as different as Chaucer's *Book of the Duchess*, *The Castle of Perseverance*, *Havelock the Dane*, and numerous devotional lyrics.[45]

---

45. In *The Book of the Duchess*, the man in black "thought hys sorwes were so smerte / And lay so colde upon hys herte" (ll. 507–8); in *The Castle of Perseverance*, the audience is told, "God asketh no more but sorwe of hert for all thi synnys smert" (l. 1389); in the romance *Havelock the Dane*, Ubbe, the Danish nobleman, has "mikel sorwe in his herte / For his [Havelock's] wundes, that wer so smerte." The rhyme is particularly common in devotional lyrics such as *When Y se blosmes spring* and *I syke when*

In the *Book* the rhyme functions as a snapshot of lay affective devotion, and draws on ideas about love as romance (in both secular and devotional contexts) that would have been very familiar to Kempe and her readers.[46] Writers routinely recommended that readers focus on Jesus' physical pain at the crucifixion to intensify feelings of spiritual love.[47] The phrase appears in Richard Caister's "Prayer to Jesus":

Ihesu, for thi woundis smerte
On feet and on thin hondis two,
Make me meeke and low of herte,
And thee to loue as y schulde do!
Ihesu, for thi bitter wounde
That wente to thin herte roote,
For synne that hath myn herte bounde,
Thi blessid bloode mote be my bote.[48]

Caister, vicar of St. Stephen's in Norwich, whom the *Book* describes as "exalted" by God and "preved" holy by "mervelyows werkys," was another of Kempe's celebrated supporters.[49] Her visit with him, which occurred in 1413, is described in chapter seventeen. In this passage, the *Book* represents Kempe as having asked Caister if she might "speke wyth him an owyr or ellys tweyn," to which it says he replied: "Benedicité. What cowd a woman occupyn an owyr er tweyn owyrs in the lofe of owyr Lord? I schal nevyr ete mete tyl I wete what ye kan sey of owyr Lord God the tyme of on owyr." Following their meeting, which may easily have lasted a good bit more than two hours (the *Book* reports that Kempe told him her whole life history from childhood to the present and that the visit included an episode in which she fell into a trance and "lay stylle a gret whyle"), Caister becomes her confessor

Y singe in Harley MS 2253; see *The Complete Harley 2253 Manuscript*, ed. Susanna Fein, TEAMS Middle English Texts Series, 3 vols. (Kalamazoo: Medieval Institute Publications, 2014), 2:230–32, 2:270–72.

46. See Gray, "Medieval English Mystical Lyrics," 203–18. Gray argues that in such lyrics "an intensely 'personal' relationship is created between the poet . . . his readers . . . and Christ" (205).

47. The *Prickynge*, for example, urges readers to use thoughts about the Passion to stimulate their "longing in love" and offers six ways to use reflection on Jesus' suffering to increase the emotional intensity of devotional practice (esp. 19–27). The author is quick to note that if this does not work and one cannot "melt" in love, then he or she should have faith, trust God, and flee sin (28).

48. In *Hymns to the Virgin and Christ, The Parliament of Devils, and Other Religious Poems*, ed. Frederick J. Furnivall, EETS OS 24 (Oxford: Kegan Paul, Trench, Trübner, 1867), 15, ll. 9–16. Windeatt notes that eight of the twelve stanzas from Caister's poem can be found in earlier poems (*Book*, 113).

49. See also chapter sixty, where Kempe visits Caister's grave and cries uncontrollably, causing the people who see her to remark, "What eylith the woman?" (chap. 60, 144).

and a staunch supporter, backing her, in some cases, against the "rumowr and grutchyng of the pepyl" (chap. 17, 50–51).

Caister's poem emphasizes the speaker's effort to use reminders of the Passion to help him remain meek before God, to suffer patiently, and to ask for God's mercy for all people. The *Book*, in surprising contrast, places the quotations in passages that work through the puzzle of giving God one's whole heart—loving God only as fundamental to future perfection—while also loving other "ghostly livers," as the *Remedy* refers to them, on a personal rather than universal level. The rhyme first appears, in chapter sixty-five, a few lines below "Jhesus est amor meus" and, just before chapter sixty-six begins, in the context of Kempe's anxiety about her affection for other people (her heart is not God's alone). Jesus assures her that he has in fact drawn all "the lofe of [her] hert fro alle mennys hertys" into his "hert" and reminds her of her past struggles when she thought it "unpossybyl" to love him exclusively and suffered "ful gret peyne" in her heart on account of "fleschly affeccyons" (chap. 65, 156). Speaking in her voice, he reminds her that during these moments she had cried out, "Lord, for alle thi wowndys smert, drawe al the lofe of myn hert into thyn hert" (chap. 65, 156).

In chapter sixty-five the rhyme is identified as helping Kempe stave off her "fleshly" loves and the pain they cause her through its substitution of Jesus' pain for her own and its visualization of Jesus' heart as something like a giant pump—a machine capable of forcing the love inside her to be drawn out of her heart and into his own. But this use of the quotation is undercut by the following chapter's opening, in which the complications of human social interaction and devotional obedience make the effortless drawing of Kempe's love into Jesus' heart appear idealized. In chapter sixty-six Jesus asserts his authority over Kempe, commanding her to give up her vegetarianism and to tell her "gostly fadyrs" that they need to "don" according to his "wyl" (chap. 66, 157).

Similarly, the rhyme's next appearance, in chapter eighty-eight, occurs in the context of Kempe's relationship with her spiritual advisers. In this chapter, Jesus recalls that when her confessor was "scharp" to her, it was to her advantage because it kept her from feeling "gret affeccyon to hys persone." He reminds her, speaking again in her voice, that when this happened, she would "ronne wyth al [her] mynde to me," declare that God "alone" could be trusted, and cry out "wyth al [her] hert, 'Lord, for thi wowndys smerte drawe alle my lofe into thyn hert'" (chap. 88, 203–4).

In chapter eighty-eight, as in chapters sixty-five and sixty-six, Jesus reminds her of another instance when she had been concerned about her affection for "sum synguler persone"; to help her, Jesus performed "a gret myracle" and, again, drew all of her love to himself (chap. 88, 204).[50] As in the other passages, however, even as the rhyme is used to remind her to feel love for Jesus alone, it is modified by further commentary: Jesus says he knows that she has "ryth trewe love" for this other man and that her love is acceptable because "that persone hath plesyd" him "ryth wel" (chap. 88, 204).

The rhyme's implications are stretched even farther as the chapter goes on, and Jesus explains in detail how this particular singular person and Kempe's other spiritual advisers have deserved his love. On the one hand, he commends them because their advice to her is the same as his own. For example, he tells her that he is "hyly plesyd" with both her friend the Carmelite Alan of Lynn and the (unnamed) "singular" person's support for Kempe's visionary experiences. He also praises Robert Spryngolde, her confessor, who had just a few dozen lines back been described as causing her to feel that there was "no trost but in [God] alone" on account of his harshness, because "he biddith the that thu schuldist sittyn stille and gevyn thyn hert . . . to holy thowtys as God wyl puttyn in thi mende" (chap. 88, 204).

Yet on the other hand, even as her spiritual friends are represented as pleasing God by providing her with Jesus' instructions, they are also described as competing with Jesus for Kempe's affection and attention. Jesus, in fact, reproaches her for attending to Spryngolde's instructions but ignoring the same instructions when he himself tells her to behave in particular ways. He promises that he is not "displesyd" with her—because, he says, he is always pleased with her—but notes that she responds to his own advice "wyth meche grutchyng" but attends to Spryngolde's even though "he biddith the do the same that I bidde the do" (chap. 88, 204–5).

The rhyme appears in truncated form in the *Book*'s concluding prayer. Here the phrase is closer to the version in Caister's poem: "And geve us thin holy drede in owr hertys for thi wowndys smert" (bk. 2, chap. 10, 231). There is no reference to Jesus drawing her love into his heart, and the transfer is in the opposite direction: from God to the believer's heart. The passage is nonetheless, like the previous two, concerned with the difficulty of relinquishing love toward other people. It identifies the elusive nature of wanting to love God exclusively: "And, as anemst any erdly mannys love, as wistly as I wolde no love han but God to lovyn above al thinge and alle other creaturs lovyn for God and in God, al so wistly qwenche in me al fleschly lust" (bk. 2, chap. 10, 231).

---

50. This episode is discussed further in the present book's fifth chapter, "Loneliness."

In contrast with chapters sixty-five and eighty-eight, the *Book*'s last chapter balances Kempe's participation in the world with her identity as one perfectly united to God. As well as reversing the direction of the "flow" of the rhyme toward the believer, her prayer reverses the movement of authority and power found in the earlier chapters in which the verse appeared. Here, instead, Kempe asks that her "gostly fadirs" be made "to dredyn the [God] in me and for to lovyn the [God] in me." With Kempe at the center, her prayer then goes on to represent itself as a request for perfect balance and identity between herself and Jesus: "Good Jhesu, make my wil thi wyl and thi wil my wil that I may no wil han but thi wil only" (bk. 2, chap. 10, 231).

Making the Unworthy Worthy

Repetition and reconfiguration of the "wowndis smert/hert" rhyme allow for exploration of the emotional experience of God's love. By the end of the *Book*, the phrase captures the sense of imagined transformation implied by Jesus' promise, his paraphrase of Isidore as quoted in the *Chastising*, to judge Kempe "not as she is but as she will be." Although the *Book* relies on a number of phrases associated with seemingly sudden change to make this point, such as the rhyming lines "thi sorwe schal turnyn into joy and blysse, / the whech thu schalt nevyr mysse" (chap. 32, 87), the phrase most closely associated with the issue of shame before God occurs, along with the smert/hert rhyme, in the final prayer: "As thu hast mad of unworthi creaturys worthy, so make al this world worthi to thankyn the and preisyn the." As Kempe asks for mercy for all people, she frames this request in terms of transformation: just as Jesus has "drawn" her to him, undeserving, she asks that any other who is "undrawyn" will be brought to grace. This, she reminds God, has been his practice all along: "Good Lord, have mende that ther is many a seynt in hevyn whech sumtyme was hethen in erde" (bk. 2, chap. 10, 232).

Like the smert/hert rhyme, phrases in which the "unworthy" are transformed and become "worthy" are common in devotional lyrics from the period. Harley 2253's *Dulcis Jesu memoria*, for example, includes the following lines: "Jesu, thah Ich be unworthi . . . That ich thareto worthi be / Make me worthi that art so fre."[51] A similar lyric, *Swete Ihesu, Now Wil I Synge*, reprinted in various versions by Horstmann, includes this verse: "Ihesu, euer beseche I the / Thy luf inwardely graunte thou me; / Thof I ther-to vnworthi be /

51. *Harley 2253*, 2:254, ll. 129, 143–44. Fein provides a brief, critical background for this poem and related lyrics (2:436).

Make me worthi, that art so fre."[52] It seems likely that Kempe was familiar with the entire poem because she also includes the poem's question "When schal my soule come to the? / How longe schal I here be?" in the chapter. The poem draws attention as well to the distinction between knowing and feeling and to the need to keep God's goodness in mind on account of human sinfulness.

The *Book*'s immediate source for the phrase is another of Kempe's supporters, the Carmelite William Southfield, whom she visited in Norwich at the same time that she consulted with Julian of Norwich, and whom she met just after she had become acquainted with Richard Caister. Southfield is identified as "a good man and an holy levar" (chap. 18, 52). The EETS notes, based on Bale's account in *Anglorum Heliades*, describe Southfield's visionary experiences and his penchant for "multiplication of vocal prayers," that is, the practice of praying through vocalization of set prayers as opposed to inner, silent prayer.[53] Chapter eighteen represents Kempe's meeting with Southfield in terms similar to the description of her appointment with Caister but in a much condensed form: Kempe had been "chargyd and comawndyd in hir sowle" to meet with Southfield to show him "hir meditacyons and swech as God wrowt in hir sowle to wetyn yf sche wer dysceyved be any illusyons or not." The *Book* notes that "sche dede as sche was comawndyd" and devotes the rest of the chapter to reporting what Southfield had said to her after he held up his hands (presumably to stop her) and exclaimed: "Jhesu, mercy and gremercy. Syster . . . dredyth ye not of yowr maner of levyng, for it is the Holy Gost werkyng plentyuowsly hys grace in yowr soule" (chap. 18, 52). Although Southfield's subsequent remarks take just twenty lines or so (ll. 933–954), his conversation with Kempe—if it can be called that, since she does not report speaking again during their meeting—is packed with quotations, especially from scripture.[54]

The *Book* represents Southfield as having no doubt about the nature of Kempe's visionary experiences, and the first part of the passage is largely a pep talk aimed at encouraging Kempe to thank God for his goodness and accept God's gifts with meekness. Seemingly sensing that her anxiety is as much about her sinfulness as her visionary experiences, Kempe conveys Southfield's defense of God's prerogative to bestow his favors where he will: "He may," Southfield says, "gevyn hys gyftys wher he wyl, and

52. Horstmann, *Yorkshire Writers*, 2:22. This version is MS Reg. 17 B xvii.

53. EETS, 278, nn. 41/2–3 through 41/35; see also Appendix 3, viii, which includes the relevant passage from Bale.

54. The EETS edition identifies several of them—Wisdom 1:4, Isaiah 66:2, Psalms 1:19—and goes on to observe that "scriptural phraseology runs all through this conversation" (EETS, 278, n. 41/29).

of unworthy he maketh worthy, of synful he makyth rygtful" (chap. 18, 53, emphasis added).

Kempe notes that she was "mech comfortyd bothe in body and in sowle be this good mannys wordys and gretly strengthyd in hir feyth" (chap. 18, 53), but if she was, she must have been focusing on Southfield's guarantee that God makes the unworthy worthy, because the rest of the conversation as recorded in the *Book* is a series of scriptural quotations packaged as warnings. For example, the *Book* represents Southfield as explaining that God's mercy is "evyr redy unto us," but goes on to caution "les than the fawt be *in owyrself*" (chap. 18, 53, emphasis added), and to note, quoting Wisdom 1:4, that God "dwellyth not in a body soget to syn" (chap. 18, 53). He tells Kempe that he "trost[s]" that she is meek, contrite, and well-intentioned in either her "wyl" or her "affeccyon er ellys in bothyn," suggesting, perhaps unintentionally, of course, that she worry about this (chap. 18, 53).[55]

Southfield makes it clear that his original assessment needs qualification. He asserts that he "helde not" that God would allow those who put their trust in him to be "dysceyved endlesly" and refines his definition of those who trust God by adding that they are those people who "nothyng sekyn ne desyryn but hym only"; he then says to Kempe, "as I hope that ye don" (chap. 18, 53). The careful qualification in the latter half of the passage can be explained, as Voaden and Caciola have demonstrated, in relation to concerns about the "discretion of spirits," that is, the importance of determining that there was no "deceyte" in visionary experiences.[56]

Nevertheless, Southfield's qualifications are in turn qualified. Julian is more enthusiastic than Southfield about the inner nature of Kempe's experiences, and instead of cautioning her about possible deception, she provides her with "tokenys" that prove her visions are from God, such as tears, "mornynggys and wepyngys unspekable," and shameful treatment by the world. As she converses with Kempe about her feelings of unworthiness, Julian offers a variation on the transformative phrase, declaring that "the mor despyte, schame, and repref" experienced, "the mor is yowr meryte in the sygth of God" (chap.18, 54). The *Book*, then, strikes a balance between imagined future perfection and the pitfalls of the imperfect present, playing one verbal tag off another. In chapter twenty-one, for example, the phrases "have mende of thi wykydnesse and thynk on my goodnes," "I take no heed what a man hath ben, but I take hede what he wyl ben," and "of unworthy I make worthy, and

---

55. See Psalm 50 [51]:17 and Isaiah 66:2.
56. See Voaden, *God's Words;* Caciola, *Discerning Spirits.*

of synful I make rytful" appear nearly on top of one another (chap. 21, 59, ll. 1125–31).

There is also editorial undercutting: by shifting the order of the chapters, asking that audiences read twenty-one before seventeen, Kempe and her scribes privilege Jesus' words over those of Kempe's human supporters and, in doing so, hold fast to the possibility of worthiness in the present. In chapter twenty-one Jesus uses nearly the same phrasing as Southfield in chapter seventeen but includes none of Southfield's qualifications. When Jesus says "of unworthy I make worthy, and of synful I make rytful," he guarantees that this is true and describes Kempe as she is in the present: "And so have I mad the worthy to me, onys lovyd and evyrmor lovyd wyth me" (chap. 21, 59). When he explains what this entails, it is a description of his love for her and not a checklist of terms she must fulfill or problems she must avoid: "I love the wyth all myn hert and I may not forberyn thi lofe." The editorial change cements the power of linguistic claims for transformation and insists on Kempe's right to feel secure both in her own worth and in God's love.[57]

All Is for the Best

The assumption that future perfection makes guarantees applicable to the present is in keeping with the *Book*'s insistent emphasis on the idea that "all is for the best." When Kempe's companion, a man called Patrick, suffers "gret perel" on her account and complains to her that the mayor of Leicester had "gretly turmentyd" him because of her, she tells him, "Be not displesyd, for I schal prey for yow, and God schal rewardyn yowr labowr ryth wel; it is al for the best" (chap. 49, 119). Kempe reassures herself with the phrase after she is arrested by some of the Duke of Bedford's men as a Lollard. As they lead her toward Beverley, she tells the men "good talys" and assures one of them, who regrets having arrested her after he hears her "ryth good wordys," "I trust al

---

57. In chapter twenty-one, and throughout the *Book*, saints with "shameful" reputations are her heroes, and this too serves the function of exploring how the unworthy become worthy. Here, Jesus compares Kempe with Mary Magdalene, Mary the Egyptian, and Paul, all of whom, he implies, were unworthy but who "arn now in hevyn" (chap. 21, 59). The depth of their disgrace on earth only heightens their sanctity; Kempe assumes that her readers will feel just as awed and inspired by their example as she did herself. On the importance of proof and witnessing in/for the *Book*, see [Amy] Kathleen Howard, "The Word Made Flesh: The Perception of Holiness in the Texts of Late Medieval and Early Modern Women in England" (Ph.D. diss., University of Minnesota, 2009), 62–83. The authority of Kempe's life as a "witness" is based on the depths of her sinfulness. Michael P. Kuczynski describes this dynamic in relation to the biblical David; see *Prophetic Song: The Psalms as Moral Discourse in Late Medieval England* (Philadelphia: University of Pennsylvania Press, 1995), esp. 5–36. See also Utter, "'Fawty and Falce."

schal be for the best" (chap. 53, 130). She expresses the sentiment again after her friends urge her to leave town because "so meche pepyl was ageyn hir." Her confessor says that only "the mone and seven sterrys" are left to stand in opposition to her; she replies, "Ser, beth of a good comforte, for it schal ben ryth wel at the last" (chap. 63, 151). In chapter seventy-two of the *Book*, Romans 8:28 is offered as the source for this idea: "Aftyr the sentens of Seynt Powle, 'To hem that lovyn God al thyng turnyth into goodnes,' so it ferd wyth hir" (chap. 72, 167).

This is, obviously, at the heart of the idea of future perfection as it is expressed in the *Book*: it is not what you are but what you will be that counts. But implied in the phrase is the sense that the future will of course *be better* than the present, an assurance but also a reminder to Kempe and her readers that, despite their efforts to understand themselves as transformed, the world around them might fail to recognize this at any given moment. "Al was for the best," as Kempe's husband, John, observes, but that meant that everything "schuld comyn to good ende whan God wold" (chap. 15, 46), and the problems of the present did not necessarily disappear even if the future brought a happy conclusion. What the repetition of affirming phrases like those discussed in this chapter did, however, was submerge the present, even if temporarily, in the imagined perfection of the future, and it did this in explicitly verbal terms.[58] The "negative" impact of phrases associated with books of consolation could be modified through language that responded to such claims not as a direct challenge but as a supplement to those claims.

Past Perfect

If this sounds like a success story, one in which the *Book*'s writing solved Kempe's sense of shame and, in turn, modeled such success for its readers, the nature of that success requires qualification.[59] Kempe's linguistic strategies could go only so far in making the present perfect. The "unworthy" people around her were also practiced in the art of using proverbs, sayings, and rhythmic phrases to express their ideas and to shore up their sense of themselves, and the *Book* demonstrates that Kempe found it impossible to escape from the world's attempts to define her.

---

58. *The Chastising of God's Children* reminds its readers of the power of reciting verses from scripture and "other hooli preiers" to strengthen one against "al temptacions and tribulacions" (204). This sense of the power of words is well attested as a devotional strategy in the period.

59. "The past perfect tense is used to express action (or to help make a statement about something) completed in the past before some other past action or event." *Warriner's English Grammar and Composition*, 149.

Although the *Book* ends with a prayer that, while placing Kempe at the center, generalizes her religious experiences in terms that might apply to any believer (bk. 2, chap. 10), chapters nine and ten, the final two chapters, are startlingly specific in their representation of Kempe's person and life. Chapter ten, for example, includes the hermit Reynald's less than welcoming greeting when Kempe approaches him at Sheen following her long series of pilgrimages to the Continent. Serenely representing Kempe's ability to resolve conflicts with her "friends" created by her actions in the past, chapter ten, despite Reynald's crossness, fits with the *Book*'s representation of Kempe's ability to use her sense of optimism—all will be for the best—in accordance with divine plans.[60] With Kempe having disobeyed her confessor because God commanded her to go across the sea, the episode illustrates her increasing ability as she grew older (when she returns from pilgrimage, she is sixty-three or so) to "hear" God's words "in her soul" and to count on the support of her friends who, also over time, came to understand that she was indeed "worthy."

In contrast, chapter nine of book two represents the sinful world's sense of Kempe's reputation. Although "mech of the comown pepil magnifiid God in hir," according to its conclusion, most of the ninth chapter is taken up with her abuse at the hands of people in London—casual acquaintances who knew her only by reputation. Some of this follows the model established earlier in the *Book* in which the experience of abuse is retrospectively allegorized. Kempe "suffryrd scornys and reprevys" as she went through London speaking "boldly and mytily" against "swerars, bannars, lyars and swech other vicious pepil," and her "spekyng profityd rith mech in many personys"; she herself felt "swet dalyawns of owr Lord," so much so that "sche myth not mesuryn hirself ne governe hir spirit" (bk. 2, chap. 9, 227–28).

The chapter returns to the sense of lived shame found earlier in the *Book*—in episodes such as the seduction scene and her humiliation when she gives up vegetarianism. It opens with her feelings of mortification about her clothing. Having just returned from pilgrimage, she wears "cloth of canvas as it wer a sekkyn gelle," that is, she has on an outfit made of rough cloth, appropriate to a pilgrim. But appropriate or not, once Kempe is back in London, the *Book* describes her discomfort at appearing in such clothes in a city

---

60. The *Remedy* is similarly optimistic: "And therfore lete hym trusten veryly that it is al for his beste, though that he knowe not goddis abydynge" (chap. 5, 231). The phrase is repeated in chapter nine: "Thei must seke, in all weyes of discomfort, how thei mowe comfort hem self in god, and thenke alwey that it is for here beste" (235). Hilton, too, encourages readers to hope "steadfastly" to be one of God's chosen people, to hold fast to his idea ("stire not fro this hope"), and to believe "al schal be right weel" (*Scale*, bk. 1, chap. 21, 54).

where "mech pepil knew hir wel anow."[61] The chapter explains that "sche was not clad as sche wold a ben for defawte of money" and therefore, "desiryng to a gon unknowyn" until she could take out a loan of some sort and purchase new clothes, she "bar a kerche befor hir face" as a disguise (bk. 2, chap. 9, 226).

The sense of shame Kempe feels is directly tied to her past and the people from it. As she goes about in her disguise, "sum dissolute personys" recognize her, "not wythstondyng" the kerchief. Although the chapter establishes her clothing as the grounds for her discomfort at being recognized, the dissolute persons go on to scorn her on another basis: they pass and remark, so she can easily hear their words of "repref," "A thu fals flesch, thu schalt no good mete etyn." Kempe, the chapter notes, does not answer them and continues on "as sche had not an herd" their words (bk. 2, chap. 9, 226). Although the scene might be read as comic and possibly even self-mocking (Kempe hiding her face with her scarf, embarrassed to be found in her sackcloth; the people who recognize her identifying her in some way with meat-eating and taunting her; Kempe pretending she does not know that they know that she is behind the kerchief), or simply as another episode of routine abuse (like the episodes in which her fellow travelers steal her sheets or cut her dress short) that will allow her to demonstrate her greater spiritual status, it is neither.[62]

Instead, this chapter tells the story of a proverbial phrase that got associated with Kempe "not long aftyr the conversyon of the sayd creatur" (bk. 2, chap. 9, 226) and represents her continued anger and shame, more than forty years later, at people's identification of her with this phrase. The chapter focuses explicitly on identity: at the same time that it tells the story of the meaning of the "repref" about false flesh, it presents the single instance in which Kempe is called by her full name in the text. The dissolute persons who insult her do so, the chapter explains, "supposyng" she "was Mar. Kempe of Lynne" (bk. 2, chap. 9, 226).[63] Although at first glance this "signature"

---

61. In *London in the Later Middle Ages: Government and People* (Oxford: Oxford University Press, 2004), Caroline Barron estimates London's population in 1300 as between fifty thousand and eighty thousand (238). This is of course before the later fourteenth-century plague years, but it is useful for contextualizing Kempe's sense that she was known by people in a fairly large city.

62. Staley, *Dissenting Fictions*, argues that the scene can "be read two ways, as a crucial moment in the spiritual development of Margery, or as a trenchant commentary" on London society (55). Edwin Craun, "*Fama* and Pastoral Constraints on Rebuking Sinners: *The Book of Margery Kempe*," in *Fama: The Politics of Talk and Reputation*, ed. Thelma Fenster and Daniel Lord Smail (Cornell: Cornell University Press, 2003), 185–209, argues, alluding to the scene, that "slandered Margery has no way to manifest publicly her internal experience before and during her extraordinary public acts of affective piety" (196).

63. Stephanie A. Viereck Gibbs Kamath observes that first-person voice is routinely identified with narrator, character, and the author's proper name; see *Authorship and First-Person Allegory in Late Medieval France and England* (Cambridge: D. S. Brewer, 2012), esp. 173–76. See also Anne Middleton,

may not seem particularly striking, the passage goes on to present a story of Kempe's life, encapsulated by the proverb, that functions as a kind of "naming." Even before explaining what the story is, Kempe insists that "the forseyd wordys," the saying about false flesh, "wer nevyr of hir spekyng" and objects, further, that they were attributed to her at all (bk. 2, chap. 9, 226). She is vehement in her denials.

The chapter provides a vivid and overly emphatic description of the words' satanic creation by people whom "the devyl, fadyr of lesynges," had "favowryd, maynteynd, and born forth of hys membrys." Satan's spawn, envious of Kempe's "vertuows levyng," are said to have repeated the phrase because they had no "powyr to hyndryn hir but thorw her fals tungys." Repeating her denials, no man or woman, the *Book* explains, "evyr myth prevyn that sche [Kempe herself] seyd swech wordys"; people got the story from "other lyars," the "autorys" of the saying and malicious gossips. Kempe is so focused on denying that she is the source of the saying that even as she begins to explain what the proverb means, she cannot resist another mention that "sum on person er ellys mo personys, deceyvyd be her gostly enmy, contrivyd this tale" (bk. 2, chap. 9, 226).

One might guess that Kempe was angry on any number of grounds: perhaps people were saying that her visions were fraudulent, or that she had continued to have sexual relations with her husband after her vow of chastity, or maybe that her crying was simply for show. But in fact the "reproof" in chapter nine is about something, seemingly at least, far less important: Kempe's delight in food. The rumor started "not long aftyr the conversyon of the sayd creatur"—probably sometime in the mid-1390s—when she sat at a meal at a "good mannys table" on a "fisch day," that is, a day of fasting from meat. At the meal she was served "divers" kinds of fish such "as reed heryng and good pyke and sweche other." The rumor started after she supposedly said to herself aloud, "A thu fals flesch, thu woldist now etyn reed heryng, but thu schalt not han thi wille," and then, after rejecting the herring, which was considered a less desirable fish than the others, she "ete the good pike" instead (bk. 2, chap. 9, 226–27). In today's food economy, her alleged actions would be something like "denying" herself the pleasure of eating inexpensive canned tuna and instead choosing to enjoy lobster.

Chapter nine describes the linguistic power of the phrase: "Thus it sprong into a maner of proverbe" (bk. 2, chap. 9, 227). Like her own use of phrases

"William Langland's Kynde Name: Authorial Signature and Social Identity in Late Fourteenth-Century England," in *Literary Practice and Social Change in Britain: 1380–1530* (Berkeley: University of California Press, 1990), 15–82.

to promote a sense of worthiness, the people who use the proverb about Kempe's false flesh use it to define her identity as "Mar. Kempe of Lynn." But unlike Kempe's phrases, the false flesh proverb ties that identity to the past instead of the future. Her love of meat, mentioned periodically in the *Book* even by Jesus, is who she *was*, but it is not who she wants to have been or wants to be in the future.[64] The sting of the proverb comes in part from its truth, even if she did not say the actual words or actually eat the pike, and its ability to diminish her and the lived life that the *Book* describes as hers.[65] It is a funny story, but it turns her into a punch line, and it is a punch line that tells her insistently that she must be who she *was* (a lover of meat above all else) and where she is *from* (Lynn). The harmfulness of the proverb, forty years after the incident, was fresh: "The wordys the whech arn beforn wretyn" were all "fals, but yet wer thei not forgetyn; thei [the words] wer rehersyd in many a place wher sche was nevyr kyd ne knowyn" (bk. 2, chap. 9, 227). The saying's ability to fix her identity in the past, even to people who had never met her, continued to hurt and left no room for triumphant celebration of tribulation at the hands of the unworthy.

This scene is a reminder of the seriousness of the lived experience of shame and its social dimension. In the *Book*, anxiety about God's love, about sinfulness, about personal worth is wrapped up with the impossibility of escaping fully from the world's definition of who she is, as far as Kempe is concerned. When Jesus, using wordplay and rhyme, again tells her in chapter seventy-seven, "Thow other men settyn lityl be the / I sett but the more prys be the" (chap. 77, 175), the reassurance encompasses the experiences of social rejection that the *Book* can only sometimes re-envision as triumphs.

The memory in chapter nine of the proverb's ability to harm is linked to the *Book*'s sense of the power of sayings, proverbs, and rhymes to create identity. On this ground, the chapter asks if the phrases Kempe claims for herself and her readers, and which she deploys against shame and negative thinking, can really work if false language works the same way. Can Kempe and her readers create and expand their own identities as worthy people by incorporating these phrases into their lives if "worthless" people can do the same thing?

---

64. The lack of desire for meat was a common trope in lives of the holy; see, for example, the Middle English life of Marie of Oignies, which explains that Marie survived on hard black bread, fruit, herbs, and potage but drank no wine and ate no meat, and almost no fish (Marie of Oignies, "Life," 140).

65. Kempe's sense of rebuke was probably spiritual as well as personal; on gluttony (and speculation about the nature of Jesus' first meal after fasting), see Love's *Mirror*, 73–75.

The *Book* tries to answer in the affirmative by returning to London of 1434 and expanding on Kempe's responses to the proverb. In the second half of the chapter another meal is described, but this time Kempe is in London at the home of a "worschepful woman" and dining with people she was "unknowyn onto."[66] They have "a gret fest and ferdyn ryth wel," and when "thei wer in her myrthys," someone "rehersyd the wordys beforn wretyn er other liche," that is, the proverb about Kempe, even though they had not known her before and did not know that she was the butt of the false flesh joke. This time, however, the *Book* lets Kempe respond to the proverb (rather than pretending, as she does at the beginning of the chapter, that she did not hear it). The people at the dinner had "gret game of the inperfeccyon" of the "fals feynyd ypocrite" from "Lynne" until Kempe asks them if they know who that person is (chap. 9, 227). They do not, of course, and she first reprimands them for passing along gossip and then reveals that she herself is Mar. Kempe of Lynn.

The *Book* takes the opportunity to reclaim the upper hand in relation to the power of proverbial language. When Kempe reprimands the other diners, she says, "Ye awt to seyn no wers than ye knowyn and yet not so evyl as ye knowyn," generating her own saying about gossip and knowledge, which she then uses as a personal introduction: "Nevyrthelesse her ye seyn wers than ye knowyn, God forgeve it yow, *for I am that same persone* to whom thes wordys ben arectyd" (bk.2, chap. 9, 227 emphasis added).[67] By doing so, Kempe reclaims her right to define herself: she asserts she is that "same persone," and yet by doing so she refuses to accept the definition and takes the opportunity to state again that she never said the words. The tone of the passage, in contrast with the angry denunciation of the devil's minions who spread the gossip in the first place, is measured. The other people at the dinner party are finally brought to see the truth of her words and are driven to make amends for speaking out of turn.

Having reasserted control over language, the *Book* concludes with Kempe's prayer, which incorporates many of the phrases employed throughout the *Book*, including the heart/smart rhyme (l. 702), the unworthy/worthy transformation (l. 726), and the mutuality of presence in my will/thy will (l. 704). The phrases' repetition at the end of the *Book* testifies to their centrality in

---

66. The *Book* observes that some of them were from Cardinal Beaufort's house (Windeatt, 416, n. 8224), but also mentions that Kempe knew this only because someone at the meal told her so; emphasis is laid on anonymity.

67. Kempe's new proverb sounds proverbial, that is, like a saying she already knew, but I have not found another source for it.

the text's linguistic approach to counteracting the power of negative thinking. The history of the *Book*'s reception, however, is a reminder of how Kempe should have been worried about the way that proverbial language might be used against her.

When Wynkyn de Worde published extracts from the *Book* in 1501, his tract was referred to in the explicit as "a shorte treatyse called Margerie Kempe de Lynn," suggesting that this seven-page pamphlet *was* Kempe.[68] It was introduced in the incipit, however, as "a shorte treatyse of contemplacyon taught by our Lorde Jhesu Cryste, or taken out of the boke of Margerie Kempe of Lynn." The incipit is the more accurate rendering of the pamphlet, which is largely a collection of proverbs taken from the *Book*. Many of them are spoken by Jesus rather than Kempe herself, and include passages discussed in the present chapter, such as "Have mynde of thy wyckednes, and thynke on my goodnes," which appears twice, and "Love me with all thy herte."

De Worde's extracts provide valuable evidence for the popularity of proverbial thinking in the period, which, I argue here, was central to Kempe's spirituality and was instrumental in shaping the *Book*. But it seems likely to me that Kempe would have disliked de Worde's proverbial version because his "Margerie Kempe of Lynn" undoes the work that her *Book* does. Certainly Kempe would have been in agreement with the devotional value of the phrases from her *Book*, but de Worde's excision of any evidence of the difficulty with which she came to find the truth in those proverbs is at odds with the *Book*'s method of demonstrating how such language could be used.

De Worde strips the *Book* of the lived experience of shame. His extract concludes with Jesus' comments on the subject: "Nay, nay, doughter, for that I love best, that they love not, and that is shames, repreves, scornes and despytes of the people; and therfore they shall not have this grace; for, doughter, he that dredeth the shames of this worlde may not *parfyghtly* love God" (emphasis added). Kempe's sense of worthiness was hard fought; her *Book* insists that her readers, just as she did, needed to see how difficult it was to get to the point of loving God "parfyghtly," that is, of approaching future perfection.

---

68. Windeatt includes de Worde's tract in his edition of the *Book* (430–34), and notes that there are divisions between extracts (there are twenty-eight). He also supplies the relevant line numbers from the *Book* for comparison.

🍃 Chapter Four

Fear

> When she looked at the waves, she was always *frightened. Our Lord, speaking to her spirit, bade her lay down her head so that she should not see the waves, and she did so. But still she was always afraid. . . . [And then] her dread was much the more, and ever among [her fears] our Lord spake to her mind, "Why are you afraid? No one will do harm to you, nor to any who travel with you* (bk. 2, chaps. 4–5, 216–17).

This passage, from the second part of Kempe's *Book*, echoes the rendition of the gospel account of Peter's near drowning and rescue in *The Mirror of the Blessed Life of Jesus Christ*. In Matthew 14:24–32, Peter and the other disciples are on a boat at sea when a storm comes up. During the night the winds pick up, and, as the *Mirror* puts it, in the early hours of the morning the disciples experience "grete disese" because the boat was "in poynt of perishyng thorh the grete wawes and the gret tempeste that was risyne in that tyme." In order to comfort them, Jesus, who has prayed alone in the mountains the entire night, walks on the water toward the boat. Instead of calming them, however, this makes the disciples even more afraid: they fear Jesus is a "fantasme." In response to their heightened distress, Jesus identifies himself: "I am he that ye desiren: bethe not adrede." Peter, still frightened but "more feruent" than the others, starts to walk toward Jesus to prove his faith, but "anone . . . a gret wynd blewe" and he "failed in byleue and dredde and so began to drench," making it necessary for Jesus to reach out and save him from drowning.[1]

Like Peter and the other disciples, Kempe, in the second book, is in great distress on account of the wind and the rising waves during a storm at sea. Her *Book* draws particular attention to her great and ongoing fear, just as the disciples in the scriptural account are described as desperate to be rescued.[2] Furthermore, Jesus' verbal responses to Kempe and the disciples are similar.[3] In the *Book*, Jesus asks Kempe, rhetorically, "Why dredist the?"—just as he instructed the disciples, "I *am* he that ye desiren *bethe not adrede*," and as he asked Peter in the gospel account, when Peter nearly drowns, "O thou of little faith, why didst thou doubt?"[4]

Although Kempe refers to Peter directly at several points in her *Book*—he is mentioned along with her favorite saints, including the Virgin Mary, Paul, Mary Magdalene, Katherine, and Margaret as speaking "to her mend" (chap. 17, 51; chap. 87, 202)—book two, chapters four and five, merely allude to the gospel story in which he appears. There is no need to identify the disciple because Kempe represents *herself* as Peter; his actual presence in *her* story is unnecessary.[5] Instead, what the gospel account lends the *Book* is a dramatic structure. Kempe is, like Peter, a disciple in crisis, caught between her desire to believe and free herself from fear and her unassuageable "drede" of the dangers of storms at sea. The disciple / woman-in-crisis genre—the gospel story concerning Peter and the disciples and other narratives such as the woman taken in adultery and Susanna in the bath—provide Kempe with models for understanding and representing her own experiences of fear.[6]

---

1. *Mirror*, 109–10. Kempe draws on Love's language in her description of her fear at sea.

2. They are "desturblet and trauailede" (*Mirror*, 110).

3. The sequence in the *Book* begins with an earlier storm at sea. Kempe, like the disciples, wants proof that Jesus is not an evil spirit: "Schewe thu art sothfast God and non evyl spiryt that hast browte me hedyr into the perellys of the see." Jesus "blamyd hir of hyr feerdnes," as he did Peter in the gospels, "seying, 'Why dredist the? Why art thu so aferd?'" (bk. 2, chap. 3, 214).

4. *Mirror*, 110; Matthew 14:31. Love minimizes Peter's role in order to draw a generalized moral about tribulation. The differences among the three versions (Kempe, Love, and Matthew) are instructive. Matthew ascribes most of the disciples' fear to their belief that Jesus is a ghost (14:26); Kempe represents her situation as entirely singular (she has no fellow disciples, only unsympathetic fellow travelers who are delighted that the waves have picked up to speed them along); Love enjoys the drama of Jesus as rescuer, mentions the disciples' fear of apparitions,and greatly intensifies their fear of the waves.

5. Barbara Newman, *God and the Goddesses: Vision, Poetry, and Belief in the Middle Ages* (Philadelphia: University of Pennsylvania Press, 2003), observes that Kempe performs the same kind of identification / substitution with the Virgin Mary (280).

6. Watson, "The Making," remarks on the significance of fear in the context of Kempe's relationship with readers (422–24).

Woman-in-crisis episodes appear throughout the *Book*, and they reinforce the exemplary function that the author and her scribes claim for its composition. In contrast with its treatment of shame, which, with a few exceptional episodes, the *Book* allegorizes retrospectively to diminish the lived quality of shame and then manages through the multiplicity of phrases that undercut its power, the *Book* represents fear as alive and lived in an ever-returning present. Kempe is "evyr feryd," and Jesus speaks to her "evyr among," that is, always in the midst of, those fears. The continuousness of both terror and rescue is, furthermore, not merely experiential but structural: fear is encoded in these scenes in visual and visceral terms that associate the episodes (anachronistically, of course) with film. In the *Book*, Kempe's fear is ever present, and, as in a film, a sense of immediacy is invoked each time the experience is "replayed" or retold.[7]

If, as I argued in the previous chapter, Kempe and her readers are drawn together by the shared experience of shame, it is the excitement and pleasure of dramatized fear that reminds her why she has written the *Book* and that, in turn, compels readers to identify with the *Book*'s author/reader. The present chapter is about the ways the *Book* demonstrates how Kempe came to embrace fear: fear allowed her to know emotionally and intellectually that she mattered, that she was, as Jesus tells her throughout the *Book*, his "singular love," and a "wonder," inspiring to herself and to other people.

They Say Fear Is a Man's Best Friend

Late medieval devotional writers struggled to articulate the relationship between fear and spiritual growth. Their difficulties arose in part from long-held ideas about passions, which involved both bodily transformation and cognition, and affections, which were understood as "higher" than the passions because they involved intellect and will rather than sensation. This tension arises especially in writing that attempts to teach readers about "affective devotion": Is fear a "first step" in a spiritual process, or is it as an affective, embodied response, essential to spiritual engagement?

---

7. See Yoshikawa, *Margery Kempe's Meditations*, for a discussion of Kempe's transportation "through her imagination . . . to an eternal present" (8, 37–40). C. David Benson also remarks on the way images "seem to come fully alive" for Kempe and become "present reality"; see *Public Piers Plowman: Modern Scholarship and Late Medieval English Culture* (University Park: Pennsylvania State University Press, 2004), 143. Elisabeth Hansen, "Temporality in Fourteenth-Century English Contemplative Writing" (Ph.D. diss., University of Minnesota, 2012), draws attention to Kempe's emphasis on the present; see esp. 1–5.

Love's widely circulating *Mirror*, for instance, identifies intense, embodied emotion as preliminary to deeper spiritual understanding.[8] The *Mirror* is aimed at readers who feel bound up in bodily things but want to move beyond this feeling as they "fede" and "stire" their devotion.[9] Love insists that his readers should be responding on a spiritual level, even if their initial engagement is affective, and he returns to the subject frequently, as he does after he tells the story, alluded to earlier, of Peter's rescue: "In this processe touching the disciples, we haue gostly doctrine and ensaumple of pacience in tribulacion and of profite therof. . . . Wherfore we shole vndurstonde that as it felle with the disciples *bodily* so it falleth with vs alday *gostly*."[10] Peter's experience is bodily, but ours, Love insists, should be spiritual.

What one should fear, if one should fear, and what the meaning of fear was—if it indeed was allowed at all—were questions that occupied devotional writers. Some writers were firmly in favor of fear. In the homily for the fourth Sunday in Lent, Mirk, for instance, asserts that constant fear is the believer's best friend, remarking, "He that ys allgate [constantly] aferde, he schall do well."[11] He insists, casually and in passing, suggesting how pervasive the idea was, that constant fear is desirable because it keeps the believer from returning to sin and allows for "persauaracyon" to the end of one's life.[12] Fear of the sort he describes was referred to as "expectant fear," and its value was grounded in its ability to lead to action.[13] Since fear, in Mirk's view, could keep people from falling into sin, it was a desirable emotional experience and should be embraced rather than assuaged.

In contrast, some devotional writers present fear as an emotion that might best be avoided. So, for example, in *The Boke of Comforte agaynste all Tribulacyons*, Jesus tells the "poor sinner" that she should stop feeling afraid: "Leue

---

8. The *Mirror* is frequently identified as the source of Kempe's "dramatic" principles—her vivid animation of the Holy Family and the saints, for example—but Love actually insists that the point of his book is to teach devotion and spirituality that transcend the physical understandings of "symple soule[s]" (*Mirror*, 10).

9. Ibid., 10.

10. Ibid., 110, emphasis added.

11. *Mirk's Festial*, ed. Theodor Erbe, EETS, e.s., 96 (London: Kegan Paul, Trench, Trübner, 1905), 103 / 31–32, referring to Matthew 14, as does the quotation from Love.

12. Fear of God was routinely understood as essential to devotion. Hilton, for example, employs the image of a mortar and pestle to describe how dread of God (the pestle) should be used to crush everything seen, heard, felt, or experienced in the "mortar of meekness" (*Scale*, bk. 1, chap. 23, 56–57). *Contemplations of the Dread and Love of God* agrees: "It is more spedful to drede wiel than to triste amys" (20). "Perseveration" is discussed at length later in this chapter.

13. On the linguistic history of the term, see Erik Carlson, "The Gothic Vocabulary of Fear," *Journal of English and Germanic Philology* 111 (2012): 285–303. The *Prickynge* describes this type of fear in physical terms—the sinner "quaketh and shaketh for drede . . . as dothe an aspen leefe" (chap. 6, 53)—and calls such fear a "gift" of God.

leue this drede and so fere not the dethe eternall ne the greuous tormentes of helle." A few pages later, he reminds the reader of the solace that he brings and encourages her "often for to thynke and to recorde" this "swete comforte."[14] The text's strong modulation of the hygienic value of fear follows a long-standing tradition of distinguishing between fear that inspires and fear "associated with surprise and paralysis," which was thought to possess "low moral value."[15]

There is extensive scriptural support for conflicting attitudes toward fear. On the one hand, the idea that the fear of God is the beginning of wisdom (Prov. 9:10; Ps. 111:10) was not just scriptural but proverbial. Philippians 2:12 instructs the believer to "work out your salvation with fear and trembling," and Matthew 10:28 is similarly insistent that fear of God, who "mai sende [both] bodi and soule into euerlasting fuir," is necessary.[16] On the other, biblical instructions to "fear not" are numerous, and evidence that "dread," the Middle English word that is most often used in the *Book* for this feeling, can be destructive is also scriptural. And 1 John 4:18 supports the idea that believers in harmony with God do not fear: "There is no fear in love; put perfect love casts out fear because fear hath torment. He that feareth is not made perfect in love." The verse draws attention, especially, to the antipathy between love and torment.

Devotional writers looked for ways to explain fear in order to separate the experience of fear, which was of little concern to most of them, from its meaning, which was of great importance. This approach to emotional experience—it is the same approach that Kempe adapts in relation to shame caused by unworthy people—assumes that feelings arise in response to some kind of "trigger," they are registered by the body, the intellectualized name of the emotion is applied, and, finally, the whole experience is moralized. In contrast, for Kempe, fear is expected, recognized *because* it is experienced bodily, and remains unmoralized.

This explains why distinctions between bodily and spiritual fear are absent from the *Book*. In chapter twenty-two, for example, fear of purgatory, the Godhead, and the devil are mixed in with fear of a painful death and of violent storms. One might describe this, condescendingly, as marking Kempe as

---

14. *The Boke of Comforte agaynste all Tribulacyons*, STC 3295, Wynkyn de Worde, 1505, A.ii, A iv.

15. See Carlson, "The Gothic Vocabulary of Fear," 285–303. Douglas Gray observes that the rest of *The Boke of Comforte* is largely "an affective meditation on the passion," and, despite the book's title and opening, in this dialogue "the tribulations which afflict men are mentioned almost in passing"; see "Books of Comfort," in *Medieval English Religious and Ethical Literature*, ed. Gregory Kratzmann and James Simpson (Cambridge: D. S. Brewer, 1986), 214.

16. The Middle English version is found in *Contemplations of the Dread and Love of God*, 8.

lacking in spiritual knowledge, carnal, or merely simpleminded. I would argue, instead, that we think of it in terms of her realistic portrayal of emotional experience. Whatever fear was, Kempe felt it and recognized it as the *same* emotion she experienced when she was in physical danger and when she was threatened emotionally and spiritually.[17]

Kempe's *Book* absorbs some of the devotional rhetoric of fear, found in books of consolation as well as scripture, without using that rhetoric to fix its representation of the significance of fear. Instead, it focuses on the *experience* of fear and not on its meaning, and represents the importance of fear as immediate—concerned, in other words, with the present. In this way, Kempe rewrites the "scripts" that devotional writers constructed to explain what fear is and how it is significant. The *Book* represents fear as expectant rather than reactive. Kempe is already afraid whenever she comes to experience fear because she *always* expects to be frightened: the *Book* describes her feelings of "great dread" as always already present. For example, in the episode with which the present chapter began, this is put in terms of continuity. As she traveled on her way to Wilsnak, she was "ever afeared" and Jesus comforted her "ever among" these ongoing feelings. To be alive, for Kempe, was to be afraid.

In contrast with positive emotions like love, fear, as it is represented in the *Book*, is immediately recognizable and requires no qualification. When she is afraid, Kempe does not ask herself the kinds of questions she keeps asking about love—an issue she returns to incessantly: Did Jesus love her as much as and in the same way that she loved him? Did he know how much she loved him? Was it enough? In contrast, she never asks herself: "Am I afraid? Is this actually fear?" Her responses to fear require no worried reflection on the precise nature of her emotional experiences. When she worries about fear, her worries are, instead, about her inability to control the situations in which she finds herself.

Tears and Pain

The propulsive physiological nature of fear forms the backdrop for the *Book*'s account of Kempe's crying.[18] Her tears are described as an uncontrollable

---

17. Some writers, like the author of the *Prickynge*, make claims for "feelinglessness": "bi-twene tribulaciouns and recreaciouns" the believer "schulde passe forth as un-felable as yif he wist no thynge of al this but ay felande god" (chap. 18, 111). The person who can do this is, however, a "seelden seen brid" (chap. 18, 112).
18. On tears, see Elina Gertsman, ed., *Crying in the Middle Ages: Tears of History* (New York: Routledge, 2012), esp. Gertsman's introduction and Lyn A. Blanchfield's "Prolegomenon: Considerations of Weeping and Sincerity in the Middle Ages," xxi–xxx.

physical force: "Sche kept hir fro crying as long as sche myth," but, unable to hold in her tears, "at the last sche brast owte [burst out] wyth a gret cry and cryid wondyr sor" (chap. 61, 146). The *Book* repeatedly refers to her crying as explosive—as causing her body or her heart to burst.[19] Although her crying is also frequently identified as a special gift of sweetness and holiness, these tears, like her "feelings," make her afraid. They are "wondirful," a Middle English term used in the *Book* to refer to things that are not just surprising and unusual but frightening (chap. 77, 174). Her distress over the spectacular nature of these episodes troubles her so deeply that she asks God to take them away or, if he wishes that she should "algate" cry, to allow her to do so "alone in my chambyr as meche as evyr thu wilt" (chap. 77, 174).

The unexpectedness of Kempe's crying, as well as the volume of her sobbing, is represented as profoundly upsetting. At Mount Calvary she has her first experience of contemplation while crying, and from that time on "sche knew nevyr tyme ne owyr whan thei schulde come" (chap. 28, 76). When she visits Mount Quarentyne, near Jericho, the *Book* again says that she "myth not wythstonde whan God wold send" her "wepyng, sobbyng, and crying" (chap. 30, 81). Even after Jesus promises her, several years later, to "takyn awey fro" her the very loud crying and she instead cries in another "maner," now "sumtyme lowde and sumtyme stille" (chap. 63, 151–52), she is unable to control her tears: it lay not "in hir powyr to cryen ne wepyn but what God wolde" (chap. 68, 160). In representing her early experiences, the *Book* observes repeatedly that people think Kempe is able to predict when she will weep and capable of modulating the sound of her sobbing (chap. 3, 27), even though she was not.

Kempe's fear of her sudden and uncontrollable weeping is traceable to the very end of the *Book*'s representation of her life. This is true, according to chapter forty-one, even after Saint Jerome has come to her, in a vision, to persuade her to see this unexpectedness as a mark of singular grace. He tells her, "Dowtyr, drede the nowt," and calls her "welle of teerys" a "specyal gyft that God hath govyn" and "whech schal nevyr man take fro" her (chap. 41, 103).[20] It even continues to be true when she comes to desire tears and to feel

---

19. See, for example, chap. 21, 59; chap. 28, 75; chap. 39, 98; chap. 73, 168; chap. 78, 177; chap. 80, 182.

20. See also the reference to the well of tears in bk. 2, chap. 10, 231. The phrase appears in Jeremiah 9:1. See also Fiona Somerset, "Excitative Speech: Theories of Emotive Response from Richard Fitzralph to Margery Kempe," in *The Vernacular Spirit: Essays on Medieval Religious Literature*, ed. Renate Blumenfeld-Kosinski, Duncan Robertson, and Nancy Warren (New York: Palgrave Macmillan, 2002), 67–73.

pain when she cannot cry, as chapter eighty-two relates.[21] And when Kempe visits Aachen, in 1433, the uncontrollable and unpredictable nature of her crying continues to plague her at the same time that she insists tears bring spiritual joy.[22]

By the end of the *Book*, the nature of the fear she feels as well as the emotional significance of crying itself are firmly established. Her tears are, finally, as critics frequently observe, a sign of her devotion, the exceptional grace shown to her, and her extraordinary spirituality. But they are also terrifying to her. Why does the *Book* return, incessantly, to Kempe's fear of the unexpectedness and spectacular nature of her tears? Why not, as is the case with shame, rewrite these scenes to highlight spiritual triumph?

In describing Kempe's longing for tears, chapter eighty-two draws attention to a fundamental association between fear and pain. In this chapter, "to weep is to pray," as Windeatt puts it, and pain comes when she *cannot* cry.[23] Here she thinks in terms of an economy of pain: her barrenness of tears causes her pain; she would like to trade the whole world for tears, or if that is impossible, to suffer bodily pain to "purchase" them. It is an exchange, then, of pain (caused by lack of tears) for physical suffering (bodily pain) to purchase the sweetness of crying, which, the chapter remarks, she could "buy" in no other way.[24] In describing her tears in this way, the *Book* comes close to the idea that love is measured in pain.[25] The difference, however, is the completeness associated with the idea of purchase: in chapter eighty-two, the economic axis of the exchange removes the anxious desperation of *measuring*

---

21. By chapter eighty-two, though still terrifying, this fearful experience is represented as the thing Kempe most desires. Here we are told that Kempe was "sumtyme so bareyn fro teerys" for a day or half a day and that this caused her "gret peyne for desyr that sche had of hem." Without her tears, she "thowt it was no savowr ne swetnesse," and she would, the chapter recounts, have given "al this worlde" or even "suffryd ryth gret bodily peyne" to have "gotyn hem." Weeping, she feels, enables prayer (chap. 82, 189). This is comparable to narratives concerning other holy women, such as Marie of Oignies. It is true of Kempe, however, only after years of feeling upset by her crying.

22. When her traveling companions became angry and complain about her crying, she responds "'Qui seminant in lacrimis' and cetera 'eutes ibant et flebant' and cetera'" (bk. 2, chap. 6, 219), a reference to Psalm 126 [125]: "They that sow in tears shall reap in joy. Going they went and wept, casting their seeds. But coming they shall come with joyfulness, carrying their sheaves" (5–7).

23. Windeatt, 29.

24. Atkinson, *Mystic and Pilgrim*, calls Kempe's tears "her religious capital, wealth that she could and did share with other people" (59). Susan Dickman argues that Kempe's writing becomes "a replacement for lost tears"; see "A Showing of God's Grace: *The Book of Margery Kempe*," in Pollard and Boenig, *Mysticism and Spirituality in Medieval England*, 175.

25. According to *Lyfe of the Soule* (ed. Helen Moon [Lewiston, N.Y.: Edwin Mellen Press, 1978]), believers should "louen so myche oure god that we wulden for his loue sufferen the dethe" (32). The impulse to describe love in terms of ideas of exchange is common. The *Lyfe* goes on to explain that Mary Magdalene's "many synnes" were forgiven because "sche loued myche" (36–37).

love (worrying about whether one has done enough versus knowing the price and paying it matter-of-factly).

The advantage of pain over knowledge, from this "economic" point of view, is that pain can be felt; even imagined pain—like that which Kempe experienced when she performed imaginative exercises in which she pictured herself being slain three times a day for seven years or lying naked on a hurdle—allowed for the sensation of "dread." This is made explicit in chapter seventy-seven, when Jesus asserts emphatically that she will experience her fear and pain of crying "whan I wil, and wher I wil" because this is how she will *know* God. Just as "gret wyndys" may not be "seyn" but "may wel be *felt*," Jesus tells her, divine power, too, cannot be seen but "may wel be *felt*" (chap. 77, 174, emphasis added). What fear does is take away the guesswork: it guarantees that Kempe has paid the price required for the experience of feeling, and knowing that she feels, "true" spiritual joy.

Kempe's insistence that she would suffer pain to buy her tears is nonetheless surprising since the *Book* is uncompromising in its description of her lifelong *fear* of physical pain, and especially of dying a painful death. Anxious about her inability to withstand pain on her deathbed, Kempe is assured that she will "have mor mynde" of the pain Jesus suffered at the Passion than she will have of her own suffering (chap. 22, 60). This assurance accords with devotional advice concerning the imitation of Christ: focusing on divine suffering makes human pain insignificant. Kempe's concern, however, is not just theological but specific to her. In chapter seventy-seven she is offered personal reassurance: again addressing her concerns, Jesus promises that she will "no peyn felyn" when she is "comyn owt of this worlde" and will have little pain at the time of her death (chap. 77, 175).

In the *Book*, Kempe's fear of pain is coupled with personal disgust at her inability to withstand physical and emotional suffering. Her failure to deal with such suffering is detailed at length. The sharp pains she experienced during her eight-year-long illness, which cause her to "voydyn that was in hir stomak as bittyr as it had ben galle, neythyr etyng ne drynkyng whil the sekenes enduryd but evyr gronyng tyl it was gon," lead her to ask God why she "can not suffyr this lityl peyne?" (chap. 56, 136). When she meditates on the Passion and imagines the Virgin Mary's suffering, she experiences one of her crying episodes and is in such great pain that she prays: "Lord, I am not thi moder. Take awey this peyn fro me, for I may not beryn it" (chap. 67, 159).

There are layers and layers to Kempe's sense of personal, rather than strictly devotional, disappointment. Books of consolation, of course, encouraged patient suffering as the proper response to every circumstance. Jesus was the model for this, and works like the *Prickynge* recommended the practice of meditation on divine suffering to stimulate greater love of God. Kempe, how-ever, fails to succeed in patience because of her personal characteristics and psychology, as represented in the *Book*. Her personal, idiosyncratic experience of pain is often represented, as in the description of her illness just quoted, as impeding her devotional efforts.[26] Kempe's attention to the subjects of pain and her inability to suffer it patiently highlights the *Book*'s efforts to revise ideas about fear found in books of consolation. Rather than advocating stoic suffering, a frequent model in devotional writing, or treating the subject alle-gorically, the *Book* shows Kempe working to find ways to experience pain even when she is unwilling to do so.

Kempe proceeds to engage in meditative practices to attempt to overcome her fears. In chapter fourteen she tries to imagine "what deth sche mygth deyn for Crystys sake" (chap. 14, 43). The idea of desiring martyrdom was widely espoused in popular literature from the period; the thrill of the heroic was part of the idea's appeal, of course, even at the level of fiction. She can-not, however, enjoy even imaginary martyrdom because, when she thinks about being "slayn for Goddys lofe," she is so afraid that she can only envision for "hyrself the most soft deth" (chap. 14, 43). In order to "please" God, she makes repeated attempts to imagine her own death, but she has little success.

Although Kempe's efforts to imagine martyrdom may seem surprising, models can be found in devotional writings describing "mystical death," such as those of Catherine of Siena.[27] The concept became part of the popular devotional tradition and would have been familiar to readers of books of con-solation. It is alluded to, in somewhat veiled terms, in *The Chastising of God's Children*. Here the author carefully distinguishes between the desire to die for God's love, which is spiritually beneficial, and violent impulses that arise "whan a man desireth hem awei for his owne ease, and nat to the pleasynge of god."[28] The author assures his reader that as long as the death wish comes from the desire to please God, it is "no synne" but, rather, "high encres of

---

26. Even the pain caused by imagining Jesus' warning to Mary Magdalene—"Touch me not"—proves too much for her (chap. 81, 188). There is a self-absorbed (and competitive) element to her disgust with herself, a sense that she is incapable of measuring up to the kind of suffering required of a saint.

27. See Karen Scott, "Mystical Death, Bodily Death: Catherine of Siena and Raymond of Capua on the Mystic's Encounter with God," in *Gendered Voices: Medieval Saints and Their Interpreters*, ed. Catherine M. Mooney (Philadelphia: University of Pennsylvania Press, 1999), 136–67; and Dan Merkur, *Crucified with Christ: Meditation on the Passion, Mystical Death, and the Medieval Invention of Psychotherapy* (Albany: SUNY Press, 2007).

28. *Chastising*, 118. The *Book*, too, distinguishes between suicidal inclinations (chapter one) and the desire to leave this world because to be parted from God is so painful (in chapters seventy-three and seventy-four, for example, where Kempe sighs for her death).

merit."[29] The *Prickynge* and the *Scale* also teach readers to feel pain, that is, to suffer for God in vivid, physical terms.[30]

The *Book*, however, differs from those works in its realistic description of Kempe's efforts at *practicing* such exercises. As she tries to imagine dying for love, she comes up against her fear of pain (the desire for a "soft deth") and her fear of "inpacyens," the term used to describe what made people unable to "persevere" to the end, that is, her fear that she will be unable to go through with the martyrdom. To counter these fears, she thinks up the quickest death possible: "to be bowndyn hyr hed and hir fet to a stokke and hir hed to be smet of wyth a scharp ex for Goddys lofe" (chap. 14, 43). Kempe's detailed account of her failures at bravery—she imagines herself as an animal about to be slaughtered, bound head and foot and butchered with a very sharp ax—suggests conscious awareness of the clumsiness of her attempts.

Despite her inadequacy, Jesus assures her he will love her "wythowtyn ende" and guarantees her physical safety. The point, according to chapter fourteen, was not to succeed but to try. Achieving perfect imaginative martyrdom was unimportant: Jesus guarantees her "the same mede in hevyn" for her efforts that she would have earned if she really had suffered "the same deth" (chap. 14, 43). Without dismissing the value of the exercise, subsequent references to imagined death are largely rhetorical.[31] Chapter fifty-four, for example, shows her waking up in fear after recounting her bravery the day before when she was imprisoned in Beverley, and being reassured by Jesus that her brave suffering there was "mor plesyng" to him than if she had her head "smet of thre tymes on the day every day in sevyn yer" (chap. 54, 131). The ritualization of the slaughter through enumeration (smitten off three times a day for seven years!) points toward the sense of this as a repetitive exercise, and one, as Jesus tells her, that she need not endure (or even perform). The episodes feel more like gestures than ritual practices.

Chapter seventy-seven, for instance, shows Kempe imagining that even if she could be slain "an hundryd sithys [times] on a day" for God's love, it would be inadequate to the love that God has already shown her. At the very end of the same chapter, just after Jesus tells her that all he wants from her is

---

29. Ibid. He carefully observes that this "desire without plesynge of god is synne, as I seide bifore," to make sure the reader is clear on the distinction (119).

30. "Practicing" pain, both physical and imagined, is central to the *Prickynge*. See, for example, chapter two, where self-infliction of pain is recommended: "Scourge thi bodi nobli wel, spare nought [though] thow fele smerte, but wenne thou fele smertyng and peyne, lifte up thenne thi thought to ihesu" (*Prickynge*, 16).

31. Yoshikawa, in contrast, believes that these episodes are successful and lead Kempe "closer to contemplative experience" (*Margery Kempe's Meditations*, 71).

for her to give him "not ellys but lofe," she tells him she would like to be laid "nakyd" on a "hyrdil" (hurdle) so that all the people would "wonderyn" at her on account of her love for God. As they gaze at this spectacle, she says, she would like it if they threw "slory and slugge" on her and dragged her from town to town "every day" of her "lyfetyme" if it would please God, and if it would not put the spectators' souls in jeopardy (chap. 77, 175–76). In the same way, Jesus assures her, in chapter eighty-six, that he is grateful for her efforts to imagine dying for love but that the thing that pleases him most is to be allowed "to speke to [her] in [her] sowle" (chap. 86, 198); he tells her that he knows she would like to try to "aqwityn" the love he has shown her, if she could, by being "slayn a thowsend tymys on the day yyf it wer possibyl" (chap. 86, 199) but assures her that this is not necessary.[32]

If Kempe fails at imagining a brave death, and if such imaginings are not what God wanted in any case, why does she keep trying to imagine herself in these situations and why does the *Book* record these attempts? The answer lies in the value that Kempe placed on her fear of pain as a means for *knowing* how she felt. In contrast with modern psychologists, medieval devotional authors were concerned with feelings that were "false" as well as those that were true. The entire genre of remedies/books of consolation arose at least in part in order to tell their readers how they *should* feel. Kempe, too, wanted to be sure that what she felt was true.

Wounds You Cannot Feel

A subset of devotional writing about pain discussed the issue of being unable to recognize the real nature of one's emotional experience. The problems of "vainglory," "presumption," and "impatience" were of particular concern.[33] The three temptations, all related to pride, were thought to attack "ghostly livers"; the three were seen as especially dangerous because they tripped up "holy" believers in their attempts to live lives of virtue and devotion.[34] Those

32. Similarly, Jesus thanks her for her "general charité" concerning the salvation of her fellow believers and assures her that he knows she would be "hakkyd as smal as flesche to the potte for her lofe" (chap. 84, 193).

33. Morton Bloomfield, *The Seven Deadly Sins*, has little to say about distinctions among the three. Robert Stanton counts vainglory as "a form of pride" and discusses it in those terms; see "Lechery, Pride, and the Uses of Sin in *The Book of Margery Kempe*," *Journal of Medieval Religious Cultures* 36 (2010): 169–204. Cassian, one of the earliest writers on the sins and remedies, is the source for the particular sense of vainglory found in Kempe's *Book*. See Cassian, book eleven, *The Spirit of Vainglory*. *The Chastising of God's Children* shows Cassian's influence as well.

34. The *Chastising*, for example, describes these temptations as more "perilous" than all others (121).

people especially desirous of special gifts from God were particularly at risk because mistaken notions of righteousness could lead them to believe that their own actions were meritorious. Unaware that they are under attack, these "ghostly livers" become unable to find "comforte" since they "knowen nat what hem lackith."[35]

The three all involve a lack of genuine emotional understanding. Presumption refers to a false sense of certainty about one's salvation, based on belief in one's holiness and not in God's mercy alone.[36] Vainglory, too, involves false feelings of worthiness and was associated especially with the public impression of holiness: vainglory arises because good works are done without the knowledge of the believer about her motivations for performing virtuous deeds. "Impatience," failure to endure to the end of one's life—the enduring known as "perseverance"—was also represented in relation to a lack of knowledge of one's self. In Kempe's *Book* it is described repeatedly in terms of her inability to be *sure* she would remain faithful at the moment of her death.[37]

All three temptations arise from the effort to live a virtuous life and from the performance of good deeds; if these temptations are left unchecked, believers who fall into these sins "perish" without knowing why. The only remedy is to understand completely that "al goodnes is, was, and euer shal be in god"—and not in one's own efforts.[38] Hilton observes that the person who suffers from these temptations does not choose "wilfulli" to sin but, rather, falls into temptation out of delight in goodness "withouten displesynge or agenstondynge of wille, for he weneth it were *joie in God.*"[39] The three were dangerous because they left believers worried about their inability to know, fully and with certainty, how they felt, whether what they felt was true, and what motivated them.

---

35. Ibid., 135. Colledge asserts that this passage relates to the (worthy) "repression of enthusiasm" undertaken by orthodox writers and aimed at people like Kempe, the "queen among enthusiasts" (ibid., 55). He would, I expect, be displeased at the suggestion that Kempe was concerned with the same issues as the author of the *Chastising*.

36. The *Prickynge* defines presumption as "fals sikernesse" and suggests that believers firmly hope for God's mercy but always remain afraid (chap. 13, 90–91).

37. The problem of how to be aware of how one felt was addressed explicitly in books of consolation. *Contemplations of the Dread and Love of God*, for example, includes a section on how to be "war" [aware] of "temptations" which addresses the issue of understanding what it is that one feels (32–36, sec. X). Patience and perseverance are then taken up in sections Y and Z. Augustine makes it clear that no one knows if he or she has persevered during this lifetime; only death brings certainty that one has endured to the end. Traditionally, there were five temptations understood to afflict the dying: unbelief, despair, impatience, vainglory, and avarice.

38. James Yonge, *Secret of Secrets*, in *Three Prose Versions of the Secreta Secretorum*, ed. Robert Steele, EETS, e.s., 74 (London: Kegan Paul, Trench, Trübner, 1898), 132.

39. *Scale*, bk. 1, chap. 59, 97, emphasis added. Hilton uses the term "hypocrisy" instead of "vainglory" (distinguishing a deadly from a venial sin). Kempe uses both interchangeably.

Vainglory, in particular, like suicide, required special care when it was discussed. When Kempe, in chapter four, is "smet wyth the dedly wownd of veyneglory," she and her scribes are reluctant to provide too many details. They include them, finally, as a caution to the reader, an "exampyl of hem that com aftyr," so that they do not trust in themselves or find joy in their virtue "as this creatur had" (chap. 4, 28). The *Book* takes particular pains to define the term with precision and clarity: it refers to Kempe's belief that she loved God "mor than he hir," which resulted in a wound that was undetectable by the author (she "felt it not" [chap. 4, 28]).

The problem, of course, is that if this is a wound that one cannot feel, how is it possible to recover? If you do not know you've been injured, how do you even begin to look for remedies? Furthermore, how, if you are offering spiritual advice, do you encourage readers to act bravely, virtuously, heroically if such powerful and confusing enemies lie in wait? The first chapters of the *Book* reflect on the difficulties of recognizing this "hidden" problem by mimicking tensions between spiritual confidence and presumption, or misunderstanding, on a structural level. Chapters one and two work to model things that are "upsodown"—dramatic shifts between the lack of understanding and the experience of grace—until, at the end of chapter two, Kempe describes herself as having finally entered into the "wey of evyrlestyng lyfe" (chap. 2, 25); chapters three and four show her halting steps along this "way" and represent the constant struggles against sinfulness as part of the struggle against misunderstanding one's self.

By chapter ten, Kempe reports that she had learned to recognize the problem, even though she could not feel it; the chapter notes that at this point she had "gret dred of veynglory" and "mech was aferde" even after Jesus assured her he would "take veynglory" away from her (chap. 10, 36). By divorcing feeling from truth, chapter fourteen explores an experimental strategy to manage the problem. Jesus tells her to try to understand why she sometimes is unable to know things emotionally; he explains that he is "an hyd God" and she should, he says, understand that he sometimes will "wythdrawe . . . the felyng of grace" so she will know that these gifts come from God "wythowtyn" her "meryte" (chap. 14, 43). Her inability to feel his love is proof of his love for her, a way for her to know by *not feeling* it that he protects her from invisible enemies like vainglory.

For Kempe, this is only a partial answer to the problem. She is assured that the failure to feel grace at any given time is not the same as falling into sin, but this guarantee is useful only in thinking about discrete moments in the present. As her worries become increasingly associated with anxiety about future events, which she cannot control, fear of vainglory is replaced by fear of the failure to "persevere unto the end."[40] The possibility of being unable to remain perseverant to the end of her life because she cannot feel the reality of her "perfeccyon" becomes her "most dred" (chap. 18, 54). The scribe at the end of the first book concludes that God "gaf hir encres of vertu wyth perseverawns" (chap. 89, 206), but Kempe's prayer in the last chapter of the second part of the *Book* asks for perseverance for "alle that arn in grace . . . into her lyvys ende" and for "grace for me and for alle my gostly fadrys and perseverawns into owr lyvys ende" (bk. 2, chap. 10, 232, 234).

From a logical perspective, Kempe's fear that she should "turnyn and not kepyn hir perfeccyon" (chap. 18, 54) makes no sense at all. Jesus had already promised that all of her sins would be forgiven "to the utterest poynt" and that at her death she would have the "blysse of hevyn" in "the twynkelyng of an eye." To reassure her further, he declares, "I grawnt the contrysyon into the lyves ende" (chap. 5, 30–31). With these additional guarantees, on top of the usual assurances concerning mercy and forgiveness, her anxiety, even with the perilousness of sins that cannot be felt, such as vainglory and failure to persevere, seems excessive. But she was not, apparently, unusual in her fears concerning perseverance and salvation.[41] To assuage such fears, late medieval devotional writers sought to build up their readers' confidence in God's mercy. Thomas Betson, for example, in a treatise printed by Wynkyn de Worde in 1500, provides a "devoute prayer" in which the supplicant asks Jesus for "grace and mercy" so that she "may be one of them that shall be saved."[42]

---

40. For the term's origins, see Matthew 10:22b, "But he that shall persevere unto the end, he shall be saved," and Wisdom 11:24–27: "But thou hast mercy upon all, because thou canst do all things and overlookst the sins of men for the sake of repentance. For thou lovest all things that are, and hatest none of the things which thou hast made: for thou didst not appoint, or make anything hating it. And how could anything endure, if thou wouldst not? or be preserved, if not called by thee? But thou sparest all: because they are thine, O Lord, who lovest souls." Discussed by Augustine in *De Dono Perseverantiae*; Prosper of Aquitaine takes up Augustine's arguments and makes the influential statement "Predestination is for many the cause of perseverance, for none the cause of falling away" (*Pro Augustino responsiones ad capitula objectionum Vincentianarum*; for a summary, see the *Catholic Encyclopedia*, s.v. "predestination").

41. Perseverance may strike modern readers as a rarefied spiritual concern, but it was widely discussed. See, for example, Yonge's rendition of the pseudo-Aristotelian *Secret of Secrets*: " 'Sine me nichil potestis facere' / 'Wythout me ye may nothynge do.' In anothyr Place he Saythe, 'qui perseuerauerit vsque in finem, hic Saluus erit.' 'Who-so contynuyth into the Ende, he shal be sawid' " (133). In the dream vision *The Assembly of Gods*, a knight called Perseverance—who is described as having taken the field that was nearly lost—signifies "contynuaunce of vertuous lyuyng tyll dethe hath owrgoon" (*The Assembly of Gods*, ed. Jane Chance, TEAMS Middle English Texts Series (Kalamazoo: Medieval Institute Publications, 1999), l. 1837). The subject is common in morality plays; see the discussion later in this chapter.

42. Thomas Betson, *Treatyse to Dyspose Men to Be Vertuously Occupyd* (Amsterdam: Theatrum Orbis Terrarum, 1977), bii. This is the same treatise as *A Ryght Profytable Treatyse Compendiously Drawen Out of Many and Dyvers Wrtynges of Holy Men* (Wynkyn de Worde's edition, STC 1978).

In the treatise, Betson, on the authority of Jean Gerson, insists that anyone who says "three truths" can be "sure that he is in the state of helth and grace and he shal have ever lastynge lyf though he had done all the synnes of the worlde." The truths amount to three short prayers in which the petitioner (1) makes an acknowledgment of sin and agrees to do penance; (2) expresses ongoing awareness of sinfulness and promises not to sin again; and (3) consents explicitly to make a clean confession, according to the dictates of the Church, when "place and tyme convenient may be had."[43] The concept of the three truths was influential and widespread. It can be found in various works including Julian's *Revelations*, Mirk's *Festial*, Eleanor Hull's translation of the Penitential Psalms, and the morality play *Everyman*.[44]

Devotional tracts took up the subject as well, indicating that at least some people wanted greater emotional assurance than they found in conventional religious practices.[45] Works expounding methods for securing a "free and sure passage to [God's] kyngdome" were among the earliest printed books available, and the tracts' popularity arose from their articulation of easily managed ritualistic practices. De Worde, for example, printed one in which it is suggested that believers fast on Wednesdays because doing so guarantees the person who fasts, even under the most dire circumstances, the opportunity to confess to a priest before dying and be absolved of sin. The tract illustrates its point with "real life" examples: the seemingly dead body of a man who had fasted on Wednesdays was cast overboard from a ship but "spake and had his rightes"; another man who followed the practice, having fallen from his horse and broken his neck, "ever spake" despite his mortal injuries and said, "Until I have a preest shall I never be deed."[46]

The existence of such tracts points out a seeming contradiction in late medieval devotion: although there was a general sense that believers should trust in God's mercy, at least some people were anxious enough about perseverance and salvation that they wanted to read books that *guaranteed*, if one followed the book's directions, perfection to life's end. There was a difference, in other words, between what late medieval believers *knew* was true, as a

---

43. Betson, *Treatyse*, aiii.

44. Certain knowledge of salvation was deemed possible only for people who experienced direct revelation from God—as the thief on the cross did—but believers were nonetheless encouraged to place confidence in God's mercy. As *Lyfe of the Soule* puts it, "Thof we lyue not so parfytliche as he [Jesus] taught us and as he lyuede hymsilf, we hopen to ben saued" (4).

45. See, for example, Caxton's *Ars Moriendi*, STC 786, printed in 1491.

46. *A Little Treatise That Shows How Every Man and Woman Ought to Fast on Wednesday*, de Worde, STC 24224, printed in 1500. Sections of *A Little Treatise* are identical with Caxton's *Ars Moriendi*.

theological principle, and their feelings about that truth. Readers understood they should rely on God's mercy, as long as they were careful to follow the Church's dictates, but they wanted to *feel* certain that they could do so.

Drama

Despite earlier critics' dismissal of Kempe as an "enthusiast," based largely on the *Book*'s insistence on the embodied nature of emotional experience, the relationship between sensation and devotion was emphasized in "mainstream" late medieval writing, including the *Chastising* and the *Prickynge*, in sermons, and in the visual arts. Given the widespread significance of the embodied and experiential nature of devotion in late medieval popular writing, it is unsurprising that Kempe turns to the visual and dramatic to explain how she experienced fear. Drama in particular provided her with a method for understanding fear that was both visual and embodied: dramatic fear could be seen and felt by both the characters on stage and the audience.[47]

Morality plays explored the audience's understanding of the relationship between devotion and sensation by taking abstract principles and bringing them to life. The most obvious English example of this is *The Castle of Perseverance*, whose title indicates the centrality of this schematic theological idea to the embodied but universally applicable narrative.[48] Treating life as easily divided between sinful existence and righteous living, the *Castle* invites its audience to watch "Humanum Genus," Mankind, as he inhabits the "Castle of Perseverance." Humility personified explains that whoever lives in the castle "schal nevere fallyn in dedly sinne; It is the Castel of Perseveranse. *Qui perseveraverit usque in finem, hic salvus erit*" (Bevington, 846).[49] The play's moral (Be perseverant) is established early on, when the flag bearers introduce the

---

47. Although we have no explicit record of Kempe's attendance at these plays, Claire Sponsler persuasively argues for their influence on the *Book*; see "Drama and Piety: Margery Kempe," in Arnold and Lewis, *Companion to* The Book of Margery Kempe, 129–43. Atkinson also assumes this is the case (*Mystic and Pilgrim*, 94–97), traces the plays production history in the late fourteenth century, and describes Kempe's probable attendance at the cycle plays in York when Kempe was a girl. Windeatt suggests that chapter eleven of the *Book* describes Kempe and her husband returning from seeing the cycle plays at York in 1413 (Windeatt, 86 n. 708). See also Gibson, *The Theater of Devotion*; Coletti, *Mary Magdalene and the Drama of Saints*, esp. 190–217; McAvoy, *Authority and the Female Body*, 122–25; and Jesse Njus, "Margery Kempe and the Spectatorship of Medieval Drama," *Fifteenth-Century Studies* 38 (2013): 123–52.

48. Bevington, *Medieval Drama*, 796–900. Subsequent references to plays from this volume are cited parenthetically by page in the text.

49. The Latin is the verse on which the concept of perseverance is based (Matthew 10:22).

action of the play, thank the audience, and go on to "preye" they will be "of good continuance / To our livys ende" (Bevington, 803).[50]

What Kempe learns from plays like the *Castle* are structural principles: drama creates affective dynamics in which a central character and audience are directly linked. The effect, as it is in the *Book*, depends on the audience's envisioning the main character's predicament as their own.[51] This effect is often produced by focusing on issues of danger and safety. The *Castle*, for example, makes the audience's desire for Mankind's physical safety central to its didactic message. Mankind has barely gotten to the physical and spiritual safety of the Castle when things fall apart: there is a physical battle between the virtues and the sins; Covetousness successfully lures Mankind out of the castle; Mankind is on his deathbed (things do not look good for our hero). At this dramatic high point of the play, Mankind cries for mercy.[52] The feeling of relief when God makes his final judgment in favor of Mercy-personified is palpable. As God reminds the audience what perseverance is, relief and gratitude replace the audience's fears for Mankind. Despite relying on abstraction, the play is intensely focused on the audience's emotional investment in Mankind, encouraging each spectator to see himself or herself as the play's Everyman figure—as frightened, vulnerable, and just barely "deserving" of any attention from God at all.

The morality play *Mankind*, like the *Castle*, treats perseverance in terms of physical embodiment and points toward sensation, just as Kempe's *Book* does, as the means by which truth is known. It juxtaposes intellectual and emotional knowledge as Mankind learns from Mercy, stumbles, confesses, and repents. Furthermore, the play might be seen, more perhaps than other moralities, as aware of the problem of learning embodied truth through abstract devotional language.[53] Like the *Castle*, *Mankind* juxtaposes and intertwines emotional

---

50. "Continuance" is a synonym for perseverance. See *Contemplations*: "Take hed than what goodnes God putteth in the, and thonk him mekeliche and prei hem of continuans" (20). Having a "perseverant wil" is central to the *Contemplations*; Matthew 10:22 (Matthew 24:13 is identical) is quoted in section R.

51. McAvoy, *Authority and the Female Body*, describes this response by audiences and links drama with Kempe's *Book* (125).

52. Even this feeling of assurance is immediately taken away from the audience. The debate among the Four Daughters of God prolongs the anxiety concerning Mankind's safety: Will this last-minute cry count as perseverance?

53. Hilton offers extensive comment on the superiority of knowledge over affect. Things that "mai be feelyd bi bodili wit, though it be never so comfortable and lykande" are "symple and secudarie though thei be good"; the aim is "goostli knowynge' [spiritual understanding] and loovyng of God" (*Scale*, bk. 1, chap. 10, 40). Feeling is suspect because, in contrast with knowledge, it "lasteth not so longe" (bk. 1, chap. 6, 36). It is also problematic in its pleasurableness (41). In contrast, the "feith of Holi Chirche is thi feith, though thou neither see it ne fele it" (bk. 1, chap. 21, 53).

and intellectual truth in its textualized structure and in doing so invites the audience into the process of spiritual discovery. The play opens with the priest-like Mercy's exposition of the nature of God's mercy. Even as he conveys essential truths to his audience, the efficacy of Mercy's intellectualized approach to faith is interrogated. The play acknowledges the ponderous nature of Mercy's "English Latin" and undercuts his labored exposition with the hilarious antics of Mischief, New Guise, Nought, and Nowadays. The effectiveness of Mercy's delivery of intellectualized truth is shown to be only temporary. Mankind *thinks* he believes, but that belief is represented as merely abstract, the repetition of Latinate phrases he memorized as he listened to Mercy. A hundred or so lines later, as he is attacked by the vices, Mankind's overconfidence in his ability to keep his bodily condition under control leads him to declare that his soul is "saciatt" (satiated) with Mercy's doctrine and that he has conquered his sinful condition (Bevington, 914).

Although Mercy argues for subordination of the body to the soul, the play—particularly in performance—exhibits awareness of the embodied nature of spiritual understanding. Mankind's overconfidence is similar to Kempe's vainglory, and it makes him oblivious to his true condition. This blindness is performed on stage: it is the *invisible* Titivillus who is able to persuade Mankind to give up on Mercy's teachings. Vainglory has made Mankind unaware of the true nature of his feelings. Titivillus whispers in his ear and, as if he were a hypnotist, encourages Mankind to recognize that he is "holier then ever was ony of [his] kin" (Bevington, 923). Mankind must experience his fall from grace in explicitly physical terms (he nearly commits suicide) before he is able to understand the dangers of allowing feelings alone to dictate belief.

After drawing their audiences into the emotional crisis of Mankind's near destruction, both *Castle* and *Mankind* invite them to make the same active choice on their own behalf. Cycle plays, based on biblical incident and not on abstract morals, also depend on the same dynamic, drawing audiences into the didactic lesson represented on stage and creating opportunities for personalized response, but do so by insisting on the particularity and humanity of the biblical figures at the center of the drama rather than by offering embodied allegory. In the context of Kempe's *Book*, the N-Town *Woman Taken in Adultery*, a cycle play, is an important example of this for two reasons.[54] First, like the story of Peter's near drowning with which the present chapter began, it is a believer-in-crisis story, and this model shaped Kempe's

---

54. McAvoy, *Authority and the Female Body*, associates Kempe's *Book* with the N-Town play (104–5).

understanding of fear. Second, the *Book* assigns particular significance to the gospel story about the woman taken in adultery. According to chapter twenty-seven, Kempe thought of the story daily: "This creatur had every day mend of the Gospel whech tellyth of the woman whech was takyn in avowtré and browt beforn owyr Lord" (chap. 27, 73). The emphasis in these lines, as it is in the play itself, is on the dramatic action: the woman is "taken" by the scribes and Pharisees, "brought" before Jesus for judgment, and then forgiven and told to "go and sin no more" (John 8:11).[55]

In turning toward an embodied understanding of mercy, the N-Town play, like the *Book*, makes forgiveness synonymous with love. Jesus speaks directly to the audience: "Into the erth from hevyn above, / Thy sorwe to sese and joy to restore, / Man, I cam down all for thy love. / Love me ageyn—I aske no more" (Bevington, 461). The same idea is found repeatedly in Kempe's *Book*, which offers a near quotation of the passage: Jesus tells her, "I aske no mor of the but thin hert for to lovyn that lovyth the" (chap. 36, 95). In the play, the emotional truth of this love is offered to the audience at the outset of the dramatic performance, and the performance itself is, then, an enactment of God's mercy as it is realized in the episode concerning the woman taken in adultery. The play's resolution is about the promise of mercy, and the story of her sin is used to highlight both the danger inherent in sin and God's miraculous ability to forgive and rescue.

After dragging the woman out of the house where she had been involved in illicit sexual relations, the scribes and Pharisees bring her before Jesus and demand that he give true "dom" and "just sentence" for her crimes. The woman stands powerless between her accusers, who repeatedly insist that Jesus make a judgment. Jesus, meanwhile, seeming to ignore the situation, squats on the ground and writes words in the earth. As the accusers continue to demand judgment, the woman calls herself a "wrecch" deserving "bodily

---

55. It is likely that Kempe identified the biblical episode with God's protection against despair: in the *Remedy*, the story of the woman taken in adultery is interpreted as offering assurance that regardless of how sinful one is, "thei schulden neuere the rathere dispeire of the mercy of god ne be discumforted" (chap. 4, 227). The starting point for *Woman Taken in Adultery* is God's mercy, and the play opens with a quotation from Ezekiel, "Nolo mortem peccatoris" (I [God] do not wish the sinner's death)," that is also found in Kempe's *Book* (chap. 64) and in Mercy's speech to Mankind (Bevington, 461). Ezekiel 33:11 is routinely cited in discussions of perseverance. Worried about salvation, Kempe "reminds" Jesus of this verse: "It semyth, Lord, in my sowle that thu art ful of charité, for thu seyst thu wilt not the deth of a synful man. And thu seyst also thu wilt alle men ben savyd" (chap. 64, 154). The N-Town play incorporates standard devotional wisdom into its script. At its end, for example, Jesus tells the audience, "What man of sinne be repentaunt, / Of God if he wil mercy crave, / God of mercy is so habundawnt / that, what man haske it, he shal it have" (Bevington, 469). But this advice is the intellectualized and rationalized version of truth, much like Mercy's exposition at the beginning of *Mankind*, for example, and not the dramatic heart of the play.

deth and werldly shame," declares her sorrow for her sins, and asks Jesus to be merciful (Bevington, 467). Jesus finally stands up and, addressing the woman's accusers, suggests that the one who is sinless should cast the first stone. He then returns to his writing. As the accusers look at the ground on which he writes, they discover he has written their own crimes in the earth. They slink away, leaving the woman alone with Jesus.[56]

The woman's response to the ordeal shifts from fear of violence and exposure to uncertainty. Her accusers have disappeared, but Jesus, a figure of masculine authority, remains, and the woman's uncertainty is underscored. She is not yet sure if he has actually saved her—or if she even deserves to be rescued. Desperate to feel that she has truly been saved, the woman exclaims, "Sey me sum wurde of consolacion!" Jesus finally assures her that he has no plans to condemn her. She is, he tells her, free to "Go hom ageyn," but that when she does, she should "loke that" she lives "in honesté" and "wil no more to sinne."[57] Her rescue complete, she thanks Jesus enthusiastically for the "grett grace" he has shown her and, promising to attempt to be "Goddys trewe servaunt," leaves the stage (Bevington, 469).

There are, as this summary suggests, thematic associations between Kempe's representation of her life and the narrative. The *Book* draws attention to Kempe's affinity for saints like Paul and Mary Magdalene, who undergo remarkable transformations—from the worst of sinners to God's beloved. Furthermore, as in the N-Town play, themes of mercy and perseverance are central to Kempe's understanding of herself and her experiences. Go and sin no more is the only real answer to her worries about perseverance, for example, and there are direct parallels between the *Book*'s representation of her fears and the resonant, well-known phrase.

This is all true, but what is most useful about the N-Town play is the way it allows us to see, through comparison, how Kempe came to understand the nature of the frightening episodes in her life. When she writes that she thought about the woman taken in adultery on a daily basis, it suggests that the narrative provided her with a way of seeing herself and the world. Like the moralities, the N-Town play represents the "unstable" nature of

---

56. The tradition associating Jesus' writing with their crimes can be traced back to the *Glossa Ordinaria*. See Jennifer Knust and Tommy Wasserman, "Earth Accuses Earth: Tracing What Jesus Wrote on the Ground" *Harvard Theological Review* 103 (2010): 407–46. They associate this version with a sermon by Jacobus de Voragine; another tradition, which Voragine traces back to Ambrose and Augustine, argues that Jesus wrote "terra terram accusat" (444–45).

57. *Mankind* also uses as an example of a "grievous sinner" the woman taken in adultery. The advice to the woman "Go and sin no more" is cited three times in the play, once in Latin, and twice in English, to underscore the significance of Jesus' words: "He seyde to her theis wordys, 'Go and sin no more.' So to yow [that is, to the audience]: 'Go, and sin no more'" (Bevington, 935–36).

believers and the impossibility of remaining "perseverant" without mercy, but in contrast with *Mankind* and *Castle*, it insists on the particularized nature of this experience, and especially on the gendered aspects of the woman's experiences. The narrative of the woman taken in adultery provided Kempe with a model for feeling her "perfection," and it did so through the imaginative experience of revisiting episodes in which she had been afraid.

A Woman in Crisis

In the N-Town play, the woman is frightened by the threat of becoming a public spectacle. Though expressed in relation to her crying rather than exposure of sin, the same fear of the public's attention troubled Kempe. The *Book* makes frequent mention of her role as devotion-inducing "wonder." For example, just before the record of her departure from England to go on pilgrimage, "many men merveyled and wonderyd of the gret grace that God wrowt in hys creatur" (chap. 26, 69). Although the *Book* notes her discomfort with this attention, it is also careful to underscore the value of this display. During her stop in Jerusalem, described in chapter twenty-nine, the Virgin Mary tells Kempe that she is blessed and that Jesus will "flowyn so mech grace in" her that "all the world schal wondryn" at her (chap. 29, 79).

The *Book* acknowledges both the difficulty and glamour of being such a wonder. On the one hand, it is frightening and requires self-sacrifice. In chapter five, the first place in which Jesus tells Kempe, "I schal flowe so mych grace in the that alle the world schal mervelyn therof," he also tells her she will "ben etyn and knawyn of the pepul of the world as any raton knawyth the stokfysch" (chap. 5, 31).[58] The same image occurs at the end of chapter sixty-two, where, on account of the grace shown to her, she was "slawnderyd, etyn, and knawyn of the pepil" (chap. 62, 150). She is one of God's chosen marvels, but this "gnawing" is the price she has to pay for being chosen.

On the other hand, the *Book* highlights the excitement and desirability of being a wonder. First, there is the promise of fame. In chapter twenty-nine Kempe reminds herself, after a friar identifies her as "the woman of Inglond" of whom they have heard told that she "spak wyth God" (chap. 29, 80), that his remark proved the truth of Jesus' promise to make "al the werld to wondryn" at her (chap. 29, 80). Her fame is such that the Virgin discusses it with her earlier in the same chapter. She is so important that the Holy Family speaks of the world's wonder of her in similar terms.[59]

---

58. This occurs in the same chapter in which Kempe's salvation is guaranteed by Jesus.

59. Chapter twenty-nine includes Mary's quotation of Jesus' original statement, found in chapter five, and Kempe's repetition of his words.

Like any work written from a first-person perspective, the *Book* records the "wonder" of other people through the eyes of the object of fascination. This means that as Kempe imagines herself watching the people who "marvel" at her, she imagines herself as a spectator. She watches herself being watched, and she imagines the experience of viewing herself, of identifying with her past self, *as if* she were reading her own life.[60]

This has explicit consequences for understanding the *Book* as gendered and implicitly concerned with feminization. Literary scholars are familiar with "the gaze"—mostly from film theory, derived from psychoanalytic theory—and the idea that looking, in patriarchal societies, is coded as masculine.[61] We can see this in a great deal of medieval art, such as the images of Susanna bathing (passive female object) as the elders (powerful masculine agents) look on. This, however, is not the way Kempe's self-objectification works. Rather, imagining looking-at-herself-having-been-looked-at, in situations of danger especially, allows Kempe, in retrospect, to experience, appreciate, and enjoy her own fear as triumph. This is the dynamic found in the N-Town *Woman Taken in Adultery* as well. The "looking" is coded as feminine, even as the woman is placed, in Eve Kosofsky Sedgwick's phrase, "between men." Kempe's retrospective glance at herself as object, first between men, and then on the path to starting over again (going and sinning no more), is in this way empowering for her and for readers who understand themselves in direct relation to her struggles.[62]

In fact, the *Book* couples episodes of assurance with episodes of fear to emphasize this idea. So, for example, chapter fourteen shows Jesus assuring Kempe, and by extension the reader, that she need never fear violence against her—murder, burning by fire, drowning, and windstorms—nor God's anger. Here, it seems, the *Book* follows the model found in books of consolation as they seek to reassure rather than terrify. But chapter thirteen, in contrast, insists on a much more complicated sense of the nature and value of fear. In chapter thirteen she is temporarily left on her own, by her husband, "in the cherch among the monkys" in Canterbury. This is the occasion when Kempe tells the story about the man who gets free abuse at the hands of his tormentors. When she leaves the monastery, the men who have heard her story follow her out and, pointing at a cartful of thorns, threaten to set her on fire.

60. On devotional looking and identification, see Claire Sponsler, *Drama and Resistance: Bodies, Goods, and Theatricality in Late Medieval England* (Minneapolis: University of Minnesota Press, 1997), 104–35.

61. Most significantly, Laura Mulvey, "Visual Pleasure and Narrative Cinema," *Screen* 16 (1975): 6–18.

62. Eve Kosofsky Sedgwick, *Between Men: English Literature and Male Homosocial Desire* (New York: Columbia University Press, 1985).

The situation becomes even more dire: as she stands "wythowtyn the gatys at Cawntrybery . . . mech pepyl" gather, "wonderyng on hir," and calling out "Tak and bren hir" (chap. 13, 40–42).

Kempe is ultimately rescued by "tweyn fayr yong men" who help her escape from the crowd, but before she is rescued, the *Book* describes her extreme fear in graphic, physical terms: "The creatur stod stylle, tremelyng and whakyng [quaking] ful sor in hir flesch wythowtyn ony erdly comfort" (chap. 13, 42). As readers, we know she will be rescued (the *Book* goes on for over 150 more pages), but it is important, too, that the text draws our attention to the danger-ous predicament in which she found herself. Kempe's trembling and quaking in chapter thirteen precede chapter fourteen's assurance of safety and descrip-tion of an imaginative exercise aimed at inducing terror: she thinks about the fact that she would like to "be slayn for Goddys lofe," but her fear of pain is so great that she can imagine only a "soft deth" (chap. 14, 43).

The contrast between the two chapters—the "real" danger of chapter thir-teen and the "imagined" pain of chapter fourteen—illustrates the way Kempe responds to devotional rhetoric.[63] In contrast with the, at best, partial success of her pain-driven devotional exercises, the incidents in which Kempe records her responses to actual fear-inducing situations are moments of triumph. The memory of these triumphs and her successes are then shared with her readers and offered, in turn, for them to use for their own "comfort."[64]

Chapter twenty-seven, in which Kempe records her daily thoughts about the woman taken in adultery, makes this identification between fear and tri-umph explicit. When she finds herself in need of a guide to help her on her way to Bologna from Constance, William Weaver, an old man from Devon-shire, appears in answer to her prayers. But William, like Kempe, is terrified of travel, and they go "forth togydder in gret drede and hevynes." He fears she will be "take fro" him and that he himself will be beaten and stripped of his "tabbarde," his outer coat. Kempe, who had just been abandoned by the company with whom she has traveled, is equally fearful. She has "gret hevynes inasmeche as sche was in strawnge cuntré and cowde no langage ne the man" who is her guide (chap. 27, 73).

---

63. In the "schort meditacion of the passion" found in section AB of the *Contemplations* (which frequently circulated as a separate tract), Jesus is described as "chiuering and quaking" (42).

64. This section of the *Book* covers the span of her life when she began going on pilgrimages (rep-resented in chapter twenty-seven) until she became ill for eight years (described in chapter fifty-six). Structurally, the *Book* closes this "unit" by turning, in chapter fifty-nine, to an overlapping sequence, the eight years during which she read books with her lister. Kempe connects the pilgrimage chapters through a series of reconstructions of episodes in which she imagines herself playing the role of the woman taken in adultery.

Yet despite their mutual apprehensiveness, the chapter draws attention to the way that trying to feel heroic makes it possible to face one's fears. William's fright, chapter twenty-seven recalls, made Kempe less fearful because it provided an opportunity for her to think about how to conquer terror. Imitating Jesus rescuing Peter, she reminds William of God's promise to protect them: "Willyam, dredyth yow not; God schal kepyn us rygth wel." She then recalls the woman taken in adultery, her model for experiencing God's protective power despite feeling frightened. Kempe "preyde, 'Lord, as thow dreve awey hir [the woman taken in adultery's] enmys, so dryfe awey myn enmys, and kepe wel my chastité that I vowyd to the." But Kempe vows, in an inversion of Jesus' admonition to the woman to return home, that she "wyl nevyr" return to England "whil I leve" if God does not protect her and she is "defowlyd" (chap. 27, 73). Although the vow seems strange, it is similar to Kempe's experiments imagining pain—the imagined "defouling"—but more effective because it acts as a promise of faith in God's protection rather than a clumsy effort to prove her own love for God. Kempe's self-observation, then, is about replaying the fearful episode in terms of triumph and rescue. She is both truly afraid *and* truly happy because she has lived through both aspects of the experience.

Each successive episode in which she describes herself in danger and then being rescued confirms the positive nature of this kind of recollection. Instead of displacing fear, the reenacted scenes heighten her terror, her pleasure in remembering that terror, and her sense of success and confidence at the episode's conclusion. The delight she takes in these recollections creates strong, tangible bonds between her past and present selves and her *Book*'s readers. Chapter forty-seven draws attention, again, to the gendered nature of such identification. Kempe recalls the incident in Leicester when she was locked in prison and the steward "toke hir be the hand and led hir into hys chawmbyr and spak many fowyl rebawdy wordys unto hir, purposyng and desyryng, as it semyd hir, to opressyn hir and forlyn [have sex with] hir." His menacing behavior is described in detail, and so is its effect on Kempe—"Than had sche meche drede and meche sorwe, crying hym mercy"—another woman-taken-in-adultery-like scene that leads Kempe to ask to be spared because she is "a mannys wife" (chap. 47, 115).

The steward's villainy makes Kempe, even in recollection, recoil in horror: the unsavory steward "strobelyd [struggled] wyth hir, schewyng unclene tokenys and ungoodly cuntewans" (chap. 47, 115; the alliterative "s" sounds certainly underscore his villainy). In this chapter Kempe admires the bravery of her younger self and creates a space in which the reader feels the same way about the chapter's heroine. The steward is the same kind of villain that the woman encountered in the N-Town play: as soon as Kempe stands up to him and admits, out of fear, the truth of the matter, that "hyr speche and hir dalyawns" came from the "Holy Gost and not of hir owyn cunyng," he is surprised by her "boldenes" and leaves her, unharmed, with the jailer. As she describes it, the steward, "al astoyned of hir wordys, left hys besynes and hys lewydnes, seying to hir as many man had do beforn, 'Eythyr thu art a ryth good woman er ellys a ryth wikked woman'" (chap. 47, 115).

"Astonied," from which modern English "astonished" derives, conveys the sense of being stunned, both figuratively—terribly surprised by—and literally, as in having been deprived of sensation. Instead of paralyzing Kempe with fear, however, the steward is himself stupefied. This lack of sensation contrasts with the visceral excitement the *Book* associates with Kempe's terror and, more important, with her triumphs. During the series of conflicts with secular and ecclesiastical authorities, she emerges as a heroine, one with a reputation for having such power over (evil) men like the steward.

Although actively ascribing this power to God, the *Book* nonetheless emphasizes the emotional impact of *Kempe's* actions on the people around her. Her feelings of fear and triumph, as described by the *Book*, are produced through her interactions in crowds. In chapter forty-eight, for instance, she recounts the excitement that people felt when she came to the Church of All Saints in Leicester: "Ther was so meche pepyl that thei stodyn upon stolys for to beheldyn hir and wonderyn upon hir" (chap. 48, 116). In chapter forty-nine, after recovering from a vision and an episode of crying (so intense that she was afraid she would fall), Kempe describes herself matter-of-factly procuring documentation to demonstrate her orthodoxy and leaving Leicester surrounded by the "good folke" who came to "cheryn hir, thankyng God that had preservyd hir and govyn hir the victory of hir enmyis." They accompany her all the way to the edge of town and promise that if she ever comes to Leicester again, she "schuld han bettyr cher among hem than evyr sche had beforn" (chap. 49, 119).

The *Book's* reconstruction of Kempe's struggles against the authorities from Leicester unites the author and her readers as members of a community, along with the community of "good people" in Leicester, who recognize Kempe's righteousness and who identify with it as an expression of obedience to a higher authority. Like her arrest and the subsequent events in Leicester, Kempe's legal troubles in York, Hull, Hessle, Beverley, and Ely (chapters fifty through fifty-five) are presented with an eye toward representing the *Book's* author, the citizens of the cities she travels through, and the *Book's* readers as spectators who choose to side either with Kempe or against her. In chapter fifty, for example, before her examination by the archbishop, the people around her respond both favorably and negatively to her. Those who "madyn hir ryth good cher" were happy to listen to her, "havyng gret merveyle of hir speche" because it was "fruteful"; those "many enmyis" against her "slawndryd," "scornyd," and "despysed hir." Her enemies hurl insults at her, like the priest who looks at her clothes (God had commanded her to dress in white), grabs her by the collar, and says, "Thu wolf, what is this cloth that thu hast on?" (chap. 50, 121).

The priest's violent behavior and Kempe's response work to draw reader and author closer and closer together. Although the priest's suggestion that Kempe is a wolf among sheep is represented as unsettling—so much so that she "stod stylle" and refused to answer, leaving children passing by to tell the priest, "Ser, it is wulle"—she then speaks "for Goddys cawse," and the *Book* insists she was "not aferd." But she was afraid, of course, even if she no longer was as she recounted the episode, and the reader certainly is, because she is pushed into the position of sharing Kempe's silence as she is held by the collar. Our fear is relieved only by the humor of the children's answer, which makes the priest savagely angry and causes him "to sweryn many gret othis" (chap. 50, 121). This narrative shift allows the reader to step back from her identification with Kempe, and the priest's anger becomes an invitation for Kempe to offer pious lectures on keeping God's commandments.

The *Book* employs close identification of author, former self, and reader in its descriptions of the most frightening experiences from Kempe's life and in doing so represents these episodes as existing continuously in the present. In these narrative sequences, the author watches her younger self as if she were still that younger self; the reader is similarly drawn into the narrative as a spectator who watches another person as if she were that person.

Chapter fifty-one describes a much briefer examination by a lone clerk and another at the chapterhouse in York. In both cases Kempe uses her wits to defend herself—she answers "thorw the grace of God" and the clerks are "wel plesyd"—but is nonetheless required to appear before the archbishop at his residence in Cawood, seven miles from York. In chapter fifty-two her public denunciation during a sermon is recounted; despite the preacher's slanderous remarks about her, she was "meche the mor mery," but her friends "that lovyd hir wel wer ful sory and hevy therof." After the sermon, a "doctowr of dyvinyté" asks her how she is doing, and a man and his wife and other people accompany her the entire seven miles to Cawood. These chapters argue for Kempe's righteousness and the public support that it generated among worthy people. Their worthiness stands in contrast with the archbishop's men, who insult Kempe as she enters the archbishop's chapel, calling her "loller and heretyke," and swear "many an horrybyl othe that sche schulde be brent" (chap. 52, 124).

Chapter fifty-two's focus on the community's observation—and their support or abuse of Kempe—shifts to Kempe's own perspective as it progresses. The archbishop's men, like the accusers in the N-Town play, "gedyn awey as thei had ben aschamyd" (chap. 52, 124) after she speaks out against their swearing.[65] This has the dramatic effect of heightening the tension and then, immediately after, creating a sense of stasis by trotting out minor villains who are easily defeated. The reader—like Kempe herself—knows that this difficulty is a prelude to the climactic event, the archbishop's examination. The chapter builds up to the most serious and most threatening confrontation by removing its concentration on minor characters: the archbishop's men slink away ashamed; the supporters are present but become part of the background and are undifferentiated throughout the rest of the chapter.

The account of events shifts to Kempe's observations of herself as she is examined. The chapter emphasizes her confidence in God's power, as was the case in chapter forty-eight's recounting of the events in Leicester. In fact, her prayer before the archbishop, recorded in chapter fifty-two, is nearly identical to her prayer before her examination in Leicester. The effect of the repetition is to underscore the heroic nature of her trials.[66] Kempe represents herself as God's servant, as at Leicester, and as happy to suffer for the truth. Even the beginning of the examination proper allows for an exhibition of her bravery. In York, once the archbishop enters the room, the chapter records his questions and Kempe's answers: "At the last the seyd Erchebischop cam into the chapel wyth hys clerkys, and scharply he seyde to hir, 'Why gost thu in white? Art thu a mayden?' Sche, knelyng on hir knes befor hym, seyd, 'Nay, ser, I am no mayden; I am a wife'" (chap. 52, 124). Though much more respectful than her chastising of his men for swearing, her answer is confident and filled with conviction.

Yet the impulse to describe herself, retrospectively, in terms of spiritual confidence dissolves as the precise details of the examination are remembered. In particular, the recollected threat of physical violence jolts the narrative into an intense visual and physical description of Kempe's predicament. The archbishop "comawndyd hys mené to fettyn a peyr of feterys and seyd sche schulde ben feteryd, for sche was a fals heretyke. And than sche seyd, 'I am non hertyke, ne ye schal non preve me.' The Erchebisshop went awey and let hir stondyn alone" (chap. 52, 124). Frightened by the archbishop's order that manacles be fetched to restrain her, but still emphatic, she denies the

---

65. On fraternal correction, see Craun, "*Fama* and Pastoral Constraints on Rebuking Sinners; and Edwin Craun, *Ethics and Power in Medieval English Reformist Writing* (Cambridge: Cambridge University Press, 2010), 132–46.

66. At Leicester she prays "that sche myth han grace, wytte, and wysdam so to answeryn that day as myth ben most plesawns and worschep to hym, most profyth to hir sowle, and best exampyl to the pepyl" (chap. 48, 116).

charges. Her fear escalates as she is left standing, alone and isolated, after the archbishop leaves the room.

As the chapter reconstructs Kempe's memories of the ordeal, it moves from observation of the events from the outside, as a spectator, to presentation of embodied experience, observed from the inside. She prays, again following her understanding of the story of the woman taken in adultery, for God to "helpyn hir and socowryn hir ageyn alle hir enmyis, gostly and bodily" (chap. 52, 124); the phrase draws attention to bodily experience by describing those opposed to her as both spiritual and *physical* enemies. The chapter then shows Kempe reliving her experience in explicitly visceral terms: the *Book* relates that she prays for "a long while," and as she does, "hir flesch tremelyd and whakyd wondirly that sche was fayn to puttyn hir handys undyr hir clothis that it schulde not ben aspyed" (chap. 52, 124–25). The trembling and quaking—the same words are used to describe her experience when she was threatened with burning as she stood at the gates in Canterbury in chapter thirteen—betray her fear, which she tries to hide by pushing her quivering hands under her garments so they will not be noticed by the people who are watching her.

The moment is recalled in the *Book* as one of Kempe's experiments with pain, but in this case the fear is real. She does not just imagine suffering for God's love but she actually *feels* the painful terror. The embodied nature of the experience and her observation of herself extends in the next few lines to her sudden "melting" into tears: "The seyd creatur stod al behyndyn, makyng hir preyerys for help and socowr ageyn hir enmiis wyth hy devocyon so long that sche meltyd al into teerys" (chap. 52, 125). The crying overtakes her, and after it is over, she falls "down on hir kneys" before the archbishop. It looks, for a few lines, as if the archbishop has become Jesus from the N-Town play and Kempe has assumed the role of the woman taken in adultery.

Tale-Telling and Bodily Betrayal

Scholars often associate Kempe with "bodiliness." But what is especially interesting about the episodes in which she recounts her fears is the way these scenes of physiologically experienced fear are juxtaposed with an intensely *verbal* narrative. In chapter fifty-two, Kempe's story of the priest, the pear tree, and the bear underscores the *Book*'s linking of the visceral and verbal.

The *Book* introduces that story by shifting from the visualized narrative of fear to a dialogue between the archbishop and Kempe. The chapter drops the framework of the woman taken in adultery as soon as Kempe falls on her knees before the Archbishop: instead of a beneficent scene of forgiveness, the two of them begin squabbling. The archbishop demands to know why she is crying, and Kempe responds, "Syr, ye schal welyn [wish] sum day that ye had wept as sor as I." He goes on to examine her on the Articles of Faith, but even after her success in answering, they continue to argue. The archbishop tells her he has heard she is a "wikked woman," and she snaps back, "So I her seyn that ye arn a wikkyd man." Emboldened by her cleverness, she goes on, at least in memory, to celebrate her witty challenges to the archbishop's commands: she refuses to accept the short amount of time that the archbishop grants her to stay in York; she refuses to swear that she will not teach others about God, insisting that "the gospel gevyth me leve to speken of God"; and she denies preaching, saying, "I come in no pulpytt. I use but comownycacyon and good wordys" (chap. 52, 125–26).

By drawing attention to her verbal mastery over the situation, the chapter pushes aside the experience of fear and replaces it with linguistic success. In chapters fifty-two through fifty-four, Kempe's success at telling "tales" is mentioned repeatedly.[67] In chapter fifty-four she tells the story of a woman who was damned because she did not love her enemies and a bailiff who was saved, despite his reputation as "an evyl man," because he forgave his enemies. The archbishop approves of her story: he "seyd it was a good tale" (chap. 54, 133). In chapter fifty-three she tells tales as the Duke of Bedford's men accompany her to the room in Beverley in which she is to be held. She keeps telling stories, even as she is locked in, relating "many good talys" to the women who gather outside the window of the room in which she is imprisoned. In chapter fifty-two, the chapter in which she appears before the archbishop, she tells the heavily alliterative story of the priest, the pear tree, and the bear when the archbishop demands to hear it after one of her examiners blurts out that she told him "the werst talys of prestys that evyr I herde" (chap. 52, 126).

In this sequence of chapters, the triumph first associated with fearful, embodied experiences is replaced by triumph associated with verbal dexterity and cleverness. The story of the priest, the pear tree, and the bear, which takes up more than a page in Staley's edition, is the most extensive example of this reinvention of the impact of fear. In Kempe's story, a priest sleeping in an arbor beside a beautiful pear tree in flower is surprised by a bear who shakes the blossoms off the tree, eats them, and then, "turnyng his tayl ende in the prestys presens, voyded" the blossoms "owt ageyn at the hymyr party." The heavily alliterative passage—a technique common in popular

---

67. See Rebecca L. Schoff, *Reformations: Three Medieval Authors in Manuscript and Movable Type* (Turnhout: Brepols, 2007), 91–110, on Kempe's tale-telling. On the discursive power of tale-telling, see Phillips, *Transforming Talk*, 65–117.

preaching—is interpreted allegorically by a "pilgrim" who has come upon the priest as he ponders his experience with "gret drede and hevynes." Like John Holmes's angel, the palmer first asks what is the "cawse" of the priest's "hevynes." After he hears the story, Kempe's pilgrim explains to the priest, "Preste, thu thiself art the pertre, sumdel florischyng and floweryng thorw thi servyse seyyng and the sacramentys ministryng," although he does so "undevowtly"; and he is also the bear—"Lych onto the lothly ber, thu devowryst and destroist the flowerys and blomys of vertuows levyng"—and this will lead to his own damnation and injury to his fellow believers unless he mends his ways. The archbishop pronounces it yet another "good tale"; the *Book* observes he "likyd wel the tale and comendyd it" (chap. 52, 127).

In practicing fear—replaying fearful events over and over in the present as an exercise in pain—Kempe works toward representing an immediacy of emotional experience. Bursts of tears, shaking, quivering, swooning all overcome her and fix her in the present moment, suspended in time. Describing these episodes in vivid, visceral terms becomes a means of taking control of these experiences through a kind of bodily narration. Kempe's tale-telling, by contrast, allows for the illusion of disembodiedness.

When, in chapter fifty-four the archbishop is reported as having asserted, "I leve ther was nevyr woman in Inglond so ferd [feared] wythal as sche is and hath ben" (chap. 54, 133), it is provided as evidence of Kempe's power in her community. Instead of being afraid, she re-categorizes herself, through the archbishop's words, as the one who is feared. The archbishop, in fact, encourages Kempe's storytelling at multiple points in the *Book*: when he asks her to retell the story of the priest, the pear tree, and the bear; when he asks her to rehearse the story she had told to the Lady Westmorland (chap. 54, 133); and even when he asks "ful boistowsly," after she says she has heard he is a "wikkyd man," "Why, thow, what sey men of me?" (chap. 52, 125). Even as the archbishop's men continue to suggest that bodily fear would teach Kempe a thing or two (one is reported as saying, "Putte hir forty days in preson and sche schal lovyn God the bettyr whyl sche levyth" [chap. 54, 133]), the *Book* looks for ways to circumvent human embodiment through narration.[68]

The *Book*'s representation of the archbishop as both terrifying and playfully engaged with Kempe's outrageousness and outspokenness is so disarming that we might actually believe that he and Kempe thought verbal dexterity trumped physical danger. We would be entirely mistaken to think this,

---

68. Lochrie argues that Kempe's "laughter" and tale-telling replace threats; see *Translations of the Flesh*, 143, 151. I think this is only a temporary state.

however, given the world in which we know they lived. Although it is easy to miss if we are reading the *Book* only for knowledge about Kempe, Henry Bowet, the archbishop, had been actively involved in the suppression of heresy. When Kempe trembles before him, it is with the awareness that he had taken part in the infamous trial of John Badby, a Lollard burnt at the stake in 1410, as one of Arundel's assistants. For his own part, Bowet was no stranger to threats of physical destruction, having been sentenced to be executed by Richard II in 1399. Although the sentence was commuted to banishment for life, Bowet's political entanglements were such that he was careful "to secure papal absolution for his part in warlike acts, homicides, and mutilations."[69]

Threaded among threatening legal, ecclesiastical, and personal entanglements, the exchanges between Kempe and the archbishop function as breaks, albeit temporary ones, in the pressing fearfulness and bodiliness of human experience as represented in the *Book*. Kempe and Bowet met in 1417, the same year that Bowet, "already in his seventies and so infirm that he could only be carried in a litter," took part in the English victory over the Scots.[70] Kempe describes him taking his own seat (chap. 52, 125), so even if he was sickly at the time of her examination, he was nonetheless still able to walk. He was certainly elderly, if not completely infirm. Kempe, by contrast, was in her mid-forties and in good health—although she was about to fall severely ill for an eight-year period. She records their exchanges with specific attention to this fact: chapter fifty-six begins with a detailed discussion of the "many gret and divers sekenes" that she suffered from 1417 through 1425. But that comes later, and chapter fifty-four concludes with merriment rather than pain: "Sche lowgh and made good cher" (chap. 54, 134). In full health, Kempe can forget, for a brief space of time, her body and the experience of pain. The terrifying scenes and the constant threat of physical violence could be represented as circumstantial and subject to human control, even if Kempe and Bowet both knew better.

Traffic and Weather

From chapter fifty-six through the rest of the *Book*, Kempe concentrates on seemingly mundane fears—of sickness, travel, and especially the weather— instead of on visualized moments of intense danger and triumph. Her fantasy of power as the most feared woman in England dissolves in chapter fifty-six into impatience with her inability to withstand physical pain. She ascribes her

---

69. *Oxford Dictionary of National Biography*, online edition 2007, s.v. Bowet, Henry.
70. Ibid.

illnesses, as books of consolation routinely suggested one should, to God's chastisement: "God ponyschyd hir" with many sicknesses. Yet in contrast with the consolation genre, her *Book* is heavily invested in the precise details of her suffering. Chapter fifty-six is like a medieval version of a patient file: Kempe suffers from dysentery for so long and so severely that she is anointed for dead; she survives, but is so weak that she is unable to hold "a spon hir hand"; she experiences illnesses that attack her head—causing her to believe she will fall into insanity, so that she "feryd to a lost hir witte"—and her back. She recovers for a brief period, but then "an other sekenes" comes upon her, afflicting her right side, for eight whole years, with the exception of eight weeks of respite, and occurring sometimes weekly and for two to thirty hours at a time. She suffered tremendous pain during these episodes, which caused her to vomit and left her unable to eat or drink, "evyr gronyng" until the pain left her (chap. 56, 136).

Once again, it is her inability to withstand the pain that upsets Kempe. Her fear is concentrated, again, on her bodily experience, but the chapter marks a distinct sense of her physicality that differs from the woman-in-crisis sequences. She is not presented as struggling bravely against terrifying human forces; instead, as the *Book* winds down, it is almost exclusively the physical world—her body, the weather, the waves—that cause her to be afraid. From this point on, her heroism, as Kempe represents it, is constituted by her efforts to "suffyr this lityl peyne," as she calls it, comparing its smallness to the greatness of Jesus' suffering; but it is in no way "small" in terms of its effect on her, as the description at the end of chapter fifty-six makes clear. After quickly noting that the eight years of illness had ended but that her episodes of sobbing, in turn, had become more intense—so much so that she received Holy Communion in private—chapter fifty-six goes on to suggest that there was a conflict between her "parts": she cried "as yyf hir sowle and hir body schulde a partyd asundyr." The violent force of her crying required that "tweyn men" should "heldyn hir in her armys tyl hir cryng was cesyd" (chap. 56, 137).

The shift from heroic woman-in-crisis moments and masterly narration to pitiful cataloguing of illness and bodily distress is precipitated by the previous chapters' somewhat obscured return to the issues of fear and perseverance. In chapter fifty-four, Kempe's "cunnyng," her verbal mastery and ability to answer "in Goddys cawse wythowtyn any lettyng" (chap. 54, 134), cause men of law to ask her where she learned to speak in this manner. She replies that her speech is from "the Holy Gost" and asserts that this is just what Jesus meant when he said, "Stody not what ye schal sey, for it schal not be yowr spiryt that schal spekyn in yow, but it schal be the spiryt of the Holy Gost" (chap. 54, 134). The rest of Matthew 10 lingers behind Kempe's chapter, including verse twenty-two, where perseverance is defined, and verse twenty-eight, in which Jesus tells his disciples, "Fear ye not them that kill the body, and are not able to kill the soul: but rather fear him that can destroy both soul and body in hell."[71]

Although Kempe speaks out against the authorities openly "in the light," as Jesus tells the disciples to do, and represents her actions as heroic and brave in chapters forty-six through fifty-five, the rest of the *Book* is shaped by the eight years of illness and the isolation it brought. She takes up pilgrimages again after 1431, but the years in between—she was ill from sometime around 1418 through 1426 and then took care of her husband until his death—were focused on physical difficulties associated with ill health and aging. In describing Kempe's life after 1426, the *Book* relies on patterning, found earlier in the *Book* but to a lesser extent, in which she is constantly forced to face fears that seem small in comparison with those during her legal troubles but which loom larger and larger in Kempe's life: fear of sickness, fear of the weather, and fear of travel.[72]

The present chapter began with a discussion of Kempe's fear of the weather, and in particular of the waves at sea, described very near the end of the *Book*.[73] Earlier in the book, her anxiety about the weather is associated with her mistreatment by her traveling companions or by her anxiety about understanding divine secrets. For example, on Kempe's way to visit the pilgrimage site at the Abbey of Hailes in Gloucestershire, described in chapter forty-five, just before her troubles in Leicester, she prays before boarding a ship that God will preserve her and her fellow travelers from "venjawns, tem-

---

71. *Contemplations of the Dread and Love of God* also relies on Matthew 10:28 in its definition of "dread" (8–10). Although Matthew 10:22 itself is not quoted in the *Book*, chapter fifty-five goes on to describe Kempe's encounter with another group of men, "gret lordys" who "sworyn many gret othys," who wanted to know, as they had heard, if Kempe could "tellyn us whethyr we schal be savyd er damnyd" (chap. 55, 134–35) in terms of perseverance. Her answer is a restatement of the theory and not the prophetic utterance that they had hoped for. On Kempe and prophecy, see Diane Watt, *Secretaries of God: Women Prophets in Late Medieval and Early Modern England* (Cambridge: D. S. Brewer, 1997), 15–50.

72. The shift in emphasis coincides with the escalation of anti-Lollard measures in and around Norwich during the late 1420s. The *Book*'s reticence concerning the period from 1421 through 1431 reflects Kempe's ill health and involvement in familial obligations such as caring for her husband. But the volatile political situation in Norwich was clearly of concern as well, and many of the church officials with whom Kempe interacted were involved in the suppression of heresy, including Henry Bowet, Thomas Peverel, and Thomas Netter. Kempe would have been fully aware of the heightened concern with heresy (and her own legal difficulties are largely described in relation to questions about her orthodoxy). William White, the influential Lollard teacher, provided instruction to dissident groups in East Anglia beginning in 1426. White was tried in Norwich in 1428 and burned as a relapsed heretic under Bishop Alnwick, who conducted a series of prosecutions from 1428 to 1431.

73. Atkinson, *Mystic and Pilgrim*, comments wryly on Kempe's ongoing fear of the sea and remarks, in an aside that draws attention to the persistence of Kempe's fears, "Perhaps even the Lord was annoyed with her by this time" (57).

pestys, and perellys in the se that thei myth go and come in safté," not just because she is afraid of storms but because she has been told by her companions that if there is a storm, they will treat her as Jonah's fellow travelers did him, casting her into the sea, because, they say, "the schip was the wers for sche was therin" (chap. 45, 112).

Even earlier in the *Book*, in chapter forty-four, her fear is coupled with the symbolic value of bad weather as a "token" confirming the nature of God's will. In this chapter, Kempe asks God to "grawnt me a tokne of levyn [lightning], thundyr, and reyn" so she will know that it is God's will that she wear white clothes (chap. 44, 107). Similarly, during her time in Rome, described in chapter thirty-nine, weather is a sign demonstrating that Saint Bridget's Day, the day on which Kempe has the experience, "schulde ben halwyd and the seynt had in mor worshep than sche was at that tyme." On this day "owr Lord sent swech tempestys of wyndys and reynes and dyvers impressyons of eyrs [disturbances in the atmosphere] . . . [as] tokenys" (chap. 39, 99–100).

Nevertheless, even Kempe's stylized responses to the weather are based on literal experiences of fear and suggest that this was, in reality, a lifelong problem. In chapter forty-three, her fear is so great that she kisses the ground when the boat makes it to shore following "gret tempestys and dyrke wedyr." When they reach land, "the forseyd creatur fel downe on hir knes kyssyng the grownde" (chap. 43, 105). Similarly, in the previous chapter, she is so frightened by "perlyows" weather that she thinks it will kill her. As she scurries home, by "wey" and "feldys" during a storm that includes "gret levenys [bolts of lightning] wyth hedows thundrys, gresely and grevows," she is terrified, frightened that she will be "smet . . . to deth" (chap. 42, 105).

At several points in the first half of the *Book*, Kempe's fear of the weather is mentioned in relation to the idea that she should conquer it and learn to trust that God will protect her. In Rome, for example, when she learns to read the violent storms as signs of God's intentions, she remarks both on the intensity of the weather and on divine assurance. Chapter thirty-nine notes that during that year there had been such intense storms "of thunderys and levenys, of gret reynes and dyvers wederyngys" that old men said they "had nevyr seyn swech beforn"; the lightening was so frequent and bright that they feared it "schulde a brent her howsys wyth contentys." God tells her, "Dowtyr, be not aferd, for ther schal no wedyr ne tempest noyin the, and therfor mystrost me not" (chap. 39, 100). Similarly, at the end of chapter forty-two, after she has worried that she will be killed during the storm, Jesus tells her to stop being afraid because he is with her and he is "as mythy to kepyn her" out in the open as he is "in the strengest chirche." After he tells her this, the chapter notes, "sche was not so gretly aferd a sche was beforn" (chap. 42, 105).

It looks as if the lesson of chapters thirty-nine and forty-two is that believers should learn to trust God and that if they do this, they will become less afraid over time. What is perhaps surprising, however, is that this dramatic and effort-based method is abandoned in the second half of the *Book* and replaced by acceptance of constant fear as part of daily life. The *Book* suggests that Kempe came to reject the belief that fear would diminish over time, as some books of consolation taught.

Instead, in the second half of the *Book*, Kempe associates fear with the mundane and "unheroic." Rather than highlighting the excitement of terror, episodes in which she is afraid after her eight-year illness are represented as purposefully repetitive and frequent. In these experiences there is no progression, no personal "growth." Instead, by virtue of their very mundaneness, they are presented as opportunities, which come constantly and which Kempe and her readers might experience at every moment, to practice faith. Kempe moves forward, goes on voyages that scare her, suffers through storms, exposes herself to those who are ill, not because she stops being afraid of these things but, rather, because she believes that God wants her to do so.

Indeed, it is her *failure* to overcome fear that becomes the focus of the *Book* following Kempe's reflections on her long illness in chapter fifty-six. As the *Book* progresses, she becomes a different kind of "wonder," one whose claim to people's attention was based on following God's commands *despite being afraid*, rather than on heroism. The episode, described in chapter eighty-four, when God orders her to visit the nuns at Denny during the time of plague offers extensive illustration of this shift.

In this chapter, Kempe describes her changed understanding of herself in relation to fear. Rather than trying to hide her trembling hands—so to speak—she exposes the exact nature of her fear. First, she thinks she will put off the visit because it will be too hard on her and she "myth evyl duryn the labowr." God commands her to go, speaking directly to her, but, she goes on to explain, she is still "loth to gon, for it was pestylens [plague] tyme," and she does not, under any circumstances, want to die there. He orders her, again, to go and promises that she will "go saf and com saf agen." At this, she reports, despite the fact that she continues to feel "mech hevynes," she prepares for the trip; she felt she had to go. Even after a friend whose husband is ill urges her not to take the journey, Kempe explains to her that she must—even if her friend gave her "an hundryd pownde" not to do so (chap. 84, 192).

The moral of the story about traveling during times of plague is to trust God. Jesus tells her in her soul that "sche schulde not ben sory ne hevy, for sche schulde ben ordeynyd for [provided for, taken care of]" (ch. 84, 192). The chapter goes on to assure her that she should feel secure in her thoughts and feelings. But even with this guaranteee Kempe's experience is of fear, and the *Book* illustrates the repetitive but necessary motions of feeling afraid, feeling secure, and starting all over again. Even though the last chapters of the first book are filled with encouragement from Jesus that Kempe should trust her feelings, the last chapter, eighty-nine, describes her ongoing dread of visionary experiences and her feelings of uncertainty, as discussed earlier in the present chapter, as "the grettest scorge that sche had in erde" (chap. 89, 206).

The second book's account of Kempe's mundane fears is even more extensive. When her daughter-in-law tells Kempe she plans to return home to Germany, by herself, after Kempe's son, her husband, has died, Kempe is relieved. She notes that she herself is "ryth glad and mery" that her daughter-in-law will travel alone. Kempe is afraid of taking the journey and relieved that she "schulde not gon ovyr the see." Her fear, the *Book* explains, comes from bad experiences in the past, "for sche had ben in gret perell on the see afor tyme and was in purpos nevyr to comyn theron mor be hir owyn wille" (bk. 2, chap. 2, 211). And in addition, she is not only afraid but also injured and elderly. The second chapter notes that her confessor tells her, when Kempe finds that God wants her to travel over the ocean with her daughter-in-law: "Ye hirtyd but late yowr foote, and ye ar not yet al hool, and also ye arn an elde woman. Ye may not gon" (bk. 2, chap. 2, 211).

Kempe's fearfulness, infirmity, and elderliness are highlighted in the second book, and in this way she shows herself and her readers a new way of thinking about fear. Being afraid becomes an opportunity instead of a hindrance. It allows her to begin over and over again. This, in fact, is what allows her to understand herself as "perseverant"; like the main characters in the *Castle, Mankind*, and the N-Town play, she is "variable" but also able to begin anew in each instance. According to the *Book*, she becomes a much greater, though less dramatic, kind of "wonder" than she was in Leicester and York by repeatedly experiencing fear and repeatedly, nonetheless, listening to God's commands and obeying them (even when she is forbidden to do so by her confessor).

At the end of book two, chapter two, Kempe records other people's speculation about the reasons why she travels with her daughter-in-law, who is adamantly opposed to having Kempe accompany her. The passage is worth quoting at length, in translation, for its explanation of her actions: "The people who heard about this had great wonder and said what they liked about it. Some said it was a woman's 'wit' and a great folly for her to put herself, a woman of great age, through the perils of the sea in order to go into a strange country—where she had not been before and when she knew not how she would get home again—out of love for her daughter-in-law. Some maintained it was a deed of great charity. Just as her daughter-in-law had left her friends and her country, . . . now she would help her in the same way. . . . But others who knew more of the creature's manner of living supposed and trusted that it was the will and the working of almighty God to the magnifying of his own name" (bk. 2, chap. 2, 213).

At the end of the *Book*, Kempe's fears keep coming, but they do not stop her from moving forward. Although she is "evyr aferd . . . whedir sche had cawse or non" (bk. 2, chap. 7, 224), she keeps trying. If the *Book* represents her as heroic, as capable of maintaining her "perfection" to the end, this ability to keep going, despite her fears, was the basis of her perseverance.

🍎 CHAPTER FIVE

Loneliness

> *Now you have, Lord, taken from me the anchor—I trust to your mercy—the most special and singular comfort that ever I had on earth, for he always loved me for thy love and would never forsake me, not on account of anything that anyone could say or do, while he lived. And Master Alan is kept from seeing me and I from him. Sir Thomas Andrew and Sir John Amy are beneficed and have left town. Master Robert hardly dares speak with me. Now I have in a way no comfort from either man or child* (chap. 69, 163).

The reproachful tone of Kempe's complaint about her loneliness, written years after her friend the anchor had died, highlights the intense feelings of isolation that she experienced over the course of her life. When she recalled this time, she remained distraught over her losses: in addition to the anchor's death, her friend Alan of Lynn, a friar, had been commanded to refrain from talking with her by Thomas Netter, the provincial of the English Carmelites; other clerical friends had moved away to take up ecclesiastical livings; and her confessor, Robert Spryngolde, had grown concerned enough about her reputation to be cautious about interacting with her. Her mournful complaint that she had "no comfort" from "man" or "child" is an exaggeration, of course, but her question is a fair one: Why were her friends repeatedly taken from her? Why did she feel so lonely, and what, the *Book* asks, could she do to feel less desolate?

Instead of pushing Kempe's questions aside, insisting "ther is no trost but in" God—an easy and perfectly orthodox answer—the *Book* wrestles with the human experience of loneliness.[1] Responding to various, and sometimes contradictory, teachings on the subject, Kempe's *Book* illustrates her lifelong efforts to escape from loneliness and to find spiritual communities of "high desire" in which she might participate. It traces her repeated experiences of isolation and loss of fellowship as well as her successes in finding new friends and companions.

Ultimately, the *Book* itself is represented as Kempe's solution to the problem of loneliness. By creating a community of like-minded readers who find in it answers to the problems they face, it becomes a remedy to this situation. The physical book stops the perpetual loss of friends and companions by making permanent Kempe's interaction with her readers through the written account of her life. It resolves loneliness by offering a lasting solution to the problem of the fracturing of friendship and fellowship that she experienced repeatedly: she and her readers become companions with a perfect and enduring understanding of one another. Writing the *Book* allows her to find herself in her own book, and the self she discovers is offered to her readers as a vehicle through which they too can find themselves.

Furthermore, the *Book* reshapes the "real" communities in which Kempe and readers like her find themselves. As both the reader and writer of the text, she becomes a witness to the actual writing (the process of textualizing experience) and also to the multiple and contradictory layers of lived experience through which this self is created. In this way, as Jeanne Perreault suggests of twentieth-century "autographers"—feminist authors who write from an autobiographical perspective that includes the reader in configurations of subjectivity—Kempe's "process of the self-in-the-making" is shared, offered to readers as their own opportunity for participation and self-creation.[2]

Kempe's is a therapeutic model: textual involvement (writing and reading) are linked, and definitive statements about "wholeness" characterize the final chapter of the first book. The moment when Kempe feels complete—"heil and hoole" (hale and whole [chap. 89, 205])—is when she writes in the company of her scribe and in the service of sharing her "singular" experiences with her readers. But despite this, the finality and permanence of this solution to loneliness is thrown into question by what serves as a coda to the first eighty-nine chapters—book two—in which textualized conclusiveness

---

1. Jesus reports that Kempe herself says this ("ther is no trost but in the alone") in chapter eighty-eight (204).
2. Perreault, *Writing Selves*, 2.

conflicts with representation of the always unfinished nature of lived life. The *Book* leaves readers with a question: Is it really possible to build a community, to fend off loneliness, by treating a physical book as a vehicle for companionship?

Jesus Alone

The first fifteen chapters of the *Book* show Kempe gradually separating herself from her biological family. Devotional writers asserted that anything that detracted from one's complete love of God should be eliminated from one's life. This included one's family, and when her *Book* represents her struggle to love God "alone," it frames that struggle in relation to her role as her husband, John's, wife. In chapter three, she tells John she "may not deny" him her "body," but "the lofe of myn hert and myn affeccyon is drawyn fro alle erdly creaturys and sett only in God" (chap. 3, 26). The *Book*'s preface offers a succinct, if somewhat exaggerated, account of this separation: "Her kynred and thei that had ben frendys wer now hyr most enmys" (preface, 18). Authoritative advice insisted that love of family detracted from spirituality. Kempe tried to follow this advice.

Despite the fact that John supports her spiritual searching throughout their lives, the process of separation is gradual but unmistakable. Kempe represents herself as traveling farther and farther away from conventional domestic life, moving from the first chapter, in which her breakdown is described; through chapters two through five, in which her separation from the world is initiated (business failures, revulsion toward sexual relations with her husband, failed seduction by her "friend'); to chapters six through eight, in which Jesus makes spiritual promises to her and she is "present" at Jesus' birth; through to her bargain with John to cease sexual relations in chapter eleven; followed by her visits to nearby towns, accompanied by John, up to chapter fifteen, in which Jesus commands her to go on pilgrimage and dress in white clothing, visible signs of her removal from the domestic life of a wife and mother from Lynn.[3]

Though perhaps surprising to modern readers, Kempe's decision to separate herself from her family was among the usual paths suggested to people looking for more intense spiritual experiences. In *Contemplations of the Dread and Love of God*, for example, a work written for lay readers, the author distinguishes among three types of love for God (from lowest to highest): obedience

---

3. Just as John continues to support her throughout their lives, she in turn cares for him when he is sick and elderly. The practical realities of family life are sometimes suppressed in the *Book*. I discuss this near the end of the present chapter.

to God's commands; forsaking of family and the world; and isolated, contemplative life. Kempe's seemingly extreme decision was, at least according to the author of the *Contemplations*, only the second-most demanding of the ways to love God.[4]

The image of family-as-obstacle figured in much of the devotional writing that Kempe read during her tutorials with the young priest. In *The Fire of Love*, Rolle, for instance, defines the "lyfe of parfyt" as requiring one "to kest away" all worldly business including "ffadyr and modyr and all thi gudis"; he lumps those loves in with "warldly desyres" such as lechery and "unlefull meuyngis" (unlawful stirrings).[5] In the Middle English version of Bridget's *Revelations*, Jesus commands the saint to reject her family: she must "desyr no thing bott" Jesus; that is, "all thynges" including her "children and kynne" are obstacles to that love.[6] Even popular literature alluded to the mistakenness of rating family and friends over God. A well-known example is the morality play *Everyman*, in which Felawship, Kinrede, and Cosyn are among the first to leave Everyman as he makes his way toward his final "accounting." Lyric poetry, too, often castigated the fickleness and changeability of familial relations and secular friendships. In *God Send Us Patience in Our Old Age*, the speaker observes that those who are our friends and love us best will "have us but in hate" in old age. There is no "truste" in companionship; God is our only true friend.[7]

Kempe's *Book*, however, endorses separation from intimate domestic attachments but also insists on familial responsibility. In Kempe's early life, this is conveyed in relation to her desire to live chastely with John: she does not want to have sex with him but continues to do so because it is her duty. Later in the *Book*, her sense of familial obligation is presented in the context of her physical care of the now elderly John. After he had been injured falling down the stairs, she cared for him until he died. The *Book* notes that she "had ful mech labowr wyth hym" because he was incontinent and that she was sometimes tempted to feel "yrkyd" because of this "labowr" but saw it as justified punishment for her sinful delight and "inordinat" love for her husband in her youth (chap. 76, 173).

---

4. *Contemplations*, 7. See Matthew 10:35–37, where Jesus explains that instead of peace, he brings "variance": "For I came to set a man at variance against his father, and the daughter against her mother, and the daughter-in-law against her mother-in-law. And a man's enemies shall be they of his own household. He that loveth father or mother more than me, is not worthy of me; and he that loveth son or daughter more than me, is not worthy of me."

5. *Fire*, bk. 1, chap. 23, 50.

6. *Revelations*, EETS, o.s., 178, 2.

7. Brown, *Religious Lyrics*, no. 148, 234.

Excessive love for another person, including members of one's family, was routinely denounced because such love was thought to stand in the way of one's love of God. But devotional rhetoric often left out the qualifier (inordinate) and emphasized exclusivity. Rolle, for instance, advises "Godis lufar" that she cannot be "knyttid . . . parfitely" to God while she is "bune" (bound) to "any creature."[8] At certain points, Kempe's *Book* also follows this model. In chapter thirty-seven, for instance, Jesus reminds her that it is impossible for her to forgo his love and that she has no other "comforth but me only, whech am I, thi God, and am al joy and blysse to the" (chap. 37, 95–96).[9]

An understanding of human nature as both affectionate and possessive underlies the idea that love of family stands in the way of one's love of God. The love between God and believer was understood as reciprocal, and God's definition of himself as a "jealous" God was frequently mentioned to explain his demands of humans. In the *Fire*, Rolle declares that the reader should know, "with oute dowt," that if she "deuidys" (divides) her heart and "dredis not" to love another at the same time, that God will "forsakyn" her love.[10] Similarly, *The Book of Tribulation*, in a horticultural metaphor, suggests the reader saw off "braunches of flesshely frendes" to make sure his heart does not "drawe to fer from him" or "goo spredyng . . . by vnkynde braunches of foreyn thynges."[11] A jealous God requires all the believer's attention.

In return for single-minded devotion, the believer is promised perfect love, a companionship with God so complete that the beloved will never even notice her loneliness and longing for human friends. Although at first this isolation will feel like labor, when one finds it "light and likinge," he or she can be sure that "God putteth in the grace to konne loue."[12] The "work" of loving God should feel like pleasure. The *Contemplations* uses an interesting comparison between lovers of God and hunters to make this point: like people who are avid hunters and who work hard as they go about their sport, believers who love God will feel, despite strenuous efforts, that the work of loving him is a pleasure.[13]

The joy of the lover's labor is coupled with perfect acceptance and responsiveness between God and the beloved. Jesus' relationship with Mary Magdalene was frequently alluded to in this context. The *Mirror*, for example, describes the couple as "tweyn trewe louers" who "standen & speken togeder

---

8. See *Fire*, bk. 1, chap. 11, 23.

9. That Jesus makes this observation in Rome is significant; see the discussion later in this chapter.

10. *Fire*, bk. 1, chap. 24, 51. Exodus 20:5 and Deuteronomy 4:24 describe God as jealous.

11. *Book of Tribulation*, 65.

12. *Contemplations*, 10.

13. Ibid., 10–11.

with grete *likyng* & ioy."[14] The ideal is to feel *at ease* with God in the same way that human friends and companions who like one another feel "grete likyng," as the *Mirror* puts it. Kempe's *Book*, too, shows that perfect love allows lover and beloved to express themselves freely and with the expectation of acceptance by the other. Jesus and Kempe's "swet dalyawnce" is represented as intimate conversation between friends (chap. 87, 201). Congeniality and affection between God and believer is central to the *Book*'s definition of love, and all that is asked is the exchange of one's own heart for Jesus'.

And yet, although the *Book* repeatedly celebrates the "parfyte lof that owr Lord Jhesu Crist had to mankynde" (chap. 78, 177), the promised perfection, the guarantee that Kempe would feel complete, delighted in God's love, and in no need of human companionship, was never fully realized. Along with moments of rapturous joy, the *Book* records dark experiences of loneliness and isolation. Instead of the sublime perfection of spiritual love, the practical result of Jesus's "alienation" of Kempe's affections is that it deprived this daughter of the city's former mayor, wife of a very kind and understanding man, and mother of numerous children of her "natural" community of family and friends. Although the *Book* makes categorical statements about the desirability of this situation, references to family matters such as her husband's support during her travels and her concern about the salvation of her children provide glimpses of her "past" life as a mother and wife.

Some devotional writers anticipated the loneliness created by the discrepancy between idealized theory and the reality of human experience. *The Book of Tribulation*, for example, argues that troubles free one's heart from human attachments and states that losing a friend (to death) is an aid that helps the believer set her heart on God. But it also reflects on the loss entailed in turning from friends to God. Although its advice is, ultimately, to be patient and keep pursuing God's love, *The Book of Tribulation* also describes the difficulties faced by the believer for whom the "tauerne" of "worldly solace" and "the tauerne of heuen" are both "forclosed"—one because she has turned to God's love completely and the other because she still lives in this world and not in the next.[15]

Similarly, Rolle's endorsement of solitude is tempered by a keen sense of the pleasures and importance of human companionship. He is, of course, aware that believers are commanded to "love their neighbors as themselves," and insists that they love their neighbors and friends "in God" by

---

14. *Mirror*, 200, emphasis added. Louise M. Bishop discusses this passage in the context of Kempe's relationship with Jesus; see *Words, Stones, and Herbs: The Healing Word in Medieval and Early Modern England* (Syracuse: Syracuse University Press, 2007), 172–75.

15. *Book of Tribulations*, 106–9.

acting charitably.[16] His categorization of charity includes affection between people; an entire chapter of the second book of the *Fire* is concerned with the nature of friendship and the human desire for a "trew frende."[17] Rolle, in fact, expresses his own, unfulfilled wish for a "fela [companion] in the way" with whom to have shared his experiences. With this friend, he says, he would have "restyd" and enjoyed "gude spech withouten stryfe"; they would have been "glad" and lived "truly in myrth of lufe togidyr."[18]

Despite her attempts to love God "alone," Kempe's longing for her absent friends, described at the beginning of the present chapter, fits with the description of unfulfilled companionship in the *Fire*. She came, like Rolle, to assume a clear (at least theoretical) understanding of the hierarchy of affection with love of God as the highest priority. And yet, although she "casts off" her family, removing herself from shared domestic space, she, like Rolle, values the importance of human relationships that are "in God" and is concerned with shared spiritual understandings, with community, and with friendship.

Kempe's representation of her desire for fellowship was in keeping with devotional writers' encouragement of communication among "ghostly livers," as the *Chastising* calls them. Alongside the "Jesus alone" model, readers were urged to form strong spiritual friendships.[19] The *Consilia Isidori*, for example, encourages believers to search for "good felowschype": "Ioyne the with good men, desyre the felouschyppe of dyscrete men, seke the companyes of vertues men."[20] In the *Chastising*, companionship is among the remedies offered to combat despair and uncertainty. The author includes it as part of one's spiritual "strength," a gift from God, which is "conceyued of ioie, of liberte, of armour and of felawship."[21] The person who has chosen a life of devotion is, as a consequence, no longer "aloone" but instead "associed to al the company of rightful men."[22]

But in reality, it was not so easy to enter into the company of rightful men. Kempe's *Book* traces her great efforts to seek such a fellowship. Although she finds a great deal of local clerical support early on—from her confessor,

---

16. *Fire*, bk. 1, chap. 20, 44; chap. 26, 56; chap. 30, 64. *Contemplations of the Dread and Love of God* makes the same point: "Thou schalt loue thi neighbour for God . . . thou schalt loue God for himself, with al thin herte, and thi neighbour for God as thiself" (14).

17. *Fire*, bk. 2, chap. 9, 91.

18. Ibid., chap. 5, 78.

19. On the "discourse of familiarity," see Anne Clark Bartlett, *Male Authors and Female Readers: Representation and Subjectivity in Middle English Devotional Literature* (Ithaca: Cornell University Press, 1995), 86–114. For earlier traditions of spiritual fellowship, see Brian Patrick McGuire, *Friendship and Community: The Monastic Experience, 350–1250* (Kalamazoo: Cistercian Publications, 1988).

20. Horstmann, *Yorkshire Writers*, 2:370.

21. *Chastising*, 153.

22. Ibid., 153–54. See Staley, *Dissenting Fictions*, on the substitution of "spiritual kinship" for "natural" familial relations (124).

Spryngolde; from her friend the anchor; and from "celebrities" including the bishop of Lincoln, Southfield, Julian of Norwich, Caister, and Arundel—the *Book* records a series of unpleasant clashes with others who one might have assumed would have been like-minded allies.

Companions in the Way

The *Book*'s earliest account of Kempe's efforts to join communities of fellow spiritual seekers focuses on her vexed relationships with three devout widows.[23] Although they must have seemed the perfect solution to her desire for this kind of community, the widows prove to be her competitors and enemies rather than fellow spiritual seekers and friends. Kempe and the first widow become embroiled in a feud that lasts twelve years. Kempe has heard "in hir spyryt" that the widow should leave her confessor; the woman refuses to believe her, and snarls back when Kempe suggests she should do so that "it had ben good" if Kempe's love for her own confessor "wer set as hir was" (chap. 18, 55).

The second widow refuses to believe Kempe when she tells the woman that her deceased husband is in purgatory and requires more frequent prayers; she angrily declares to Kempe's friend the anchor that if he continues to support Kempe, he "schuld lesyn" her own "frenshep" as well (chap. 19, 56).[24] The third widow turns on Kempe, like the second, after she feels insulted when she hears that her deceased husband will spend thirty years in purgatory "les than he had bettyr frendys in erthe" (chap. 19, 57). Unwilling to accept Kempe's spiritual insights, the widows do not merely distance themselves from her but attack her and attempt to turn her friends against her. Entangled in petty jealousies and personal feuding, the widows bear no resemblance to the company of "rightful" people with whom Kempe hoped to interact. Soon after these episodes with the widows, Kempe begins to plan a series of pilgrimages. It must have seemed like a natural solution to her failure to find friends among the "devout" people at home.

But it is no solution at all. Instead of finding a community of right-minded men and women, Kempe experiences unrelenting loneliness as she makes her way to the Holy Land. Already in chapter twenty-six, the first in the sequence about pilgrimage, she recounts the hostility of her fellow pilgrims. They, and

---

23. See Katherine French, *The Good Women of the Parish: Gender and Religion after the Black Death* (Philadelphia: University of Pennsylvania Press, 2008), esp. 85–156.

24. Kempe's friend the anchor had been promised "gret frenschepys" if he would break off his relationship with her (chap. 16).

even their confessor, tire almost immediately of her crying, her vegetarianism, and her talk "of the lofe and goodnes of owyr Lord" (chap. 26, 69). In fact,
they suggest that she would have been better off staying home; they taunt
her and tell her they will "not suffren hir *as hir husbond dede* whan sche was at
hom and in Inglond" (chap. 26, 70, emphasis added). A supposedly spiritual
community, they fail to demonstrate even the sense of like-mindedness and
support that Kempe had at home.

Rather than companions in the way, her fellow travelers turn out to be
tormentors. They make repeated plans to abandon her, cut her dress short to
"disguise" her as a fool, force her to sit far from them at meals, and routinely
mock her for speaking of spiritual matters. By the end of chapter twenty-six,
she reports that she prayed, as they made their way to Constance, having
barely begun their time together, that God would protect her from "her
enmys" (chap. 26, 71); already at this point in the narrative it is difficult to
discern if she meant strangers or her traveling companions. More than devoid
of spiritual aspirations, her fellow travelers are cruel and undependable to
such an extent that Kempe comes to stereotype her "cuntremen" as the worst
people in the world: she found "alle pepyl good onto hir and gentyl saf only
hir owyn cuntremen."[25]

Not only do her fellow pilgrims never become the spiritual community she
hoped for but they also refuse to appreciate what she has to contribute to the
experience of pilgrimage. Instead, they repeatedly insist that she change to
conform with *their* behavioral norms. Obsessed with creating a community
of uniformity, they demand that the pope's legate, whom they meet in Constance, order Kempe "to etyn flesch as thei dedyn and levyn hir wepyng and
that sche schulde not speke so mech of holynes." The legate refuses, having
heard Kempe's confession earlier and given her "wordys of gret comfort"
(chap. 27, 71–72), but the pilgrims continue to insist, and when they do not
get their way, they abandon her.

Although Kempe's companions were no company of right-minded believers, and they surely needed to examine their spiritual commitments, Kempe,
too, needed to revise her understanding of communal relations. Her desire
to belong to the group was so strong that she attempted to conform to their
emotional and behavioral dictates. Her fellow pilgrims, after abandoning her
in Bologna, discover that she has made better time than they have and invite
her back into their fellowship. But with certain conditions. If she wishes to

---

25. "Countrymen" has negative connotations in most instances from this point on in the *Book*:
see ll. 1489, 1723, 1754, 1779, 1780, 1860, 1942, and 2295 (Staley ed.). Weaver, her guide, is from
Devonshire and an exception to Kempe's feelings about her countrymen.

travel with them to Venice, she must enter into a new "comnawnt" with specific terms: she may not "speke of the Gospel," and she must "makyn mery," as they do, at meals. Once they reach Venice, she realizes she has made a mistake. When she starts to tell a gospel story at dinner one evening, her fellow pilgrims jump in and accuse her of breaking her "comenawnt." In response, she tells them she can no longer hold to the agreement and explains, "I must nedys speke of my Lord Jhesu Crist thow al this world had forbodyn it me (chap. 27, 73–74).

The *Book*'s recollection of the experience demonstrates how the desire for friends can go too far. If these are the people from whom you must choose, it is clearly better to have no friends at all. But what is surprising, given the clear identification of her fellow travelers as spiritually unsuitable, is how often the *Book* meditates on Kempe's own flawed response to other pilgrims. She does what is right, but she continues to feel upset about their disapproval and dislike. The *Book* looks for ways to understand these feelings by going back over the situations that caused her to feel this way.

After she records her breaking of the "covenant," she goes on to recall the emotional cost of her decision. After she refuses to keep up the bargain, she breaks off all communal interaction, takes to her "chawmbre," and eats by herself for six weeks, after which time she falls so ill that "sche wend to a be ded" (chap. 27, 74).[26] Even her maid leaves her and gets employment caring for some of Kempe's former companions. Although Kempe is suddenly and miraculously made "hool agen" after her illness, the chapter's conclusion focuses on her unhappiness about being excluded from the group—dining for weeks by herself and becoming terribly ill with no one to care for her—rather than on God's protection.

The company's cruelty is described in terms of behavior and actions—stealing her sheets, cutting her dress short, repeatedly abandoning her in various locations and banning her from communal dining—but their rejection of Kempe is based on their desire for *emotional* conformity. Her fellow pilgrims were the sort of people, the *Book* suggests, who only want to be with people who are just like them. Lacking all empathy, they were, apparently, quite satisfied to see Kempe alone and suffering precisely because her responses and feelings were different from theirs.

---

26. Eating alone becomes the *Book*'s shorthand for loneliness and lack of community. Kempe's fellow pilgrims are defined by the fact that they "had putt the forseyd creatur fro her tabyl that sche schulde no lengar etyn among hem" (chap. 28, 74). In chapter twenty-nine, her crying in Bethlehem leads her fellow pilgrims to forbid her, again, to eat with them, and "therfor sche ete hir mete be hirselfe alone" (chap. 29, 80).

Kempe's first impulse, once she understands this is no company of right-minded men looking for spiritual "high desire," is to withdraw from interaction with them completely. She does so, in part, by acknowledging her own lack of emotional symmetry with the pilgrims, making an "apology" in which she snippily declares that she is "in charité" with them and hopes that they will be "in charité" with her (chap. 28, 75). This is a willed, rather than felt, response to the situation, and in accordance with traditional notions concerning *caritas*. But theological correctness aside, as she prepares to enter Jerusalem, what the *Book* shows Kempe looking for is a fellowship bound together by the same emotional understanding and intensity that she herself feels. When she does not find it, she retreats from her earthly companions and looks for alternatives. Once she enters the city, she discovers that it is really three places: the earthly city, the city in her soul, and the city "abovyn"—that is, the "cyté of hevyn" (chap. 28, 75).[27] She takes refuge in the cities in her soul and in heaven.

Three Jerusalems and Rome

As in the moments when a relationship with "Jesus alone" satisfies her, Kempe's representation of her time in Jerusalem is filled with tears, dalliance, and "the unspekabyl lofe that wrowt so fervently in [her] sowle" (chap. 28, 77); the contrast with her recent experiences of loneliness heightened these feelings. With the exception of a few lines mentioning the ceremonies conducted and the famous dozen lines—borrowed in places from a text ascribed to Rolle—about Jesus' crucified body, chapter twenty-eight is taken up entirely with Kempe's inner devotion: the cities in her soul and above.[28] Flesh-and-blood pilgrims seem to have disappeared from this pilgrimage.

In Jerusalem, *Kempe's* feelings are identified as the natural ones. *Her* spectacular expressions of grief, as she imagines Jesus' death, are the appropriate response to every situation. The chapter suggests that if her fellow travelers really understood spiritual truth, they would see this too. In the world outside

27. The New Jerusalem is the city of the saints (Revelations 20:3) and a new earthly city brought down from heaven to earth (Revelations 21; Ezekiel 36–48). Hebrews 11–13 figures the believer as a wanderer on this earth who longs for a better country, the heavenly Jerusalem.

28. See Windeatt, 166, n. 2270, for the passage in which Jesus' body is compared to a "dufhouse" filled with holes in which doves chased by hawks seek refuge. On late medieval cities and bodies, see Alex Mueller, *Translating Troy: Provincial Politics in Alliterative Romance* (Columbus: Ohio State University Press, 2013), 68–80. On the New Jerusalem in late medieval poetry, see Ann R. Meyers, *Medieval Allegory and the Building of the New Jerusalem* (Cambridge: D. S. Brewer, 2003).

Jerusalem, people "cryen and roryn and wryngyn her handys as yyf thei had no wytte ne non mende" when their friends die (chap. 28, 77). In Jerusalem, earthly experiences are, the *Book* insists, nothing more than triggers for thinking about Jesus' Passion. When she sees any evidence of violence such as a person or an animal with a wound or a man beating a child or a horse, "hir thowt sche saw owyr Lord be betyn er wowndyd" (chap. 28, 76). It is the truth of transcendent reality, she claims, that occupies her.

The subsequent chapter, which describes Kempe's visits to sites associated with the Passion, is similarly effusive about the "city" in her soul and dismissive of her fellow travelers. At Mount Calvary, she was "ful of holy thowtys and medytacyons and holy contemplacyons . . . and holy dalyawns" which were so "holy" that "sche cowde nevyr expressyn hem aftyr" (chap. 29, 78). At Sion, where Jesus washed the disciples' feet, she was filled with "gret devocyon, wyth plenteuows teerys, and wyth boystows sobbyngys" (chap. 29, 79). The chapter connects this inner city with the heavenly Jerusalem, observing that Kempe's responses are the same as those of the inhabitants of the city "abovyn." In contrast with her experiences out in the world, where people judged her unfairly for her crying because "thei knewyn ful lytyl what sche felt," during her three weeks there she felt divine love and acceptance (chap. 29, 76, 78–79). In Jerusalem, "holy dalyawns," dramatic encounters in her soul, replace the narratives of pettiness and casual cruelty that marked the entire journey to the Holy Land. Little wonder that she thinks about staying in Jerusalem, a place that allows her to withdraw from this world into the cities of her soul and above.[29]

Chapter twenty-nine, however, also shows Kempe's awareness, in recollection certainly, and perhaps during her time in Jerusalem as well, that this refuge from earthly communities could only be temporary. The chapter reflects on her right to choose (by her "own self") whether to "reenter" the earthly world by continuing on to Rome. As Jesus observes, she did not need to do so for penitential reasons because her sins were already forgiven. But her right to decide is revoked. Jesus insists she go on: "Notwythstondyng al this, I comawnde the . . . that thu go vysite thes holy placys . . . for I am above al Holy Cherch" (chap. 29, 79). The Virgin Mary's reassurance that leaving Jerusalem might not be so bad—Kempe is, after all, "blyssyd" and should not feel "aschamyd" of her special spiritual gifts as she returns to the world of fellow pilgrims (chap. 29, 79–80)—draws attention to Kempe's reluctance. Mary

---

29. See *The Prickynge of Love*'s joyful description of the fellowship, love, happiness, freedom, and comfort in heavenly Jerusalem at the very end of the treatise (208–10).

reminds her it is her duty to continue on, to be a "wonder," and to help people in this world. She has to, they insist, continue on to Rome.

Rome is the place in the *Book* where she could try to bring the heavenly city, her own New Jerusalem, down to earth. If Jerusalem was a refuge for her, Rome was a magical space in which other people, especially those who were unable to speak her language, understood her emotional experiences and appreciated her special spiritual status as a woman moved to tears for God's love and whom God, in turn, spoke to directly.

Nonetheless, her journey to Rome, like her earlier travels, was fraught with difficulty: she was abandoned repeatedly and forced to rely on the kindness of strangers to make her way. Things did not get much easier upon her arrival in the city; the *Book* records experiences of rejection and loneliness similar to those described in relation to the journey to the Holy Land. The English are, again, the primary cause of her misery.

Although she is eagerly welcomed at the hospital of St. Thomas Canterbury, she is soon thereafter ejected from the hospice after an English priest of her fellowship "slawndryd so hir name" throughout the city (chap. 31, 86). Once she leaves the hospice, she no longer has a confessor, and it begins to look as if she is about to retreat to the city in her soul again. Jesus sympathizes with her predicament and sends John the Evangelist to hear her confession "in her soul."[30] The Roman experience seems about to repeat the same patterns as the rest of the pilgrimage. But it does not. Instead of retreating, the *Book* shows Kempe learning to integrate all three Jerusalems, and Rome becomes the place in which she learns to begin again, and to form new relations with other people.

In Rome, Kempe's active participation in the world intensifies as she embraces poverty as a spiritual exercise. Being impoverished forces her to interact directly with other people. Like the imaginative exercises involving physical pain, this "practice" poverty is more about effort than outcomes. Her attempts, as an act of penance, to serve an elderly indigent woman for six weeks are illustrative. She cares for the woman, according to chapter thirty-four, as she "wolde a don owyr Lady," carrying water and wood, caring for her physical health (she picks "vermyn" off her), and acquiring their food by begging. Although it may seem odd, or even comical, as the chapter also reports, that Kempe drank the indigent old woman's sour wine and gave the woman in turn the good wine she had bought for herself, the point is not that this is practical or logical or even particularly generous but, rather, that she

---

30. Kempe's mystical marriage to the Godhead also takes place in Rome and affirms the significance of the inner experiences as well as the outer ones.

learns compassion by performing compassionate *exercises* involving people who inhabit this world.[31]

Furthermore, just as Kempe finds opportunities to practice emotional responsiveness toward others through their poverty, others learn to enter into her spiritual community by interacting with her.[32] This begins in chapter thirty-eight, when Jesus insists that she must "folwyn" her "owyn cownsel" to other people and give up her money and goods. (She gives up those of her guide, Richard, as well, and Richard is not at all happy about this.) The comic element is again part of the recollection of clumsiness. She is no better at exercises in poverty than she was at the calisthenics of pain, but that is the point. Practicing "voluntary" poverty forces her to find ways to resist the temptation to give up on human relationships and creates opportunities for other people to act according to the principles of spiritual solidarity that first drew Kempe to go on pilgrimage.[33]

Necessity brings people to her aid. For example, upon learning that Kempe is destitute, Dame Margaret Florentyne invites Kempe to dine with her every Sunday, seating Kempe at her own table and serving Kempe "wyth hir owyn handys" (chap. 38, 97).[34] Kempe's poverty allows the two to form a spiritual community, and despite the linguistic barrier, Dame Margaret and Kempe become friends. The personalized service, the companionable intimacy of Dame Margaret feeding Kempe with her own hands, is as important, as described in chapter thirty-eight, as the sustenance itself. Other people also feed Kempe and become part of her circle. Another acquaintance, Marcel, invites Kempe to meals twice a week; a "holy mayden" feeds her on Wednesdays.[35] The *Book* represents the experience of poverty as an opportunity to find spiritual fellowship and to enjoy relationships that are emotionally as well as physically sustaining. In fact, it is the companionable intimacy produced by the situation, much more than the food itself, that Kempe emphasizes in this section of the *Book*. In Rome, warmth and reciprocity characterize her inter-

---

31. The same is true of the episodes, in the subsequent chapter, when she kisses children "in the stede of Criste" (chap. 35, 91).

32. Benson, *Public Piers Plowman*, observes that for Kempe, "material necessities of daily life . . . are used to approach the sacred in ways beyond the control of the institutional Church" (151).

33. The lives of both Marie of Oignies and Elizabeth of Hungary include similar representations of the desire to practice poverty.

34. Florentyne allows Kempe to travel with her entourage—composed of Knights of Rhodes, who acted as guides to pilgrims in Rome, and gentlewomen from Assisi—to Rome after the English pilgrims abandon Kempe yet again. In addition to dining with her on Sundays, each week Dame Margaret packs a hamper of foodstuffs and wine to feed Kempe for several days.

35. Benson, *Public Piers Plowman*, calls these "sacramental secular meals" (151–52). Staley describes them as "acts of kindness in the form of . . . social rituals" (*Dissenting Fictions*, 64–65).

actions with other people, and sanctity is identified with the performance of kindness toward others.[36]

In this context, Saint Bridget emerges as the ideal holy woman, a spiritual seeker whose sanctity is matched by her kindness, affection, and humility. Kempe's efforts to live a life of spiritual desire in this world, to bring the New Jerusalem to earth, are intensified by her visit to the room in Rome in which the Swedish saint died.[37] During her visit to Bridget's room, the maid tells Kempe, through a translator, that the saint was "goodly and meke to every creatur and that sche had a lawhyng cher." The chapter dwells on Bridget's warmth, her personality, and, as a German priests calls it, "hir maner of levyng" (chap. 39, 99). Although her revelations are mentioned in the *Book*, it is Bridget's compassionate affability and love that draw particular comment. The host at Kempe's lodgings, for example, tells her that he had not known that Bridget was such a "holy woman" because she was never aloof but rather always "homly and goodly to alle creaturys" (chap. 39, 99). Her holiness is equated with personal warmth and humility. Bridget's kindness and "laughing cheer" become ideals of interpersonal relations in the *Book* and serve as the basis for a categorization of sanctity that includes all believers.

The *Book* develops this idea in relation to Kempe's interactions with unnamed Italian women in two brief vignettes that lead into the description of Bridget's "manner of living." The first is a stylized set piece in which a poor woman with an infant invites Kempe into her home to "sytten be hir lytyl fyer" and drink wine out of a "cuppe of ston," while the baby runs between the two women. As Kempe visits with the woman and her child, she thinks of them in relation to the Virgin and Jesus, which causes her to "brast al into wepyng" (chap. 39, 98).

Although the *Book* often records earthly interactions as triggers for spiritual reflections (the inner city) concerning the saints above (heavenly), chapter thirty-nine goes on to make the human element (the earthly city) central to the interaction as well. At the home of the woman with the stone cup, Kempe responds to both the woman's poverty and the spiritual significance

---

36. Kempe's affinity with Rome was due to the fact that it was not her home: dislocation made it possible for her to teach. On this kind of association see Claire Waters, *Angels and Earthly Creatures: Preaching, Performance, and Gender in the Later Middle Ages* (Philadelphia: University of Pennsylvania Press, 2004), 121–42.

37. Before this, Kempe felt competitive uneasiness toward the saint. In chapter twenty, when Kempe sees Jesus in the guise of the sacrament flickering back and forth like a dove, she relishes the fact that Bridget never saw him "in this wyse" (chap. 20, 58). Kempe struggles with competitiveness repeatedly; see chapters twenty through twenty-two, for example, which include Kempe's mournful comments on her lack of virginity and her checkered past: "Maydonys dawnsyn now meryly in hevyn. Schal not I don so?" (chap. 22, 60).

of the scene. As she weeps, Jesus declares to her, "Thys place is holy" (chap. 39, 98), indicating that Rome's holiness extends beyond its official, and important, status as "an unparalleled well of mercy, a sure remedy for the human burden of sin," to lived experiences of spiritual connection.[38] Although the Italian woman does not understand why Kempe weeps, the woman shows compassion and concern for her visitor (chap. 39, 98). As Kempe leaves, she sees herself reflected in the poor woman and thanks God for her own poverty.

In the second vignette, the *Book* links Kempe's active participation in the earthly city with the city above and the city in her soul. In this instance, a "gentylwoman" from Rome asks Kempe to serve as godmother to a child named Bridget, after the saint (chap. 39, 98).[39] The child, like the poor woman and her male baby in the first vignette, occupies both the earthly city and, symbolically, through her identification with the saint, the city above. Kempe's description of her own behavior, like her description of eyewitness accounts of Bridget's, draws attention to the way that spiritual kinship brings heaven to earth. Here again, Saint Bridget's reputation for kindness toward "alle creaturys" is as important as her prophetic gifts. Through her role as godmother to the child, she links the earthly and the heavenly.

Like the saint, Kempe looks to new kinds of familial networks to sustain her devotional impulses and inclinations. The Roman people become for her, just as they had for Bridget, family and neighbors; she serves this community, and they in turn show her "lofe" and "favowr." Participation in this fellowship is so powerful that even the "maystyr and brothyr" at the English Hospital of Saint Thomas asks her to return after hearing about her reputation "in the cyté." The English community makes her "wolcomear than evyr sche was beforn," shows her "ryth good cher," and is "rith glad of hir comyng" (chap. 39, 98–99).

Rome provided Kempe with an environment for exploring passionate emotional responsiveness and social engagement because, in contrast with English parish life, it was, at least as far as the *Book* is concerned, a place where such responses were valued, encouraged, or, at the very least, accepted. When Roman citizens judge Kempe, as the women did when she stopped wearing white, their judgment—in contrast with the dogged and unchanging animos-

38. C. David Benson, "The *Stacions of Rome*: Rome as City of Divine Grace," unpublished essay (2015), 5.

39. Ties between godparents and biological parents, "compaternitas," were more important than the relationship between godparent and child; see Guido Alfani and Vincent Gourdon, "Spiritual Kinship and Godparenthood: An Introduction," in *Spiritual Kinship in Europe, 1500–1900*, ed. Guido Alfani and Vincent Gourdon (Basingstoke: Palgrave Macmillan, 2012), 1–46.

ity of Kempe's "countrymen"—is temporary; the Italians' opinions are open to change (chap. 34).

The *Book* traces Kempe's efforts to surround herself with people who *feel* the way she does. The "like-minded" people she looks for are emotionally constituted, as she is, in opposition to prevailing normative models (the judgmental, vindictive, and joyless English pilgrims). She and the people she describes as part of her own true fellowship feel, as it is referred to in Marie of Oignies's Middle English life, "high desire of heart."[40]

Even the linguistic barrier between Kempe and the Italians produces goodwill. A conversation in broken English using "syngnys er tokenys and in fewe comown wordys" results in Margaret Florentyne's dinner invitation (chap. 38, 97), and in chapter forty-one, sympathetic Roman women use gestures to comfort Kempe. Despite the lack of verbal understanding, in witnessing her crying, the women "lovyd hir" all the more (chap. 41, 102).

Although her Italian friends approximate this level of high desire, the *Book* nevertheless represents the linguistic barrier between Kempe and the Italians as preventing her from forming completely fulfilling friendships with them.[41] Ultimately, goodwill is not enough. Even as she continues to interact with the Roman people, and feels satisfaction and success in doing so, the *Book* comments repeatedly on the fact that "sche undirstod not" the "speche" of the people with whom she was living and records her longing for "sum crumme of gostly undirstondyng" (chap. 41, 102) that depends on linguistic understanding. Kempe's inability to talk with other people directly is identified as another source of loneliness.[42]

Spiritual Sons: Rome, Bristol, Lynn

Instead of continuing to emphasize her bonds with the Romans, the *Book* turns to Kempe's relationship with the high-ranking German priest Wenslawe to describe her discovery of the kind of friendship that, she finds, staves off loneliness. Although scholars have been preoccupied with Wenslawe and the "language miracle"—Wenslawe and Kempe come to understand each other, despite his inability to speak English and her inability to comprehend German, after two weeks of interaction via an interpreter and prayer—there

---

40. Marie's life is discussed later in this chapter in relation to the third scribe.

41. Armstrong, "Understanding by Feeling," characterizes this idea in terms of a "spirit of intimacy" and places it in the context of later religious movements that focus on emotionality (see esp. 28–34).

42. See Cooper-Rompato, *The Gift of Tongues*, 108–42, on xenoglossia and Kempe's "negotiation of lay status."

is something equally amazing but perhaps less miraculous about their relationship than this. Wenslawe steps aside for a time from his elevated position as one of the "grettest" priests in Rome in order to support Kempe "in hir sobbyng and in hir crying" (chap. 33, 88–89). Before Kempe's appearance he was "hily belovyd, wel cherschyd, and myche trostyd in Rome," but while he supported her, he "sufferd many evyl wordys and meche tribulacyon"; he was attacked by the "enmys of vertu" as severely as Kempe was herself (chap. 33, 89). His decision to support her during her time in Rome had serious consequences.

The *Book* reflects on various ways in which people join Kempe in her community of spiritual, affective intensity. Institutionally superior to Kempe—and therefore possessing greater spiritual authority, Wenslawe is nonetheless transformed by *his* interaction with *her*. He might, in fact, be described as an emotional convert to the life of "high desire" that he experienced, at least vicariously, through Kempe's intervention. She, by contrast, seems to have known that he was always meant to belong to her emotional community; she represents herself as having an intuitive sense of his underlying emotionality and sympathy toward such a life. When she first meets him, according to chapter thirty-three, her impression, based only on having heard him say mass, is that he "semyd a good man and devowte," and again, acting solely only on the basis of this, she is "sor mevyd in spiryt" to go and speak to him (chap. 33, 87–88).

They are quickly united by bonds of affection, as she guessed they would be. Wenslawe welcomes Kempe "ful mekely and reverently as for hys modyr and for hys syster" (chap. 33, 89), and their relationship intensifies during her sojourn in Rome. By the time she must leave the city, they have become spiritual soul mates who, united in "charité," expect to meet again in their "kendly [kindly] cuntré"—heaven—when they have left this "wretchyd" world's "exile" (chap. 42, 104). This ascetic, otherworldly rhetoric is used to describe their parting, but Wenslawe and Kempe's farewells are as effusive as those of the "secular" people criticized in the Jerusalem sequence. They are desperately unhappy to say good-bye: their parting "was ful lamentabyl," the "pur watyrdropys rennyng down" their "chekys" serving as witnesses to their affection (chap. 42, 104).

The *Book* describes Wenslawe's conversion to Kempe's spirituality of high desire by way of their conversations and his "astonishing" experience of witnessing her crying. His growing faith in the truth of Kempe's spiritual gifts is confirmed by an experiment in which he watches her, unobserved, and proves that she cries as "plentyuowsly" when alone as in public. In contrast with her English companions, who would much have preferred that she "neythyr a sobbyd ne cryed" and who never come to understand her, Wenslawe learns to value her tears. Kempe, he discovers, "myth nowt chesyn" to refrain from crying (chap. 33, 89), and when he recognizes this, his own life is altered.

Before his interactions with her, he was already, as chapter thirty-three states, a "good man . . . a good clerke, and a wel lernyd man" (chap. 33, 88), but he did not "belong" to the same world of passionate spirituality that the *Book* represents as Kempe's "natural" affective state. By the time they part, "charité" has "joyned bothyn in oon" (chap. 42, 104). We might think of this as the sympathetic-clerical model of high desire: Wenslawe needed to have his intuitive sense of Kempe's exceptional spirituality confirmed, just as the priest does in the life of Marie of Oignies, discussed later, by observation. This clerical model is repeated in chapter eighty-three when two priests run a similar test on her.

In contrast with the *Book*'s representation of Wenslawe—whose compassion and emotional sympathy are first tempered by doubt—are portrayals of Kempe's interactions with others who seem, like Kempe herself, to have been born with an ecstatic affective character and who embrace emotional expressiveness implicitly. One of these is an English priest who travels from England to Rome simply because he "herd tellyn of" her at home and "longyd hyly to spekyn" with her (chap. 40, 100). His search for Kempe is described as a spiritual quest; his efforts to track her down in Rome are dogged. Eager and attracted to her without having a scientific explanation of her spiritual validity, he goes "speryng [inquiring, with the sense of "tracking down" evidence] and inqwyryng diligently aftyr the seyd creatur" and stops only when he finds her.

The *Book* refers to people who have a natural affinity for Kempe's brand of ecstatic emotional spirituality as her spiritual "sons," as the priest is described.[43] As soon as he finds Kempe, he immediately calls her "modyr" and asks her to "receyven hym as hir sone" (chap. 40, 100). He cares for her in Rome, refusing to allow her to beg any longer, and accompanies her part of the way home to England "as yyf he had ben hir owyn sone born of hir body" (chap. 42, 104). The pope's legate, too, whom Kempe met in Constance, is another "son" who cares for her "ful benyngly" as if she had been "hys modyr"(chap. 27, 72).

Middle English *moder* was a respectful term for an older woman, but the *Book* makes it clear that Kempe's use of familial vocabulary is pointedly emotional and spiritual. Once Kempe leaves Rome, this is most explicit in the portrayal of another of her "sons," Thomas Marchale, who is identified as a

---

43. See Staley, *Dissenting Fictions*, on the term "son" for "Margery's male converts" (121–22).

member of her emotional community and one of the few English pilgrims who becomes a companion in the way.[44]

They meet in Bristol, after her return home from Rome, and on her way to Santiago de Compostela. In Bristol she begins to attract a following, as she does in Rome: some people "wonderyd upon hir" and puzzled over "what hir eyled [ailed]" but others came to "lofe hir and cherschyn hir ryth meche" and invite her to dine with them, listening to her "dalyin in owre Lord" with "ful gret gladnes" (chap. 45, 110). Like the young priest who tracks her down in Rome, Marchale responds to her with immediate enthusiasm and warmth: he has "ful gret gladnes" to listen to her and invites her to dinner repeatedly so that he can talk with her. He has been, he explains to her, a "ful rekles man and mysgovernyd," and this "sore rewyd hym." Marchale is "drawyn" by her conversation and responds emotionally: he is "al mevyd as he had ben a new man" (chap. 45, 110–11). Through their "dalyawns" she becomes a catalyst for his religious transformation.

Marchale's conversion, in contrast with Wenslawe's, is entirely spiritual. In terms of affective expressiveness, he appears to have already been a member of the same emotional community as Kempe, and takes to her particular expressive habits with surprising instinctiveness. Immediately after he becomes a "new man," the *Book* recounts his noisy response to his former life. He cries "terys of contricyon and compunccyon, bothe days and nyghtys, as owr Lord wolde visiten hys hert wyth grace," again like Kempe, "sumtyme" crying so forcefully that "he fel down and myth not beryn in" (chap. 45, 110–11). When God visits "hys hert with grace," Marchale, drawn to extreme emotional expression, runs out to the fields and cries "so sor for hys synnes and hys trespas" (chap. 45, 110).

Marchale's filial identity is based on the similarity between his emotional responses and Kempe's. He is a "son" because he "takes after her" in terms of ecstatic and enthusiastic embrace of spiritual *feeling*. His "maner of werkyng" is the same as Kempe's when she visits Caister's grave in chapter sixty. She "cryed, sche roryd, sche wept, sche fel down to the grownd. . . . Sche had so holy thowtys and so holy mendys that sche myth not mesuryn hir wepyng ne hir crying" (chap. 60, 144). Although the people who see Kempe do this are baffled by her behavior, true "sons" like Marchale are described by the *Book* as instinctively grasping the appropriateness and desirability of such action.

---

44. For more on Marchale, see chapter 1.

They, like Kempe, "wolde not for al this world sey otherwyse than" they "felt" (chap. 60, 147).

Marchale comes as close to Rolle's "fellow in the way" as any character in Kempe's *Book*. After accompanying her to Santiago and back to Bristol, then going with her to Gloucestershire to visit another pilgrimage site, Marchale travels with her to Leicester. Chapter forty-six describes their stop at a "fayr cherch" there, where, upon seeing a crucifix, she "gan meltyn and al to relen-tyn by terys of pyté and compassyown." Marchale is with her as "the fyer of lofe kyndelyd" her heart and she breaks "owte wyth a lowde voys" and cries "merveylowslyche" and "ful hedowslyche that many a man and woman wondryd on hir therfor." He accompanies her and takes part in her devotional responses, and as he does so, his experiences become those of the empathetic reader. Like Marchale, we watch and are invited to identify with Kempe as she "melts" into tears "whedyr sche wolde er not" (chap. 46, 113).

The *Book* draws attention to differences among people who respond to Kempe's expressiveness. Marchale and other "bystanders" who form part of Kempe's emotional community are distinguished from people who ask ques-tions such as that asked by a man who stopped her "at the chirche dore" and "toke hir be the sleve," saying, "Damsel, why wepist thu so sor?" (chap. 46, 113). Kempe's rude answer, "Ser . . . it is not yow to telle," underscores the dif-ference between the curious man and members of her inner emotional circle, like Marchale and the sympathetic reader, who "accompany" her as she "went forth and toke hir hostel and ther etyn her mete" (chap. 46, 113). Marchale and sympathetic readers like him become Kempe's confidants; the intimacy between them is emphasized by the exclusion of bystanders who do not "get" what it is she experiences.

Those who do understand, according to the *Book*, have such a deep spiri-tual and emotional commitment to one another that they will risk their lives for their friends. When Kempe is arrested in Leicester, two of "hyr felaws," Marchale—her "sayd sone"—and another companion, identified only as a man from Wisbeach, Cambridgeshire, are also imprisoned "for cawse of hyr" (chap. 47, 115).[45] Although all three of them are released, the group is alert to the dangers of Leicester and arrange to have another friend and fellow pil-grim, Patrick, escort Kempe out of town. Kempe forgets her bag, and when

---

45. Though hostile toward her before she leaves Bristol, Kempe's pilgrim "fellowship" to Santiago de Compostela is friendlier than her companions on the trip to the Holy Land. Kempe makes close friends on this pilgrimage, including the man from Cambridgeshire and Patrick of Melton Mowbray, Leicestershire.

Patrick runs back to fetch it, he too is nearly arrested. When he finally returns to Kempe's side, she exclaims, "Patryk, sone, wher ha ye ben so long fro me?" Although he replies, "Ya, ya, modyr . . . I have ben in gret perel for yow" (chap. 49, 119), possibly suggesting frustration or impatience with her, the scene ends with jubilation. They ride back to Patrick's house, where they are reunited with Marchale. The three, delighted to be together again, celebrate "in owr Lord al that nyth" (chap. 49, 119).[46]

Kempe's travels, and with them her efforts to find spiritual friendship, dominate chapters twenty-six through forty-nine, making up a quarter of the entire book. Although only four years of her life are covered in these chapters, the extensiveness of the *Book*'s account of that time makes it clear that these experiences were central to her understanding of her search for fellowship.

Home Again

Upon returning home, Kempe resumes her reading tutorials with the young priest whom she met in 1413 (chap. 58). When they first became acquainted, the young priest had been "gretly mevyd to speke wyth hir" and, like the priest in Rome, "speryd of other folke what maner woman sche was" (chap. 58, 140). Satisfied with the answers he received, he and his mother invited Kempe into their home and entertained her with "ryth good cher." During the visit, the priest read a passage from Luke (19:41–44) in which Jesus weeps as he imagines Jerusalem's future destruction. Kempe, in response, started to cry. Although the priest and his mother, like the unnamed Italian women, did not understand what was happening, they decided Kempe was a "good woman" and determined to "spekyn mor wyth hir" (141), initiating the start of their devotional studies and proving, the *Book* explains, that their tutorials were divinely ordained.[47] By the time Kempe returns from Santiago and endures her legal difficulties in Leicester, York, and Beverley (late 1413 through 1418), the young priest has become one of Kempe's "sons," a close confidant, and a vital part of her spiritual life.

---

46. On her way home she stops to see the bishop of Lincoln, Philip Repingdon. Repingdon's endorsement of Wycliffite teachings early in his career might make Kempe's visit, at the moment when she is called a "Lollard," surprising—but this was well after his career as an orthodox clergyman was settled. Kempe's enthusiasm for the bishop seems to have had to do with his support of and involvement with the poor: his feeding, with his own hands, of thirteen poor people daily "steryd" her "to hy devocyon" in chapter fifteen. His excitement to meet her, warm welcome of her, and excited urging that she write down "hir felyngs" in the same chapter indicate that Kempe considered him part of the same fellowship of "high desire" to which she herself belonged.

47. "Ther schal come on fro fer," God tells Kempe (chap. 58, 140), to satisfy her desire to hear books read aloud. The priest's mother is never mentioned again. No explanation for this is given.

During the time when Kempe read with the young priest, until 1420 or 1421, despite suffering abuse at the hands of people who were unable or unwilling to understand her crying, she was sustained by the spiritual communities around her. She became occupied with local politics, listened to sermons, and spent time with friends talking over spiritual ideas and hearing books read aloud. Despite opposition, she found ways to continue pursuing her spirituality of high desire and steadfastly worked to integrate all three of her Jerusalems. Even when the preaching friar forbade her to attend his sermons, because her crying was disruptive, she refrained from withdrawing into her "inner city" and instead declared that she would stay in Lynn: "In this town have I synned. Therfor it is worthy that I suffyr sorwe in this town ther ageyn" (chap. 63, 151).

But Kempe's satisfaction with her experience of spiritual fellowship plummeted after her lister left, probably in 1421, for a new position. Her bitterest complaints about loneliness, quoted at the beginning of the present chapter, refer to this time. In fact, with a few exceptions, details of her life during the years from 1421, after Kempe and her lister's tutorials had ended, until approximately a decade later, in the early 1430s, when Kempe began composing the *Book*, are entirely missing from the account of Kempe's life.[48] After 1421, Kempe spends far less time in long spiritual conversations with other people and, at least as far as we know from the *Book*, no time at all in devotional reading. A brief series of subsequent chapters returns to her involvement in the world—beginning in chapter seventy-four with her interaction with lepers, going on in chapter seventy-five to describe her care of a mentally ill woman suffering from postpartum depression, and followed by chapter seventy-six's record of her long-term care of her elderly and ailing husband following a fall—but most of the rest of book one is taken up with inner experiences and meditations. (Chapters sixty-three through sixty-six dwell on inner conversations with Jesus; chapters seventy-three through eighty-two focus on revelations involving events leading up to the Passion.)

Surprisingly, however, despite this concentration on inner experience, book one ceases, after Kempe's outburst in chapter sixty-nine, to comment on her loneliness. We might expect, given the pattern of withdrawal into her "inner city" developed in the *Book*, that loneliness would go hand in hand with this sequence. Why don't we hear about her loneliness? It is, of course, possible that she had truly become content with spiritual things—that in fact she was satisfied with "Jesus alone" and the heavenly city above and had given

---

48. Kempe's ill health (lasting eight years) and miraculous quenching of the fire at the church in Lynn in 1421 are notable exceptions (chap. 56 and chap. 67).

up on human fellowship—but it seems more likely, given the record of lone-liness found earlier in the *Book*, that she is silent on the subject because her social life, except for the years immediately after her lister left and leading up to her reunion with Alan of Lynn (probably from 1420 through the early to mid-1420s) was in fact *not* as lonely. She was busy caring for her husband until his death in the early 1430s. And, most important for understanding why she wrote the *Book*, she had found human companionship through the experience of working with her scribes.

Kempe turned to reading and writing precisely because they were, for her, communal activities; they were, very literally, ways for her to keep from experiencing loneliness. The *Book* ultimately shows no interest in a life of permanent isolation from other people, and when Kempe is forced to spend time alone, it is described in negative terms. Jesus even apologizes to her for asking her to spend time by herself: "Be not yrke of me in erde to syttyn alone be thiself and thynkyn of my lofe, for I am not yrke of the" (chap. 66, 156).

Obviously, the modern autobiographer can wrestle with her narrative on her own; Kempe, however, needed the assistance of a scribe. Because of this, for Kempe, writing, just like reading, even from the outset, happened *along with* another person. The act of composition was immediately and directly collaborative and, necessarily, accomplished through shared experience. Con-temporary theorists often talk about the "myth" of lone authorship and the "fantasy" of an autonomous self. Kempe, for concrete practical reasons, could never have harbored such illusions; reading and writing both involved com-munal interaction.

Kempe and her first scribe made up the *Book*'s first audience. Linked together through shared emotional understanding, they compose book one as readers and writers simultaneously. As they create the self-in-the-making found in its pages, Kempe's life becomes something they share through creative practice as well as through emotional symmetry. In the process of composition, the *Book* itself functions both as the object that brings them together and as a third "person" created through their collaborative efforts. It is in effect another "companion in the way," as it "speaks" back to its creators about how they have constructed themselves through its vocabulary, struc-ture, and engagement with multiple discourses.

Similarities between the description of the first scribe and the biography of Kempe's son, found in book two, suggest that they may have been one and the same person.[49] At the time when God finally commanded Kempe to

---

49. Hope Emily Allen originally suggested this idea in her notes to the EETS edition.

begin writing the *Book*, she had "no wryter that wold fulfyllyn hyr desyr ne geve credens to hir felingys" until an Englishman living in Germany, "havyng good knowlach of this creatur and of hir desyr," was "mevyd" by the Holy Spirit to come, with his German wife and their child and all their belongings to live with Kempe and write for her (preface, 19). We know that the third scribe (the one who rewrote whatever the draft of book one looked like and wrote, from scratch, all of book two) began his work in 1436 after putting the job off for four or so years. This makes 1432 the terminus a quo for his efforts. As scholars have become increasingly convinced, it is possible that Kempe's son was the first scribe.

Moreover, her biological son was also a spiritual son, like Marchale, and his participation in the same devotional culture of high desire makes him a likely candidate for the work of reporting his mother's revelatory and affective experiences. Book two describes the son's transformation from a lecherous, fashionable young man to one whose "dalyawns was ful of vertu." Changed by the "mervelyows drawt of owr Lord," he embarks on "many pilgrimagys." Significantly, he believes in his mother's spiritual gifts without insisting on observational tests like those conducted by Wenslawe and, on another occasion, by two priests at an isolated church two miles from her home (chap. 83): her son "trustyd meche in hys moderys cownsel" and believed that her manner of living "was of the Holy Gost" (bk. 2, chap. 2, 209–10).[50]

Living in her house and working on the project together meant that this relationship, like that with her lister, allowed for the kind of active, engaged, and ongoing fellowship that Kempe sought. In writing the *Book* together, she and the first scribe are united in the same emotional community of "high desire" that she found in Rome with Wenslawe, with Thomas Marchale and Patrick on the way back from pilgrimage, and with her lister at home in Lynn.[51]

For subsequent readers, the readers whom Kempe and her scribes imagined as themselves-in-the-making, the collaborative creative process is found in reading. The reader in tune with Kempe—that is, the reader whose emotional experiences make her part of the community of high desire, along with

---

50. I have, only half-facetiously, suggested to students that Kempe's daughter-in-law may have been the first scribe. I do not think so (not because of her gender but, instead, on account of the conflicted nature of Kempe's relationship with her, discussed later in this chapter). I recently discovered that Ute Stargardt makes the same suggestion (cited in Lochrie, *Translations of the Flesh*, 127, n. 7) in "The Influence of Dorothea von Montau on the Mysticism of Margery Kempe" (Ph.D. diss., University of Tennessee, 1981).

51. Related to this idea of high desire, see Lochrie's description of Methley's *amor sensibilis* (in conjunction with a later reader's annotation in the manuscript of Kempe's *Book*) in *Translations of the Flesh*, 212–20.

Kempe, her spiritual sons, and the first scribe—also gets a "companion in the way," but instead of the scribe or Kempe it is the *Book* itself. The lonely reader, however—the person who, like Kempe and the first scribe, already feels that her emotional experiences place her outside the "normal" patterns of Kempe's "countrymen"—is not the only reader for whom, and with whom, the *Book* was written. If the first scribe was already, when he became Kempe's amanuensis, a spiritual son, the third, in contrast, was a spiritual-son-in-the-making. Scribe Three becomes another "companion in the way," but he does not start there, and the *Book* identifies him, and individuals like him, with a different reading experience. Readers like the third amanuensis need to be converted to the spirituality of high desire, and this conversion depends on their ability to understand lived experience in relation to the representation of experience found in books.

The Third Scribe

With the death of the first scribe, Kempe lost both a spiritual (possibly biological, too) "son"—a companion in the way—and an amanuensis. When she asked the third scribe to take up the work, it must have been with the idea that he was suitable on both counts. The preface suggests that when she approached him, she was looking for another spiritual son to complete the work with her. She feels great "affecyon" for him, and even before she gives him the draft to look at, they "comown" together about it. Kempe's eagerness to show him a draft, given the long delay in its composition (despite encouragement from high-ranking clerics like Repingdon) and the secrecy to which she apparently swore the second amanuensis, indicates her enthusiastic embrace of the third scribe as another of her spiritual "sons." His feelings, however, were not the same as hers. He tells her he will take up the task with "good wylle," but he puts off the work for several years, anxious about the "evel spekyng" about Kempe and unwilling to tackle the first scribe's difficult hand. The third amanuensis distinguishes himself from individuals like the first scribe and Thomas Marchale. He becomes a spiritual son in the process of rewriting the *Book*, but he did not feel that he was one when Kempe first approached him, sometime around 1431, to take on this work.[52]

---

52. Lochrie remarks that Kempe's scribe was "both her *scriptor* and her reader" (ibid., 119). Staley calls the scribe a "witness" (*Dissenting Fictions*, 34–35). Chapter eighty-three remarks on Kempe's confessors' role in remembering her visionary experiences. When her confessors happened to find her just after a visionary experience, she was able to tell them "meche thyng of the dalyawnce" but she herself "in a schort tyme aftyr" had "forgetyn the most party therof and ny everydeel" (chap. 83, 191).

Put off by the first scribe's handwriting and, more important, worried about the "perel" he might be in if he did take up the task, the third amanuensis resists Kempe's request for four years.[53] Finally, driven by guilt over his promise (but not, apparently, by a sense of urgency about God's command that Kempe's life get written), he suggests Kempe ask an acquaintance familiar with the first scribe's hand to take a stab at writing a fresh copy of the manuscript. She then brings the manuscript to the second amanuensis, makes him promise not to reveal what she has written during her lifetime, and pays him "a grett summe of good for hys labowr" (preface, 20).

This payment draws attention to the difference between the third and second scribes. Kempe asks the third to do the work because she has "gret affeccyon" for him; she recognizes, even before he does, that he belongs to her emotional community. When she asks the second scribe to take up the work, no personal relationship is articulated. Instead, she offers him a "grett summe" of money and begs him not to "bewreyn" the contents of the *Book* until after her death (preface, 20). The second amanuensis gives up after copying over a page, unable to make his way through the first's handwriting. With no personal motivation, the effort to earn the great sum of money must not have seemed worth it. Kempe goes back to the third scribe and begs him to try again.

But the third scribe knew, even if Kempe did not, that his own feelings about her were conflicted; it appears that he did not think of himself as a spiritual son until he *finished* the process of rewriting the manuscript. As he explains in an aside in chapter sixty-two, during the episode in which the famous friar speaks against Kempe and ultimately threatens to "schamyn alle hyr mayntenowrys [supporters]," he initially had "lityl affeccyon" toward Kempe and had "fled and enchewyd [eschewed: turned away from]" her after the friar's

---

Did her confessors keep notes about her visions? There is no evidence that they did, of course, but the passage invites us to speculate about the nature of memory and the record presented in the *Book*.

53. The preface may imply that the first scribe's draft included both German and English words—and perhaps it did—but the emphasis is on the nature of the handwriting itself and not the language: "The booke was so evel wretyn that he cowd lytyl skyll theron, for it was neithyr good Englysch ne Dewch, ne the lettyr was not schapyn ne formyd as other letters ben. Therfor the prest leved fully ther schuld nevyr man redyn it, but it wer special grace" (preface, 19). It seems likely that the third scribe's difficulty lay in part in the use of different cursive hands in England and on the Continent. (On the distinction between Anglicana and secretary—English provinces versus the Continent and London—see Malcolm Parkes, *English Cursive Book Hands: 1250–1500* [Oxford: Clarendon Press, 1969].) The third scribe goes on to complain further that "the boke was so evel sett and so unresonably wretyn." He reads the whole draft "ovyr beforn this creatur every word," and when he does, she "help[s]" him if there is "ony difficulté" (preface, 20). Unless Kempe had learned German later in life (we know at least that when she was in Rome she knew none, since she and Wenslawe needed their language miracle to communicate), it seems unlikely that her help involved translation from German into English.

denunciation of her and her friends. He had determined, in fact, "nevyr to a levyd hir felyngys aftyr" the friar's condemnation (chap. 62, 148–50).

This all changed after he read the life of Marie of Oignies. Although critics often think of Marie's life as a "source" for Kempe's conduct, the *Book*'s references to Marie occur in the context of her life as a text *read* by Kempe and Kempe's clerical friends. This is important because it means that the life functions primarily as a model for *reading*, and only secondarily as a model for conduct. In fact, the life's narrator, in the Middle English version, carefully suggests that readers *refrain* from considering the book as a guide to conduct. Marie's extreme behavior, he explains, is described in order to convey "the feruore" of her devotion—not the excessiveness of her actions. The narrator insists, in regard to Marie's actions, that the "priuilege of a fewe makith not a commun lawe."[54]

In the Middle English version of Marie's life, emphasis is placed on "hygh desyre of herte," "naturel pite," and, especially, on crying as an emotional response to joy and love.[55] The life draws attention to the distinction between the world's understanding of emotional expression and that of people like Marie whose emotions seem to overwhelm them. "Men of the worlde," the life states, never "merueile" if people "crye for angwysshe and ache, as it fallith in a trauelynge woman," but they have "wondir and meruel if any man criynge for ioye of plente of herte maye not holde his pees."[56]

The third scribe appears to have been on the fence about Kempe's experiences of high desire. He was surely attracted to them, or he would never have persuaded her to think of him as a spiritual son or have agreed to work on her book, but he was also frightened by pronouncements against her by clerical authorities and unsure that her uncontrollable weeping was an authentic gift from God. His view of things, he reports, changed entirely after a chance reading of Marie of Oignies's life. Impressed by Marie's "maner of levyng," including the "wondirful swetnesse" she felt when she heard scripture, the "wondirful compassyon" she had when she thought of the Passion, and the "plentyuows teerys that sche wept," the scribe says he came to feel differently about Kempe. Instead of "eschewing" her whenever he could, he began to "lov[e]" her and to trust more and more in her "wepyng" and "crying" than "evyr he dede beforn" (chap. 62, 149–50).

---

54. Marie of Oignies, "Life," 136.

55. Ibid., 137, 135. Marie's tears *appear to others* to be a burden to her but are in reality miraculously refreshing (138).

56. Ibid., 178.

The detail from the life that particularly influenced him, as it did Kempe's longtime friend the "worschepful doctowr" Master Custawns, was its account of the impact of Marie's crying on a priest who asked her to stop crying during his sermons.[57] The priest who had objected to her crying ends up having the same experience of high desire as Marie herself. Kempe's scribe explains that this priest felt such "grace" and "devocyon" when he read scripture and wept so "wondirly" that his vestments were soaked with tears and, like Marie, he was unable to "restryn" his crying (chap. 62, 149).

The scribe's account of the story focuses on the written narrative's ability to validate Kempe's experiences. Marie's emotionality is not a "source" but rather an explanation of a pattern of feeling that, in lived time, feels chaotic and unaccountable but, given the textual precedent, is systematic and understandable. His reading of Marie's life made him understand that Kempe's crying was not a sign of hypocrisy or insanity but instead a kind of emotional experience that he had never encountered before and had never personally experienced. Kempe's ecstatic outpourings became understandable, even appealing, precisely because something very similar *was mentioned in a book*. The third amanuensis enters into Kempe's emotional community by reading books; he in turn helps her compose her own book of consolation because books, they both discover, can change people. [58]

I have argued throughout the present chapter that Kempe sought out fellow spiritual seekers with whom she shared emotional experiences. These were people, to use William Reddy's terminology, who found themselves dissatisfied with the prevailing "emotional regime," the normative mainstream culture of affective experience and expression, and who looked for emotional "refuge" against normative emotional expression.[59] The *Book* includes its

---

57. Master Custawns's version of the story draws greater attention to the fact that the priest had "no conseyt" (no belief) in her crying (chap. 68, 160). In Master Custawns's retelling, Marie prays to God that the priest should have the same feeling of grace that she did so he would understand that her crying was beyond her control (chap. 68, 160). Custawns's priest, like the third scribe's, has a similar experience to Marie's. Although he does not, interestingly, cry, his feeling of "devocyon" at mass is so great after Marie's prayer that "he myth not mesuryn hymself." In turn, instead of despising and disbelieving her, he comforts her (chap. 68, 160).

58. Ji-Soo Kang, "Clerical Anxiety, Margery's Crying, and Her *Book*," in *Global Perspectives on Medieval English Literature, Language, and Culture*, ed. Noel Howard Kaylor and Richard Scott Nokes (Kalamazoo: Medieval Institute Publications, 2007), 41–58, describes the way the scribe is assimilated into Kempe's affective community. See also Ji-Soo Kang, "Lollard Repression, Affective Piety, and Margery Kempe," *Feminist Studies in English* 11 (2003): 1–29. The scribe's reading is not limited to Marie's life; he mentions books he had read including works from her "syllabus," such as *The Prickynge of Love* and Rolle's *Incendium Amoris*, as well as the life of Elizabeth of Hungary (chap. 62), as books that help him understand life.

59. Reddy describes the range of such regimes (and is more heavily invested in the political dimension of these regimes than I am here—although Kempe's difficulties with legal/religious authorities

readers in this community, and by doing so, invites them to see themselves as companions in the way, fellow collaborators who learn to change by reading books.

The third scribe's excitement about discovering that reading changed his emotional understanding convinced him of the necessity of Kempe's *Book*. His conviction that we learn from reading must have put pressure on him, finally, to help her finish writing. As the first book draws to a close, that pressure is inscribed in the *Book* itself. There is, for example, a "progress report" in chapter seventy-two where things in her life begin to be summed up with a sense of finality. The chapter begins, "So be process of tyme hir mende and hir thowt was so joynyd to God that sche nevyr forgate hym. . . . And evyr the mor that sche encresyd in lofe and in devocyon" (chap. 72, 166). With only seventeen more chapters to go, the process of getting to the end has begun in earnest.

The final chapters of book one are primarily directed toward biographical and textual conclusiveness. Kempe's thoughts seem fixed, so complete that in chapter eighty-nine, the last chapter of book one, the scribe can conclude that God "mad hir alwey mor myty and mor strong in hys love and in hys drede and gaf hir encres of vertu wyth perseverawns" (chap. 89, 206). The *Book* itself is, like Kempe, identified as having come to completion: the last sentence begins, "Her endith this tretys," refers to the death of the first scribe who "wrot the copy of this boke," and concludes by stating that everything in the original version has been "trewly drawyn owt of the copy into this lityl boke" (chap. 89, 206). By the end of book one, the completed version of the book has become a source of proof of the validity and significance of the life Kempe had led. As they look back over the book, hearing it read aloud, as the scribe observes they did together, "every word" (preface, 20), became a means of enjoying the fixity of God's comfort—which Kempe had sought throughout her life. In this way the book itself became evidence: proof of the "very trewth schewyd in experiens." The book, not as a process but as a finished object, told her that, despite difficulties, "hir dred and hir hevynes turnyd into gret gostly comforte and gladnes" (chap. 89, 206).

Together, Kempe and the scribe construct the final version of book one as a vehicle for solving the difficulties that believers confronted in relation to both their own spiritual lives and their reading. Book one is a conclusion, an

---

in Leicester and York make it clear that this aspect is also important) in *Navigation of Feeling*, esp. 124–28. See also Rosenfeld, "Envy and Exemplarity": "The *Book* . . . sees ideal community in terms of shared singularity . . . affiliations rooted in a desire to both acknowledge and transcend certain social ideals" (117–18).

answer, and a companion for lonely readers. As such, it provides examples for readers to reexperience, both positive and negative, as if they were the readers' own, but at the same time, it draws attention to the hopefulness of surviving a life that is "upsodown," as the scribe refers to it in the preface, and finding comfort in the progressive nature of spiritual certainty. Both kinds of lonely readers, the Thomas Marchales and the Wenslawes, both of whom Kempe herself identifies with by the time the revision of book one is completed, are invited to reach for the *Book* as a companion in the way, one who will not be "taken" but, instead, will remain permanently with the reader for as long as he needs it.

So why, then, if the final, conclusive, perfected revision worked this way—why, if it was so effective in reaching out to the lonely readers with whom Kempe and her scribes identified and so convincing to the collaborators themselves—did they bother to write book two?

Unfinished Business

The obvious answer, provided in the first chapter of book two, is that, although the "little book" may have been finished, Kempe's life was not over: the second book was to be a description of the grace the "Lord wrowt in hys sympyl creatur" during the time that "sche levyd aftyr" book one's completion (bk. 2, chap. 1, 207): more life, more wonders, more grace. Yet this disruption of the stylistic conclusiveness of book one makes this answer fraught with inconsistency. Chapter one addresses this too, noting that this was, in fact, the case: the conclusion was only temporary.[60] Kempe, it explains, had withdrawn from the world in the earlier book, had "forsakyn the occupasyon of the worlde and was joynyd in hir mende to God." But a crisis arose that forced her to come out of retirement: her son, an assistant to a merchant in Lynn, had been ensnared in the "perellys of this wretchyd and unstabyl worlde," and her goal was to "drawyn" him "owt" of this life (bk. 2, chap. 1, 207).

Book two, a coda to book one, adds Kempe's son's conversion to the miracles that she and the scribe considered "notabyl mater" (bk. 2, chap. 1, 207). Her son's life follows Kempe's own preferred model of spiritual reclamation, beginning, like Thomas Marchale's, Kempe's, and those of some

---

60. See Yoshikawa, who argues for "maturity" and settled spiritual progress (*Margery Kempe's Meditations*, 120–135). Sheila Delaney, by contrast, remarks that it is not a book of devotion but rather an autobiographical account of Kempe's "personal agony": "We are constantly aware of Margery in relation to her society; and it is the peculiar quality of her religious experience—unsatisfying for Chambers; fascinating for us—that it is so inadequate an instrument of transcendence"; see "Sexual Economics, Chaucer's Wife of Bath, and the *Book of Margery Kempe*," *Minnesota Review*, n.s., 5 (1975): 108.

of her favorite saints—Paul, Mary Magdalene—in sin and involving a highly charged spiritual conversion. Kempe and the amanuensis might, however, just as well have left this out if the purpose of adding on to the book was merely to give "solas and comfort" to readers: the son's conversion is just another example of God's mercy toward sinners, and the *Book* is already filled with similar examples.

In a provocative essay about Lollard trial transcripts, Steven Justice argues that passages in the vernacular may have been added to the Latin out of simple boredom on the scribe's part.[61] Along the same lines, it seems to me very likely that Kempe and the scribe resumed their collaboration because they, as much as anything else, were *lonely*. Although the didactic claims in the preface and at the opening of book two are certainly plausible, the return to their labors, after the eager rush of rewriting and anticipation of the final version of the "little book," suggests that the personal enjoyment of the collaboration was at least as important as the spiritual value of more examples from Kempe's life.

The description of Kempe's son's conversion, visit to his parent's house, and death belongs, chronologically, to the previous book. John Kempe died just after his son, and his death is mentioned in chapter seventy-six; and of course if her son was the first scribe, his death, too, is alluded to in the first book.[62] In inserting the story in the first two chapters of book two, Kempe and her amanuensis use it as a bridge between the parts: here is the story of another conversion, of another spiritual son, another companion in the way, admired. The daughter-in-law's actions, by contrast, come on the other side of this bridge between books one and two. After Kempe's son dies, the daughter-in-law stays with Kempe, according to book two, for another year and a half. More important, though, it is the daughter-in-law's representation as a hostile, *un-spiritual daughter* that helps explain what happens to the conclusiveness of book one.

Scholarship about the *Book* is surprisingly quiet as to Kempe's competiveness toward other women. Instead, critics tend to draw attention to her identification with female figures. To be fair, this is partially because many of the saintly figures mentioned in the *Book* are indeed women: Marie of Oignies, Bridget of Sweden, Elizabeth of Hungary, the Virgin Mary, Mary Magdalene, and so on. Yet at the same time, the people in Kempe's community and in her own family—with very few exceptions, such as Margaret Florentyne and the unidentified "worshipful woman" who was "a specyal frende to this

---

61. Steven Justice, "Inquisition, Speech, and Writing," *Representations* 48 (1994): 1–29.
62. John's death may, of course, have been a later addition to draft one.

creatur"—who are described as her closest companions, those with whom she might "makyn ful mery togedyr and han ful good comunycacyon" (chap. 23, 63), were all men.[63] Although much of the *Book* is written from a gendered perspective—the seducer "friend's" treatment of her in chapter four, for example, and her marriage to the Godhead in chapter thirty-five—and it places readers who identify with Kempe in female roles, her efforts to find like-minded friends, as represented in the *Book*, are largely concerned with finding *male* friends.

Women, in contrast, frequently cause Kempe pain: the *Book* includes women like the devout widow who feuds with her for twelve years; the maid who abandons her to care for other people in Rome; the fur-wearing woman in London who "forschod," "bannyd," and "seyd ful cursydly to hir," "I wold thu wer in Smythfeld, and I wold beryn a fagot to bren the wyth; it is pety that thow levyst" (chap. 16, 48); and the "worthy" woman who refuses to allow her to travel with her and tells her so with "rith schort cher" and "rith scharp langage" (bk. 2, chap.7, 223). The women in the *Book* who do support Kempe are usually bystanders or casual acquaintances: the women in Beverley who listen to her stories, weep, and say with "gret hevynes of her hertys, 'Alas, woman, why schalt thu be brent?" (chap. 53, 130); the Roman women who are moved by her tears even though they do not understand why she cries; the innkeeper's wife near Calais who tries to help her find a place on a "wayne" so she does not have to travel alone; the woman in the town near Aachen who arranges for two girls to sleep with Kempe because she is afraid of being assaulted. By contrast, the women she knew intimately and with whom she spent any amount of time are frequently represented in the *Book* in negative terms.

In book one, women with whom Kempe has conflicts are allegorized, in retrospect, as oppressors of the sort whose abuse she re-understands and reconstructs in the *Book*: suffering at their hands becomes proof of God's love. Their cruelty is described, but they are, as actual people, unimportant. This changes, however, in book two, where the fraught nature of Kempe's relationship with her daughter-in-law is presented as disappointing, a cause for serious regret, and a third category of acquaintances and readers emerges.

---

63. In chapter eight, Jesus promises Kempe that her father, husband, and all her children will be saved but makes no mention of her mother. Perhaps her mother was already dead, but the omission is curious and fits with her frequent difficulties with women in the *Book*. Atkinson notes that the *Book* "is populated largely by men" (*Mystic and Pilgrim*, 190–91). Clementine Oliver, too, states that "most of the characters that inhabit Margery's world are men" and notes that Kempe makes "infrequent references to women"; see "Why Margery Kempe Is Annoying and Why We Should Care," in *The Middle Ages in Texts and Textures: Reflections on Medieval Sources*, ed. Jason Glenn (Toronto: University of Toronto Press, 2011), 323–31.

In addition to natural, spiritual sons and converts like Wenslawe, book two attends to those individuals who show no inclination toward "high desire" but whom Kempe nonetheless comes to consider as potential readers.

It seems highly unlikely that all of Kempe's fourteen biological children were male, but whatever the realities of her family life, it is only when her daughter-in-law becomes part of her life story that the *Book* reflects explicitly on her relationship with women in her family. Her recalcitrant daughter-in-law is not a "Margery"—she is not emotionally the same as Kempe and her "sons"—but she is also not a personally insignificant irritant who can be neatly depersonalized and turned into an allegory of oppression. So, for example, when Kempe, following a spiritual "mevyng," decides, without her confessor's permission and against her own wishes (because of her fear of travel), to accompany her daughter-in-law back to Germany and her daughter-in-law repulses her, Kempe's resentment and disappointment are pointedly expressed: "Ther was non so meche ageyn hir as was hir dowtyr," Kempe notes, who "awt most to a ben wyth hir" (bk. 2, chap. 2, 213). "Awt" (ought)—expressing a sense of familial obligation—makes it clear that Kempe's response to the daughter-in-law's opposition differs from her reconstruction of abuse at the hands of other women.

Chapter two of the second book concludes with Kempe's report of speculations about her motivations for sailing to Germany. The final hypothesis—that she does so because it is God's will—is the only one that is not directly concerned with gender. It was "womanys witte" and "lofe of hir dowtyr" that moved her, a "woman in gret age," to go; or it was "charité" toward her daughter-in-law—in fact a debt—that she owed, since the daughter-in-law whom Kempe should "halpyn . . . home ageyn into the cuntré that sche cam fro" had done the same thing for Kempe by leaving Germany and coming to live in Lynn (bk. 2, chap. 2, 213). Although the spiritual explanation is clearly the "answer," the hypotheses based on a woman's love for her daughter-in-law, coupled with Kempe's disappointment at her daughter-in-law's displeasure and lack of gratitude, highlight the passage's concentration on gendered familial relationships in book two.

Although there is no easy solution to the problem of the daughter-in-law's antipathy, book two incorporates Kempe's struggles to garner her daughter-in-law's approval as part of its reflection on the role of her *Book* in her readers' lives.[64] She never wins her daughter-in-law over. When, after a desperate and dangerous sea journey, they arrive in Danzig, Kempe stays with her for "five

---

64. On "female homoerotic bonding," see Kathy Lavezzo, "Sighs and Sobs between Women: The Homoerotics of Compassion in *The Book of Margery Kempe*," in Fradenburg and Freccero, *Premodern*

er six wekys" and finds "ryth good cher of meche pepil for owr Lordys lofe" but is still rejected by her daughter-in-law: "Ther was non so meche ageyn hir as was hir dowtryr in lawe, the whech was most bowndyn and beholdyng to a comfortyd hir yf sche had ben kende" (bk. 2, chap. 4, 215). The daughter-in-law's resistance is a reminder that the conclusiveness of book one could work only for readers who were already convinced. How, book two asks, do you reach recalcitrant readers?

Book two answers this question by refusing the idea of Kempe's life as "concluded." Although the second book is littered with episodes in which Kempe is afraid, fails to reach her goals, and suffers rejection from people she wishes would care for her, it is also insistent about the need to keep trying. In chapter three, as Kempe describes being tossed on the waves and says that her experience of "sorwe and care" had "nevyr" been "so mech beforn" (bk. 2, chap. 3, 214), she nonetheless clings to the idea that perseverance to the end means that there is no conclusiveness until the end. In this chapter Jesus, "spekyng in hir mende," reminds her, "Wavyr nowt in the feith" and "have trost in my mercy" (bk. 2, chap. 3, 214), ideas that recur throughout the *Book* In doing so, he places great emphasis on the results of enacting her faith for herself and for the people with whom she interacts. Instead of giving in to fear and giving up, Jesus reminds her, "thu maist han gret comfort in thi self and mythis comfortyn al thy felaschep wher ye ben now alle in gret drede and hevynes" (bk. 2, chap. 3, 214). Her life of consolation, he tells her, is consoling to her and to the people around her. This dual purpose is, ultimately, the force that drives her to draft the first book, to ask the third scribe to rewrite it, and to begin again by composing book two.

The second book's refusal of conclusiveness makes Kempe's anxiety in the face of danger as important as her steadfastness. Being "evyr . . . afeered"—so important to book two that the phrase occurs here in chapter four and twice again in chapter seven—is part of the lived experience of faith that the stable conclusions of book one gloss over. The second book erases the finality of the first because part of the consolation of Kempe's life, constructed for herself as well as her readers, is that simply failing to "waver" is not synonymous with perfect balance. Kempe's "upsodown" life is a guarantee of comfort not because it offers a model of clear-cut progress but because it shows how lived faith involves stumbling but keeping on nonetheless.

The *Book* offers its consolation to all three kinds of readers, but its gendered positioning of potential readers like the daughter-in-law comes only

---

Sexualities, 175–98. On Kempe's desire to find a "spiritual and actual *famiglia*" in Danzig, see David Wallace, *Strong Women: Life, Text, and Territory* (Oxford: Oxford University Press, 2011), 89.

at the end, in book two, because it is, finally, the point in Kempe's life when she can see herself in people *outside* of her emotional community. The vulnerability that the *Book* allows its readers to view is part of the point: in her daughter-in-law, Kempe glimpses herself in both emotional and gendered terms. Although she goes on to cultivate yet another spiritual son—the young man in chapter ten whose "fervent desir to have undirstondyng" draws him to ask her why she cries (bk. 2, chap. 10, 229)—her anxieties in the second book are largely gendered and focused on her physical vulnerability: her fear of the salacious priests who call her "Englisch sterte" (chap. 6); her inability to keep up with her male companions because "sche was to agyd and to weyke to holdyn foot wyth hem" (chap. 7); her embarrassment on account of her pilgrim dress when she arrives in London (chap. 9); her dependence on a male companion to escort her in safety as she made her way from London back to Lynn (chap. 10).

It would be going too far to say that Kempe recognized herself as a "woman author" or that she thought of herself as empowering her *female* readers, but by the end of book two, it is safe to say that her questioning of the advice found in books of consolation expanded out to include an awareness of the particular gendered contours of spiritual engagement and possibility. Even as she keeps reaching out to spiritual sons, the *Book* represents her longing to find a spiritual daughter to call her own. She never achieves this, and her last potential daughter, a "worschepful woman of London," is cruelly disappointing in her tricky schemes to avoid traveling with Kempe.

It must have seemed to Kempe that this worshipful woman would count as a Roman-level female friend: she listened to Kempe's complaints that she had "no felaschep," "dede hir etyn and drynkyn wyth hir, and made hir ryth good cher" (bk. 2, chap. 7, 221). But the worthy widow was no Margaret Florentyne, and when it came time to leave Aachen, she "sped fast owt" and left Kempe—who was under the impression that she had been invited to travel with her back to London—behind. Like her daughter-in-law's rejection, the worthy woman's causes Kempe "gret hevynes" (bk. 2, chap. 7, 222), but she remains unsure if the cruelty was intentional or an accident. They meet again and this time the woman's dislike for her is unquestionable. After Kempe approaches her "wenyng to a be receyvyd wyth a rith glad cher," the woman tells her she wants nothing to do with her. This rebuke causes Kempe such pain that "sche wist not what to do." Rejected and afraid to go on without fellow travelers, she feels "gret diswer and hevynes, the grettest, as hir thowt, that sche had suffyrd syn sche was comyn owt of Inglond" (bk. 2, chap. 7, 223).

Although Kempe never wins over the worthy woman, the latter nevertheless plays an important role in Kempe's realization, as suggested by her *Book*, that she needed to reach out to people beyond her community of spiritual seekers. The challenge of continuing on was the challenge of interacting with people who did not naturally respond to her ecstatic spirituality. Perhaps she needed, to put it in other terms, to learn not to allegorize her enemies. Maybe future perfection meant aiming at present perfection.

After a series of movements from one ship to another, Kempe eventually ends up on the same one as the worthy woman, the person who, the chapter carefully reminds us, "had refusyd hir as is beforn wretyn." Kempe sees "thorw her cher and cuntenawnce" that the woman "had lityl affeccyon to hir persone." As they travel from Calais to Dover, the widow and the other passengers suffer from terrible seasickness. Kempe, however, had prayed that God "preservyn hir fro voidyng of unclene mater," and while the others are busy "voydyng and castyng ful boistowsly and unclenly," she is able to help the other passengers, who "mervel" at her ability to keep from vomiting (bk. 2, chap. 8, 225).

The scene is described in terms very similar to the earlier episodes of triumph as others abuse Kempe. There is a difference here, however: in this case, she refrains from denouncing the widow and thereby depersonalizing her. Instead, she explains that she helps the violently ill widow "for owr Lordys love." She does this, the chapter remarks tartly, out of "charité" alone because "other cawse had sche non" (bk. 2, chap. 8, 225). Although this looks like an attempt to make herself feel better about the woman's rejection of her, and probably is, it is also about the literal truth: she really does not have any other cause—no personal affection, no obligation for favors done—to help the woman. Oddly enough, it is in its representation of this malicious, unkind, and disgustingly sick woman that the *Book* really seems to acknowledge the limitations of the model of "high desire": acting in God's love requires Kempe to act in charity whether she likes the other person or not.

Kempe's ungrateful daughter-in-law and the violently ill widow allow Kempe to see something, even temporarily, that her desire to escape from loneliness by spending time exclusively with other "fervent" people had obscured: bringing consolation meant seeing herself in people toward whom she felt no thrill of delightful compatibility. The gendered connections she felt with the daughter-in-law and the widow, though ultimately disappointing, provide the opportunity to recognize herself in these women. Her vulnerability to them as people, furthermore, lets her pay attention to that connection despite her "great heaviness" over their rejection.

That lesson gets translated into the book's final prayer, which pushes for the inclusion of all humanity in Kempe's gratitude: "Lord, for alle thos synnys that thu hast kept me fro whech I have not do, and gramercy, Lord, for al the sorwe that thu hast govyn me for tho that I have do, for thes gracys and for alle other gracys whech arn nedful to me and *to alle the creaturys in erthe*" (bk. 2, chap. 10, 234, emphasis added). The second book makes it clear that this kind of expansive identification with others is part of the unfinished and partial nature of Kempe's spiritual exploration and not a conclusion. It is a prayer that, the chapter states, forms part of her ongoing daily spiritual practice for many years. As such, it is part of the *Book*'s identification of itself as the kind of book of consolation that insists its readers see themselves, too, as ongoing: not as they are, but as they will be.

Afterword

> But poems are like dreams: in them you put what you don't know you know.
>
> —Adrienne Rich, "When We Dead Awaken"

Like Kempe's scribe, I cannot resist underscoring the neat conclusiveness of my own "lityl boke" about her treatise of "felyng and werkyng." The emotions that the *Book* rewrites in response to her lifelong search for spiritual joy and comfort, and especially in relation to her reading of books of consolation, are integral to its very first chapter and recur at the very end of the second book. Despair, shame, fear, and loneliness—the emotions that Kempe's reading made central to her literate engagements as a writer searching for comfort—form an arc from the beginning to the end of her *Book*.

Just as the scene of Kempe's breakdown encapsulates all four emotions at the *Book*'s opening, the second book locates all four in its description of Kempe's last journey home. In chapter seven of book two, as Kempe makes her way to Calais with a lone friar, she is "evyr aferd," and experiences "gret drede and hevynes" because they are surrounded by "a perlyows pepil" (bk. 2, chap. 7, 223). The effort of making her way in such conditions brings her very close to the brink of despair: she is "so wery and so ovyrcomyn wyth labowr" that, nearly giving up, she "thowt hir spiryt schulde a departyd fro hir body as sche went in the wey" (bk. 2, chap. 7, 224). When she is on the ship from Calais to Dover, she prays that God will prevent her from vomiting so she will not experience shame by causing her fellow travelers to feel "abhominacyon" (bk. 2, chap. 8, 225). Finally, having reached Dover, she again confronts the intense lack of companionship that plagues her throughout her life. She is the only one among her companions who "myth getyn no felawe to hir ese" and she must, therefore, make her way "be hir self alone, sory and hevy"" (bk. 2, chap. 8, 225).

Despite all this, Kempe perseveres, making her way home, and finding, as she believed she would, that the friends who loved her before she left still loved her "whan sche come hom" (bk. 2, chap. 10, 230). Although I have emphasized the "wobble" in Kempe's steadfastness—that is, in her search for comfort as an ongoing, unfinished process—I might, out of my wish to wrap all this up, conclude, like her scribe, that her *Book* does indeed show, within certain limits, how "hir dred and hir hevynes turnyd into gret gostly comforte and gladnes" (chap. 89, 206), and that it encourages its readers to find consolation in Kempe's textualized life by accepting her invitation to join the community of high desire and follow the instructions for making sense of the human life of upsodownness in just the same way that she has. If there is stumbling and error, there is also joy and satisfaction in Kempe's *Book*—and in her life as it is found there. The comfort she herself finds in this representation of her struggles with negative emotions becomes the comfort that she offers the *Book*'s readers, too. The addition of the second book to the entire "treatise" reminds us that this life is not really completed, but it also promises and reassures that the misery of rejection by friends, the taunting by strangers, and the frightening feeling of having no idea what to do next are just temporary setbacks: Margeries wobble but they don't fall down.[1]

Although a proper conclusion might go on to explain, perhaps, what this tells us about late medieval literate practice or emotions or late medieval devotion on a broader, historical level, this chapter is, instead, like Kempe's second book, a coda to the previous chapters; that is, it is a freestanding defense, or at least an explanation and extension, of the reasons why this is the book that it is.

In particular, it seems important to draw attention to the great emphasis I place on the *Book* as a written work. The topics of my chapters are about emotional experience, but my method of analysis is explicitly literary / textual and only secondarily historical. What I mean by this is that my attention is drawn to form and language: *How* does the *Book* say what it says? Why is *this* the book that Kempe finally writes? I am no longer certain whether this is a cunningly avant-garde practice (the new formalism) or ploddingly "old

---

1. See Szell, "From Woe to Weal and Weal to Woe," which traces the "pattern of repeated loss followed by gain" in the *Book* (79). The reference to Weebles is, of course, my own. See also Denise Despres, *Ghostly Sights: Visual Meditation in Late Medieval Literature* (Norman, Okla.: Pilgrim Books, 1989), describes the "organic, experiential movement" of the *Book* and argues that this shows that "the path to salvation is cyclical" (83).

school," but it is, regardless, what I think yields the most interesting results in relation to Kempe's *Book*.[2]

Several years ago I wrote an essay about the *Book* as a "treatise," the word Kempe and her scribes use to describe their "little book," instead of an autobiography. My interest in the subject came directly out of the word Kempe and her scribes used. Why call it a treatise if it was not a treatise? And in any case, what exactly did it mean for them to call it one? Instead of assuming that this was an autobiography, I found myself wondering if "treatise" let me see something that the idea of autobiography had obscured. I concluded that it does: it let me think about the *Book* as offering some kind of instruction that differed dramatically from our usual ideas about autobiography. As I taught and reread the *Book* over the years, studied the secondary criticism, and wrote several other pieces about Kempe, I found myself returning to the ways in which ideas were expressed in the *Book*. The present account of Kempe's writing comes out of many years of trying to notice how the nature of the *Book*'s literariness—as made up of particular words in a particular order—was as important to understanding what the *Book* is as ideas about power, authority, vernacular theology, heresy, and gender.

Other theoretical interests, of course, shape my analysis in particular ways. The work I did on literate practice, for example, in my first book means that I understand close analysis as allowing us to see, in detail, how individuals enact (perform) their literacy. It also makes me stubborn about treating literate practices discretely. To make a claim about Kempe's writing, I try to make sense of as much as I could sort out about Kempe's consumption of texts (as an aural reader and as a passive consumer of information from books—something like inhaling secondhand smoke). I worried over the issue of her Latinity or lack thereof, thought further about the relationship between dictation and composition, and looked for ways to think about the nature of the delay in the *Book*'s writing.

Furthermore, my curiosity about emotions as expressed in different ways at different, historical points means that William Reddy's work is keenly interesting to me and, closer in time period, Barbara Rosenwein's allows me to see my work as part of a larger trend in medieval studies.[3] Farther afield, but intellectually engaging and stimulating to me, is recent work loosely labeled

---

2. See Andrew Galloway, "Introduction: The Medieval Literary," in *Answerable Style: The Idea of the Literary in Medieval England*, ed. Frank Grady and Andrew Galloway (Columbus: Ohio State University Press, 2013), 1–12. In 1991 Nancy Partner drew attention to the "poetics of Margery's *Book*" and its "private symbolism" ("Reading *The Book of Margery Kempe*," 45) but also observed that the language of the *Book* had rarely been discussed in poetic and structural terms (33).

3. Krug, "Natural Feeling and Unnatural Mothers," is about this subject, for example.

"affect theory," which emphasizes the embodiedness of emotional experience and, following Deleuze's reading of Spinoza, frequently makes a sharp distinction between conventional designations of emotions and affect, which these theorists generally see as intrapersonal, experiential states of interaction. For medievalists schooled in scholastic distinctions between anima, affectio, and passio, contemporary theory is often disorienting but also thrilling in its similar interest in bodily transformation (or the lack thereof) when distinguishing between affect and emotion.

While this theoretical material helped me think about Kempe's *Book*, I have, however, been primarily concerned in the present book with the ways that *the language of its writing* tells us about Kempe's literate practice and emotional experiences. Although some of the writers whose works Kempe and her lister read display a considerable awareness of distinctions between passionless affects and emotional responses that entailed bodily transformation, her *Book* shows no interest in this whatsoever. Rather, like a great deal of late medieval literature, Kempe's *Book* represents emotion in ways that appear to be very similar to modern understandings of the experience as both personal and communal, embodied, and psychological, with little if any concern with philosophical or scientific theory. Although there is a great deal left to discover in terms of affect theory, and I am eager to read other scholars' work in the area of theories of emotion in the Middle Ages, *Margery Kempe and the Lonely Reader* turns, instead, to literary and linguistic structure to explain how its author came to write her *Book*.

Linguistic patterning, the idea that the choice of words and their placement in a book tells us more than a simple summary of ideas does, is central to this book's analysis. For example, the origin of the chapter on despair is similar to my essay distinguishing between a "treatise" and an autobiography. Scholars of medieval literary works are familiar with the term "wanhope," which appears in widely studied works such as *Piers Plowman* and the morality play *Mankind*, which I discuss in the chapter on fear. Was Kempe's despair "wanhope"? Were they the same thing? Working through as many references to "despair" as I could find, I saw that it was used in a precise theological sense in some cases, but also, in others, and sometimes in the same works that defined it with precision, it referred, loosely, to the same emotional condition with which we associate it today. This is similar to the clinical and casual definitions of "depression" in modern speech, and that similarity reminded me to see if Kempe's *Book* also relied on both the technical and the emotional in its definition of her condition. (I argue, as is now obvious, that it does.)

The episodes of despair in Kempe's *Book*, of course, occurred at particular points in the narrative. My chapter on despair is concerned with the structural implications of beginning with this episode of mental breakdown. This would be important in any work, but it seemed to me especially vital to consider it in a *Book* that announced its author's "origins," a starting point for the textualized life that her readers encounter. A similar concern with structure exerted force on my chapter about shame. There, I catalogued episodes that involve abuse and humiliation and noticed distinct differences between those that were allegorized in retrospect and those that continued to feel rawly shameful. In doing this cataloguing, I began to think about the reader in relation to the stories of abuse and to ask how we were to think, especially, about point of view as the stories are told. If readers refused the invitation to experience Kempe's (retrospective) glee, how did that disrupt the narrative experience? If readers felt the shame of, for example, Kempe's acquiescence to her seducer's demands and subsequent rejection and humiliation, what resources did the reader discover in the *Book* that kept shame from canceling the thrilling pattern of identification?

As I gathered passages in which the word "shame" appeared and collected related words—synonyms and antonyms—I noticed many passages in proximity to the representation of shameful and painful experiences in the *Book* that acted like refrains to songs. After collecting as many of these proverbial or verse-like phrases as I could find, I sorted them into thematic groups and discovered, in some cases, that the "refrains" were repeated, or very nearly repeated. As I became more interested in the sound of these phrases—my attention drawn to sound largely because of the phrases' repetition—I started to wonder if thinking about Kempe's prose in stylistic terms might help me see more clearly why the phrases were repeated. Going back through the *Book* again, I found heavy alliteration and a number of rhythmic and rhyming passages. I discuss many of these rhyming lines in "Shame," but there are several more, including one that I did not discuss earlier but which is worth including to draw attention to the importance of poetic style in the *Book*:

> For I schal make the buxom to my wil
> That thu schalt criyn whan I wil
> And wher I wil
> Bothyn lowde and stille.
> For I telde the, dowtyr,
> Thu art myn

And I am thyn,

And so schalt thu be wythowtyn ende.

(chap. 77, 174)[4]

In Hope Emily Allen's deeply learned, influential, and extensive notes to the EETS edition of the *Book*, she remarks, with her usual authority, that poetic effects such as alliteration and rhyme are rarely used in the *Book*. This is simply not true.[5]

When I discuss the incorporation of poems and rhyming phrases in the *Book*, my aim is to demonstrate that their inclusion has a cumulative effect on the reader. Just as the phrases become "part" of Kempe, explaining how she feels to herself, they are internalized by the *Book*'s readers and produce a particular emotional impact in which their very sound moves the reader to experience the same hopefulness expressed by the *Book*'s author. This is an antidote to the un-narrativized accounts of shame that might be read as preventing the reader from optimistic responsiveness. The chapter on fear argues that the dynamic narrative of fear that offers Kempe and her readers a pleasurable, rather than pain-filled, experience of danger and uncertainty performs a similar replacement, but in this case the substitution is visual instead of aural. The literary models in this chapter are dramatic: medieval morality and cycle plays that position the central, often female, figure in a crisis from which she is rescued.

Structurally, the representation of fear in the *Book* is episodic and recurring. Although an episode concludes, the structure is cyclical and resists both linearity and conclusiveness. Repetition forms the dramatic principle in these scenes, and the *Book*'s return to the same episode, at least in structural terms, is strikingly opposed to ideas of character as involving organic growth and

---

4. This is Jesus speaking to Kempe in the chapter in which he compares his love to an earthquake.

5. Concerning the passage describing Jesus' solution (he will teach her himself) to Kempe's lack of understanding when she attended sermons by German preachers in Rome, Allen states: "The frequent rhythm and alliteration in this passage should be compared with that which is perceptible in [ten lines in chapter forty-two, the passage in which Kempe and Wenslawe must part]. No other similar passages have been noted, and no clue is given as to the element in Margery's reminiscences (probably a special emotion connected with her mysticism in some way) which has made her break out into these patches of poetical style. In each example she is describing a contact with 'Duchemen'" (EETS, 305, n. 98/20–35). Allen's suggestive speculation about alliteration as keyed to passages concerned with Germanic mysticism is fascinating, and compels the note's reader to think about the relation between this limited application of poetic style and nationality. As interesting as the assertion is, however, it is nonetheless entirely wrong. The *Book* is filled with alliterative passages (and many of them have nothing to do with Germans), including Kempe's tale about the bear and the pear tree ("al floreschyd wyth flowerys and belschyd and blomys ful delectabil") as well as the preface ("Sadly he trad it and dewly he went"; "And thei alle that sche schewed hyr secretys unto seyd sche"). Nor is her remark about rhythm in any way accurate.

development. This, too, is a dramatic principle that can be found in medieval moralities and, moreover, in literary works from the period that are often considered more sophisticated than drama, such as the Prologue to Chaucer's *Pardoner's Tale*. Like fear, loneliness is also episodic, but its structural patterning, in contrast, is only partially recurring. Instead, although episodes of disjunction among Kempe's three "cities"—inner, outer, above—are repeated, there is also a structural progression that shapes the *Book* even as it allows for these recurrences: from familial separation, to fellowship based on common activities (pilgrimage), to the embrace of similarly fervent individuals, to the inclusion of "converts," and, finally, to the difficult work of trying to reach out to people for whom she feels no affection whatsoever.

In the chapter on loneliness, the vocabulary of "high desire" employed by Kempe and her spiritual sons can be found in the *Book* itself, but it also occurs in other texts to which Kempe and her scribes refer. The Middle English life of Marie of Oignies is particularly significant in this regard, and in rereading the life, I was able to see how it was important intertextually and not simply as a source from which Kempe copied. Instead, the Middle English life modeled fervent, ecstatic emotionality, and its modeling resonated with the emotional responses of Kempe and people like the third scribe and her friend Master Custawns who read the life. Readers entered into a dynamic relationship with the text. This meant the book became an active but not necessarily determining force in their lives. We can see this very clearly in the scribe's reevaluation of Kempe in light of his reading.

The devotional books that Kempe read with her lister, all of which might, in a loose way, be called books of consolation, had the same dynamic potential as Marie's life. In trying to understand Kempe's *Book*, I worked with as many of the likely texts from her "syllabus" as I could: those explicitly named, those to which the *Book* directly alludes or at least hints at alluding to, and other books that might have fallen under the category of "good" books "of hy contemplacyon." My purpose was to understand how these books might allow me to see why Kempe needed to write her own book: What, I kept asking, was the dynamic relationship between Kempe and the books of consolation? Was there something in them that compelled her to write in response? And if there was, how did she frame her response? For many years I thought about Kempe's *Book* as working through emotional experiences that were largely negative in an effort to align herself with the "positive power of negative thinking" on which books like Hilton's *Scale* and the *Prickynge* depend. I still think that this was one of the ways she responded to her reading and that some of the language in the *Book* occurs precisely because her thinking about such negativity was not consistent. Why should it be?

But, finally, after paying close attention to the particular strands of negative emotional experience in the *Book* and in the devotional writings Kempe may have read, I found that despite frequent expressions of conformity with the basic principles of negative thinking, Kempe's *Book*, perhaps without clear awareness of what it is doing, constantly reframes the advice found in such books. She would no doubt have agreed with the basic principles of these books if asked: one is worthless, should feel shame, deserves to be afraid, must live in isolation. Yet the *Book* nonetheless resists these principles even when it claims to be in agreement with them.

The best example of this, which I discuss in "Shame," is the reframing of "have mynde of thi wykkydnes and thynk on my goodnes" in rhyming, comparative terms:

> Lord, for thy gret goodness
> Have mercy on al my wykkydnes
> As wistly as I was nevyr so wykkyd
> As thu art good
> Ne nevyr may be
> Thow I wolde,
> For thu art so good
> That thu mayst no bettyr be.
>   (chap. 85, 196)

In Kempe's reframing, the difference between God's infinite goodness and her wickedness, however wicked she is, is so great that it overturns the purpose of the advice, which is to encourage self-loathing. The point is underscored by the lack of a rhyming partner for "wykkyd." The connection between "goodnes" and "wykkydnes" formed in the first two lines is disrupted by "wykkyd's" isolation. Instead, the rhyming triplets "good," "wolde," and "good" dominate the sounds of the line; the perfect rhyme of "be" and "be" gives the reframing its own infinite and complete status without batting an eye at the changes wrought. Rhyme itself makes the nature of the comparison more precise, more distinct, and more significant in its ability to convey the sense of emotional resistance found in this rewriting of the consolation genre.

The verse revision marks an important aspect of Kempe's rewriting of the books she read: her *Book*'s re-imagining of the truths embedded in books of consolation is driven by *formal literary* considerations and not just by some abstract sense of "content." Ideas in books are always shaped by their linguistic packaging. The rhyme just noted, for example, might be described in terms of its content—as I label it, it is a comparison between the infinite goodness of God and Kempe's less than infinite wickedness—but even in calling it a "comparison," I describe the linguistic shapes and relations among the words.

More broadly, the poem is part of the *Book*'s response to the devotional lyric as a genre. Late medieval religious lyrics were repositories of the kind of "high desire" that defined Kempe's emotional community. These poems are emotive rather than philosophical. They stimulate affective responses in their audiences and show little interest in deeper theology. They tend, like Kempe's poem, to concentrate on aural patterning rather than logic to move their readers. For Kempe, they were at least as important in forming her emotional understanding as were texts like the lives of Marie of Oignies or Elizabeth of Hungary that made their claims through narrative.

Kempe was familiar with a range of literary and linguistic forms, and much of her knowledge must have come through informal channels. In addition to religious lyric, which was popular, common, and widespread in the same way that lines from popular songs and advertisements are today, the *Book* demonstrates intimate knowledge of drama, which I discuss in the chapter on fear. The moralities and cycle plays in particular, as I argue in that chapter, gave Kempe a structural framework for understanding herself in relation to other people and God, a visual and emotional pattern for seeing herself in context. Another genre, the prose tale, was also familiar to her and performed a similar structural function. The prose tales that made up collections used by preachers such as the *Gesta Romanorum* and the *Alphabet of Tales* provided Kempe with the means for placing herself, again a structural placement, in a position of interpretive linguistic authority.[6]

Tales, like jokes, follow the setup/premise plus punch line structure. Kempe's story about the pleasure of free abuse in chapter thirteen, for example, follows this structure: the premise is the man's need, at his confessor's orders, to pay men to chide him for his sins; the man finds himself, incidentally, among a crowd of great men who verbally abuse him; the punch line is the answer to one of the abuser's questions, "Why lawhyst thu, brothel, and art thow gretly despysed?": "A, ser, I have a gret cause to lawh, for I have many days put sylver owt of my purse . . . to chyde me for remyssyon of my synne, and this day I may kepe my sylver in my purs" (chap. 13, 41). Tales appear frequently in the *Book*: for example, the priest and the elderly bookseller (chap. 24); the priest, the bear, and the pear tree (chap. 52); the lady damned/the bailiff saved

---

6. *The Early English Versions of the Gesta Romanorum*, ed. Sidney J. Herrtage, EETS e.s. 33 (London: Oxford University Press, 1962); *The Alphabet of Tales*, ed. Mary Macleod Banks, 2 vols., EETS o.s. 126–27 (London: K. Paul, Trench, Trübner, 1904–5).

(chap. 54). By following this structure, these tales are weighted toward the creation of emotional identification between the audience and the storyteller/ the deliverer of the punch line. They provide a linguistic structure that packs emotional weight through form and diminishes the possibility of multiple points of view: to use Kempe's example in chapter thirteen, the punch line wrests all of the power from the abusers and places it all in the hands of the penitent/Kempe.

Medieval collections of tales, like the *Gesta Romanorum*, for example, combine the structure of the tale, as I have described it, with an allegorical moral, appended after the tale. Kempe's tales usually identify the moral in relation to the circumstances in which she finds herself: the penitent's punch line in chapter thirteen, for instance, is used by Kempe to make a point about her own abuse at the hands of the monks in Canterbury. But the allegorization of narrative is also used in the *Book*, especially in relation to the scorn and abuse that Kempe experiences, retrospectively, as spiritual gain. Instead of the spiritual allegories appended to tales such as those in the *Gesta Romanorum*, in which the stories are interpreted as conveying truths about the soul and God, Kempe's moralizations are personally protective.

The *Book*'s incorporation of parables and quotations from scripture is similarly personalized. Kempe's application of scripture to herself occurs through identification with particular kinds of characters in these stories, like Peter or the woman taken in adultery, who she becomes through a sense of emotional sameness and situation, and through direct application of scriptural promises to herself. In chapter seventy-two, incidentally one of the *Book*'s most conclusive chapters, Kempe combines the person of Paul and the language of scripture and claims both his words and his life as her own. The chapter cites Romans 8:28 and identifies it with Paul as a character: "Ther was neithyr worschep ne preysyng, lofe ne lakkyng, schame ne despite that myth drawyn hir lofe fro God, but, aftyr the sentens of Seynt Powle, 'To hem that lovyn God al thyng turnyth into goodnes,' so it ferd wyth hir" (chap. 72, 167). Paul's traditional characterization as the worst of sinners but, nonetheless, a convert to whom God promises, as the Digby *Conversion of Saint Paul* remarks, "socor in every dere [harm]," is used to underscore the dramatic structure of Kempe's identification (Bevington, 672).[7] "Seynt Powle's" person—a "chosen vessell" who will suffer "many sharpe shoures" for God—is tied in the passage to the quotation from Romans, which Kempe claims as her own (Bevington, 673).

---

7. See Utter, "Fawty and Falce."

Paul's life and his language, too, become Kempe's own, an explanation and extension of her identity.[8] The devotional works on Kempe's reading list also encouraged identification but did so, whether intentionally or not, in terms which implied that such identification was bound by distinctions between the reader and the author. When the *Prickynge*, for example, provides its readers with "how to" advice, the author imagines those readers as his contemporaries. The connection that the *Prickynge* offers its readers comes via its use of the second person; the narrative perspective places the author in direct relation to the reader: the *Prickynge*'s "I" speaks to its reader as "you." Intimacy is created as the author provides the reader with exercises to work through, suggesting similarity between author and audience, but the relationship created is also exclusive to the "I" and the "you" and bound by the powerful implied agreement: "I" am helping "you," but if you agree to follow my advice, it means that "I" am also distinct from and superior to "you" in knowledge and experience.

Kempe's *Book* refuses this distinction. Her strenuous insistence on her own singularity in no way excludes her readers or places them in a subordinate position. The *Book* is filled with "ifs" and "whens" that make the truths of Kempe's spirituality identical with those of the reader. In chapter seventy-three, Jesus tells her "Yyf" people "wyl forsakyn her synne and ben in ful wylle no more to turnyn ageyn therto but ben sory and hevy . . . and wil don dew penawnce . . . thei schal have *the same pardon* that is grawntyd *to thiselfe*" (chap. 73, 169 emphasis added). The reader needs to do exactly what Kempe does. The *Book*'s "how to" advice is the same for reader and writer. This, the *Book* tells its readers, is reassuringly easy to do. When the "gret lordys men" in Lincoln ask her if they will be damned or saved in chapter fifty-five, the simplicity of divine requirements is part of the point. She tells the men that if they "wil not levyn" their sin, then they will be damned. If, however, they will be "contrite and schrevyn of" sin, perform penance, and "wil no mor to turne" to sin "agen," she tells them, "I dar wel say ye schal be savyd" (chap. 55, 135). Their disappointment at the simplicity of the advice— "What, canst thu noon otherwise tellyn us but thus?"—underscores the tale's moral: they do not need Kempe's revelations, feelings, or second sight for this truth to be known.

And yet the *Book*'s representation of the clarity of truth in no way erases the difficulty of finding ways to live that truth. The explanatory mission

8. Kuczynski, *Prophetic Song*, demonstrates this dynamic in relation to the psalmist David (51–77).

of books of consolation is what made them so popular in the later Middle Ages, and the urgency with which readers approached the question of finding consolation and community is not to be underestimated. Such urgency is written into the *Book* as it represents Kempe's constant struggle to find this truth for herself. God urges her to venture out into the world and, especially, to talk to strangers about her experiences and spiritual longings. As Jesus tells her in Norwich, "Speke to this man, speke to this man" (chap. 44, 107).

The comfort that the *Book* offers its author and its readers comes, finally, through the linguistic representation of Kempe's ongoing attempts to talk to God, herself, and her fellow believers/readers. How she says what she says is as important to her as the things she tells us. If the *Book* reaches out and speaks to us now, it does so by way of its words and not merely by way of historical categories and ideas. If we want the consolation the *Book* offers, no matter what modern readers believe that consolation is, it has to come through the words found in the *Book*.

❦ BIBLIOGRAPHY

Aelred of Rievaulx's De Institutione Inclusarum. Edited by John Ayto and Alexandra Barratt. EETS 287. Oxford: Oxford University Press, 1984.

Aers, David. "The Self Mourning: Reflections on *Pearl*." *Speculum* 68 (1993): 54–73.

Alfani, Guido, and Vincent Gourdon. "Spiritual Kinship and Godparenthood: An Introduction." In *Spiritual Kinship in Europe, 1500–1900*, edited by Guido Alfani and Vincent Gourdon, 1–46. Basingstoke: Palgrave Macmillan, 2012.

Alighieri, Dante. *The Divine Comedy*. Volume 1, *Inferno*. Rev. ed. Translated by Mark Musa. New York: Penguin, 2003.

An Alphabet of Tales. Edited by Mary Macleod Banks. EETS o.s. 126–27. 2 vols. London: K. Paul, Trench, Trübner, 1904–5.

Ancrene Wisse. Edited by Robert Hasenfratz. TEAMS Middle English Texts Series. Kalamazoo: Medieval Institute Publications, 2000.

Appleford, Amy. *Learning to Die in London, 1380–1540*. Philadelphia: University of Pennsylvania Press, 2014.

Armstrong, Elizabeth Psakis. "'Understanding by Feeling' in Margery Kempe's *Book*." In McEntire, 17–34.

Arnold, John, and Katherine J. Lewis. *A Companion to* The Book of Margery Kempe. Cambridge: D. S. Brewer, 2004.

Ars Moriendi. STC 786. 1491.

Asad, Talal. *Genealogies of Religion: Discipline and Reasons of Power in Christianity and Islam*. Baltimore: Johns Hopkins University Press, 1993.

The Assembly of Gods. Edited by Jane Chance. TEAMS Middle English Texts Series. Kalamazoo: Medieval Institute Publications, 1999.

Atkinson, Clarissa. *Mystic and Pilgrim: The Book and the World of Margery Kempe*. Ithaca: Cornell University Press, 1983.

Auer, P. Albert. *Johannes von Dambach und die Trostbücher vom 11 bis zum 16 Jahrhundert. Beiträge zur Geschichte der Philosophie und Theologie des Mittelalters: Texte und Untersuchungen* 27. Münster: Verlag der Aschendorffschen Verlagsbuchhandlung, 1928.

———. *Leidungstheologie im Spätmittelalter*. St. Ottilien: EOS Verlag der Erzabtei, 1952.

Auerbach, Erich. "Passio als Leidenschaft." In *Gesammelte Aufsätze zur romanischen Philologie*, 161–75. Bern: Francke, 1967.

Augustine. *De Dono Perseverantiae*. PL 45:993–1034.

Baltussen, Han, ed. *Greek and Roman Consolation: Eight Studies of a Tradition and Its Afterlife*. Swansea: Classical Press of Wales, 2013.

———. Introduction. In Baltussen, xiii–xxv.

Barasch, Moshe. *Gestures of Despair in Medieval and Early Renaissance Art*. New York: New York University Press, 1976.

Baraz, Yelena. *A Written Republic: Cicero's Philosophical Politics.* Princeton: Princeton University Press, 2012.

Barratt, Alexandra. "Dame Eleanor Hull: The Translator at Work." *Medium Aevum* 72 (2003): 277–96.

——. "*Stabant matres dolorosae:* Women as Readers and Writers of Passion Prayers, Meditations and Visions." In *The Broken Body: Passion Devotion in Late-Medieval Culture,* edited by A. A. MacDonald, H. N. B. Ridderbos, and R. M. Schlusemann, 55–71. Groningen: Egbert and Forsten, 1998.

——. *Women's Writing in Middle English: An Annotated Anthology.* London: Longman, 1992.

Barron, Caroline. *London in the Later Middle Ages: Government and People.* Oxford: Oxford University Press, 2004.

Barthes, Roland. *Image-Music-Text.* Translated by Stephen Heath. New York: Hill and Wang, 1977.

——. *S/Z: An Essay.* Translated by Richard Miller. New York: Hill and Wang, 1975.

Bartlett, Anne Clark. *Male Authors, Female Readers: Representation and Subjectivity in Middle English Devotional Literature.* Ithaca: Cornell University Press, 1995.

Benson, C. David. *Public Piers Plowman: Modern Scholarship and Late Medieval English Culture.* University Park: Pennsylvania State University Press, 2004.

——. "The *Stacions of Rome*: Rome as City of Divine Grace." Unpublished essay, 2015.

Besnier, Niko. *Literacy, Emotion, and Authority: Reading and Writing on a Polynesian Atoll.* Cambridge: Cambridge University Press, 1995.

Betson, Thomas. *Treatyse to Dyspose Men to be Vertuously Occupyd.* Amsterdam: Theatrum Orbis Terrarum, 1977.

Bevington, David, ed. *Medieval Drama.* Boston: Houghton Mifflin, 1975.

Bhattacharji, Santha. "Medieval Contemplation and Mystical Experience." In *Approaching Medieval English Anchoritic and Mystical Texts,* edited by Dee Dyas, Valerie Edden, and Roger Ellis, 51–59. Cambridge: D. S. Brewer, 2005.

Bishop, Ian. *Pearl in Its Setting.* Oxford: Blackwell, 1968.

Bishop, Louise M. *Words, Stones, and Herbs: The Healing Word in Medieval and Early Modern England.* Syracuse: Syracuse University Press, 2007.

Blanchfield, Lyn A. "Prolegomenon: Considerations of Weeping and Sincerity in the Middle Ages." In *Crying in the Middle Ages: Tears of History,* edited by Elina Gertsman, xxi–xxx. New York: Routledge, 2012.

Bloomfield, Morton. *The Seven Deadly Sins: An Introduction to the History of a Religious Concept.* 1952. Reprint. East Lansing: Michigan State University Press 1967.

The Boke of Comforte agaynste all Tribulacyons. STC 3295. 1505.

The Book of Tribulation. Edited by Alexandra Barratt. Heidelberg: Carl Winter, 1983.

Brantley, Jessica. *Reading in the Wilderness: Private Devotion and Public Performance in Late Medieval England.* Chicago: University of Chicago Press, 2007.

Breen, Katharine. *Imagining an English Reading Public, 1150–1400.* Cambridge: Cambridge University Press, 2010.

Brown, Carleton, ed. *Religious Lyrics of the Fifteenth Century.* 1939. Reprint. Oxford: Clarendon, 1952.

Bryan, Jennifer. *Looking Inward: Devotional Reading and the Private Self in Late Medieval England.* Philadelphia: University of Pennsylvania Press, 2008.

Caciola, Nancy. *Discerning Spirits: Divine and Demonic Possession in the Middle Ages.* Ithaca: Cornell University Press, 2003.

Carlson, Erik. "The Gothic Vocabulary of Fear." *Journal of English and Germanic Philology* 111 (2012): 285–303.

Cathcart, Kevin J. "The Phoenician Inscriptions from Arslan Tash and Some Old Testament Texts." In *On Stone and Scroll: Essays in Honour of Graham Ivor Davies*, edited by James K. Aitken, Katharine Julia Dell, and Brian A. Mastin, 87–99. Berlin: Walter de Gruyter, 2011.

Catto, Jeremy. "Religious Change under Henry V." In *Henry V: The Practice of Kingship*, edited by G. L. Harriss, 97–115. Oxford: Oxford University Press, 1985.

Chaganti, Seeta. *Medieval Poetics of the Reliquary: Enshrinement, Inscription, Performance.* New York: Palgrave Macmillan, 2008.

The Chastising of God's Children. Edited by Joyce Bazire and Eric Colledge. Oxford: Blackwell, 1957.

Clanchy, Michael T. *From Memory to Written Record, England, 1066–1307.* Cambridge: Harvard University Press, 1979.

Clark, John P. H. "Walter Hilton and the Psalm Commentary *Qui Habitat.*" *Downside Review* 100 (1982): 235–62.

The Cloud of Unknowing. Edited by Patrick J. Gallacher. TEAMS Middle English Texts Series. Kalamazoo: Medieval Institute Publications, 1997.

Coleman, Joyce. *Public Reading and the Reading Public in Late Medieval England and France.* Cambridge: Cambridge University Press, 1996.

Coletti, Theresa. *Mary Magdalene and the Drama of Saints: Theater, Gender, and Religion in Late Medieval England.* Philadelphia: University of Pennsylvania Press, 2004.

The Complete Harley 2253 Manuscript. Edited by Susanna Fein. TEAMS Middle English Texts Series. 3 vols. Kalamazoo: Medieval Institute Publications, 2014.

Connolly, Margaret. "Mapping Manuscripts and Readers of the *Contemplations of the Dread and Love of God.*" In *Design and Distribution of Late Medieval Manuscripts in England*, edited by Margaret Connolly and Linne R. Mooney, 261–78. York: York Medieval Press, 2008.

Contemplations of the Dread and Love of God. Edited by Margaret Connolly. EETS 303. Oxford: Oxford University Press, 1993.

Cooper-Rompato, Christine. *The Gift of Tongues: Women's Xenoglossia in the Later Middle Ages.* University Park: Pennsylvania State University Press, 2010.

Craun, Edwin. *Ethics and Power in Medieval English Reformist Writing.* Cambridge: Cambridge University Press, 2010.

——. "*Fama* and Pastoral Constraints on Rebuking Sinners: *The Book of Margery Kempe.*" In *Fama: The Politics of Talk and Reputation*, edited by Thelma Fenster and Daniel Lord Smail, 187–209. Ithaca: Cornell University Press, 2003.

Davis, Mary Beth L. "Spekyn for Goddys Cawse: Margery Kempe and the Seven Spiritual Works of Mercy." In *The Man of Many Devices, Who Wandered Full Many Ways: Festschrift in Honour of János M. Bak*, edited by Balázs Nagy and Marcell Sebők, 250–68. Budapest: Central European University Press, 1999.

Delaney, Sheila. "Sexual Economics, Chaucer's Wife of Bath, and the *Book of Margery Kempe.*" *Minnesota Review*, n.s., 5 (1975): 104–15.

Despres, Denise. *Ghostly Sights: Visual Meditation in Late-Medieval Literature.* Norman, Okla.: Pilgrim Books, 1989.

Dickman, Susan. "Margery Kempe and the English Devotional Tradition." In *The Medieval Mystical Tradition in England: Papers Read at the Exeter Symposium, July 1980*, edited by Marion Glasscoe, 156–72. Exeter: Exeter University Press, 1980.

———. "A Showing of God's Grace: *The Book of Margery Kempe.*" In *Mysticism and Spirituality in Medieval England*, edited by William F. Pollard and Robert Boenig, 159–76. Woodbridge, Suffolk: D. S. Brewer, 1997.

Eakin, Paul John. *Living Autobiographically: How We Create Identity in Narrative.* Ithaca: Cornell University Press, 2008.

Early English Versions of the Gesta Romanorum. Edited by Sidney J. Herrtage. EETS, e.s., 33. London: Oxford University Press, 1962.

Ehrenreich, Barbara. *Bright-Sided: How the Relentless Promotion of Positive Thinking Has Undermined America.* New York: Metropolitan Books, 2009.

Erler, Mary C. "Devotional Literature." In *The Cambridge History of the Book in Britain.* Volume 3, *1400–1557*, edited by Lotte Hellinga and J. B. Trapp, 495–525. Cambridge: Cambridge University Press, 1999.

———. *Women, Reading, and Piety in Late Medieval England.* Cambridge: Cambridge University Press, 2002.

An Exposition of "Qui Habitat" and "Bonum Est" in English. Edited by Bjorn Wallner. Lund Studies in English 23. Lund: C. W. K. Gleerup, 1954.

Fabian, Johannes. "Keep Listening: Enthnography and Reading." In *The Ethnography of Reading*, edited by Jonathan Boyarin, 80–97. Berkeley: University of California Press, 1993.

The Faits and Passion of Our Lord Jesu Crist. In *Women's Writing in Middle English: An Annotated Anthology*, edited by Alexandra Barratt, 205–18. London: Longman, 1992.

The Fire of Love and The Mending of Life or The Rule of Living of Richard Rolle, Translated by Richard Misyn. Edited by Ralph Harvey. EETS, o.s., 106. London: Kegan Paul, Trench, Trübner and Company, 1896.

Fisher, John. *The Works of John Fisher.* Edited by J. E. B. Mayor. EETS, e.s., 27. London: Trübner, 1876.

Flete, William. "Remedies against Temptations: The Third English Version of William of Flete." Edited by Edmund Colledge and Noel Chadwick. *Archivo Italiano per la Storia della Pieta* 14 (1967): 201–40.

French, Katherine. *The Good Women of the Parish: Gender and Religion after the Black Death.* Philadelphia: University of Pennsylvania Press, 2008.

Fulton, Rachel. *From Judgment to Passion: Devotion to Christ and the Virgin Mary, 800–1200.* New York: Columbia University Press, 2005.

Galloway, Andrew S. "Petrarch's Pleasures, Chaucer's Revulsions, and the Aesthetics of Renunciation in Late-Medieval Culture." In *Answerable Style: The Idea of the Literary in Medieval England*, edited by Andrew S. Galloway and Frank Grady, 140–66. Columbus: Ohio State University Press, 2013.

Gallyon, Margaret. *Margery Kempe of Lynn and Medieval England.* Norwich: Canterbury Press, 1995.

Garber, Rebecca L. R. *Feminae Figurae: Representations of Gender in Religious Texts by Medieval German Women Writers, 1100–1475.* New York: Routledge, 2003.

Garrison, Jennifer. "Liturgy and Loss: *Pearl* and the Ritual Reform of the Aristocratic Subject." *Chaucer Review* 44 (2010): 294–322.

Georgianna, Linda. *The Solitary Self: Individuality in the Ancrene Wisse.* Cambridge: Harvard University Press, 1981.

Gertsman, Elina, ed. *Crying in the Middle Ages: Tears of History.* New York: Routledge, 2012.

Gibson, Gail McMurray. *The Theater of Devotion: East Anglian Drama and Society in the Late Middle Ages.* Chicago: University of Chicago Press, 1989.

Gillespie, Vincent. "Anonymous Devotional Writings." In *A Companion to Middle English Prose*, edited by A. S. G. Edwards, 127–49. Cambridge: D. S. Brewer, 2004.

——. "Religious Writing." In *The Oxford History of Literary Translation in English*. Volume 1, edited by Roger Ellis, 234–83. Oxford: Oxford University Press, 2008.

——. "Vernacular Books of Religion." In *Book Production and Publishing in Britain, 1375–1475*, edited by Jeremy Griffiths and Derek Pearsall, 317–44. Cambridge: Cambridge University Press, 1989.

Gilmore, Leigh. *Autobiographics: A Feminist Theory of Women's Self-Representation.* Ithaca: Cornell University Press, 1994.

Goodman, Anthony. *Margery Kempe and Her World.* London: Pearson, 2002.

Graff, Harvey J. *Literacy Myths, Legacies, and Lessons: New Studies on Literacy.* 2010. Reprint, New Brunswick, N.J.: Transaction Publishers, 2012.

Gray, Douglas. "Books of Comfort." In *Medieval English Religious and Ethical Literature*, edited by Gregory Kratzmann and James Simpson, 209–21. Cambridge: D. S. Brewer, 1986.

——. "Medieval English Mystical Lyrics." In *Mysticism and Spirituality in Medieval England*, edited by William F. Pollard and Robert Boenig, 203–18. Woodbridge, Suffolk: D. S. Brewer, 1997.

Green, Richard Firth. *A Crisis of Truth: Literature and Law in Richardian England.* Philadelphia: University of Pennsylvania Press, 1999.

Greenspan, Kate. "The Autohagiographical Tradition in Medieval Women's Devotional Writing." *a/b: Auto/Biography Studies* 6 (1991): 157–68.

Gregg, Melissa, and Gregory J. Seigworth. *The Affect Theory Reader.* Durham: Duke University Press, 2010.

Hamm, Berndt. "Was Ist Frömmigkeitstheologie? Überlegungen zum 14. bis 16. Jahrhundert." In *Praxis Pietatis: Beiträge zu Theologie und Frömmigkeit in der Neuzeit; Wolfgang Sommer zum 60. Geburtstag*, edited by Hans-Jörg Nieden and Marcel Nieden, 9–45. Stuttgart: Kolhammer, 1999.

Hanna, Ralph. "Brewing Trouble: On Literature and History—and Alewives." In *Bodies and Disciplines: Intersections of Literature and History in Fifteenth-Century England*, edited by Barbara A. Hanawalt and David Wallace, 1–17. Minneapolis: University of Minnesota Press, 1996.

——. "Miscellaneity and Vernacularity: Conditions of Literary Production in Late Medieval England." In *The Whole Book: Cultural Perspectives on the Medieval Miscellany*, edited by Stephen G. Nichols and Siegfried Wenzel, 37–52. Ann Arbor: University of Michigan Press, 1996.

——. "Some Commonplaces of Late Medieval Patience Discussions: An Introduction." In *The Triumph of Patience: Medieval and Renaissance Studies*, edited by Gerald J. Schiffhorst, 65–87. Orlando: University Presses of Florida, 1978.

Hansen, Elisabeth. "Making a Place: Imitatio Mariae in Julian of Norwich's Self-construction." In *Reading Memory and Identity in the Texts of Medieval European Holy Women*, edited by Margaret Cotter-Lynch and Brad Herzog, 187–209. New York: Palgrave Macmillan, 2012.

——. "Temporality in Fourteenth-Century English Contemplative Writing." Ph.D. diss., University of Minnesota, 2012.

Herzog, Brad. "Portrait of a Holy Life: Mnemonic Inventiveness in *The Book of Margery Kempe.*" In *Reading Memory and Identity in the Texts of Medieval European Holy Women*, edited by Margaret Cotter-Lynch and Brad Herzog, 211–33. New York: Palgrave Macmillan, 2012.

Hill, Gabriel. "Pedagogy, Devotion, and Marginalia: Using *The Pore Caitif* in Fifteenth-Century England." *Journal of Medieval Religious Cultures* 41 (2015): 187–207.

——. "Reading Religious Miscellanies in Fifteenth-Century England." Ph.D. diss., University of Minnesota, 2012.

Hindsley, Leonard P. *The Mystics of Engelthal: Writings from a Medieval Monastery.* New York: St. Martin's, 1998.

Hirsh, John C. "Author and Scribe in *The Book of Margery Kempe.*" *Medium Aevum* 44 (1975): 145–50.

——. *The Revelations of Margery Kempe: Paramystical Practices in Late Medieval England.* Medieval and Renaissance Authors Series. Volume 10. Leiden: E. J. Brill, 1989.

Holbrook, Sue Ellen. "'About Her': Margery Kempe's Book of Feeling and Working." In *The Idea of Medieval Literature*, edited by James M. Dean and Christian K. Zacher, 265–84. Newark: University of Delaware Press, 1992.

Holsinger, Bruce. *Music, Body, and Desire in Medieval Culture: Hildegard of Bingen to Chaucer.* Stanford: Stanford University Press, 2001.

Horsley, Katharine. "Poetic Visions of London Civic Ceremony, 1360–1440." Ph.D. diss., Harvard University, 2004.

Horstmann, Carl, ed. *Yorkshire Writers: Richard Rolle of Hampole and His Followers.* 2 vols. London: Swan Sonnenschein, 1895–96.

Howard, [Amy] Kathleen. "The Word Made Flesh: The Perception of Holiness in the Texts of Late Medieval and Early Modern Women in England." Ph.D. diss., University of Minnesota, 2009.

Huber, Emily. "Margery Kempe's Institutional Sorrow." Paper presented at the Annual Meeting of the Medieval Academy of America, Chicago, 2009.

Hymns to the Virgin and Christ, The Parliament of Devils, and Other Religious Poems. Edited by Frederick J. Furnivall. EETS, o.s., 24. Oxford: Kegan Paul, Trench, Trübner, 1867.

Ibsen, Henrik. *When We Dead Awaken.* Translated by William Archer. Chicago: Herbert S. Stone, 1900.

Iser, Wolfgang. *The Act of Reading: A Theory of Aesthetic Response.* Baltimore: Johns Hopkins University Press, 1978.

James, Mervyn. "Ritual Drama and Social Body in the Late Medieval English Town." In *Society, Politics and Culture: Studies in Early Modern England*, 16–47. Cambridge: Cambridge University Press, 1986.

Jauss, Hans Robert. "Literary History as Challenge to Literary Theory." In *Toward an Aesthetics of Receptions*, translated by Timothy Bahti, 3–45. Minneapolis: University of Minnesota Press, 1983.

Jenkins, Jacqueline. "Reading and the *Book of Margery Kempe.*" In Arnold and Lewis, 113–28.

Johnson, Lynn Staley. "The Trope of the Scribe and the Question of Literary Authority in the Works of Julian of Norwich and Margery Kempe." *Speculum* 66 (1991): 820–38.

Jollife, P. S. *A Check-List of Middle English Prose Writings of Spiritual Guidance.* Toronto: Pontifical Institute, 1974.

Justice, Steven. "Inquisition, Speech, and Writing." *Representations* 48 (1994): 1–29.

——. *Writing and Rebellion: England in 1381*. Berkeley: University of California Press, 1994.

Kamath, Stephanie A. Viereck Gibbs. *Authorship and First-Person Allegory in Late Medieval France and England*. Cambridge: D. S. Brewer, 2012.

Kang, Ji-Soo. "Clerical Anxiety, Margery's Crying, and Her *Book.*" In *Global Perspectives on Medieval English Literature, Language, and Culture*, edited by Noel Howard Kaylor and Richard Scott Nokes, 41–58. Kalamazoo: Medieval Institute Publications, 2007.

——. "Lollard Repression, Affective Piety, and Margery Kempe." *Feminist Studies in English* 11 (2003): 1–29.

Karant-Nunn, Susan. *The Reformation of Feeling: Shaping the Religious Emotions in Early Modern Germany*. Oxford: Oxford University Press, 2010.

Keiser, George R. "The Mystics and the Early English Printers: The Economics of Devotionalism." In *The Medieval Mystical Tradition in England*. Exeter Symposium IV, edited by Marion Glasscoe, 9–26. Cambridge: D. S. Brewer, 1987.

——. "Scientific, Medical, and Utilitarian Prose." In *A Companion to Middle English Prose*, edited by A. S. G. Edwards, 231–48. Cambridge: D. S. Brewer, 2004.

Kemp, Theresa D. "The Knight of the Tower and the Queen in Sanctuary: Elizabeth Woodville's Use of Meaningful Silence and Absence." *New Medieval Literatures* 4 (2001): 171–88.

——. *Women in the Age of Shakespeare*. Santa Barbara: Greenwood Press, 2010.

Kempe, Margery. *The Book of Margery Kempe*. Edited by Sanford Brown Meech and Hope Emily Allen. EETS 212. 1940. Reprint, Oxford: Oxford University Press, 1993.

——. *The Book of Margery Kempe*. Edited by Lynn Staley. TEAMS Middle English Texts Series. Kalamazoo: Medieval Institute Publications, 1996.

——. *The Book of Margery Kempe*. Edited by Barry Windeatt. Longman Annotated Texts. Harlow: Pearson Education, 2000.

Kerby-Fulton, Kathryn. *Books under Suspicion: Censorship and Tolerance of Revelatory Writing in Late Medieval England*. Notre Dame: University of Notre Dame Press, 2006.

Kieckhefer, Richard. *Unquiet Souls: Fourteenth-Century Saints and Their Religious Milieu*. Chicago: University of Chicago Press, 1984.

Kinane, Karolyn. "Sanctity Deferred: The Problem of Imitation in Early English Saints Lives." Ph.D. diss., University of Minnesota, 2005.

——. "To Imitate and Inspire Awe: Enclosure and Audience in the Katherine Group of Saints' Lives," *Magistra: Journal of Women's Spirituality in History* 2011 (17): 32–52.

Knust, Jennifer, and Tommy Wasserman. "Earth Accuses Earth: Tracing What Jesus Wrote on the Ground." *Harvard Theological Review* 103 (2010): 407–46.

Krug, Rebecca. "The Idea of Sanctity and the Uncanonized Life of Margery Kempe." In *Cambridge Companion to Medieval English Culture*, edited by Andrew Galloway, 129–45. Cambridge: Cambridge University Press, 2011.

——. "Jesus' Voice: Dialogue and Late-Medieval Readers." In *Form and Reform: Reading across the Fifteenth Century*, edited by Shannon Gayk and Kathleen Tonry, 110–29. Columbus: Ohio State University Press, 2011.

——. "Margery Kempe." In *Cambridge Companion to Medieval English Literature, 1100–1500*, edited by Larry Scanlon, 217–28. Cambridge: Cambridge University Press, 2009.

——. "Natural Feeling and Unnatural Mothers: *Herod the Great*, The Life of Saint Bridget, and Chaucer's *Clerk's Tale*." In *Laments for the Lost in Medieval Literature*, edited by Jane Tolmie and M. J. Toswell, 225–41. Turnhout: Brepols, 2010.

——. "*Piers Plowman* and the Secrets of Health." In *Chaucer, Langland, and Company: Studies in Middle English Literature in Honor of C. David Benson*, edited by Daniel Donoghue, Susanna Fein, David Raybin, James Simpson, and Nicholas Watson. *Chaucer Review* 46 (2011): 166–81.

——. *Reading Families: Women's Literate Practice in Late Medieval England*. Ithaca: Cornell University Press, 2002.

Kuczynski, Michael P. *Prophetic Song: The Psalms as Moral Discourse in Late Medieval England*. Philadelphia: University of Pennsylvania Press, 1995.

Langmann, Adelheid. *Quellen und Forschungen zur Sprach und Kulturgeschichte der germanische Völker* 26 (1878).

Langston, Albert Douglas Beach. "Tudor Books of Consolation." Ph.D. diss, University of North Carolina, 1940.

Larsen, Vickie, and Mary-Katherine Curnow. "Hagiographic Ambition, Fabliau Humor, and Creature Comforts in *The Book of Margery Kempe*." *Exemplaria* 25 (2013): 284–302.

Lavezzo, Kathy. "Sighs and Sobs between Women: The Homoerotics of Compassion in *The Book of Margery Kempe*." In *Premodern Sexualities*, edited by Louise Fradenburg and Carla Freccero, 175–98. London: Routledge, 1996.

Lavinsky, David. "'Speke to me be thowt': Affectivity, *Incendium Amoris*, and the *Book of Margery Kempe*." *Journal of English and Germanic Philology* 112 (2013): 340–64.

Lawlor, Leonard. "The Beginnings of Thought: The Fundamental Experience in Derrida and Deleuze." In *Between Deleuze and Derrida*, edited by Paul Patton and John Protevi, 67–83. London: Continuum, 2003.

Lawton, David. "English Literary Voices, 1350–1500." In *The Cambridge Companion to Medieval English Culture*, edited by Andrew Galloway, 237–58. Cambridge: Cambridge University Press, 2011.

Liber Celestis of St Bridget of Sweden. Edited by Roger Ellis. EETS 291. Oxford: Oxford University Press, 1987.

A Little Treatise That Shows How Every Man and Woman Ought to Fast on Wednesday. STC 24224. 1500.

Lipton, Emma. *Affections of the Mind: The Politics of Sacramental Marriage*. Notre Dame: University of Notre Dame Press, 2007.

Little, Katherine C. *Confession and Resistance: Defining the Self in Late Medieval England*. Notre Dame: University of Notre Dame Press, 2006.

Lochrie, Karma. *Margery Kempe and Translations of the Flesh*. Philadelphia: University of Pennsylvania Press, 1991.

Lyfe of the Soule. Edited by Helen Moon. Lewiston, N.Y.: Edwin Mellen Press, 1978.

Marie of Oignies. "Life." In "Prosalegenden: Die Legenden des MS. Douce 114." Edited by C. Horstmann. *Anglia* 8 (1885): 134–84.

Martz, Louis L., and Frank Manley. "The Tradition of Comfort." In *The Complete Works of St. Thomas More*, cxvii–cxx. Volume 12. New Haven: Yale University Press, 1976.

McAvoy, Liz Herbert. *Authority and the Female Body in the Writings of Julian of Norwich and Margery Kempe*. Cambridge: D. S. Brewer, 2004.

McEntire, Sandra J., ed. *Margery Kempe: A Book of Essays*. New York: Garland, 1992.

McGuire, Brian Patrick. *Friendship and Community: The Monastic Experience, 350–1250*. Kalamazoo: Cistercian Publications, 1988.

McNamer, Sarah. *Affective Meditation and the Invention of Medieval Compassion*. Philadelphia: University of Pennsylvania Press, 2009.

McTaggart, Anne. *Shame and Guilt in Chaucer*. New York: Palgrave Macmillan, 2012.

Mechthild of Hackeborn. *Book of Ghostly Grace*. Edited by Teresa A. Halligan. Toronto: Pontifical Institute, 1979.

Merkur, Dan. *Crucified with Christ: Meditation on the Passion, Mystical Death, and the Medieval Invention of Psychotherapy*. Albany: SUNY Press, 2007.

Meyers, Ann R. *Medieval Allegory and the Building of the New Jerusalem*. Cambridge: D. S. Brewer, 2003.

Middleton, Anne. "William Langland's Kynde Name: Authorial Signature and Social Identity in Late Fourteenth-Century England." In *Literary Practice and Social Change in Britain: 1380–1530*, edited by Lee Patterson, 15–82. Berkeley: University of California Press, 1990.

Mirk's Festial. Edited by Theodor Erbe. EETS, e.s., 96. London: Kegan Paul, Trench, Trübner, 1905.

Mitchell, Marea. The Book of Margery Kempe: *Scholarship, Community, and Criticism*. New York: Peter Lang, 2005.

Moss, Rachel. *Fatherhood and Its Representations in Middle English Texts*. Cambridge: D. S. Brewer, 2013.

Mueller, Alex. *Translating Troy: Provincial Politics in Alliterative Romance*. Columbus: Ohio State University Press, 2013.

Mueller, Janel. "The Autobiography of a New 'Creatur': Female Spirituality, Selfhood, and Authorship in *The Book of Margery Kempe*." In *The Female Autograph: Theory and Practice of Autobiography from the Tenth to the Twentieth Century*, edited by Domna C. Stanton, 57–69. Chicago: University of Chicago Press, 1987.

Mulvey, Laura. "Visual Pleasure and Narrative Cinema." *Screen* 16 (1975): 6–18.

Murray, Alexander. *Suicide in the Middle Ages*. Volume 1, *The Violent against Themselves*. Oxford: Oxford University Press, 1998.

——. *Suicide in the Middle Ages*. Volume 2, *The Curse on Self-Murder*. Oxford: Oxford University Press, 2000.

Murtan, Megan. "Praying with Boethius in *Troilus and Criseyde*." *Chaucer Review* 49 (2015): 294–319.

Newman, Barbara. *God and the Goddesses: Vision, Poetry, and Belief in the Middle Ages*. Philadelphia: University of Pennsylvania Press, 2003.

——. "What Did It Mean to Say 'I Saw'? The Clash between Theory and Practice in Medieval Visionary Culture." *Speculum* 80 (2005): 1–43.

Nicholas Love's Mirror of the Blessed Life of Jesus Christ. Edited by Michael G. Sargent. New York: Garland Publishing, 1992.

Norem, Julie K. *The Positive Power of Negative Thinking*. Cambridge, Mass.: Basic Books, 2001.

Njus, Jesse. "Margery Kempe and the Spectatorship of Medieval Drama." *Fifteenth-Century Studies* 38 (2013): 123–52.

Oliver, Clementine. "Why Margery Kempe Is Annoying and Why We Should Care." In *The Middle Ages in Texts and Textures: Reflections on Medieval Sources*, edited by Jason Glenn, 323–31. Toronto: University of Toronto Press, 2011.

Olson, Glending. *Literature as Recreation in the Later Middle Ages*. Ithaca: Cornell University Press, 1982.

Orlemanski, Julie. "Margery's 'Noyse' and Distributed Expressivity." In *Voice and Voicelessness in Medieval Europe*, edited by Irit Ruth Kleiman, 123–38. New York: Palgrave Macmillan, 2015.

"Orologium Sapientiae or The Seven Poyntes of Trewe Wisdom." Edited by Carl Horstmann. *Anglia* 10 (1887): 323–89.

Ortner, Sherry B. *Making Gender: The Politics and Erotics of Culture*. Boston: Beacon Press, 1996.

Parkes, Malcolm. *English Cursive Book Hands, 1250–1500*. Oxford: Clarendon Press, 1969.

Partner, Nancy. "'And Most of All for Inordinate Love': Desire and Denial in the *Book of Margery Kempe*." *Thought* 64 (1989): 250–67.

——. "Reading *The Book of Margery Kempe*." *Exemplaria* 3 (1991): 29–66.

The Paston Letters and Papers of the Fifteenth Century. Edited by Norman Davis. 2 vols. Oxford: Clarendon Press, 1971.

Perreault, Jeanne. *Writing Selves: Contemporary Feminist Autography*. Minneapolis: University of Minnesota Press, 1995.

Phillips, Helen. "Structure and Consolation in the *Book of the Duchess*." *Chaucer Review* 16 (1981): 107–18.

Phillips, Kim M. "Margery Kempe and the Ages of Women." In Arnold and Lewis, 17–34.

Phillips, Susan E. *Transforming Talk: The Problem with Gossip in Late Medieval England*. University Park: Pennsylvania State University Press, 2007.

Poems of the Pearl Manuscript. Edited by Malcolm Andrew and Ronald Waldron. York Medieval Texts. 2nd ser. Berkeley: University of California Press, 1982.

The Pore Caitif: Edited from MS Harley 2336. Edited by Mary Teresa Brady. Ph D. diss., Fordham University, 1954.

Powell, Susan. "Preaching at Syon Abbey." *Leeds Studies in English*, n.s., 31 (2000): 229–67.

The Prickynge of Love. Edited by Harold Kane. Salzburg: Institut für Anglistik und Amerikanistik, 1983.

The Pricke of Conscience. Edited by Richard Morris. Berlin: A. Asher, 1863.

Provost, William. "Margery Kempe and Her Calling," in McEntire, 3–15.

Rakoff, David. *Half-Empty*. New York: Doubleday, 2010.

Reddy, William M. *The Navigation of Feeling: A Framework for the History of Emotions*. Cambridge: Cambridge University Press, 2001.

Rees Jones, Sarah. "Margery Kempe and the Bishops." In *Medieval Women: Texts and Contexts in Late Medieval Britain*, edited by Jocelyn Wogan-Browne, 371–91. Turnhout: Brepols, 2000.

Remedy ayenst the troubles of temptacyons. STC 21263. Wynkyn de Worde, 1525.

The Revelations of Saint Birgitta. Edited by William Patterson Cumming. EETS, o.s., 178. London: Oxford University Press, 1929.

Rich, Adrienne, "When We Dead Awaken: Writing as Re-Vision." *College English* 34 (1972): 18–30.

Rickert, Edith, ed. *Ancient English Christmas Carols, 1400–1700*. New York: Duffield and Co., 1915.

Riddy, Felicity. "Text and Self in *The Book of Margery Kempe*." In *Voices in Dialogue: Reading Women in the Middle Ages*, edited by Kathryn Kerby-Fulton and Linda Olson, 435–53. Notre Dame: University of Notre Dame Press, 2005.

Riehle, Wolfgang. *The Secret Within: Hermits, Recluses, and Spiritual Outsiders in Medieval England*. Ithaca: Cornell University Press, 2014.

Rittgers, Ronald K. *The Reformation of Suffering: Pastoral Theology and Lay Piety in Late Medieval and Early Modern Germany*. Oxford: Oxford University Press, 2012.

The Riverside Chaucer. 3rd edition. Edited by Larry D. Benson. Boston: Houghton Mifflin, 1987.

Robertson, Elizabeth. *Early English Devotional Prose and the Female Audience*. Knoxville: University of Tennessee Press, 1990.

Robison, Katherine. "The Path to Wholeness: The Therapeutic Potential of Bodily Writing in Late Medieval Dream Visions." Ph.D. diss., University of Minnesota, 2016.

——. " 'Thou wolt make . . . thyn hed to ake': A Post-Chaucerian Treatment for Madness in Christine de Pizan's *Chemin de long estude*." *Chaucer Review* 49 (2014): 184–203.

Rosenfeld, Jessica. "Envy and Exemplarity in *The Book of Margery Kempe*." *Exemplaria* 26 (2014): 105–21.

Rosenwein, Barbara H. *Anger's Past: The Social Uses of an Emotion in the Middle Ages*. Ithaca: Cornell University Press, 1998.

——. *Emotional Communities in the Early Middle Ages*. Ithaca: Cornell University Press, 2007.

——. "Theories of Change in the History of Emotions." In *A History of Emotions, 1200–1800*, edited by Jonas Liliequist, 7–20. Ithaca: Cornell University Press, 2012.

——. "Transmitting Despair by Manuscript and Print." In *Crying in the Middle Ages: Tears of History*, edited by Elina Gertsman, 249–57. New York: Routledge, 2012.

Rosser, Gervase. *The Art of Solidarity in the Middle Ages: Guilds in England, 1250–1550*. Oxford: Oxford University Press, 2015.

Salih, Sarah. "Margery's Bodies: Piety, Work and Penance." In Arnold and Lewis, 161–76.

——. *Versions of Virginity in Late Medieval England*. Woodbridge, Suffolk: D. S. Brewer, 2001.

Sanok, Catherine. *Her Life Historical: Exemplarity and Female Saints' Lives in Late Medieval England*. Philadelphia: University of Pennsylvania Press, 2007.

Schoff, Rebecca L. *Reformations: Three Medieval Authors in Manuscript and Movable Type*. Turnhout: Brepols, 2007.

Scott, Karen. "Mystical Death, Bodily Death: Catherine of Siena and Raymond of Capua on the Mystic's Encounter with God." In *Gendered Voices: Medieval Saints and Their Interpreters*, edited by Catherine M. Mooney, 136–67. Philadelphia: University of Pennsylvania Press, 1999.

Scourfield, J. H. D. "Towards a Genre of Consolation." In Baltussen, 1–36.

Sedgwick, Eve Kosofsky. *Between Men: English Literature and Male Homosocial Desire.* New York: Columbia University Press, 1985.

Silverstein, Theodore, ed. *English Lyrics before 1500.* York Medieval Texts. 1971. Reprint, Chicago: Northwestern University Press, 1989.

Smith, Sidonie. *A Poetics of Women's Autobiography.* Bloomington: Indiana University Press, 1987.

Snyder, Susan. "The Left Hand of God: Despair in Medieval and Renaissance Tradition." *Studies in the Renaissance* 12 (1965): 18–59.

Sobecki, Sebastian. "'The writyng of this tretys': Margery Kempe's Son and the Authorship of Her *Book,*" *Studies in the Age of Chaucer* 37 (2015): 257–83.

Solomon, Michael. *Fictions of Well-Being: Sickly Readers and Vernacular Medical Writing in Late Medieval and Early Modern Spain.* Philadelphia: University of Pennsylvania Press, 2010.

Somerset, Fiona. "Excitative Speech: Theories of Emotive Response from Richard Fitzralph to Margery Kempe." In *The Vernacular Spirit: Essays on Medieval Religious Literature,* edited by Renate Blumenfeld-Kosinski, Duncan Robertson, and Nancy Warren, 59–79. New York: Palgrave Macmillan, 2002.

Spearing, A. C. "Margery Kempe." In *A Companion to Middle English Prose,* edited by A S. G. Edwards, 83–97. Cambridge: D. S. Brewer, 2004.

Speculum Gy de Warewyke. Edited by Georgianna Lea Morrill. EETS, e.s., 75. Millwood, N.Y.: Kraus Reprint, 1973.

Sponsler, Claire. "Drama and Piety: Margery Kempe." In Arnold and Lewis, 129–43.

——. *Drama and Resistance: Bodies, Goods, and Theatricality in Late Medieval England.* Minneapolis: University of Minnesota Press, 1997.

Staley, Lynn. *Margery Kempe's Dissenting Fictions.* University Park: Pennsylvania State University Press, 1994.

Stanton, Robert. "Lechery, Pride, and the Uses of Sin in *The Book of Margery Kempe.*" *Journal of Medieval Religious Cultures* 36 (2010): 169–204.

Stargardt, Ute. "The Influence of Dorothea von Montau on the Mysticism of Margery Kempe." Ph.D. diss., University of Tennessee, 1981.

Stock, Brian. *Augustine the Reader: Meditation, Self-Knowledge, and the Ethics of Interpretation.* Cambridge: Belknap Press of Harvard University Press, 1996.

Stone, Robert Karl. *Middle English Prose Style: Margery Kempe and Julian of Norwich.* The Hague: Mouton, 1970.

Street, Brian V. *Literacy in Theory and Practice.* Cambridge: Cambridge University Press, 1984.

Summa Virtutum de Remediis Anime. Edited by S. Wenzel. Athens: University of Georgia Press, 1984.

Sutherland, Annie. "'Oure feyth is groundyd in goddes worde': Julian of Norwich and the Bible." In *The Medieval Mystical Tradition in England.* Exeter Symposium VII. *Papers Read at Charney Manor,* edited by Edward Alexander Jones, 1–20. Cambridge: D. S. Brewer, 2004.

Szell, Timea. "From Woe to Weal and Weal to Woe," in McEntire, 73–91.

Taylor, Jamie. *Fictions of Evidence: Witnessing, Literature, and Community in the Late Middle Ages.* Columbus: Ohio State University Press, 2013.

Tentler, Thomas N. *Sin and Confession on the Eve of the Reformation.* Princeton: Princeton University Press, 1977.

Three Prose Versions of the Secreta Secretorum. Edited by Robert Steele. EETS, e.s., 74. London: Kegan Paul, Trench, Trübner, 1898.

Tomkins, Silvan. *Shame and Its Sisters: A Silvan Tomkins Reader.* Edited by Eve Kosofsky Sedgwick and Adam Frank. Durham: Duke University Press, 1995.

The Twelve Profits of Tribulation. In Horstmann, *Yorkshire Writers,* 2:45–60.

The Two Middle English Translations of the Revelations of St. Elizabeth of Hungary. Edited by Sarah McNamer. Heidelberg: C. Winter, 1996.

Uhlman, Diana R. "The Comfort of Voice, the Solace of Script: Orality and Literacy in *The Book of Margery Kempe.*" *Studies in Philology* 91 (1994): 50–69.

Utter, Benjamin D. "Gawain and Goliath: Davidic Parallels and the Problem of Penance in *Sir Gawain and the Green Knight.*" *Comitatus* 44 (2013): 121–55.

——. "'Fawty and Falce': Sin, Sanctity, and the Heroics of Devotion in Late-Medieval English Literature." Ph.D. diss., University of Minnesota, 2016.

Van Engen, John. *Sisters and Brothers of the Common Life: The Devotio Moderna and the World of the Later Middle Ages.* Philadelphia: University of Pennsylvania Press, 2008.

Vines, Amy N. *Women's Power in Late Medieval Romance.* Cambridge: D. S. Brewer, 2011.

Voaden, Rosalynn. *God's Words, Women's Voices: The Discernment of Spirits in the Writing of Late-Medieval Women Visionaries.* York: York Medieval Press, 1999.

Voragine, Jacobus de. *The Golden Legend: Readings on the Saints.* Translated by William Granger Ryan. Princeton: Princeton University Press, 1993.

Wallace, David. *Strong Women: Life, Text, and Territory.* Oxford: Oxford University Press, 2011.

Walter Hilton's The Scale of Perfection. Edited by Thomas H. Bestul. TEAMS Middle English Texts Series. Kalamazoo: Medieval Institute Publications, 2000.

Walters, Barbara R., Vincent Corrigan, and Peter T. Ricketts. *The Feast of Corpus Christi.* University Park: Pennsylvania State University Press, 2006.

Warren, Martin L. *Asceticism in the Christian Transformation of Self in Margery Kempe, William Thorpe, and John Rogers.* Lewiston, N.Y.: Edwin Mellen Press, 2003.

Warren, Nancy Bradley. *The Embodied Word: Female Spiritualities, Contested Orthodoxies, and English Religious Cultures, 1350–1700.* Notre Dame: University of Notre Dame Press, 2010.

Warriner's English Grammar and Composition. New York: Harcourt Brace, 1951.

Waters, Claire M. *Angels and Earthly Creatures: Preaching, Performance, and Gender in the Later Middle Ages.* Philadelphia: University of Pennsylvania Press, 2004.

Watson, Nicholas. "Despair." In *Cultural Reformations: Medieval and Renaissance in Literary History,* edited by Brian Cummings and James Simpson, 342–57. Oxford: Oxford University Press, 2010.

——. "The Making of *The Book of Margery Kempe.*" In *Voices in Dialogue: Reading Women in the Middle Ages,* edited by Linda Olson and Kathryn Kerby-Fulton, 395–434, 454–57. Notre Dame: University of Notre Dame Press, 2005.

——. "The Methods and Objectives of Thirteenth-Century Anchoritic Devotion." In *The Medieval Mystical Tradition in England,* edited by Marion Glasscoe, 132–53. Exeter: University of Exeter Press, 1987.

——. "The Politics of Middle English Writing." In Wogan-Browne, 331–52.

——. "Visions of Inclusion: Universal Salvation and Vernacular Theology in Pre-Reformation England," *Journal of Medieval and Early Modern Studies* 27 (1997): 145–87.

Watt, Diane. *Secretaries of God: Women Prophets in Late Medieval and Early Modern England*. Cambridge: D. S. Brewer, 1997.

Weatherbee, Winthrop. "The *Consolation* and Medieval Literature." In *The Cambridge Companion to Boethius*, edited by John Marenbon, 279–302. Cambridge: Cambridge University Press, 2009.

Wenzel, Siegfried. *The Sin of Sloth: Acedia in Medieval Thought and Literature*. Chapel Hill: University of North Carolina Press, 1967.

Whetter, K. S. *Understanding Genre in Medieval Romance*. Aldershot: Ashgate, 2008.

Wilcox, A. R. "Sympathetic Rivals: Consolation in Cicero's Letters." *American Journal of Philology* 126 (2005): 237–55.

Williams, Tara. *Inventing Womanhood: Gender and Language in Later Middle English Writing*. Columbus: Ohio State University Press, 2011.

Windeatt, Barry. "'I Use but Comownycacyon and Good Wordys': Teaching and *The Book of Margery Kempe*." In *Approaching Medieval English Anchoritic and Mystical Texts*, edited by Dee Dyas, Valerie Edden, and Roger Ellis, 115–28. Cambridge: D. S. Brewer, 2005.

Wogan-Browne, Jocelyn, Nicholas Watson, Andrew Taylor, and Ruth Evans, eds. *The Idea of the Vernacular: An Anthology of Middle English Literary Theory, 1280–1520*. University Park: Pennsylvania State University Press, 1999.

The Writings of Julian of Norwich: A Vision Showed to a Devout Woman and A Revelation of Love. Edited by Jacqueline Jenkins and Nicholas Watson. University Park: Pennsylvania State University Press, 2006.

Yonge, James. *Secret of Secrets*. In *Three Prose Versions of the Secreta Secretorum*, edited by Robert Steele. EETS, e.s., 74. London: Kegan Paul, Trench, Trübner, 1898.

Yoshikawa, Naoë Kukita. *Margery Kempe's Meditations: The Context of Medieval Devotional Literature, Liturgy and Iconography*. Cardiff: University of Wales Press, 2007.

Zeeman, Nicolette. *Piers Plowman and the Medieval Discourse of Desire*. Cambridge: Cambridge University Press, 2006.

✤ INDEX

CPSIA information can be obtained
at www.ICGtesting.com
Printed in the USA
BVOW08*0249100317

477893BV00002B/4/P